DATE DUE

D1010663

Cat. No. 23-221

Organizational Psychology
in Cross-Cultural Perspective

Organizational Psychology in Cross-Cultural Perspective

Colin P. Silverthorne

NEW YORK UNIVERSITY PRESS
New York and London

NEW YORK UNIVERSITY PRESS
New York and London
www.nyupress.org

Library of Congress Cataloging-in-Publication Data
Silverthorne, Colin P. (Colin Patric)
Organizational psychology in cross-cultural perspective /
Colin P. Silverthorne.
p. cm.
Includes bibliographical references and index.
ISBN 0–8147–4006–5 (cloth : alk. paper)
1. Psychology, Industrial—Cross-cultural studies.
2. Organizational behavior—Cross-cultural studies.
3. Personnel management—Cross-cultural studies.
4. Intercultural communication.   I. Title.
HF5548.8.S519   2004
158.7--dc22   2004015264

New York University Press books are printed on acid-free paper,
and their binding materials are chosen for strength and durability.

Manufactured in the United States of America

c 10 9 8 7 6 5 4 3 2 1
p 10 9 8 7 6 5 4 3 2 1

*This book is dedicated to my wife Deanna
for all her encouragenemt and support.*

Contents

1 | Introduction

Playwright George Bernard Shaw once said, "England and America are two countries divided by a common language." In many respects, this quote can be considered an analogy for the issues we will discuss in this book. Every country has managers who manage, but when we define what that means, it is not unusual to see that although we speak the same language, what we mean by what we say is quite different. Obviously, as companies operate across borders and managers manage in other countries, the potential for problems is great. Organizational psychology provides a framework for understanding individual and organizational behavior. The discipline combines research from social psychology and organizational behavior, with an emphasis on leadership, teams, motivation, values, and attitudes. Cross-cultural psychology provides a framework for understanding differences and similarities in individual and social functioning across cultures. By looking at organizational psychology in a cross-cultural context, we can prepare individuals and organizations for the current challenges facing organizations today. These challenges include an increase in the cultural diversity of the work force, particularly in the United States and Europe; the growth in international business; the emergence of many more multinational companies; mergers and acquisitions across national boundaries; the role of government in regulating, deregulating, or privatizing organizations; and the emergence of high-technology and telecommunication systems (Erez, 1994). All of these challenges and changes have accelerated cross-cultural communications and exposed more companies and individuals to the different values, norms, and behaviors that are found in other cultures.

I learned at an early age that companies operating outside their home-country environment can run into problems because of cultural differences. When I was a teenager in England, we lived near a major automobile factory. I always thought it was a British company but found out differently when the parent American company stepped in to run the factory. After years of labor problems, poor quality, and low productivity, the American parent company decided they had had enough and could run the factory much better. Within a week of the American takeover of management, the workers were involved in one of the longest strikes in company history, as the Americans tried to apply their American business practices in a British work environment. Their biggest mistakes did not concern critical organizational issues such as productivity or procedures or automation, but rather the way they treated the tea ladies and the way workers should take their breaks. The absolute ignorance of or blindness to cultural behaviors in British factories caused a bigger problem than any of the traditional conflict issues such as wages, productivity, and working conditions and, in this case, led to a very long strike. This lack of understanding of cultural differences in the workplace and the resulting problems gave me an early insight into the power of cultural differences and the serious negative consequences of ignorance and ethnocentrism.

Why Is National Culture Important in Organizations?

Organizations are operating in a global environment that has increased competition throughout the world. Countries can no longer depend on a protected domestic market while at the same time exporting to other countries to protect jobs and generate revenue. Trade barriers have come down, and countries have made significant changes to their trade policies. Now, more than ever, organizations must do everything possible to become or remain competitive.

Culture involves pervasive and deeply held implicit beliefs. Because cultures vary and different societies do not share all the same values, it is reasonable to believe that individual behavior will also vary across cultures. And there is ample evidence that national culture will have an affect on behavior at work. Cultural norms influence a manager's behavior, as well as an employee's behavior and reactions to managerial and organizational actions. Based on their research findings, L. Gardenswartz and A. Rowe (2001) identified five areas that they considered to be particularly important in organizations operating across cultures: hierarchy and status, group versus individual orientation, time consciousness, communication styles and patterns, and conflict resolution.

There are also ways to consider managerial behavioral differences across cultures, such as the simple descriptive management cultural definitions of differences based on an east, west, north, or south distinction: Western management is action oriented; Northern management is thought oriented; Southern management is family oriented; and Eastern management is group oriented (Gatley and Lessem, 1995). Clearly, culture influences how we behave in meetings, how we respond to conflict and feedback, and even how we speak and stand. There is a benefit in being able to see patterns of behavior within cultures, but there is also the danger that we are oversimplifying the complex variables that make up a culture. Understanding these issues and how they affect managers enhances our ability to create open and productive relationships.

What Is Organizational Psychology?

The earliest book on industrial/organizational psychology was published in 1913, and industrial/organizational researchers played an active role in helping the U.S. military develop tests of mental ability during World War I. These efforts led to the rapid development of the field of psychological testing. Initially, most of this research was directed toward helping the military place recruits appropriately and identify potential leaders as quickly as possible. Organizational psychology grew and developed more rapidly following the human relations movement that began in the early 1940s. Now, almost one hundred years later, psychologists continue their endeavors in a wide array of business, military, academic, and nonprofit settings.

Traditional organizational psychology has focused on understanding individual behavior within organizations and includes such topics as motivation, leadership, personnel psychology, employee behavior, employee attitudes and values, and managerial and organizational behavior. In a broad sense, personnel psychology includes all aspects of individual behavior. It places an emphasis on identifying the skills and abilities needed for particular jobs and on selecting, training, and evaluating employees. Effective selection procedures help ensure that employees will be successful, and training and evaluation ensure that employees remain effective and contributing members within the organization. Organizational behavior looks at how organizations influence employees' attitudes and behaviors while at work. Topics in organizational behavior include role-related behaviors, the impact of team and group membership, commitment to the organization, and patterns of communication. While personnel psychology focuses on the individual-level issues, organizational behavior focuses more on group-level issues.

Organizational psychology is dedicated to developing the tools to help improve organizations. The field of organizational development is concerned with changing organizations to make them more effective. In the twenty-first century, global competition is growing. One trend is to seek out the least expensive labor markets, just as companies sought out the least expensive natural resources from around the world in the seventeenth and eighteenth centuries. Companies must compete on the basis of labor costs and technological innovations.

The change in the way organizations are established and operate in the current global economy has resulted in a need to reexamine what we think we know about organizational psychology and behavior. By the early 1970s, there was a growing awareness that managerial and organizational behavior varied across nations (e.g., Massie and Luytjes, 1972). It is now generally accepted that any application of a theory of management needs to take cultural factors into consideration. This is best demonstrated by the report of a case-study exam based on a conflict between two department heads within the same company (Hofstede, 1997). All students were given the same case, but the interpretations of the cause of and best solution to the conflict were quite different. The French students saw the problem as the general manager's negligence in handling the conflict. They thought the person who was the boss of the two department heads should issue orders to settle the problem. The German students thought the problem was caused by a lack of structure, which was best resolved by establishing specific procedures. The British students saw the problem as one of human relations, best solved by giving training to the individuals involved to improve their negotiating skills. Thus, students from three different cultures attributed the same problem to three different causes and made recommendations for three unique solutions. Similarly, the importance of the role of culture was reinforced when managers from France, Germany, and the United Kingdom, working for an American multinational company, were found to be even more French, German, or British than their fellow countrymen working for domestic companies. Thus, with greater exposure to other cultures, the managers had a greater identification with their own cultural beliefs (Laurent, 1983).

Most of the organizational psychology and behavior research has been undertaken in the United States, as has been the development of many of the major theories currently in use. While the majority of theories of management have a Western and generally an American perspective, we cannot assume that management and organizational theories currently valid and/or popular within the United States have universal value or applicability (Hofstede, 1993). Fortunately, the amount of research in organizational psychology has recently been growing in countries such as the United Kingdom, Canada, Australia, New Zealand, Germany, the Netherlands, and Hong Kong.

The future challenges to organizational psychology involve being useful, relevant, and valuable to organizations. In order to maintain a viable research program, new theories need to be developed and tested using rigorous research approaches, with the goal of developing insights that can be used to help organizations function more effectively and to help employees feel valued, secure, and motivated. In a global economy where companies operate across borders and within cultures other than the home culture, differences in the perception and interpretation of the concept of management, managerial styles, leadership, and work motivation can lead to significant problems. Therefore, any application of organizational psychology theories needs to take cultural differences into consideration.

The Goals of This Book

It is time to begin to pull together ideas and research from around the world to better understand how we can apply this new and growing body of knowledge in a global environment. There is also value in applying some of the knowledge gathered from other cultures to organizations within the United States and other countries, given the increasing diversity of the work force. The purpose of this book is to help begin this process. The book is designed to consider relevant theories of organizational psychology and behavior in different cultures. From these findings, similarities and differences are considered and conclusions drawn about the applicability or nonapplicability of some of the major theories of organizational behavior and psychology to other cultures. A particular emphasis is placed on non-Western cultures where cultural value systems are the most different from those found in America and Europe.

Several areas of organizational psychology typically included in books on this subject have received little or no attention from researchers in other cultures. In addition, the emphasis of most of the research has been on highlighting differences and similarities between cultures rather than explaining why these differences and similarities exist and how they can be exploited for competitive advantage. Given these limitations in the published research in organizational behavior and psychology, perhaps this book will encourage others to explore this important and fertile research area. In this way, the mission of organizational psychology to help companies improve and prosper can be continued in a global context.

2

Foundations of
Organizations and Culture

The careless application of theories of organizational psychology across cultures is fraught with danger because research has found that, while there are similarities, the differences between organizations operating in distinct cultural and societal settings are significant (Lammers and Hickson, 1979). The similarities tend to be consistent for the same types of business and organizational structure (Hickson, Hinings and McMillan, 1981), though there can be considerable variance between organizations operating as similar organizational types but in different societies in such areas as employee-management relations, communication within the organization, and staff involvement in decision making (Maurice, Sorge, and Warner, 1980).

Even though the role of a manager is generally consistent across organizations and cultures, managerial styles can vary substantially. While the evidence available from research on managerial styles in different cultures is limited, distinct social systems can have a considerable impact on management systems, which, in turn, affects managerial styles. Further, research in international settings has clearly shown that management techniques developed in and for a particular culture or country do not always produce the same results in other cultures (Adler, 1997).

The effectiveness of a manager is, in part, based on the values that the manager holds and his or her ability to motivate employees. Values are influenced by both the nationality of the manager and the business environment within which the individual manages (Adler and Bartholomew, 1992). These values guide the selection and evaluation of managerial behaviors such as techniques for motivating subordinates (Terpstra and David, 1990) and enhancing employee job satisfaction (Trice and Beyer, 1993). Style of organizational leadership has also been shown to be a relevant variable in the implementation of management practices (Atwater and Wright, 1996). The norms established by the leader and by the organizational culture allow employees to make sense of their organizational world; if that world makes sense to them, they are likely to be more productive and more satisfied with their jobs.

Organizations in Western cultures have embraced the idea of organizational-development interventions designed to enhance organizational effectiveness at the individual and organizational levels. However, organizational-development interventions can be influenced by culture, resulting in reduced, negative, or nonexistent change outcomes. This suggests that in multinational companies some adaptation of organizational-development interventions is necessary. The primary and recurring issue is whether a subsidiary is influenced more by the parent-company culture or the local culture. A comparison of American, Japanese, European, and Hong Kong Chinese multinational companies indicates that organizational-development interventions differ by country, primarily as a function of the organization's home-country culture. American and European organizations are most likely to use, both at home and in subsidiaries, organizational-development interventions than Asian companies. Chinese firms have been found to be less open to individual-level interventions and more open to system-level changes, given their long-term orientation. Evidence indicates that organizational-development interventions that take place at a system level can be used independently of culture, while individual-level interventions are more affected by cultural differences and are, therefore, more likely to need to be adapted to local-culture needs (Lau and Ngo, 2001).

Anyone who has visited other countries knows that differences exist in language, mannerisms, dress, and customs. But in addition, there are hidden differences that are less obvious. Being able to speak the language can help to highlight these differences, but Americans are often at a disadvantage in this regard, since being fluent in another language is the exception rather than the rule for most nonimmigrants in the United States. However, culture and the perception of cultural differences are hard to define and explain, and it must be remembered that while culture suggests similarities and uniformity within a society, there is also a wide range of individual differences.

Hofstede's Classification of Culture

One of the most significant studies to look at the role of cultures within a single organization operating across many parts of the world was conducted by the Dutch researcher Geert Hofstede (1984). His research played a significant role in generating interest and additional research in multicultural settings, and it is important to discuss in some detail because of both the influence of his studies and theoretical framework on cross-cultural research and the controversy it has generated.

Specifically, Hofstede looked at the work-related attitudes and values of comparable groups of managers working in a multinational company that operated in forty countries. The research began in 1967 and continued between 1971 and 1973, when surveys completed by over one hundred thousand IBM employees in different countries were tabulated and analyzed. To help in maintaining the comparability of the groups, only employees from the marketing and servicing divisions of the company were included in the sample. The data was collected using questionnaires, and the answers from those surveyed were averaged for each country. Then scores were developed for each country, and these scores were analyzed using a factor-analysis technique designed to isolate the key factors that account for the majority of the variation in the employees' responses. Based on this analysis, Hofstede theorized that cultural differences could be usefully described by using four bipolar dimensions.

Power Distance

The bipolar ends of this dimension are high and low, and it measures the level of inequality between people that is considered normal in the culture. The concept of power distance implies that in a hierarchical organization, people in power will try to maintain their power, keeping power distance high. The level of power distance helps to define who has the power in the organization to make decisions in general and specific types of decisions in particular, as well as to help prescribe rules and procedures within the organization. In high-power-distance cultures, such as Malaysia, subordinates accept their status and respect formal hierarchical authority. Cultures low in power distance, such as Israel, will have organizations in which managers are willing to share authority.

Individualism-Collectivism

This dimension is the degree to which people prefer to work as individuals rather than as group members. Cultures high in individualism, such as the United States, respect and value personal achievement, autonomy, and innovation. Concern is for yourself as an individual rather than the group to which you belong, and people tend to classify one another on the basis of individual characteristics rather than group membership. On the other hand, cultures high in collectivism, such as Taiwan, emphasize group harmony, social order, loyalty, and personal relationships. Individual contributions are not valued if they work against group goals or interests. In order to maintain harmony in a collectivist culture, it is often necessary to be conservative and cautious. The majority of countries are collectivist, where group membership dictates a person's loyalty and identification and the interests of the group take precedence over the interests of the individual.

Masculinity-Femininity

This dimension is the degree to which perceived typically masculine attributes (e.g., assertiveness, success, and competition) prevail over perceived typically feminine attributes (e.g., sensitivity and concern for others). Cultures high in masculinity, such as Japan, are more likely to be male dominated, especially in management, whereas cultures high in femininity, such as Sweden, are more likely to have women in managerial and professional positions. In addition, masculine societies are more likely to define occupations by gender, whereas in feminine cultures women and men can do any job and are not restricted by gender-role stereotypes.

Uncertainty Avoidance

The bipolar ends of this dimension are high and low, and it measures the degree to which individuals prefer structure to a lack of structure. The concept of uncertainty avoidance suggests that countries high in this dimension have high stress levels and design rules and norms to reduce uncertainty or ambiguity to the greatest extent possible. Cultures high in uncertainty avoidance tend to be uncomfortable or insecure with risks, disorganization, and unstructured situations and will try to control their environments by creating laws, rules, and institutions. This is manifested in lifetime-employment practices in countries such as Japan and Greece. Cultures low in uncertainty avoidance are more likely to accept differences in society, and people in these cultures are more curious about discovering and trying new things. The result is more job mobility, as seen in countries such as the United States and Denmark. Uncertainty can be due to human behavior or the nature of the environment, and it shapes the organizational mechanisms that are used to control and coordinate activities (Hofstede, 1984).

While these four dimensions form the basis of Hofstede's theory of cultural classification of differences between cultures, there have been numerous changes and additions suggested to his list. For example, since Hofstede is Dutch, it is possible that his research had a bias toward Western values and that an Eastern-values-based study would produce different results. To test this possibility, a group of researchers in Hong Kong, publishing as the Chinese Culture Connection (1987), constructed a survey based on Chinese values. An analysis of the results of this survey and a follow-up study (Hofstede and Bond, 1988), conducted in a similar fashion to that originally used by Hofstede, again yielded four dimensions, three of which were similar to Hofstede's. The Chinese Culture Connection used different labels for the three overlapping dimensions. Individualism-collectivism was equated to integration, masculinity-femininity was equated to human-heartedness, and power distance was equated to moral discipline. Human-heartedness includes concepts such as kindness, patience, and courtesy. Integration includes tolerance, harmony, and solidarity. And m oral discipline includes moderation and purity of self and selflessness.

While the researchers found little support for Hofstede's uncertainty avoidance dimension, they identified a different fourth dimension, more unusual than the others. They called this dimension *Confucian dynamism* because it reflected the teachings of Confucius and a core set of Asian values including time orientation, thrift versus conspicuous expenditure, and truth as absolute rather than as dependent on the speaker. Much of the long-term economic success of Japan and other South East Asian countries has been attributed to Confucianism (Yeung and Tung, 1996). Scores on this scale are related to the teachings of Confucius, with a high score corresponding to future-oriented beliefs and a low score reflecting an emphasis on past or present beliefs. Because this dimension is clearly time oriented, Confucian dynamism was also labeled *long- and short-term orientation.* In effect, the Chinese Culture Connection discounted uncertainty avoidance but suggested a different dimension of the cultural aspects of organizations: Confucian dynamism or time orientation.

A high score on time orientation reflects a future orientation and tends to indicate a value set that includes persistence, ordering relationships by status, thrift and having a sense of shame. People from Hong Kong, Thailand, the People's Republic of China (PRC), Korea, and Japan tend to score high on this dimension (Hofstede, 1997). A low score on Confucian dynamism reflects an orientation toward the present and the past and indicates a value set that includes personal steadiness and stability, saving face, respect for tradition, and reciprocation of favors. The United States, Canada, and Pakistan score low on this dimension. While the construct of uncertainty avoidance as a totality received little support in this study, the researchers reported a link between uncertainty avoidance and the future aspect of Confucian dynamism. This link implies that individuals who avoid uncertainty may also be concerned about the future, which is, of course, uncertain. As a consequence of these findings, managers may consider that positions requiring a future orientation may be well suited to individuals who score high on Confucian dynamism.

Time orientation is an integral part of the concept of Confucian dynamism, and there is little doubt that various cultures view time in different ways. It is generally accepted that time perspective in the United States is very short-sighted, emphasizing short-term gains at the expense of long- term returns. On the other hand, Japan and other Asian countries focus on long-term returns by investing in certain industries, with a goal of maintaining national competitiveness (Lenway and Murtha, 1994). In order to verify how Western European, American, and Japanese companies actually behave with respect to time perspective, R. M. Peterson, C. C. Dibrell, and T. L. Pett (2002) studied upper-level managers from several countries. While the researchers found that time-perspective differences do exist between countries, they noted that there was in fact little difference between the Japanese and the Americans on both long- and short-term time orientations. The Western European–based companies scored high on both a short-term and a long-term perspective and so are able to compete effectively with both strategies. However, Peterson, Dibrell, and Pett studied only two specific industries (chemicals and transportation), so their results may be industry specific rather than culturally based. Specific company or industry performance may not be accurately reflected by a broad national-level approach, integrating data from many different industries, to studying organizational strategies.

In addition, individual value sets may play an important role in effectively utilizing managers in overseas assignments, particularly in 'Asia (Robertson, 2000). Although Confucian dynamism was thought to be unrelated to any of Hofstede's initial four dimensions (Franke, Hofstede, and Bond, 1991), other researchers found that when one country, Pakistan, was excluded from the analysis there was a strong negative correlation between individualism and Confucian dynamism (Yeh and Lawrence, 1995).

Subsequently, Hofstede (1997) accepted the additional dimension of Confucian dynamism but preferred to call it *long- versus short-term orientation*. The way people look at time varies across cultures, and people with a long-term orientation tend to be future oriented and enter relationships expecting a long-term relationship and knowing that any positive outcomes from that relationship may not occur for some time. On the other hand, individuals with a short-term orientation are more likely to want quick results and profits and to focus on the immediate future without concern for longer-term consequences. The current classification system, then, is generally accepted as having the four initial bipolar dimensions, individualism-collectivism, masculinity-femininity, power distance, and uncertainty avoidance, as well as the fifth dimension, which is labeled *Confucian work dynamism* by Eastern researchers and *long- and short-term orientation* by Western researchers.

Although Hofstede considered power distance and individualism-collectivism as separate factors, they are in fact strongly negatively correlated. These two factors have received the most attention from researchers and are generally accepted as being the most useful aspect of the Hofstede framework for studying cultures and organizations. Cultural differences on all the dimensions can be quite distinct. For example, Americans tend to have average power-distance and uncertainty-avoidance scores, be higher than average in individualism, and be fairly masculine and short-term oriented. On the other hand, the overseas Chinese (i.e., those outside mainland China [the PRC] in Hong Kong or Taiwan) tend to have a large power distance with weak uncertainty avoidance, low individualism, and a long-term orientation. While data from many countries were collected, Hofstede's original survey did not include significant areas of the world such as mainland China, Africa, and the former communist-bloc countries. Since a theory of cultures should be tested in as many cultures as possible, other researchers need to fill in some of the global gaps.

Hofstede's classification of culture provides one possible framework for understanding the underlying values within a country and how a country differs from other countries. Hofstede argued that where a culture falls along each of these bipolar dimensions determines the way organizations within that culture are structured and managed. So, for example, even though an organization is operating within a collectivist culture, it may be structured and managed as if the culture is individualistic. Hofstede cautioned that the dimensions he proposed are constructs and, as such, cannot be directly measured; they should be used only as tools to help analyze organizational behavior, structure, and situations. While his research is important for its breadth of cultural study, Hofstede did not investigate how the initial four dimensions of work-related values and attitudes affect the organizational structure. In other words, he labeled the differences that he found without attempting to understand if or how these differences affect organizational structure or if the organizational structure somehow affects the dimensions he identified.

One study that did use the Hofstede framework to look at its effect on organizational structure compared British and Indian organizations (Tayeb, 1988). Organizations in the two countries were found to be different in whether and how things are delegated, formal organizational structures and practices, and communication patterns but similar in the areas of centralization, joint decisions, specialization, and control strategies. Tayeb did not think that the cultural differences between the two countries could explain his results. He believed that there had to be noncultural explanations for the differences and similarities. In particular, he suggested that people's occupation and level of education play a key role in influencing variables such as trust, job security, and tolerance for ambiguity. For example, people who are better educated and/or fill executive-level positions are more likely to trust others and tolerate ambiguity.

The general level of support for the four (or five) dimensions of culture that Hofstede identified is high, and he has moved us an important step forward both in providing a theoretical basis for understanding culture and its effect on organizations and also in providing a theory that can be tested and used in research, especially since theory building is all too rare in the social science research world today. At the same time, there are serious questions that have been raised about the way the theory was developed, the way the data were used and interpreted, and some of the underlying assumptions of the framework. These criticisms raise some valid concerns and need to be carefully considered when either using the framework in research or interpreting the results of past, ongoing, and future studies that use the framework.

Criticisms of the Hofstede Approach

There has been a great deal of criticism of the Hofstede cultural framework, especially of the way that it was developed. For example, when Hofstede began his research, his questionnaire was not designed to measure culture. Rather, the questionnaire was designed to measure employee satisfaction, morale, and perception of work. Hofstede developed his dimensions of culture as an afterthought to the original purpose for the data collection. In addition, his research was not initially grounded in any theoretical framework based on cultural theory (Roberts and Boyacigiller, 1984). Another criticism of Hofstede's research is that he used an exploratory factor analysis as his statistical technique to develop the cultural dimensions. This approach is not considered statistically valid because it is based on trying a variety of options until one appears to fit rather than the more rigorous statistical approach of testing a specific set of parameters based on specific hypotheses (Fink and Monge, 1985). In addition, the results of the factor analysis, as computed, raise questions about the strength and interrelationship of the factors that were isolated. The results only demonstrated which factors could be lumped together in a particular cluster rather than establishing construct validity or the reasonable certainty that it is possible to understand what the factors actually measure (Yamagishi, Jin, and Miller, 1998).

In looking at the various items used by Hofstede in his survey, there is little apparent similarity or face validity between the operational definitions of individualism and collectivism and the questionnaire items that Hofstede claimed measured these categories (i.e., the items seem not to match what is supposed to be measured) (Kagitcibasi, 1997). In addition, Hofstede only studied employees in one company, IBM. This is a major company that had a very strong corporate culture and was predominantly male at the time of the data collection. It is unclear if the research, now almost thirty-five years old, would generate the same results today, given the changes within IBM and other factors. One study that suggests that the results would probably be different today involved students from ten

European countries and found that different work goals were endorsed in the mid-1990s than had been identified in Hofstede's earlier IBM-based data (Hofstede, Kolman, Niclescu, and Pajumaa, 1996).

As long as it is remembered that Hofstede's variables are general trends averaged across large numbers of individuals rather than predictors of individual behavior, his approach does provide an interesting framework for research and theorizing about organizations and cultural differences. While the issue of whether individualism and collectivism are two ends of a continuum remains unclear, this particular aspect of cultural difference has frequently been used with success in a variety of research settings.

Culture and Economic Growth

Cultural variables have also been linked to economic growth, because a nation's cultural values probably affect its economic success or failure (Hofstede and Bond, 1988). Researchers have attempted to explain why some countries, such as Taiwan, Hong Kong, and Singapore, have experienced high levels of economic growth while other countries have not. Indeed, Hofstede and his fellow researchers have been very forceful in articulating their belief that "differences in cultural values, rather than in managerial and structural conditions, are the ultimate determinants of human organization and behavior, and thus of economic growth" (Franke, Hofstede, and Bond, 1991, p. 166). Others disagree with this conclusion, arguing that it is based on flawed research and that, for a link to be established between national culture and economic growth, culture needs to be appropriately defined and measured and economic factors need to be more fully defined (Yeh and Lawrence, 1995). In considering the issues raised by this research approach, the mere presence or absence of cultural values is insufficient to explain economic growth within a country or to prove that economic freedom is the key link in the relationship between culture and economic growth. It appears that culture may well play a role in economic growth, but if it does, it is not the only factor and it does so in complex ways (Johnson and Lenartowicz, 1998).

Human Resource Issues and Culture

When organizations operate across cultures, human resource issues can create special challenges for organizations. For example, if managers are assigned overseas and individuals from other countries have been sent as part of or to head up a management team, they will have to manage employees from other and different cultures than their home culture. As stated earlier, research has shown that management techniques developed in one culture do not always produce the same results in a different culture (Adler, 1997). Human resource issues, therefore, require special attention in an international framework. Human resource management can have a direct and significant impact on managerial and employee behavior, so it is especially important to realize that Western management models and concepts do not necessarily transfer to other cultures. For example, a comparison of American and Chinese management trainees found that the Chinese performed best in groups and anonymously whereas the Americans performed best when operating individually and getting credit for their actions (Early, 1989). Thus, the effectiveness of the use of teams as a management approach will be influenced by culture.

Research Issues and Culture

The question of culture is very complex. Conducting research across cultures is not easy, and numerous methodological problems need to be addressed. Even though cross-cultural studies have yet to resolve many conceptual and methodological issues and societal culture or nationality are commonly accepted definitions of group culture, a common framework provides a good starting point, since the commonly used approaches to cultural assessment are inadequate when used independently. Because looking at a single country in isolation does not permit the elimination of alternative or competing explanations for any findings, standard research approaches dictate that it is better to conduct concurrent studies in several countries at the same time. By attempting to compare groups that are equivalent in every way but one (e.g., culture), it is possible to be reasonably certain that any differences can be attributed to that single variable. If that single variable is the country or cultural background, then conclusions can reasonably be drawn about differences between the cultures.

There are basically two different approaches to assessing culture. Culture-centered approaches are qualitative and explore more global, societal, or sociological or anthropological issues, while personality-centered approaches tend to use more quantitative measures and explore more individual and psychological issues (Clark, 1990).

The four most common approaches in cross-cultural research are (1) ethnological description, (2) direct values inference, (3) validated regional affiliation, and (4) validated benchmarks. Ethnological description is a qualitative approach based on observing and describing social structures and behaviors. This approach is more anthropological or sociological than psychological. The direct-values-inference approach measures the values within a sample or population, and cultural characteristics are then assigned based on the prevailing measures found within that culture. The value dimensions identified by Hofstede and others discussed earlier reflect this approach. Validated regional affiliation, a common approach in business research, is based on the assumptions that national character exists and that core cultural values are shared within countries (Hofstede, 1984). The fourth approach, using validated benchmarks, makes use of cultural characteristics identified in other studies, which are then used as benchmarks. Studies using the Hofstede measures are examples of this approach.

In all of the approaches, problems can occur if the assumption is made that the particular population or sample being studied shares the values of the larger culture when in fact it does not. A cultural-assessment framework has been proposed that includes the establishment and validation of the existence of a specific cultural grouping and provides valid measures for the type of study, including several, rather than just a single, assessment approaches. This framework includes the idea that multiple subcultures need to be identified within the country being studied, and then a value-based cultural assessment needs to be used to verify the distinctiveness of these subcultures. In this way, the question of whether there is a subculture effect on organizations can be answered. This approach is particularly relevant in complex countries where many distinct subcultures coexist, because only if subculture differences are minimal can a country be classified as located at a single point on any dimension of culture (Lenartowicz and Roth, 1999).

Research in Organizations

Research conducted in organizations is difficult to do effectively, because research is generally stronger and more valid if variables can be manipulated and controlled. For example, if a researcher wishes to study the impact of an increase in salary on performance, from a research perspective, a simple and valid approach to conducting the study is to randomly select individuals and assign them to one of two groups. One group is then given an increase in salary while the other is not. The performance of the two groups can be measured before and after the manipulation and the results compared. If the two groups are equivalent in performance before but different after, then given that all other things are the same, any differences in performance can be attributed to the increase in salary. While this approach has merit from a research perspective, finding organizations willing to participate in this type of controlled study is difficult. Further, it is almost certainly not possible to completely isolate one group from another. Word that one group of colleagues has received a raise while another has not is sure to spread. The result may well be that rather than having a happy productive group and an unchanged group after the raise, the group that did not get a raise will be unhappy and less productive. Thus, despite the good research design, the results are still open to alternative explanations, and the impact on the organization may not be what was wanted or desirable.

If we add the issue of working across cultures to this mix, the problem becomes even more difficult. Research in organizations, therefore, requires trade-offs. The more control we have in our research, the less realistic it tends to be, even though we have controlled for confounding variables. On the other hand, "real world" research, such as case studies and field research, is more realistic but is also more likely to fail to minimize or eliminate confounding variables, making the results less valid and subject to different interpretations.

Even the issue of equivalency of samples can be problematic. First, there is the issue of which countries to sample and the basis for their selection. The second issue is which individuals should be selected to represent the culture. For example, many studies use MBA students because they are readily available as research subjects, and some researchers consider MBA students from different countries to be equivalent. However, it is a lot easier to attend graduate school in the United States than it is in other countries. It is reasonable to assume that 20 percent or more of applicants get into an MBA program somewhere in America, while in Thailand it is less than 1 percent.

In this example, membership in our sample is related to availability of programs, to cultural values, and to the relative need for undergraduate and graduate degrees both within the culture and at the educational level of the programs. This leads to the possibility not only that two samples are not equivalent but also that one or both of the samples may not in fact be representative of the population being studied. Another example of these sampling concerns is that a British student who completes A-level courses before leaving high school is generally given six units of undergraduate credit for each A-level successfully completed if the student enters an American university. Thus, the American educational system systematically accepts that an education obtained at the high-school level in Britain is equivalent to first-year university-level education in the United States. Along the same lines, census data, electoral rolls, a sampling of equal numbers of male and female managers, and telephone or business directories all are based on different cultural standards, procedures, and values. Thus, the equivalency of samples cannot be taken for granted even if the samples appear on the surface to be equal in education, status, role, or occupation. One way to mitigate this problem is to select a sampling procedure based on several national or cultural populations.

One of the other primary concerns about conducting research in different cultures is the question of language. Since most questionnaires and other instruments developed for measuring different components of organizational behavior are written in English, they need to be translated. The process of translating an instrument is theoretically straightforward but in reality is not necessarily easy to do correctly. To ensure equivalency of two different language instruments, the accepted procedure is to use back-translation (Brislin, Lonner, and Thorndike, 1973). This approach requires that the instrument or document be translated from one language to another by someone experienced in translation and knowledgeable about the culture of the country of the new language. Once the translation is completed, it is given to a second and independent translator who translates it back to the original language. The original and the double-translated document, which should be the same, are then compared, and adjustments are made to reconcile any differences. While this allows for an accurate and relatively literal translation, it does not always accommodate subtle differences in the meaning of the words. For example, in one research project, I had to have a scale translated that included the phrase "Feeling in on things," which was one of the items on a ranking of motivators (Silverthorne, 1992). Capturing the meaning of this phrase in the translation to Russian was difficult and took several attempts. Eventually, the final translation, which was less literal but more accurate than the initial one, hopefully completely captured the intent and meaning behind the phrase. Even words that are easily translated, such as *trust,* cannot be assumed to have the same meaning in different cultures. In German, trust is expressed with two verbs, *trauen* and *vertrauen.* While both verbs translate as "to trust," one is used in the negative sense while the other is used in the positive sense, reflecting a cultural value that starts with mistrust and moves toward trust. In English, *trust* means reliance on and confidence in the truth and worth of a person. It begins with the assumption of trust and moves toward mistrust. The result is that the same word is subject to the subtlety of the linguistic interpretation of it, which will shade how it is used and interpreted. Other words that are common in English and organizational research may not exist in other languages. For example, Chinese lacks tenses, and words such as *autonomy* cannot be adequately translated into Chinese.

Even if the scale is translated accurately, there is another potential culturally based problem that needs to be considered. Often, the typical American research instrument uses a Likert Scale. Respondents are given a statement and generally a five- or seven-point response scale that provides for a range of responses from "strongly agree" to "strongly disagree." While Americans tend to be willing to use all the available response options as they see fit, people from some cultures are less willing to vary their responses from the central or neutral response option. This tendency can be offset somewhat by eliminating the neutral or midpoint of the scale, thus forcing respondents to choose a response toward one of the two ends of the scale. Other respondents may show a response bias based on what they think the researcher wants, and in this way their responses show generalized acquiescence. To help address some of these problems, M. H. Bond (1988) proposed a procedure he called *within-subject standardization.* In this approach, each subject's score on a scale is expressed relative to responses on other scales. In this way, the data can be reshaped to indicate any bias and more easily compared to different response sets in different cultures. (For a fuller discussion of these concerns about response sets in cross-cultural research, see Hui and Triandis, 1989).

It is also possible that if a graduated scale is used, interpretations of differences in the steps of the scale will vary, because language differences and the type of scale used are interrelated problems. For example, nine scale terms, allowing for responses from "excellent" to "very bad" were compared across eight languages (Sood, 1990). This comparison of the gradation steps has been called *measuring the metric equivalence of scales*. The results indicated that some languages, such as Korean, have fewer terms to express the gradation in evaluation while others, such as French, have many. When values were assigned to each of the steps on a graded scale from 1 to 100, the researcher found differences in the scores for the values in different countries. For example, the Spanish *muy malo* was rated 58 percent higher than its English equivalent, *very bad*. Challenges associated with the use of instruments developed for use in one country but used in another remain. If scales are not translated to account for language and cultural differences, then scale reliability may be compromised. On the other hand, if scales are modified to address cultural differences, then the ability to draw accurate conclusions based on direct comparison between different cultural groups may be jeopardized.

There are several other issues related to the equivalence of data. The first is whether people are willing to respond to surveys, questionnaires, or interviewers. In the United States, return rates are often as low as 3 percent, but in my experience response rates in Taiwan are likely to be around 30 percent. Honesty levels of respondents may also vary, with some cultures being more honest and truthful while others are more concerned about providing the researcher with the kind of responses the respondents think are wanted. Questions about certain topics, such as drinking behavior, are more likely to be answered honestly in Scandinavian countries than in Latin American countries, while other topics, such as sex, are taboo in countries such as India (Douglas and Craig, 1984). Individuals in some cultures may be reluctant to respond to personal questions, whether in writing or in an interview, because they either fear how the information will be used or see the questions as an invasion of their privacy. For example, the very private and reserved nature of Saudis makes them poor candidates for research involving interviews (Tuncalp, 1988). More generally, in some cultures there will be a reluctance to answer questions posed by women or by men or by people from specific other cultures or races.

On the other hand, cultural differences may dictate unique or unusual ways to collect data. For example, it has been suggested that since many

African countries have an oral tradition of passing leadership practices from one generation to the next, storytelling is a good way to collect data there. Specifically, participants are asked to tell a story about a time that they thought about or experienced some aspect of organizational behavior, such as leadership. The story is taped and then later analyzed. Since storytelling is highly valued in African culture, it serves as a way to socialize people and share information (Banutu-Gomez, 2003).

Summary

Many countries operate with and encourage the concept of a single culture or system of shared meanings. Culture is difficult to measure because our national culture shapes the way we perceive the world and is often taken for granted. Frameworks for describing or quantifying aspects of culture are useful in cross-cultural research. Hofstede has provided one theoretical framework that has been useful in structuring research and also can be useful for managers and organizations to understand some of the differences encountered when operating across cultures. While his framework of culture has been challenged, it does provide a theoretical foundation for beginning an exploration of the way that national culture affects organizations.

Conducting research across cultures and within organizations poses many challenges. Issues of control, equivalency of samples, and differences in measurement techniques all require extra attention and consideration in both cross-cultural and organizational research. Replications of research studies in different cultures are difficult to conduct, and research strategies involving both qualitative and quantitative methods should be used. The challenge is to design and conduct studies that meet the standard of following a robust experimental design while maintaining the value of being generalizable to different populations within and between cultures.

3

Culture and Organizations

Cultural differences are important variables in understanding social and organizational behavior (Leung and Bond, 1984). Culture is such an important determinant of behavior that it has been proposed that it be included when psychological theories are constructed (Triandis, 1976). However, given that we accept that culture is important, we still need to define what the concept of culture encompasses. There are unique methodological issues that arise in research on cultures. For example, as mentioned in the last chapter, cultural differences exist in the way that people respond to questionnaires and surveys. In addition, sample size takes on added importance if there are many individual differences within a culture. Because of these and other issues, individual and cultural differences require distinct approaches if we are to understand how cultural-variation patterns affect behavior. The identification of cross-cultural differences based on an analysis at either the individual or cultural level alone is not a sufficient focus in cross-cultural research; cultural differences need to be considered at both levels (Leung, 1989).

Several important aspects of cross-cultural management are influenced by cultural differences. For example, consumer preferences are often dictated by cultural values, where *culture* generally refers to the culture of a country. Researchers and theorists in organizational behavior have introduced the idea that organizational culture plays an important role in various aspects of an organization's daily life. Cultural values influence managerial and employee perceptions of their environment, expectations, and individual behavior. If people, even in the same organization, have different assumptions, then they will see events and react to them differently (Sims and Gioia, 1986). People from different cultures approach problems differently and have different ways to resolve and apply solutions to problems (Abramson, Lane, Nagai, and Takagi, 1993). When there are many cultural differences in an organization, there is a greater need to seek out suitable forms of cooperation (Olie, 1994). By being aware of cultural differences, managers and organizations can reduce the probability of failure when operating outside their home culture (Tung, 1987).

In the age of multinational organizations, the issue of organizational versus national culture is a complex and important one to consider. If a company has an organizational culture in one country (e.g., Japan), what happens when that company creates an operation in the United States? Will the organizational culture or the national culture dominate? If national culture is the critical variable, will it be the home or host culture that influences organizational behavior the most? The home-country culture and values are significant environmental factors for the company. If all of the companies being considered as part of a study operate within a single country, then it is reasonable to assume that the national culture is consistent across all the companies, while the organizational culture may differ between companies. A unique situation occurs in multinational companies (MNCs). If a company brings to a new country an organizational culture that is clearly different from the national culture of the host country, problems may result. A company such as IBM has an organizational culture that was established in the United States, which it tends to impose on subsidiaries in other countries at the expense of local differences in an attempt to maintain control and equivalency of operations (Peters and Waterman, 1982). While it can be argued that this approach appears to have worked for IBM, it is not universally effective. For example, numerous Western companies operating branches in China have encountered problems, and a high percentage of joint ventures fail. Relatedly, sometimes managers behave in different ways when interacting with others from their own country than they might with managers from other countries. In other words, their cross-cultural and intracultural behaviors may be the same when they should be different or different when they should be the same (Adler and Graham, 1989).

What Is Culture?

How culture should be defined is open to debate. In addition, there is considerable confusion in the literature about what the constructs of both organizational and national culture mean. There are two primary approaches to understanding and describing culture (Peng, Peterson, and

Shyi, 1991). One approach looks at the meaning of artifacts and behaviors within a given culture. This approach, called the *emic* approach, is culture specific. The second approach, called the *etic* approach, is culture general in that it looks for concepts that can be considered universal across cultures. The etic approach studies similarities and differences between cultures. The general consensus is that a culture reflects the shared values of its members. Further, the culture can and will influence managerial practices and approaches to employee motivation, and it can provide the standards or guidelines for defining appropriate behavior (Erez, 1994).

It has been argued that although national culture is an important construct, cultures and nations are not equivalent (Erez and Early, 1993). This premise was tested in a number of subcultures in Brazil using an instrument designed to assess differences in culture based on measures of differences in values among the subcultures (Lenartowicz and Roth, 2001). Strong differences were found in motivation and business performance among the subcultures, supporting the view that layers of culture exist within the national culture (Hofstede, 1997). In other words, the subcultures, or different cultural groups within the primary culture, held different values from one another.

In order to gain an understanding of culture, two different conceptual or research approaches have typically been used (Adler, 1984). One approach studies behaviors in a single culture. This approach is culture specific and provides a lot of information about a single culture. The second approach attempts to study a limited set of concepts but looks for universality across cultures. The latter approach is more frequently used in organizational research since it offers a greater opportunity for allowing generalizations within organizations (Peng, Peterson, and Shyi, 1991).

Other Theoretical Approaches to Defining Culture

There are several other approaches to understanding and measuring culture that are worthy of consideration. One such model, developed by the well-known organizational psychologist Edgar Schein (1985), can be applied to both national and organizational cultures. In his model, Schein states that culture operates on at least three different levels:

Behaviors and artifacts.
Beliefs and values.
Underlying assumptions or values.

Within a culture, each of these levels differs in how apparent or visible it is to people. Schein considered behaviors and artifacts to be the most readily apparent of the three levels and the underlying assumptions to be the least apparent. Thus, Schein ordered the three levels of culture from the easiest to see, behavior, to the hardest to see, values. Underlying assumptions or values have to be inferred rather than seen. While the Schein model can be applied to both organizational and national cultures, it has been argued that organizational culture only influences the first two levels of general culture but will have little effect on the deepest level of culture, that is, its underlying assumptions or values (Laurent, 1986). If this is true, multinational companies operating outside their own national culture will still be influenced by the deepest level of local culture in all branches, and the underlying assumptions of the host country's national culture will influence the organizational culture. In other words, even if the culture of a company is strong throughout the organization no matter where it is operating, the national culture of the host country will have at least some minimal impact on the organization. Further, the values prescribed by the organizational culture may be distinct from the values prescribed by the national culture of the host country.

The underlying values in a culture map out the ways that individuals evaluate their world, the self, and others. These underlying assumptions include the individual's views of both nature and human relationships. The individual's relationship with nature includes control over the environment, levels of activity or passivity, attitudes toward uncertainty, notions of time, attitudes toward change, and what determines "truth." The human-relationship aspect includes task versus social orientation, the importance of hierarchy, and the importance of the individual versus the group. The relationship-with-nature aspect of culture is particularly important. For example, Western cultures tend to view humanity as the master of nature, enabling nature to be controlled and exploited. Eastern cultures, on the other hand, tend to view humanity as subservient to nature and time; change and uncertainty are accepted as a given.

Assumptions regarding the texture of human relationships are also different between Western and Eastern cultures. The importance of social concerns over task, the role of the individual versus the group, and the role of hierarchy are clearly different between the East and West. Eastern cultures tend to place more emphasis on social or relationship issues than on the task at hand, and more emphasis on the acceptance of hierarchy and on the group than on the individual. Western cultures tend to focus more on the task and on the individual. The acceptance of hierarchy is considered to be of lesser importance. However, even these distinctions are not so clear-cut, and there are variations between the United States and Europe and even within the countries of Europe (Hofstede, 1984).

The Hofstede Approach to Defining Culture

The role of cultural differences received a great deal of attention when Hofstede published his major work, *Culture's Consequences,* in 1980. This study concentrated on personal values as they relate to the work setting. The subjects were the employees of IBM, which had subsidiaries in seventy-two countries. Employees had previously completed questionnaires that included measures of their personal values. Hofstede used the responses from the preexisting data bank of employee attitudes collected between 1967 and 1973 to facilitate comparisons of various dimensions across many countries. This was the first major quantitative study designed to look at differences and similarities of values across cultures. Since all of the individuals studied were from the same company, Hofstede argued that the differences between countries could not be caused by organizational differences and, so, must be directly related to differences in national cultures.

Hofstede's findings suggest that there is a difference between cultures in the way they look at the world, particularly in relation to a culture's values. Hofstede further argued that there was a need to distinguish between nations and societies and that the concept of culture applied more to societies than nations, since some nations are very complex and include diverse societies within national boundaries (Hofstede, 1997). To Hofstede, culture is a subjective or implicit concept that is not always easy to see or gauge. Therefore, companies operating across cultures need to fully understand the impact that the national culture has on an organization. If the national culture is indeed dominant over the organizational culture, managers may face special challenges operating in this environment, either from a theoretical perspective or in the application of management practices.

Some Different Perspectives on Hofstede's Approach

Several authors have raised questions about Hofstede's research and his interpretation of the data. B. McSweeney (2002) provides a detailed critique of the research and challenges the existence of a consistent national-culture effect. In terms of the methodology, McSweeney points out that although Hofstede reported a sample size of 11,700, this included all the data for two different surveys in all countries surveyed. While sample sizes in some countries were large, in other countries the sample included only around one hundred, leading McSweeney to question whether it was reasonable to claim that an accurate measure of national culture could be obtained from very small samples, particularly when they were convenience samples and all the respondents worked for a single company. While Hofstede argues that comparing people from the same organization means that they share the same organizational and occupational cultures, so any differences between countries must be based on national culture (Hofstede, 1984), McSweeney questions whether, in fact, it is reasonable to assume that all IBM branches or subsidiaries share the same organizational culture or that multiple organizational cultures cannot exist within the same company (see also Parker, 2000). McSweeney also raises questions about the assumption that the questionnaire responses were equivalent in each country, since there is adequate research demonstrating that different styles of questions and response alternatives and the way individuals respond to questionnaire items across cultures generally produce different results.

Finally, the notion of a culture being represented by a series of independent constructs, such as uncertainty avoidance, is also questioned. It is possible that any set of dimensions of culture interacts in some way. For example, some have argued that culture is based on a dynamic relationship between values (Schwartz, 1992). Others have maintained that the concept of a set of bipolar dimensions is not supported, pointing out that individualism and collectivism, for example, rather than being two ends of a continuum, can exist at the same time but with different emphases depending on the situation (Triandis, 1995).

In an interesting review of the use of dichotomous categories in generalizing about cultures, M. Voronov and J. A. Singer (2002) explore criticisms of the Hofstede approach by focusing on the individualism-collectivism category. They note that it is one of the most widely used constructs in cross-cultural research for explaining cultural differences in behavior, and they question its value and validity on several levels. The first is that people in collectivist cultures frequently behave in an individualistic way. When reporting his initial findings, Hofstede had assumed that a culture was a relatively consistent construct within a country, yet large variability within countries has been found, as he himself states in a later publication. For example, many differences have been found within Arab cultures (Buda and Elsayed-Elkhouly, 1998). Variation in individualism-collectivism has also been found to occur within a single culture (Wagner, 1995). A high degree of either individualism or collectivism was not found in a study that included only one region of India, even though India is generally considered a collectivist culture. In addition, younger, urban, and more-educated individuals tended to be more collectivist. Demographic variables such as level of education, type of employment, and urban versus rural environments can describe differences within cultures (Mishra, 1994). The individualism-collectivism category may be not an independent variable that affects attitudes and behaviors but, rather, a dependent variable that reflects societal conditions within a culture. Further, much of the cross-cultural research that has been done is really cross-national research, in that the focus is less on cultural differences and more on national differences. The general disagreement on both the conceptualization and measurement of the individualism-collectivism construct is also of concern, and the use of such constructs may oversimplify human behavior, which is extremely complex.

The issues of concern to McSweeney (2002) and others are significant and need to be carefully considered. They raise many serious questions about the validity and interpretation of Hofstede's findings. While many researchers have embraced Hofstede's results and used the concepts in their own studies, these results need to be carefully evaluated in the big picture. Whether we can rely on Hofstede's approach to defining culture is at best debatable. Given the enthusiasm generated by Hofstede's research, studies testing or using his concepts are reported along with other research in this book, and the reader will need to decide how much weight should be given to the results and conclusions.

Another Perspective on Culture

There have been several other approaches to defining culture. The Israeli psychologist S. H. Schwartz attempted to develop a theory of culture based on a set of dimensions from both the individual and cultural levels (1992, 1994b). His approach paralleled that of Hofstede (1984) and built on the work of other scholars as well. Schwartz collected data from forty-one cultural groups based on a list of fifty-six specific human values. Respondents were asked to indicate how much each of the values was "a guiding principle in my life." From the results obtained in several different research studies, Schwartz hypothesized and found support for seven types of values at the cultural level and ten individual-level values. The cultural-level values were conservatism, harmony, egalitarian commitment, intellectual autonomy, affection autonomy, mastery, and hierarchy. The ten individual-level value types were power, achievement, hedonism, stimulation, self-direction, universalism, benevolence, tradition, conformity, and security. All of these values were isolated using a statistical technique, called *smallest space analysis,* that allows values to be clustered in groups based on the distinctiveness of the differences. The utility of this approach is that it identifies consistent sets of values that appear to exist in most countries. At the same time, no judgments are made about the relative importance of these values within a culture.

Hofstede and Schwartz collected data in some of the same countries, which permitted some direct comparisons for same-country results. As expected, autonomy (Schwartz) and individualism (Hofstede) were positively correlated, and conservatism (Schwartz) and individualism (Hofstede) were negatively correlated. On the other hand, an unexpected positive correlation was found between egalitarian commitment (Schwartz) and individualism (Hofstede). Schwartz (1994a) used this finding to argue that Hofstede's individualism-collectivism dimension is too broad and does not allow for voluntary and independent actions by people to help others. Hofstede and Schwartz thus provide two similar but distinct perspectives on cultural values. The primary difference is that Schwartz separates the role of the individual in society from the role of individuals in pursuing group or cultural goals.

Studies examining values from a cross-cultural perspective have focused on differences in the importance attributed to various values, how differences in importance occur, and explanations for these differences (Schwartz, 1999). Schwartz and G. Sagie (2000) expanded on earlier research and investigated the degree of value homogeneity or hetero-geneity within a nation, using the ten motivationally distinct types of val-ues. The study found that value consensus and value importance both re-late to central structural characteristics of societies, socioeconomic devel-opment, and political democratization. In other words, the form a society takes reflects a consensus of which values are held within the culture and their relative importance. Further, consensus on basic values correlated negatively with democratization, so that democratic societies are more likely to reflect a wide array of values and nondemocratic societies are more likely to reflect a narrower set of values.

A Further Look at the Individualism-Collectivism Dimension

Despite Schwartz's assertion about the questionable utility of the dimen-sion, research since the 1980s has identified the individualism-collec-tivism continuum as perhaps the best means to measure values differences across cultures, especially between Eastern and Western cultures. Like-wise, Confucianism has been a deep-rooted foundation of Chinese life for over two thousand years, and Confucian work dynamism epitomizes the Eastern values of perseverance, thrift, and attaining long-term goals, and the construct indicates the importance of Confucianism to all Asian soci-eties. Confucianism creates a belief in harmonious interpersonal relation-ships, the value of hierarchy and order in society.

· As we have seen, it has been suggested that individualism and collec-tivism are really independent dimensions rather than two ends of a con-tinuum (Triandis et al., 1988) and also that individualism and collec-tivism should be considered in conjunction with the power distance con-struct. The separated dimensions capture the nuances lost by "averaging" them in with each other. The research results, while not conclusive, tend to support the perspective that individualism and collectivism are better viewed as separate dimensions (Ralston, Nguyen, and Napier, 1999). The concepts of individualism, collectivism, and power distance have been combined to create four theoretically unique culture types (Singelis, Triandis, Bhawuk, and Gelfand, 1995; Triandis and Gelfand, 1998):

> *Horizontal individualism (H-I)* is characterized by an autonomous self-concept. Self-reliance is stressed, and individuals are viewed as having equal status.

Vertical individualism (V-I) is characterized by autonomy but unequal status and generally includes a competitive thrust.

Horizontal collectivism (V-C) is characterized by the self being seen as part of a group that reflects the individual's self-concept. Individuals are seen as being on an equal level to all other members of the group.

Vertical collectivism (V-C) is characterized by individuals seeing themselves as part of a group, but inequality within the group is both accepted and expected.

The Kluckholn and Strodbeck View of Culture

One of the best models for evaluating culture is derived from an anthropological perspective provided within the work of Kluckholn and Strodbeck (1961). They describe cultures in terms of six different value orientations. A value orientation is a set of principles that directs people's lives. Kluckholn and Strodbeck argue that these six value orientations encompass differences in a culture based on three assumptions:

There are a limited number of problems that people must face, so everybody needs a solution to these problems.

There are a limited number of solutions available, but within these solutions there will be some variability.

People in different cultures will prefer different solutions depending on the different values of the culture.

The six value orientations are the following:

1. *Human nature orientation* looks at the nature of people and whether they are basically good or evil.
2. *Relationship-to-nature orientation* looks at whether people see themselves as the masters of the world or whether nature is the master; this also relates to whether people can live in harmony with nature.
3. *Time orientation* looks at whether a culture places an emphasis on the past, the present, or the future.

4. *Activity orientation* looks at whether the culture emphasizes being active and spontaneous, doing and achieving, or containing and controlling.
5. *Relational orientation* looks at whether the relationships between people are hierarchical, collective, or individually based.
6. *Space orientation* looks at whether the space around a person is perceived as either private or public. (Kluckholn and Strodbeck, 1961)

When researchers asked individuals to rank these dimensions in order of preference, respondents in a similar situation tended to rank the dimensions the same way. For example, the rank ordering tended to be the same for people within a culture and different for people outside that culture. Kluckholn and Strodbeck also noted that not all individuals fit the cultural pattern, that there were respondents in their study who could be considered "cultural deviants."

The factors identified by Kluckholn and Strodbeck (1961) are similar to those found later by Hofstede (1984). Uncertainty avoidance relates closely to the human nature and relationship-to-nature orientations. Power distance relates to the hierarchical or relational orientation. Individualism is also related to relational orientation and parallels the individualism-collectivism preferences. Finally, the long- and short-term orientation of Hofstede and Bond relates directly to the time-orientation dimension of Kluckholn and Strodbeck. The two approaches, while using different research techniques, resulted in the development of similar sets of dimensions that can be used to describe culture. The theoretical framework developed by Kluckholn and Strodbeck has been used to develop a practical measure of culture in international management. While the problem of effectively measuring culture and values remains, one measure based on the framework developed by Kluckholn and Strodbeck, the Cultural Perspectives Questionnaire, is available and appears to be a reliable and valid instrument for examining cultural values (Maznevski and DiStefano, 1995).

Yet Another View of Culture

A Dutch researcher and economist, Fons Trompenaars, also developed a model of culture using questionnaires to construct a set of bipolar dimensions. His studies involved responses from a minimum of five hundred managers from each of twenty-eight countries. The questionnaire used value dimensions based on the conceptualization of American sociologist Talcott Parsons as well as the work of Kluckholn and Strodbeck discussed earlier in this chapter. It is important to note that Trompenaars developed his questionnaire based on previously created, brief, value-laden business dilemmas, while Hofstede used existing data and regression techniques to define his dimensions. The results of Trompenaars's formulation led him to suggest the existence of seven dimensions of culture, which were subsequently supported by the results of his research (Trompenaars, 1993). Five of these dimensions are relevant in any discussion of organizational psychology and culture.

The first dimension, *individualism-collectivism,* is similar to the one proposed by Hofstede and looks at whether individuals perceive themselves primarily as individuals or as part of a group. Given the sociological roots of the theory of culture, it is not surprising that Trompenaars emphasizes the question of whether society should focus on facilitating an individual's ability and desire to contribute to society or whether the emphasis should be on collective issues shared by many. Trompenaars also points out that in collectivist societies there is often a variety of groups with which the individual can identify, such as the family or the country, and which group is selected will also vary by culture. For example, the Japanese tend to identify with their nationality first, the Chinese might identify with their family first, and the Irish might identify with their religion first.

The second dimension proposed in this theory is *universalism-particularism.* If people believe that what is true and good can be identified and applied everywhere, they are said to accept universalism. If, on the other hand, the society believes that unique circumstances and relationships prevail, then it is said to be a society based on particularism. The differences can take several forms. For example, a universalism approach will rely more on contracts and legal strategies, whereas a particularism approach will rely more on relationships and trust. Universalism is more frequently found in Western societies such as the United States and the Netherlands, while particularism is more likely to be found in Eastern societies such as China and Indonesia.

The third dimension, labeled *neutral versus affective relationships,* looks at when and how societies express emotions. In affective societies, such as Mexico and the Netherlands, expressing emotions openly is more natural. In neutral societies, such as Japan, emotions are held under control, and expressing emotions implies that you are out of control and is considered unprofessional at work. If people from countries representing the extremes of this dimension conduct business together, then people from neutral societies are likely to be seen as emotionally dead and hiding their true emotions in order to deceive, while people from affective societies are likely to be seen as out of control. This dimension relates to the emotional component of uncertainty avoidance within the Hofstede framework, but the two approaches are markedly different since the Hofstede construct is inclusive of many more aspects of human behavior.

The fourth dimension, called *specific versus diffuse relationships,* also looks at relationships. This dimension includes the degree to which individuals are involved with and feel comfortable dealing with other people. Individuals can be viewed as having two types of personal lives, one public and the other private. In specific-relationship societies, the public area is likely to be larger than the private area, and people will prefer to keep their private lives separate and closely guarded. The American and British cultures tend to be specific, and within these societies individuals have small and well-separated personal lives and larger public lives. In diffuse relationship cultures, such as Germany, individuals have large private and relatively small public lives. Because of these differences, Germans are more likely to maintain formal relationships and see Americans as intrusive and disrespectful when they ask questions such as "Where did you go to school?" Americans, on the other hand, are likely to see Germans as reserved and difficult to get to know.

The final dimension discussed here that is relevant to organizations is *achievement versus ascription.* This dimension includes how status and power are determined. Status can be achieved by either an individual's position or identity. In achievement-oriented societies, such as Austria and the United States, workers and managers are evaluated by how well they perform the tasks associated with their job, and people are judged by how they compare with others in similar positions. In ascriptive societies, such as Venezuela and China, status is associated with variables such as age, gender, qualifications, or the importance of the task or project. This dimension has no equivalent in the Hofstede framework, although it does include elements of the masculinity-femininity and power distance dimensions. In general, these dimensions add to our understanding of cultural differences that affect organizations directly, and they provide executives and managers with a framework for improving cultural under-standing on the job.

Still other researchers (e.g., Sullivan and Weaver, 2000) have suggested that culture should be examined from a cognitive perspective rather than considering culture a "latent variable." The cognitive perspective is more active and would consider how the members of a culture perceive or think about that culture rather than having culture viewed as a more passive as-pect of experience. By looking at cultural cognition, researchers are able to discover a framework by which managers interpret organizational be-haviors in particular ways. In addition, since there is a cultural perspec-tive that the researcher brings to his or her research, cognition will influence the way research is designed and interpreted. Therefore, good cross-cultural research requires that researchers be aware of their own cultural values and biases, both when conducting their research and when communicating the results, particularly to those in other cultures.

National Culture

We have seen that the definition of culture is open to interpretation and debate. This debate over substance does not, however, minimize the con-sensus view that national culture plays an important role within organi-zations (e.g., Hofstede, 1984). National culture has been shown to influence between 25 and 50 percent of the variation in employee and managerial attitudes (Gannon et al., 1994). While there is limited agree-ment on what is meant by national culture, in general, the culture of a so-ciety includes shared motives, values, and beliefs. The members of a cul-ture share common perceptions about their experiences and try to ensure that these perceptions are passed to future generations. The term *culture,* when used in this book, refers to national culture.

One of the most significant cross-cultural research projects currently underway is Project GLOBE (Global Leadership and Organizational Be-havior Effectiveness) (House, Javidan, and Dorfman, 2001). Although this group of researchers is considering leadership across cultures, they are also addressing the issue of defining culture. They effectively have defined culture by isolating nine cultural dimensions in their study:

Uncertainty avoidance: The extent to which members of an organi-zation or society strive to avoid uncertainty by reliance on social norms, rituals, and bureaucratic practices to alleviate the unpredictability of future events.

Power distance: The degree to which members of an organization or society expect and agree that power should be unequally shared.

Collectivism I: Societal collectivism: The degree to which organizational and societal institutional practices encourage and reward collective distribution of resources and collective action.

Collectivism II: In-group collectivism: The degree to which individuals express pride, loyalty, and cohesiveness in their organizations or families.

Gender egalitarianism: The extent to which an organization or a society minimizes gender-role differences and gender discrimination.

Assertiveness: The degree to which individuals in organizations or societies are assertive, confrontational, and aggressive in social relationships.

Future orientation: The degree to which individuals in organizations or societies engage in future-oriented behaviors such as planning, investing in the future, and delaying gratification.

Performance orientation: The extent to which an organization or society encourages and rewards group members for performance improvement and excellence.

Humane orientation: The degree to which individuals in organizations or societies encourage and reward individuals for being fair, altruistic, friendly, generous, caring, and kind to others. (House, Javidan, and Dorfman, 2001, p. 496)

Rather than looking at different countries independently, some researchers believe using cultural clusters that group countries together on the basis of geography or perceived similarities is a valid and more efficient alternative. This approach has the advantage of reducing the number of possible comparisons and simplifying the research process. However, for researchers who argue that considering a single country as the measure of culture ignores within-country cultural differences, the use of clusters is a step in the wrong direction. At the same time, organizations are more likely to expand into cultures that are similar to their home culture, and they are more likely to be successful if they do so than if they expand to cultures that are very different. Project GLOBE uses cultural clusters as a way to explore cultural similarities and differences. The study involves sixty-one countries, which were grouped into ten clusters. Some of the initial results are presented and discussed in chapter 6.

While there is no generally accepted process for clustering countries, geography, mass migration patterns, or religious and linguistic commonality are frequently used to guide the cluster formation (Gupta, Hanges, and Dorfman, 2002). In Project GLOBE, each country within a cluster includes more than two-thirds of the intersociety identified differences in values so that the clusters reflect the shared goals of the members. Within the categories of power distance, time orientation, and individualism-collectivism, the researchers decided that the use of societal clusters is appropriate for analysis of cultures. The Project GLOBE Arabic cluster includes Qatar, Morocco, Turkey, Egypt, and Kuwait. The Eastern European cluster includes Albania, Georgia, Greece, Hungary, Kazakhstan, Poland, Russia, and Slovenia. The Latin European cluster includes Italy, Portugal, Spain, France, French Switzerland, and Israel. The Germanic European cluster includes Austria, Germany, the Netherlands, and Switzerland. The Anglo cluster includes Australia, Canada, the United Kingdom, Ireland, New Zealand, South Africa (white sample), and the United States. The Southern Asia cluster includes India, Indonesia, the Philippines, Malaysia, Thailand, and Iran. The use of clusters allows for a broader understanding of similarities and differences but also implies that there is a great deal of similarity among the countries within a cluster. If this is true, it is easier to manage research by grouping countries into a relatively small number of clusters rather than the much more unwieldy approach of using separate countries. While this is certainly the view of the researchers involved in Project GLOBE, who feel that their analysis of country similarities supports the use of clusters, it contradicts the views of other researchers, who have argued that even a single country is too big and complex to be considered the unit of measurement.

A ten-nation study was undertaken with the aim of providing a more current validation of the four initial Hofstede classifications of national culture—individualism-collectivism, uncertainty avoidance, power distance, and masculinity-femininity—and investigating the relationship between respondents' perceptions of their actual culture and the culture they would like to live in. Using students from Belgium, Canada, Denmark, France, Germany, the United Kingdom, Greece, the Netherlands,

Spain, and the United States, support was found for the continued validity of the Hofstede dimensions. There was little difference, if any, between the culture as perceived and the culture desired. This finding was attributed to the possibility that since the subjects in this study were students in business-related topics, their ideal culture might have been influenced by the material in the courses they were taking at the time of the study (van Oudenhoven, 2001). This, in turn, raises the possibility that national culture will be transformed over time through exposure to other cultures. The issue of the convergence of cultures, so that they become more similar, or the divergence of cultures, so that they become more different, as a process in cultural change (discussed more fully chapter 8) was included in this study, but it is suggested that this issue is worthy of further study in order to better understand if organizations are in fact culture bound as Hofstede (1993) and others suggest.

Summary

The concept of culture provides the framework for providing meaning to members of the culture. In comparing cultures, we can assume that a single country shares the same culture, that any national culture includes many subcultures, or that if there is enough similarity among groups of countries, we can lump them together in clusters and then draw conclusions about all the countries at the same time. Each of these approaches has both supporters and detractors. The issue seems to rest on the level of specificity that we are studying as well as the aspect of culture. For example, in considering the values related to housing in a Western culture, there are likely to be more similarities than differences. However, if we look at an Arab culture, Arabs living in an urban environment will have quite different values about housing from those of nomadic tribes such as the Bedouin. There are several different approaches to understanding national cultures that provide a framework for cross-cultural research. Studies of value differences seem to provide the best conceptual basis for research, especially since the structure of individual values is relatively consistent across cultures and value differences among countries seem to be quite significant.

Culture plays an important role in organizational behavior and is a key element of understanding how organizational psychology theories can be applied and used in other countries.

4

Organizational and National Culture

Organizational or corporate culture is intended to represent a common perception held by all members of the organization. It emphasizes the relational and process aspects of the organization. These include power and authority relationships, coping with uncertainty and risk taking, loyalty and commitment, motivation, control and discipline, coordination and integration, communication, consultation, and participation (Tayeb, 1994). This does not mean, however, that there cannot be subcultures within any given organizational culture. In fact, most large organizations have a dominant culture and numerous sets of subcultures (Sackmann, 1992). There is also some evidence that there may be only a limited level of within-industry variation among organizations. Companies that conduct the same type of business will probably have similar standards and constraints (Gordon, 1991).

Organizational culture can be summarized as having seven primary characteristics: innovation and risk taking, attention to detail, outcome orientation, people orientation, team orientation, aggressiveness, and stability (e.g., Chatman and Jehn, 1994). Each of these characteristics exists in every organization, on a continuum from high to low. Where the organization lies on each of these dimensions creates a complete model that provides the form and shape of the organization's culture.

It has been suggested that organizational culture is implicitly an American concept reflecting American values and that looking at or measuring organizational culture in other countries is therefore a waste of time, since this would make organizational culture an invalid concept when looking at global organizations. However, research into organizations across cultures has found that there are similarities between organizations operating in different cultural and societal settings (Lammers and

Hickson, 1979). European researchers in particular have studied organizational culture in some depth. Similarities have been found to be especially consistent by type of organizational structure and type of business (Hickson, Hinings, and McMillan, 1981).

On the other hand, research has shown that there can be considerable differences between organizations operating as similar organizational types but in different societies in Europe (Maurice, Sorge, and Warner, 1980). There are differences between Japanese and American companies in such areas as employee-management relations, communication, and staff involvement in decision making. The organization of work in Japan reflects the social structure of the society, and the workplace is therefore a major source of an individual's identity. Consider, for example, recent concern in Japan over "organizational suicide," caused when employees believe they will only be successful if they are the first to arrive at work and the last to leave. This belief leads to a deterioration in employees' health to the point that so many people were dying at their desk that the government of Japan took steps to change this cultural value.

Organizational culture has received a great deal of attention during the last twenty years, beginning with the work of T. E. Deal and A. Kennedy (1982) and others. The concept of organizational culture is understood as being a culture that is unique to a particular organization. The nature of the organizational culture is communicated indirectly and is part of the socialization process that individuals experience in organizations (Deal and Kennedy, 1982). Yet, while the culture of a particular organization may include many distinct characteristics, the concept of organizational culture can be classified under one of several general and broad categories. Organizational culture can have a significant effect on the economic performance of an organization (Kotter and Heskett, 1992). A study of more than two hundred companies found close links between culture and performance. Of particular importance was the organization's ability to respond to the changing external environment. The researchers also note that a strong corporate culture is not necessarily always a positive thing. Strong cultures tend to be more arrogant and less flexible than weak cultures, making it difficult for organizations with strong cultures to be responsive to external pressures. While there is some belief that excellent companies have strong cultures (Peters and Waterman, 1982), the link between organizational culture and performance has been challenged. Different environments require that companies adopt different strategies, and the organizational culture has to fit these strategies (Schwartz and Davies, 1981). According to *Business Weekly* (November 5, 1984), by 1984, or two years after the publication of *In Search of Excellence* (Peters and Waterman, 1982), at least fourteen of the forty-three companies studied could no longer be considered "excellent," because they had failed to adapt to fundamental changes in the marketplace and were experiencing organizational and financial problems.

There is some evidence that the organizational culture affects aspects of employee motivation and job satisfaction (Trice and Beyer, 1993). Cultural norms allow employees to make sense of their organizational world, and if their world makes sense, it is likely to result in increased productivity. Similar results were found when the relationship of organizational strength to organizational culture was investigated (Smolowitz, 1996). The culture of an organization has also been found to have an impact on several other variables related to organizational effectiveness (Kopelman, Brief, and Guzzo, 1990). Companies in the same industry can have quite different cultural characteristics, and the relationship between employee retention and the organizational culture suggests that companies would do well to create cultures that are attractive to employees in order to reduce turnover and, ultimately, expenses (Sheridan, 1992).

Though the issue of the psychological contract and person-organization fit will be discussed more fully in chapter 10, it is worth introducing the concept here since culture plays an important role in its implementation. The psychological contract is the unwritten contract that defines the individual's needs and the way these needs mesh with the organization's expectations. The organization's culture provides the framework within which the psychological contract must be implemented (Robinson, Kraatz, and Rousseau, 1994). In a longitudinal study of business school alumnae, researchers looked at changes in employment obligations as perceived by employees over time. The results suggest that during the first two years on a job, employees come to perceive that they owe their employers less while their employers owe them more. The researchers found that the employee's feeling of obligation to the company decreased if the employee believed that the employer was failing to meet its obligations. The specific obligations that were reduced in the eyes of employees were such things as loyalty, commitment, and investment in the organization. These findings show the importance of the person-organization fit on organizational behavior (Ryan and Schmit, 1996).

It has been concluded that citizenship, or the level of an employee's commitment to the organization including his or her willingness to go beyond the responsibilities prescribed by the job or position, results from the employee's perception of obligation to the organization and the degree to which these feelings of obligation are reciprocated, rather than simply stemming from attachment, loyalty, or satisfaction. Since obligations and their fulfillment may underlie organizational commitment, managers need to pay more attention to regulating beliefs regarding mutual obligations and need to understand employees' perceptions of mutual obligations.

Related to the concept of obligation is the issue of loyalty. Group loyalty is predictive of involvement in group-based activities, positive attitudes toward an organization, and an inclination to perform behaviors for the benefit of one's own organization. The changing work environment caused by downsizing, economic concerns, and the creation of flatter organizational structures has led to a move toward more independence of employees and a redefinition of the psychological contract (Hall and Moss, 1998).

An organization is not a passive or stable institution. It evolves and grows but does so in the internal environment of the organizational culture. The process by which an individual learns to perform in an organization has been called *socialization* (Schein, 1968). This is the process whereby individuals come to appreciate the values, expected behaviors, and social knowledge that are essential for assuming an organizational role and performing in the organization.

Organizational culture does not have to be established from the top down. In fact, lower-level employees often develop their own cultures, and sometimes those lower-level cultures are in conflict with the organizational or primary culture desired by the organization (Kilmann, Saxton, and Serpa, 1985). One study showed that storytelling by lower-level workers to new employees was a critical aspect of forming cultural values within the organization (Eisenhart, 1995). For example, the faculty at my university is part of a union that was formed in the mid-1970s at a time of crisis within the university. New employees now experience an environment that is quite different, which has been achieved through a variety of events including the formation and actions of the union. However, it is difficult for some faculty to see the need for a union given the situation as it is now. By storytelling, the experiences and events that led to the unionization can be shared and better understood by all who participate in the same organizational culture that the union played such an important and controversial role in developing.

If organization culture is in fact an implicitly American concept (Adler and Jelinek, 1986), then variables such as the American perception of free will and the belief in the ability to control or change one's behavior need to be contrasted with perceptions in other countries where culture, God, fate, or social class may determine a person's attitudes, values, and future. Some research in countries other than the United States supports this distinction. For example, one study of organizational culture found that a measure of organizational commitment could be used effectively in Japan and that goal/value acceptance, intent to stay, and willingness to work were the three critical components of organizational culture and commitment, challenging the notion that organizational culture does not exist outside the United States.

· Further, a study in Denmark showed that organizational culture played a key role in Danish companies. The researchers started from the premise that companies can use different types of financial accounting systems and that the system the company chooses reflects the type of organizational culture. The researchers reported that this was a useful alternate approach for identifying characteristics of culture (Mouritsen, 1989). A study conducted in France examined the relationship between organizational-culture traits and economic performance and between strength of organizational culture and economic performance (Calori and Sarnin, 1991). By looking at such work-related values as attitude toward change, integrity, internal cooperation, and self-fulfillment at work, the researchers concluded that the economic performance of an organization was directly tied to the strength of the organizational culture and the match between work-related values of employees and cultural traits. The link between economic growth and the cultural dimension of collectivism was explored as a way of explaining the remarkable economic growth of the "five dragons" (Singapore, Taiwan, South Korea, Hong Kong, and Japan) between 1965 and 1985 (Hofstede and Bond, 1988). The researchers concluded that, while there was no simple explanation for the rapid economic growth, culture played an important part. These studies from France, Denmark, Japan, and elsewhere suggest that organizational culture is not a purely American phenomenon.

The probability that there will be a problem when two organizational cultures clash can be seen from a study that looked at problems between two companies in the same national culture but with distinctly different organizational cultures (Wilkof, Brown, and Selsky, 1995). The researchers reported an intervention between two companies with a long-term business relationship and a history of problems rooted in their different organizational cultures. One organization had a mechanistic culture that was very hierarchical and bureaucratic with clearly defined rules and regulations. The other organization was seen as having an organic culture, which means the organizational structure is informal, decentralized, and nonbureaucratic. An example of actions resulting from these fundamental differences in culture was that, even though both companies were anxious to resolve problems and employees wanted to have face-to-face meetings, the management of one of the companies would not permit direct employee contact with employees from the other company. Further, perceptions of the problems within both companies were filtered through these different organizational cultures, resulting in often very different problem definitions. Unless a problem is correctly defined and everyone agrees on this definition, the problem will be very difficult to solve. The researchers found that a mutual understanding of each other's organizational culture was critical to a successful relationship between the two companies. The cultural experience within the organization played a key role in the interactions between the two companies and the eventual successful resolution of their ongoing conflict.

Several other issues have been found to influence organizational culture. For example, the issue of technology adoption is a key component in organizational culture that has been found to be a predictor of success in a competitive international environment (Kitchell, 1995). Companies that are adaptive and more willing to adopt technological innovations are more likely to succeed.

One other aspect of organizational culture that has received some attention is the question of the level of empowerment given to employees by the company. Organizational culture has been enhanced when work groups in American companies have been given autonomy and strong support by the organization. Yet the existence and possibility of this kind of autonomy and support has been questioned in non-Western cultures, where emphasis is placed on a different set of values within the manager-employee relationship (Spreitzer, 1996).

Organizational versus National Culture

Some scholars have voiced the concern that the way organizational culture is currently presented focuses inside the organization and suggests that the organization is somehow separate from the society around it. They argue that global organizations necessitate an alternative managerial approach that includes both independence and autonomy of employees and the ability of employees to play a role in determining their own role and future within the organization. Further, these scholars argue that managers and organizational theorists must go beyond culture-bound models to create models and theories that can adapt to the changing global environment in which businesses currently function. There are very few studies that have attempted to look at the question of organizational and national cultures at the same time, even though organizations are operating in environments where these two aspects of culture play a simultaneous and important role. In the case of multinational companies, there is a particular need to address the fit of organizational culture with the different national cultures that the company operates within. When faced with differences in culture, multinational companies can adopt one of four different models, and which one is adopted should be based on an acknowledgement that differences exist between cultures in different countries. The four models are ethnocentrism, where the parent company's values predominate; polycentrism, where local values predominate; regiocentrism, where a blending of parent company and local values predominate; and geocentrism, where the culture of the entire company is adapted to reflect a global perspective (Ashkanasy and Jackson, 2001).

While the issues of multinational companies and culture are very complex because of the specific issue of organizational versus national culture, some studies have investigated this relationship. For example, using a sample of organizations from the Netherlands and Denmark, differences were found in respondents' beliefs based on their nationality and a distinction between shared values and shared perceptions of daily practices (Hofstede, Neuijen, Ohayv, and Sanders, 1990). However, it has been suggested that it is inappropriate to compare the organizational cultures of two different organizations if they are based in different countries. For example, the well-known organizational psychologist E. H. Schein compared an American company with a Swiss company without mentioning the different nationalities in his analysis of the differences between the two companies. This has led to the suggestion that no comparison can be made between the organizational cultures of two companies if the two companies have different national cultures. In some organizations that operate in many countries, companies' employees worldwide may share the organization's core values and goals, so that employees identify with the company first and the national subsidiary second (Allen and Meyer, 1990). But in a study conducted with subjects from India and Pakistan, researchers found that the subjects in both countries identified more strongly with the subsidiary than with the global organization (Reade, 2002).

In a 1998 study, I compared the national and organizational cultures of multinational companies operating in Taiwan (Silverthorne, 1998). Specifically, Japanese companies operating in Taiwan were compared to "equivalent" Taiwanese companies operating in Taiwan. Data was collected from a large number of companies using the Cultural Perspectives Questionnaire (CPQ) mentioned in the previous chapter, which is built around the cultural values delineated in the work of Kluckholn and Strodbeck (1961). Organizational cultural values were also obtained, and the values were then compared. The results suggest that organizational and national cultures are two quite distinct concepts, although the Japanese national culture did seem to have some influence on the organizational culture of the Japanese company operating in Taiwan. A more recent study examined the organizational cultures of public accounting firms in Taiwan (Chow, Harrison, MacKinnon, and Wu, 2002), comparing employees in Taiwanese local firms with those working in U.S.-affiliated international accounting firms. The results yielded more similarities than differences based on culture. More research is needed in additional countries to fully understand the relative importance of the two types of culture.

Questions surrounding the need for differentiation versus integration, autonomy versus control, and national versus corporate boundaries will greatly affect the management and particularly the human resource policies of an organization. It is important for multinational companies to ponder the role of a central organizational culture as they pursue a global strategy for their business (Schneider, 1988).

The relative influence of national and organizational cultures on stress has been studied in Greece (Joiner, 2001). The study emerged from the argument that an imbalance between the two types of culture is significant in many cultures and that this imbalance can lead to workplace problems, including increased levels of stress. Greece is a country with high power distance and strong uncertainty avoidance, and it is collectivist and masculine. A strong relationship was found between the predominant organizational culture in Greece and the high level of power distance and uncertainty avoidance. Based on this finding, it seems that organizational cultural values that do not relate in some way to the surrounding societal or national culture will probably prove ineffective or even dysfunctional.

There is considerable research on the influence of national culture from a Chinese perspective. There are five major approaches to business in Chinese cultures. Two of these are Western approaches while the other three are rooted in Asian cultures. Asian culture has a tradition of keeping the organization cohesive as a dynamic group that works together well and is often connected by family relationships. Since Asian organizations tend to be hierarchical and reflect the collective norms of Asian cultures, the dynamic-group approach works well in these kinds of organizations (Redding, 1992).

The overseas Chinese management style prevalent in Taiwan is based in the Chinese family business. These organizations are commonly dominated by a single owner and have a simple organizational structure. The success of this type of structure rests in the ability of the Chinese to develop sophisticated networks and maintain a high degree of flexibility. But management practices in mainland China are different from those found in Taiwan and Hong Kong, because the culture in that country still relies on societal rather than family authority figures to establish order and resolve disputes. Chinese management style is also influenced by Confucian values (Bond, 1996). This view is supported by an investigation of the organizational culture and managerial philosophy of a major Chinese company in Taiwan, which found that the Confucian philosophy was incorporated into its culture (Chao, 1990).

While the available research that specifically looks at the Chinese cultural influence in organizations is rather limited, the role of overseas Chinese in numerous Asian cultures has been explored (Chen, 1995). The predominant organizational form used by overseas Chinese is the family business (Redding, 1990). The dominant managerial system used in these organizations is best described as paternal. As a result, power and authority rest in the ownership of the organization, leadership is generally autocratic, and the style of management is personal (Hall and Xu, 1991). Generally, overseas Chinese have become successful by pursuing the type of business that is compatible to their preferred management culture. However, the success of Taiwanese companies in the high-tech sector appears to contradict this general trend, since this type of business encourages employee independence and autonomy, decentralization of decision making, and active employee participation. Research evidence suggests that management culture in Taiwan is in a state of transition but that this change is limited, at least to this point in time, to high-technology and knowledge-driven organizations and to Western approaches to management and organizational culture in these segments of the business community. As yet, these changes are not widespread in Taiwan and do not appear to be prevalent in other overseas Chinese cultures, such as Hong Kong and Singapore, who have yet to become major players in the high-technology sector (Hempel and Chang, 2002). While some organizational cultures are changing in the direction predicted by Western approaches to management in Taiwan, the cultures remain uniquely Chinese in many characteristics, such as harmony in working relationships. The underlying values of Chinese organizational cultures appear to be very resilient even in the face of pragmatic needs to adapt when the type of business requires change.

One study of the role of national and organizational culture in banks in Japan, the United States, and Taiwan, as well as an American bank operating in Taiwan, began with the assumption that organizational and national cultures are highly related. The employees of the American bank in Taiwan and the Taiwanese bank in Taiwan perceived most elements of organizational culture in the same way, except that employees in the American bank identified their bank with and were supervised from the United States. The other major difference was on the dimension of socializing with workers, which was valued in the Japanese and Taiwanese banks but not the American bank (Lee and Barnett, 1997).

Rewards and reward systems play an integral part in the organizational culture. To see the impact of implementation of reward systems on a cross-cultural basis, researchers compared samples in the United States and Taiwan. The study used a simulation where subjects could allocate rewards on the basis of seniority, social-emotional competence, or task competence. The results showed that both the American and Chinese groups allocated rewards on the basis of task competence. Among male recipients, the Chinese allocated rewards on the basis of seniority more than did the Americans. However, among the female recipients, the Americans favored seniority as the basis for their rewards (Rusbult, Insko, and Lin, 1995).

A study of work goals compared Taiwanese men and women managers who worked in numerous companies controlled by Taiwanese, Japanese, or American investors (Yeh and Granrose, 1993). When age, education, tenure, and position level were controlled, it was found that men believe work goals of contributing to company success, advancement, earnings, and task challenge are more important than women do. These results seem to support the idea that Taiwanese cultural work goals remain the same regardless of the national culture of the parent company. Since there was consistency in the valued work goals even though the companies were from different home cultures, the research seems to support the expectation that the national culture within which the company operates will predominate over any aspect of organizational culture derived from the parent company's national culture (Adler, 1997). However, there is always a possibility that individuals will select a particular company with a corporate culture that fits them as individuals. This explanation requires that applicants to a particular company have some advance idea of the organizational culture that they wish to join. In addition, the company's selection procedure may take into account an applicant's characteristics when hiring (Schneider, 1988).

A comparison of employees who worked for the same company in the United States, Mexico, Poland, and India explored the fit of empowerment and continuous-improvement practices with national culture (Robert et al., 2000). Empowerment was negatively associated with satisfaction for the supervisors in India and positively associated with satisfaction for the supervisors in the United States, Mexico, and Poland. Further, satisfaction with co-workers was positively related with empowerment in Poland, negatively related in India, and showed no effect in the United States and Mexico. Continuous improvement was positively associated with both types of satisfaction in all four countries. These findings suggest that if a strong organizational culture exists, then managers should rely on this culture. If the national culture is different from the organizational culture, then managers would be better off incorporating aspects of the organizational culture, rather than the national culture, into their actions when deciding how to manage employees.

In a related study, ten thousand employees of a cruise line, representing ninety different countries, provided a uniquely diverse population for consideration of the impact of national/organizational culture fit (Testa, Mueller, and Thomas, 2003). The results indicate that the better the fit between the employee's national culture and the organizational culture, the higher the level of employee job satisfaction. When the difference between the employee's national culture and the organization's culture is large, the employee is more likely to feel dissatisfied, uncomfortable, and less committed. For the managers in the company, the differences between organizational and national cultures had no impact on job satisfaction, probably because of other unrelated factors such as the more-limited range and type of managers' country of origin and the organizational hierarchical structure.

Organizational culture has been found to vary among Canadian, U.S., and European companies (Grey and Gelford, 1990). These findings are interesting in that it would be easy to assume that Canada and the United States represent a North American culture and would thus be very similar. While similarities between American and Canadian organizational cultures do exist because of the high amount of American participation in Canadian businesses, there are some major differences. For example, Canadian companies encourage a higher level of corporate ethics; emphasize more lateral, upward, and downward communication; and have higher levels of work expectations and personal accountability than American companies. European cultures tend to exhibit greater vitality, innovation, and responsiveness to change than North American organizations. Companies in France have the most favorable culture patterns, with high levels of clarity, decision making, and vitality.

The acceptance of the concept of a dominant national culture minimizes the cultural differences within that nation. Countries such as the United States are very diverse and include significant percentages of different ethnic groups, which have their own subcultures. The breakup of the former Soviet Union and the creation of several states from what was once Yugoslavia indicate that we should be careful in considering a single country as a single culture. From a research perspective, the presence of within-country differences requires that large samples, representative of the culture's diversity, be used. Another concern is that cultural restraints affect the way that people behave within a culture. So the search for universal characteristics or theories of behavior offers a challenging environment for researchers.

In South Africa, there is a Eurocentric-Afrocentric duality in the dominant male management culture. To explore this duality, race and gender influences on South African managers were investigated. The perceptions of the managers were measured on eight bipolar dimensions of culture. Even though the results showed that black and white males shared a universal masculine value system, there were significant differences between them on five of the eight cultural dimensions, which can be ascribed to racial influences. Black males measured significantly higher than white males on collectivism and humane orientation and significantly lower than white males on uncertainty avoidance, assertiveness, and future orientation. The culture of white, male South African managers is largely congruent with Western or Eurocentric management systems, which tend to emphasize competition and a work orientation, free enterprise, individual self-sufficiency, self-fulfillment, exclusivity, planning, and methodology. The culture of black South African managers differs to a large extent from the Eurocentric management system and is comparable to the Afrocentric management system, which emphasizes collective solidarity, inclusivity, collaboration, consensus and group significance, concern for people, patriarchy, respect, and dignity (Booysen, 2003).

If significant individual differences exist, they can only be fully understood with an analysis at the individual level. Still, the strategy of analyzing the properties of cultures as a whole is possible (Leung, 1989). Any consideration of individual differences in different cultures requires that an analysis of cultural differences must be conducted before any meaningful individual-level study can be conducted.

Managing Cultural Differences

One instance in which national and organizational cultures can come into direct contact occurs when joint ventures are undertaken. Depending on the source, it has been reported that between 37 and 70 percent of international joint ventures fail because of cultural differences between partners. Cross-national joint ventures have been reported to suffer from communication, cooperation, commitment, and conflict-resolution problems caused by partners' value and behavior differences, which in turn cause interaction problems that adversely influence joint-venture performance. Moreover, value and behavior differences between culturally distant partners influence interpretations and responses to strategic and managerial issues, compounding difficulties when making transactions and sharing information in international joint ventures (Mohr and Spekman, 1994). Japanese-American joint ventures have a shorter life span than Japanese-Japanese joint ventures, suggesting that having partner organizations of different nationalities increases the likelihood of conflict between them, which in turn results in joint-venture dissolution. While some researchers find that national-culture differences can cause conflicts and barriers to success, others have found national-culture differences a source of admiration and challenge, leading to a higher level of communication and more-sustained collaboration (Park and Ungson, 1997).

There are three broad strategies used by Western organizations in order to manage differences in cultures when operating internationally. The first is that the organization can build a strong organizational culture internationally so that all parts of the organization, wherever they are located, share the same organizational culture. This approach assumes that homogeneity of cultures creates the best way to manage the organization. IBM, as studied by Hofstede, represented a company utilizing this approach. This approach has been criticized because in the process of reducing the culture to its simplest form, for ease of understanding in many national cultures, the distinctiveness of the culture can be lost. In addition, a single culture discourages innovation and the maximizing of the competitive advantage that can be achieved when operating in different national cultures. The second approach to managing differences in cultures is to develop a common technical or professional culture. This approach does not try to ensure homogeneity within the work force but, rather, seeks uniformity through strong financial and planning systems. The organizational structure dictates procedures and processes, as well as specifying the sources of expertise and decision making within the organizational hierarchy. The third approach is to leave each culture alone, allowing each subsidiary to develop its own organizational culture, which is probably tied to the national culture with varying degrees of influence.

Organizational-culture distance generally has a negative impact on organizational outcomes, but national-culture distance can have either a positive or negative effect. National-culture differences between partners can potentially generate either positive or negative effects because differences in fundamental beliefs and values, as reflected in the national cultures, may turn out to undermine or reinforce partners' collaborative efforts (Fey and Beamish, 2001). Combined indices of national- and organizational-culture power distance influence organizational outcomes differently in terms of employee performance and satisfaction. National-culture power distances more significantly affect the efficiency and competitiveness measures of performance, while organizational-culture power distance is a better predictor of the satisfaction measurement. In addition, different dimensions of both national and organizational culture influence performance differently, and the presumed negative effect of partner dissimilarity on performance originates more from differences in organizational culture than from differences in national culture (Kale, Singh, and Perlmutter, 2000).

Given the complexity of culture, not all culture dimensions affect organizational outcomes in the same direction. While differences in some dimensions tend to generate negative outcomes, differences in others generate positive outcomes. The effect of any cultural distance is mainly generated in the interactions of the partners and is influenced by how they approach cultural differences; the approaches to cultural differences may themselves be part of an international-joint-venture organizational culture. Culture distance negatively affects all measures of performance whether the organizations are considered open- or closed-system organizations. Joint-venture success requires the ability to listen and pay attention, as well as patience, humility, and a willingness to learn, whereas mistrust and arrogance lead to failure. A crucial characteristic of the open-versus-closed dimension is information-sharing. If one partner engages in high information-sharing activity (open system) and the other does not (closed system), partners cannot capitalize on the additive effect of a joint venture, and the open-system partner may come to suspect the closed-system partner's commitment and loyalty toward the joint venture. Unless the international-joint-venture partners have a similar information-sharing tendency and foster an open communication climate, performance will suffer.

One of the remaining questions facing organizations that hire workers from other countries is to what extent differences between people are a function of the culture or are just individual differences (Arvey, Bhagat, and Salas, 1991). If, in fact, individual differences are more important than cultural differences, the selection and recruitment process needs to reflect and integrate this perspective. The reality is unclear, but the question remains and is a perplexing one for organizations. Hopefully, future research in this area will provide the kind of answer that will facilitate successful hiring practices. In the age of multinational organizations, the issue of organizational versus national culture is an important one to consider when looking at organizational commitment. The key question for multinational companies concerns the role of national culture relative to organizational culture. If a company has a distinct organizational culture in one country, say, the United States, what happens when this company sets up in Thailand?

Summary

Organizations that operate across cultures need to be concerned with both the national and the organizational culture as well as the interplay between them. When an organization operates in another culture, it has a second aspect of culture to integrate. The organizational culture will play an important role, particularly in American companies. Some companies attempt to create a consistent organizational culture in all countries within which they operate. Other companies allow more flexibility at the local level. While the organizational culture may reflect the national culture, they are not necessarily the same. When the organizational culture is strong at the local level, this should take precedence over national culture when choosing particular aspects of organizational behavior.

The managerial challenge facing organizations operating internationally has become how to identify the way a particular culture or cultures can provide advantages for the organization. These advantages may be in the form of responsiveness, technical expertise and knowledge, and longer-term perspectives. This opens up the possibility of creating centers of excellence in different countries based on that culture's unique and useful expertise or competitive advantages (Porter, 1990). Unfortunately, the anecdotal and research evidence indicates that companies are not likely to adopt strategies that can take advantage of national differences. More work needs to be done on exploring ways to fully integrate national-cultural competitive advantages into an organization's structure, procedures, and policies for the benefit of the organization as a whole.

5

Leadership in Organizations

Exploring the complex relationships in organizations is crucial to understanding the nature of leadership within them. The changing global economy means that companies are facing new challenges and must do everything possible to remain competitive. In this organizational environment, effective organizational leadership is critical to achieving organizational success, since a causal link has been demonstrated between leadership and employee and organizational performance (Morrison, 1992).

For most of the past century, leadership has been the focus of a great deal of research, as businesses, government agencies, and the military struggled to identify the characteristics of good leaders and to recognize and develop these characteristics. Over time, there have been several significant changes in accepted theories of leadership, as different approaches have been explored and theories of leadership developed.

The bulk of leadership research and theory development has occurred in the United States and other Western countries (see Anderson, 1992). The American system of leadership has been evolving over a number of years and is for the most part a participative system, meaning that employees (or followers) expect to be involved in decisions, especially those that affect them directly (Senge, 1996). However, in different parts of the world, organizations can require or need leadership with different characteristics. For example, in the Far East organizations tend to have a paternalistic leadership style, whereas in the Middle East organizations tend to be more authoritarian, and in Western cultures organizations tend to require a more participative leadership style (Hofstede, 1984). Unfortunately, there is very limited research data available about leaders and leadership in non-Western countries (Chen and Van Velsor, 1996).

Some research suggests that where cultural values such as religion and the everyday use of numerous languages are an integral part of the culture, different approaches to leadership are required (e.g., Hofstede, 1993; Triandis, 1993). Variations in leadership behavior influenced by other national cultural factors, such as individualism and collectivism, have been found in several studies (e.g., Gerstner and Day, 1994; Rodriques, 1990). Research using Hofstede's notion of collectivist and individualist cultures has shown that tests of leadership-style theories yield different results in the two cultural types (Smith and Tayeb, 1988). There is substantial empirical evidence to support the belief that cultural values and practices as well as organizational structure affect what leaders do (House, Wright, and Aditya, 1997). Conversely, other researchers have argued that universal leadership behaviors exist, such as the ability to influence and motivate others (e.g., Bass and Avolio, 1993). Still others have suggested that both culture-specific and culturally universal theories of leadership have value.

There is some evidence that countries can be clustered by culture, so that, for example, an Anglo-American cluster might include the United States, Canada, Australia, New Zealand, and the United Kingdom. Countries within a cluster are reported to have more similarities than differences. If countries can be effectively linked to a particular cluster, this would have the advantage of allowing data for groups to be presented in summary form and provide a more practical basis for comparison and application because it reduces the number of units being compared. Geography, history, language, and technological development all play a role in influencing cluster membership (Ronen and Shenkar, 1985). In general, research indicates that while leadership behaviors that include supportiveness, charisma, and reward contingency appear to be widespread, other behaviors such as directiveness tend to be specific to only a few cultures (Dorfman et al., 1997).

What Is Leadership?

Good leadership has a profound impact on organizations, government, society, and everyday activities because leadership allows organizations to achieve their goals. Excellent managers are usually expected to have a reasonably high level of leadership skills, and effective leadership is a necessary ingredient in successful companies (Bennis and Nanus, 1985).

In order to meet the responsibilities of an organization and protect its welfare, leaders must pursue a common goal. This may involve persuading, rather than forcing, other people to set aside, for a period of time, their individual concerns (Bennis, 1996). Leadership has been defined as the ability to persuade others to seek set objectives enthusiastically (Robbins, 1998). While most definitions of leadership have been developed using American samples, researchers who sampled organizational employees in fifty-six countries, and who restricted their definition to organizational leadership rather than leadership in general, concluded that leadership "is the ability to influence, motivate and contribute towards the effectiveness of the organizations of which they are members" (House and Wright, 1997). Organizational leadership is only possible when others willingly adopt the goals of the organization as their own. As a result, any consideration of leadership must also examine how to build cohesive and goal-oriented teams.

Early Approaches to Understanding Leadership

Early research on leadership focused on trying to identify traits that are characteristic of effective leaders. This approach was based on the assumption that effective leaders are individuals who, as a result of heredity or social position, possess qualities and abilities that differentiate them from people in general (e.g., Geier, 1967). If this assumption is true, then leadership effectiveness can be attributed to such special characteristics of a leader as intelligence, aggressiveness, or other personal traits. Hundreds of trait studies were conducted during the 1930s and 1940s in an attempt to determine the characteristics that differentiated leaders from followers (Yukl, 1994). The value to this approach is that personality characteristics and traits are relatively easy to measure, and this in turn would seemingly make identification of leaders easy. However, the failure of this approach to find consistent leadership characteristics across a variety of situations resulted in reducing the amount of research that considers traits and increasing the emphasis on the situational characteristics within which the leader functions and the effect of these characteristics on leadership style.

As a result of this change in emphasis, several taxonomies of leadership were developed, beginning with the Ohio State University studies of the 1940s and 1950s. Initial and subsequent approaches to describing leadership used a conceptualization of leadership that breaks it down into the two broad categories of task and relationship orientations.

Which orientation takes precedence is dictated by the nature of the situation. Studies that have focused on leadership behaviors have found that leadership styles vary considerably from leader to leader. A 1957 study identified a list of approximately eighteen hundred items describing different dimensions of leadership behavior. The list was split into nine categories or hypothetical subscales, with the majority of items assigned to several subscales. A statistical analysis of the data revealed two general leadership factors or dimensions labeled *consideration* and *initiation of structure in interaction.* The considerate leader is more concerned with subordinates' welfare and self-esteem, while the initiation-of-structure leader emphasizes organization, planning, and task completion (Hemphill and Coons, 1957). Individuals who have a high structure score focus on the "task" aspects of the job (Anderson, 1992). Interestingly, this characteristic is in line with Confucian thought and tradition, which is often an integral part of Chinese management (Punnett, 1995). Individuals who have a high consideration score focus on the "people" aspect of the job of leadership.

While this two-dimensional approach has some merit in Western organizations, the question becomes whether these two broad categories of leadership are adequate or appropriate in other cultures. It has been argued that they are not and that additional dimensions of leadership operate in other cultures, especially given the changing context of leadership in many cultures. Specifically, a third dimension of leadership, called *change-centered,* has been proposed and tested. The change-centered style of leadership relates to transformational leadership, which is discussed in more detail later in this chapter. Change-centered leadership focuses on making changes in objectives, processes, and procedures and adapting to change in the environment. This approach requires the ability to scan and interpret external events, as well as the ability to get support and implement change. A study of managers in the United States, Sweden, and Finland found that the measure of change orientation was independent of measures of task and relationship (Ekvall and Arvonen, 1991).

Situational Leadership Theories

Of significant importance to organizations in their quest to fulfill their goals is the relationship between leaders and followers, and also how leaders can moderate their leadership style to maximize their effectiveness (Hersey, Blanchard, and Johnson, 1996). An understanding of leadership and leader effectiveness is necessary in order to know how to motivate employees and thus achieve organizational goals.

Before considering the cross-cultural value of situational leadership approaches, it is worth reviewing the major American theories in some detail. Situational approaches to leadership examine the interplay among critical variables in order to find causal relationships that will lead to predictability of behavior. The common thread among the situational approaches is that effective leaders need to behave in a flexible manner, be able to diagnose the leadership style appropriate for the situation, and then be able to apply or use the appropriate style.

Situational Leadership Theory (SLT) has been popular in the United States ever since it was first proposed in 1969 (Hersey and Blanchard, 1969). The theory has periodically been revised, with the latest revision published in 1996 (Hersey, Blanchard, and Johnson, 1996). SLT focuses on the observed behavior of leaders and their followers in various situations. The theory proposes two dimensions, task and relationship behavior, that are similar to the initiation-of-structure and consideration concepts developed in the earlier Ohio State studies. By considering task and relationship importance as either high or low, a four-quadrant, two-dimensional model of leadership results. The effectiveness of a particular style of leadership is not the actual behavior of the leader but the appropriateness of the leader's behavior for that particular situation. Not only does the theory have appeal in the United States, but it also has become well known overseas and is often used as a management-training tool. Despite the popularity of the theory, there is little research available to support it.

The original model for SLT was formulated by Reddin (1967) and was later adapted by Hersey and Blanchard (1988). Reddin's (1967) Three-Dimensional Management Style theory attempted to match leadership styles to certain work environments, with a goal of increasing employee output. Like many other researchers, Reddin identified two leadership orientations, relationship and task orientation, and added a third dimension to assess effectiveness. Depending on the work environment within which they are operating, leaders need to choose from a variety of leadership styles by weighing the relative importance of the task and the relationship. The point is that a particular leadership style may or may not be effective depending on the situation.

Hersey and Blanchard (1988) modified the concept of the relationship between the two orientations by suggesting that leadership styles change with a leader's maturity as well as with the maturity of an organization and its work force. By looking at the two components of task and relationship and combining their relative importance with the level of maturity, Hersey and Blanchard developed a four-factor SLT. Low relationship and low task importance requires a delegating style of leadership. When this style is used, tasks can be passed on to subordinates for completion. High relationship and low task importance requires a participating style of leadership. When this style is used, subordinates are involved in the decision-making process. With low relationship and high task importance, a telling style of leadership is required. The telling style is structured and directive and requires the leader to tell followers what, when, where, and how to complete a task. The telling style simply informs subordinates of the decision, providing little or no justification for what actions are required. With high task and high relationship importance, a selling style of leadership should be used. The selling approach provides a guide but also allows for some dialogue with and clarification-seeking from followers so that they are more likely to "buy in" to what the leader wants. When using a selling style, subordinates are given information that will help "sell" them on the appropriateness of a course of action. It is assumed that the subordinate will not accept the decision completely unless given supporting information that helps to justify taking a particular approach. The latest formulation of this theory has relabeled the concept of employee maturity as *employee readiness,* which is a broader and clearer definition of the need to assess where the employee fits in the leadership-style selection process (Hersey, Blanchard, and Johnson, 1996).

Research on situational leadership first involved observing people who were put in charge of a group of people performing some physical task, such as scaling an obstacle or crossing a river. It was noted that the nominated leaders exhibited both task-related and relationship-related behavior (Nicholls, 1993). The focus in situational approaches is on observed behavior, rather than on any hypothetical inborn or acquired ability or potential for leadership. Emphasis is placed on understanding the behavior of leaders, the nature of the group members (followers), and the impact of various situations.

However, research results have not always provided support for SLT. A study to examine SLT's underlying assumption that subordinate maturity affects the correlation of leader task and relationship behaviors with leader effectiveness obtained results that did not support that assumption. Since a measure of psychological maturity was based on peer ratings while job maturity was based on experience, the failure to find supportive results may have occurred because different measures of maturity were used in the research (Blank, Weitzel, and Green, 1990).

Conversely, a study that examined the use and validity of SLT yielded results that fully supported SLT on all dimensions except the self-perception of effectiveness. When managers used SLT correctly after undergoing training in the theory, the gain in subordinate job performance was significant. Even though there was no strong evidence to prove the causal relationship, effective managers knew more about SLT and used it more often than less-effective managers (Hambleton and Gumpert, 1982). Similarly, SLT was strongly supported in low-maturity conditions where followers required more structure from their supervisors but not in high-maturity conditions (Vecchio, 1987). Generally, differences in the results of the studies can be attributed to differences in the way that the key variables were measured. In terms of sampling, the most popular samples were principals, supervisors, and teachers. Finally, there was no consistent use of a single research instrument to measure leadership. The distinct research approaches and the different variables studied may account for some of the discrepant conclusions reported.

As mentioned earlier, SLT has been popular in other countries. In an attempt to test the value and applicability of SLT across cultures, one study explored the interest in SLT in Taiwan and the value of relating leadership to other factors (Silverthorne, 2002). There were two primary goals of this research project. The first was to examine the relationship between styles of leadership and employee maturity. The second was to understand how styles of leadership and employee maturity affect employee job satisfaction. The results indicated that the managers and employees who were studied in Taiwan preferred the participative style of leadership, with the selling style of leadership being the second preference. This suggests that successful leaders and managers are those who are more adaptable and who rely on a participative style of management. This finding matches the conclusion of J. R. Goodson, J. W. McGee, and J. F. Cashman (1989), who found that all followers need a significant amount of consideration, which is best found in the participative leadership style. The results in the Taiwan study demonstrated a clear pattern of preferred leadership style in the sample tested and suggest that SLT can be used in Taiwan to identify the preferred and actually operating styles of leadership. These conclusions were also supported by the relatively high correlation between a leader's self-score and the leadership score as assigned by subordinates. Further, the instruments developed when conducting training or research on SLT are available in several languages other than English, and from this study they appear to be valid for use in Taiwan.

Regarding the relationship between leadership style and subordinate maturity, the results indicate that there is a difference between the preferred styles of leadership for different levels of employee maturity. This finding supports an important aspect of SLT. The relationship between style of leadership and employee maturity is complex and deserves attention from managers and leaders in organizations. A good match between the manager's and employee's perception of leadership style can lead to an increase in the employee's job satisfaction. The results indicate that matching employee expectations and leader behavior is as important or more important than the particular style a leader uses.

Two earlier studies that focused on a single type of organization in Taiwan found similar results (Silverthorne and Wang, 2001; Silverthorne, 2000). Taken together, the results of these three studies indicate that managers in Taiwan have a high level of trust in their employees with a predominant leadership style of participation. This finding is somewhat surprising given the historically paternalistic nature of Chinese management. Based on the traditional Chinese approach to management, it was expected that the telling and selling styles of leadership, described earlier, would predominate. The results did not support this expectation. The strong match between the leader's self-perception of leadership and the follower's perception of the leader further supported the presence of employee-leader trust. The results of these studies suggest that the situational leadership model may be useful in other countries.

Hersey and Blanchard provide a framework of leadership that can be introduced into an organization by training managers in the various aspects and use of the theory. Training in SLT involves teaching managers to diagnose the level of employees' readiness to participate, to assess employees' willingness to assume responsibility, to adapt by selecting the appropriate leadership style, and then to communicate these styles effectively to influence employee behavior. By conducting this training within an organization, it is possible to increase leaders' flexibility in choosing an appropriate leadership style given any organizational or national-culture constraints.

The Path-Goal Theory of Leadership

A second major American theory of leadership is the path-goal theory. While this theory is also considered a situational theory, the difference from SLT is that the task is viewed as based on a set of expectations rather than just its relative importance. The leader helps subordinates achieve their goals by providing a clear path for them to follow. This is best achieved by having a strong sense of the task to be performed, helping subordinates clarify their expectations, and providing opportunities for personal satisfaction that are contingent on effective performance. The path-goal theory, developed by R. J. House (1971) and revised over the following several years, argues that leaders can adjust their own behaviors to adapt to any contingency and find the most suitable style for any particular situation. The main aim of leadership is to help subordinates attain their goals effectively and to provide them with the necessary direction and support to achieve their own goals as well as those of the organization. A leader will be most effective when he or she supplies what is missing from a situation, and the leader motivates the employee when the employee sees that the leader is helping to achieve the goals or expectations of the situation.

In the path-goal theory, House (1971) contends that leadership theory should focus on three main points:

> effectiveness toward the subordinate (i.e., increased job satisfaction)
> work incentives (to increase job performance)
> acceptance of the leader by subordinates

According to path-goal theory, the role of the leader is dependent on the subordinate's work environment and the amount of structure in that environment. Highly structured environments that provide a large amount of organization, role, and task clarity will provide a clear path toward attaining work goals. In this situation, the leader should be concerned with his or her relationship with subordinates. The leader boosts morale and reduces the tedium of tasks as much as possible. If the nature of the work structure is unclear or changeable, the leader should assist subordinates by providing direction and guidance. In this type of situation, the leader should choose a task, rather than relationship, orientation.

House (1971) argued that there are four different kinds of leadership style: directive or instrumental, supportive, participative, and achievement oriented. An effective leader knows which style to use and when to use it. Directive or instrumental leaders tell subordinates what is expected of them, give specific guidance, and enforce rules and procedures. The supportive leader likes a friendly environment and gives strong attention to the needs and well-being of subordinates. The participative leader involves subordinates in the decision-making process. And the achievement-oriented leader seeks to improve performance, sets high standards, and shows confidence that subordinates will achieve these standards (Prasad, 1990). Which style a leader chooses depends on the nature of the task and the needs of the subordinates. For example, if the subordinates need affiliation, then the leader should be supportive and considerate. If, on the other hand, the subordinates need achievement, then the leader should emphasize the task and rewards. If the task is well defined, then less guidance is needed and the leader can be less directive, whereas if the task is poorly defined, subordinates will require more guidance and direction from the leader. Path-goal theory, like SLT, argues that a leader should be able to be either predominantly task or relationship oriented as required by the particular situation (Wren, 1994).

The path-goal theory is built around two different hypotheses or propositions (Robbins, 1998). The first is that when subordinates believe the leader's behavior is the source for their present job satisfaction, the leader's behavior is generally accepted and can lead to employee satisfaction. The behavior of the leader will be viewed as acceptable to subordinates only when they perceive it either as an immediate source of satisfaction or as instrumental to future job satisfaction. The second hypothesis or proposition offered by the theory is that leadership behavior is motivational. Therefore, the more appropriate the leader's behavior, the more motivational it is likely to be for subordinates. Motivation of subordinates is achieved by tying satisfaction of subordinates' needs to effective performance and by complementing the work environment of the subordinates by providing the necessary coaching, guidance, and rewards for their effective performance (Levanoni and Knoop, 1985). The theory focuses on one-on-one relationships with subordinates, in terms of leadership behaviors, and with peers, in terms of group performance and the ability to obtain resources.

The theory implies several alternate outcomes. If the work structure is unclear or there is a significant amount of environmental pressure, the directive leadership style will give subordinates more job satisfaction and result in more-effective work performance. If the work structure is clear, then a supportive leadership style will allow subordinates greater job satisfaction and result in more-effective work performance. When employees have a high level of ability and experience, a directive leadership style is probably not the most effective and, in fact, may hamper employee performance and job satisfaction. If the organization has a rigid and clear power system, then the leader needs to be more supportive than directive.

The results from a variety of research studies have not always provided support for the path-goal theory of leadership. This can be explained, in part, because much of the research has been based on different constructs and types of measurement. Effective leadership has not been found to be dependent on how well the leader explains the task and goal, and the aspects of achieving the task identified as getting in the way of employees being successful are not the ones predicted by the theory to cause problems. Alternately, the most effective leader might well be one who identifies the deficiencies and hindrances in a work situation and uses behaviors that will minimize or eliminate them (Woffard and Liska, 1993). Thus, communicating with employees regarding their needs and problems on the job is an effective strategy for managers.

There is little evidence of attempts to apply the path-goal theory of leadership to other cultures. However, the results from a study conducted using a Taiwanese sample of managers found some support for the theory. The questionnaires designed to test the theory were also valid and reliable for use in a Chinese sample and so may be appropriate for use in other cultures. When the organization's level of task structure, as defined by Taiwanese managers, was compared with normative data from the United States, the managers perceived the level of task structure to be higher in Taiwan than in the United States. Overall, the results provide only partial support for the path-goal theory of leadership. The theory was supported for the relationship between managers and subordinates but not supported for the relationship between managers and peers (Silverthorne, 2001b).

Implicit Leadership Theories

Another approach to assessing leadership effectiveness is to study it from two alternate perspectives that attempt to tie together elements of both the trait and the situational approaches. The first alternative is to consider an explicit theory of leadership. This approach is based on leaders' actual behaviors, which have been identified and measured through observation and evaluation. The second alternative is to consider an implicit theory of leadership based on the conceptual structure and definition of leadership and the expectations people have about how a leader should behave. Thus, explicit leadership theory is based on the observation and evaluation of overt behaviors, while implicit leadership theory explores the covert conceptual structure of leadership. The implicit/explicit approach is derived from leadership-categorization theory (Lord and Maher, 1991), which suggests that a person is more likely to be seen as a leader if the person who is evaluating sees a good fit between the leader's expected and actual behavior. Further, if the follower perceives the leader to be the kind of leader they expect, then the leader is more likely to be accepted. The better the fit between the expectations of a leader's behavior and the actual behaviors, the more influence the leader will have. Implicit leadership traits are based on the personal characteristics and attributes that subordinates expect of their leaders. Such implicit leadership traits as sensitivity, dedication, tyranny, charisma, attractiveness, masculinity, intelligence, and strength have been studied in the United Sates (Offermann, Kennedy, and Wirtz, 1994). Also, implicit leadership theory can be shaped by the culture in which the leader operates. Indeed, based on a study of Iraqi, European, and American samples, the evaluation of a leader was influenced by both the leader's overt behavior and the cultural background of the person evaluating the leader's behavior (Ayman and Chemers, 1983).

Transactional/Transformational Theories of Leadership

Another approach to understanding leadership is based on a proposal for a different dichotomy of leadership than discussed previously: the transactional versus transformational styles of leadership (Hater and Bass, 1988). J. M. Burns (1978) developed the initial concept of transformational leadership from his early descriptive research on political leaders. Initially, transformational leadership was seen as a process in which both leaders and followers push each other to higher levels of morality and motivation (Burns, 1978). The transformational style of leadership may be used by anyone and at any level in an organization and involves influencing peers, subordinates, and superiors. Transactional leadership is based on the idea that the leader identifies the needs of followers and then exchanges rewards for acceptable results. Transactional leadership is characterized by behaviors and attitudes that emphasize the quality of the exchange between leaders and followers. It was Burns who first contrasted transformational with transactional leadership. B. M. Bass (1990) later expanded and more fully developed this approach. Since then, other researchers have either elaborated on these concepts or proposed alternate theories that mirror the critical dimensions of the transactional/transformational leadership approach. While the theory accepts the existence of two different approaches to leadership, it seems to suggest that transformational leadership is generally the better and more successful approach (Meindl, 1990).

Bass (1990), one of the primary researchers and theorists interested in this approach, contends that the transformational/transactional model is a new paradigm. As such, this model neither replaces nor is explained by other models of leadership. A. Bryman (1992) has called this approach "New Leadership" because it integrates ideas from several different approaches and includes consideration of traits, leadership styles, and contingency approaches to explaining leadership.

Transformational leadership is said to transform the followers by raising awareness of the importance of outcomes to the organization, so that individuals will rise above their self-interests and work for the good of the organization. An organization can be transformed when the leader provides a clear vision and articulates the need for change within the organization (Tichy and Devanna, 1990). The leader transforms and motivates followers by (a) making them more aware of the importance of task outcomes, (b) inducing them to transcend their own self-interests for the sake of the organization or team, and (c) activating their higher-order needs.

Bass (1990) argues that all transactional theories are rooted in the fact that the relationship between leaders and followers is based on a series of transactions between them. The leader provides rewards and, in return, the subordinates provide effort and performance. Consensus on the nature of the relationship between transactional and transformational leadership has not been reached. On the one hand, Burns (1978) sees the two types of leadership as opposite ends of a single continuum. On the other hand, Bass (1990) views the two approaches to leadership as interrelated, so that transformational leadership builds on the elements of transactional leadership and is therefore a special case of it rather than something completely different. Bass further argues that both approaches share the same goals but use different processes to achieve them. Bass and B. J. Avolio (1993) conceptualize the transformational leadership model as including the dimensions of charisma or idealized influence, inspirational motivation, intellectual stimulation, and individualized consideration. These authors also argue that the best leaders can be both transformational and transactional. In addition, they see transformational leadership as additive to the transactional approach, providing a way to increase followers' motivation, understanding, maturity, and sense of self-worth.

A five-year descriptive study of innovative leaders led to the conclusion that transformational leaders have several consistent characteristics, the most important being the ability to develop a vision. The idea behind establishing a vision is that it provides a focus and agenda for the organization or group and is able to pull people into the process of fulfilling the vision and achieving future goals. In addition, transformational leaders are able to develop commitment and trust and facilitate organizational learning (Bennis and Nanus, 1985). Visionary leaders must cope with a significant amount of ambiguity and rely to a large degree on intuitive processes to guide their actions (Hill and Levenhagen, 1995).

Transactional leadership involves an exchange between the leader and the follower. When followers act according to the leader's wishes, the relationship between leader and follower can be seen as based on a cost-benefit exchange or a transaction (Burns, 1978). Leadership research has witnessed a shift from traditional transactional models to a new set of theories of transformational, or charismatic, leadership and leader-member exchange (LMX). Leader-member exchange is derived from transactional leadership theory and is a measure of the exchange process in which the leader provides rewards in return for employee performance and effort. LMX is defined as the quality of the relationship between a superior and a subordinate. Subordinates who have high-quality exchanges with the leader enjoy relationships based on mutual contribution, loyalty, trust, and affection. The quality of the exchange is directly related to the transformational/transactional dichotomy of leadership. If the quality of the exchange is high, then the interaction between the leader and the subordinate will be more relational; if it is low, the interaction will be more transactional or instrumental.

LMX has been positively related to job satisfaction, productivity, and career progress of managers and negatively related to turnover and employee grievances (Scandura, 1999). Studies in the United States have shown that charismatic leadership and LMX, in combination, generate significant predictable variation in a range of outcomes, such as innovative behavior (Graen and Uhl-Bien, 1995).

The role that organizational justice plays in new paradigms of leadership, such as transformational leadership and LMX, has only recently begun to receive research attention (Scandura, 1999). Investigations of the relationship between leadership and organizational justice and the role of fairness in the workplace in the United States suggest that they are linked. To date, little is known about this link in cultures other than the United States, but some research has looked at leadership, justice, and job satisfaction in cultures operating in differing economic climates (e.g., developed, newly industrialized, and developing economies). The results indicate that some cultures have similar core values to those found in the United States (e.g., Australia), while others have quite different core values (e.g., India, Colombia, and the Middle Eastern nations), suggesting that a sensitivity to local cultural issues is important when selecting a leadership style.

Transformational-charismatic leadership theories offer the promise of extraordinary individual and organizational outcomes, achieved by inducing employees to transcend their self-interests and put the organization's interests first. However, there is some evidence that women are more likely than men to enact charismatic leadership, since women both see themselves and are also seen by their supervisors as more transformational than men (Carless, 1998). Further, women are more likely to demonstrate superior social and emotional competencies than men, and this leads to greater charismatic leadership on their part (Groves, 2003). These findings suggest that gender may play an important role in leadership in organizations and that, to be effective, leadership and managerial training programs need to include gender difference as an important variable.

Gender differences were also considered in a study that assessed the importance of twenty-two characteristics for being a good top manager or a good lower-level manager (supervisor) in the Netherlands. The results confirm the expectation that several transformational-charismatic leader characteristics (e.g., inspirational, visionary, innovative, persuasive) are considered more important for top managers, whereas "supportive and people-oriented" characteristics (e.g., concerned for subordinates' interests, compassionate, participative) are considered more important for lower-level managers. Females consider dominance less desirable and people-oriented characteristics, a long-term orientation, and diplomacy more important for leaders than males do. Males rate inspirational, rational, and persuasive as more important characteristics than females do (den Hartog and Koopman, 2003).

While only a relatively small number of studies have been conducted in Europe, the results are interesting. In most of Europe and especially in Germany, charismatic leadership is regarded with skepticism and even considered an overemphasized American concept (Steyrer, 1999). However, research in German organizations found support for higher levels of transformational, including charismatic, leadership in smaller and entrepreneurial companies than in larger companies, where transactional leadership was more likely to be found (Felfe and Goihl, 2002).

Although not directly tied to the transformational/transactional model of leadership, differences have been found on several key dimensions of this model when leadership characteristics were compared among electronics plants in the United States, Mexico, Taiwan, Korea, and Japan. For example, leaders were rated positively in all five countries when they were supportive and tied rewards to performance. Charismatic leadership was rated positively in four of the countries but not in Japan, Mexico, Korea, and Taiwan rated directive leadership positively, whereas the U.S. sample was the only one to rate participative leadership positively (Howell et al., 1997). A more recent study has found that participative leadership is also valued in Taiwan (Silverthorne, 2002).

Transformational leadership is participative and may be more effective in influencing job attitudes in low-power-distance countries, where this approach tends to complement the cultural values. In areas where hierarchy is revered, such as the Middle East, there may be different ways of achieving empowerment, satisfaction, and commitment. The leader as "coach" rather than "boss" may not readily transfer even to countries that do not put much stock in hierarchy (Schneider and Barsoux, 1997). However, Bass (1997) points out that the transformational/transactional leadership paradigm has been studied in many cultures and that the data provides universal support for this approach. For example, the basic propositions of transformational-charismatic leadership have been validated in the United States and in other cultures such as New Zealand, India, Japan, and Singapore (Bass, 1997). Further, the robustness of the effects of such leadership on individual and organizational outcomes such as job satisfaction, organizational commitment, and performance has been demonstrated in numerous studies (Dorfman, 1996). From a cross-cultural perspective, it is important to note that transformational-charismatic leadership may be universally effective (Bass, 1997).

In some respects, the transformational/transactional approach to leadership reflects a renewed interest in personality factors but as a prerequisite rather than a predictor of leadership. It has been suggested that personality traits are an important component of effective leadership, and while personality measures alone may not be sufficient to predict successful leadership, using the "big-five model of personality," the value and usefulness of personality-trait measurement as a predictor of leadership can be enhanced (Hogan, Curphy, and Hogan, 1994). The big-five model of personality holds that personality from the view of the observer can be contained within the five broad categories of extroversion, neurotism, agreeableness, conscientiousness, and openness (McCrae and Costa, 1997). Whether this approach works in other cultures is worthy of consideration, since different cultures place emphasis on different aspects of behavior. For example, conscientiousness is highly valued within Chinese culture, whereas some aspects of extroversion, such as dominance and assertiveness, are not (Redding and Wong, 1986). However, researchers in one study looked at universal aspects of Chinese personality structure in Hong Kong and concluded that their findings were roughly comparable to those from an American sample (McCrae, Costa, and Yik, 1996). A more recent study compared samples of effective and noneffective leaders in Taiwan, Thailand, and the United States, using an instrument that measures variables based on the big-five personality factors (Silverthorne, 2001a). The results supported the relevance of four of the five factors in the Taiwan sample. Effective leaders in Taiwan were seen as emotionally stable, extroverted, agreeable, and conscientious, but not open. The effective Thai leaders were seen as emotionally stable and extroverted, but no differences were found on the other factors. While these results reveal some differences among the three countries, the lack of normative data for the scale for the Chinese and Thai samples suggests caution in drawing too strong conclusions based on this research. On the other hand, a study of the relationship between individual orientation (personality measures) and executive-leadership behavior in the United Kingdom led to the conclusion that the "contribution of these constructs and measures to our understanding of managerial behavior cannot be denied" (Church and Waclawski, 1999, p. 116).

Summary

The major theories of leadership have provided a framework for understanding leadership, but few of the theories have withstood the test of research investigations. Research supporting many of the theories is weak, and little attempt has been made to explore whether these theories can be considered universal by undertaking studies in cultures other than the United States. In this chapter, the major theories have been discussed and, where appropriate, research studies have been introduced that attempted to use the theories in other cultures. In general, the research results from many countries indicate that the most desirable leader is one who scores high on both task and relationship orientations. This two-dimensional approach to leadership, in whatever form, has merit as a tool for equating cultural approaches to understanding leadership. In addition, the concept of transformational/transactional leadership appears to have value, and transformational-charismatic leaders seem to be effective in most cultures. The application of the big-five personality structure to leadership characteristics also appears to be of value, but additional research using this construct in more countries is needed before final conclusions on its universal value can be reached. The results discussed in this and the next chapter are moving us closer to an idea of what constitute the universal characteristics of leadership and a recognition of the areas where cultural differences are significant enough to allow the identification of culture-specific unacceptable leadership behaviors.

6

Leadership in Other Cultures

In this chapter, the results from numerous research studies conducted in various countries are presented and discussed so that trends can be examined and cultural similarities and differences in preferred leadership styles more easily identified.

Project GLOBE

While the research on leadership across cultures is limited, one significant exception is Project GLOBE, a long-term, multimethod, multiphase, cross-cultural research program that looks at leadership and organizational practices and values in sixty-one countries (House et al., 1999). The project is being conducted in three stages and has several goals and objectives, but the primary emphasis is on developing a theory to "describe, understand, and predict the impact of specific cultural variables on leadership and organizational processes and the effectiveness of these processes" (House, Javidan, and Dorfman, 2001, p. 492). In other words, Project GLOBE looks at the interrelationship between organizational leadership and societal and organizational culture, since culture affects values, beliefs, and meanings and also influences leadership (Ayman, Chemers, and Fiedler, 1995). The first stage of the project involved the development of the research protocol and instruments. The second stage is focusing on the relationship between subordinates' attitudes and performance and particular leadership styles. The final phase will involve field and laboratory experiments designed to test hypotheses that have been developed from the previous two stages. Project GLOBE initially identified twenty-three leadership styles that work in one or more of the cultures included in the project. These leadership styles were then categorized into six distinct leadership models: transformational-charismatic, team oriented, humane, participative, autonomous, and self-protective. Transformational-charismatic leaders are visionary, inspirational, decisive, and performance oriented, and they have high levels of personal integrity. Team-oriented leaders are team builders, and they are collaborative and diplomatic. Humane leaders are generous and compassionate in a calm, modest, and patient way. Participative leaders act in a nonautocratic and nondictatorial manner, they delegate, and they behave in an egalitarian way. Self-protective leadership involves being self-centered, status conscious, face saving, conflict inducing, and procedural. Autonomous leaders are individualistic, independent, and unique. The results for several but not all the clusters are now available, and the general findings are discussed later in this chapter.

The first stage of the project included the development of a research protocol including a questionnaire to measure culturally endorsed implicit leadership theory, as well as interviews and focus groups designed to elicit information about the perceived attributes of ideal leaders. Implicit leadership theories look at the personal characteristics and attitudes that followers expect from their leaders. Explicit leadership theories are based on the observation and evaluation of the overt behavior of leaders. How we experience a leader and leadership is influenced by our personal implicit leadership theory. For example, if I think a leader should be very visible to his or her followers, I will perceive a person who stays in the office planning and creating as a less effective leader than someone who walks around a lot, even though the wandering may be accomplishing little. The available results for the country clusters studied are discussed in the following paragraphs.

In the South Asia cluster (India, Indonesia, the Philippines, Malaysia, Thailand, and Iran), transformational-charismatic and team-oriented leadership models were the most effective, although humane and participative leaders were also rated highly. Autonomous and self-protective leaders were seen as the least effective (Gupta, Surie, and Javidan, 2002). These research results suggest that leaders in this cluster need to be more responsive to humane considerations than they might need to be in other cultures.

Leaders who are charismatic, team oriented, and participative are seen as the most effective in the Anglo cluster (Australia, Canada, the United Kingdom, Ireland, New Zealand, and South Africa [white sample]). While these patterns were consistent across the countries studied, it was concluded that leaders still need to be sensitive to subtle differences in each culture and to which specific behaviors are perceived to be effective (Ashkanasy, Trevor-Roberts, and Earnshaw, 2002). Once again, the autonomous and self-protective leadership styles were seen as not being effective.

The samples from the Eastern European cluster (Albania, Georgia, Greece, Hungary, Kazakhstan, Poland, Russia, and Slovenia) responded in a similar way to those in the other clusters by identifying the transformational-charismatic and team-oriented leadership behaviors as the most effective, with participative leadership also being seen as valuable and self-protectiveness seen as the least valuable (Bakacsi, Sandor, Andras, and Viktor, 2002). Of the clusters reviewed to date, this cluster showed the greatest between-country differences, with Greece, Hungary, and Albania reporting somewhat different perceptions of what is needed for effective leadership than other countries in this cluster reported. Specifically, the Greek sample opposed the team-oriented approach embraced by most of the other countries in this cluster. Hungarians showed the greatest dislike for autonomous leadership, and the Albanians had a higher regard for the self-preservation approach to leadership than did the other countries in this cluster. Since many of the countries within this cluster have experienced significant social and structural change in recent years, perceptions in most of the countries have also undergone and continue to experience change. Managers and leaders thus need to be sensitive to the existence of confusion, fear, and other emotions related to the need for significant adjustment to the changing environment (Bakacsi, Sandor, Andras, and Viktor, 2002).

The Germanic European cluster (Austria, Germany, the Netherlands, and Switzerland) is characterized by a tendency for more rules and standardization, and once again charisma, team-orientation, and participation are seen as effective leadership styles (Szabo et al., 2002). In this cluster, humane orientation is also seen as helpful, but not at a high level. Autonomous leadership is seen as not contributing much, and self-protective behavior is seen as being an ineffective leadership style.

Leadership effectiveness is also associated with the charismatic, team-oriented, and participative styles in the Latin European cluster (Italy, Portugal, Spain, France, French Switzerland, and Israel). The respondents in this cluster scored lower on humane, autonomous, and self-protective leadership. The French samples from France and Switzerland generated slightly different results from the other samples in this cluster, preferring the participative style to the other styles. They also indicated that using the humane style of leadership tended to impede effective leadership (Jesuino, 2002).

The final cluster report relates to the Arabic cluster (Qatar, Morocco, Turkey, Egypt, and Kuwait). The top-two leadership characteristics of effective leaders were the same as for the other clusters, although their relative importance switched. For this cluster, team-orientation was rated the highest, with charismatic leadership also rated highly. Because these countries tend to have family and in-group societal values, this result was not unexpected (Kabasakal and Bodur, 2002). While the results obtained in this cluster mirrored those found in the other clusters, the relative value of the preferred leadership styles was lower, indicating that Arab cultures prefer a more-balanced middle-of-the-road approach rather than preferring one approach over another at a more extreme level. Leaders are expected to be competent and have modest attributes and, at the same time, be a person with a "miracle" who is able to lead to attain followers' ideals (Abdalla and Al-Homoud, 2001). Building relationships and trust are very important to managerial effectiveness. An "outstanding leader in the Arabic cluster is a person who is able to initiate change and improvement by keeping group solidarity and yet at the same time avoiding nepotism" (Kabasakal and Bodur, 2002, p. 52).

Some summary data is also available for the other three clusters. In the Latin American cluster (Argentina, Bolivia, Brazil, Colombia, Costa Rica, Ecuador, El Salvador, Guatemala, Mexico, and Venezuela), team leadership was the preferred approach, followed closely by the self-protective leadership style. In the sub-Saharan African cluster (Namibia, Zambia, Zimbabwe, Nigeria, and South Africa [black sample]), humane and self-protective leadership were by far the dominant leadership styles. Taiwan, Singapore, Hong Kong, South Korea, China, and Japan formed the Confucian Asian cluster, and here the results paralleled the sub-Saharan cluster, with the self-protective and humane leadership styles dominating the leadership preferences. Finally, the Nordic cluster (Denmark, Finland, and Sweden) preferred a participative leadership style (Gupta, Hanges, and Dorfman, 2002).

Leadership in Europe

Another large study conducted as part of Project GLOBE looked at the conceptions of leadership across twenty-two European countries (Brodbeck et al., 2000). The results indicate that leadership concepts are culturally endorsed. Relatedly, European countries with similar cultural values also shared similar leadership values. Data was compared from five European country clusters (Anglo, Nordic, Germanic, Latin, and Near East), and a sixth cluster, called Central European, which included Poland and Slovenia, was established. Four simple core dimensions—interpersonal directness, proximity, autonomy, and modesty—which can be used to compare leadership behaviors across regions, were identified, leading to the suggestion that individuals who want to be "Euromanagers" need to consider the full range of cultural differences if they are to be successful in bridging the cultural gaps. The research also implies that leaders will have an easier time leading in countries within their cultural cluster than in other European clusters.

One other Project GLOBE study reported on the similarities and differences for countries in the southern part of the European Union, namely, France, Greece, Italy, Portugal, and Spain. The results for Greece have been reported elsewhere as part of the Eastern European cluster but were included in this Southern European Union cluster because it was felt that this was a better fit. Greeks tend to question authority, have difficulty cooperating, and mistrust superiors, but at the same time, the successful Greek manager is expected to take care of employee needs within a family organizational culture (Broome, 1996). Greece was found to have the highest scores for autonomous, charismatic, and humane leadership, and it was the most individualistic country. France scored the lowest in humane and charismatic leadership and the second lowest on autonomous leadership. In this country grouping, there was a lot of similarity in the societal culture measures. These countries share a high power distance, an inclination to reward excellence, family collectivism, caring behaviors, future-oriented behaviors, and collective distribution of resources and action. The researchers conclude that, while there is some evidence that the countries in this group share some of the same values, there were considerable differences in leadership preferences. At the same time, these countries share common civilization and religious roots and are at similar levels in their economic development, indicating some convergence in their cultural values (Nikandrou, Apospori, and Papalexandris, 2003).

Comparative Leadership Studies Involving Several Countries

Managers in eight countries were asked to identify leadership capabilities that they considered crucial to effective leadership (Yeung and Ready, 1995). The countries included in this study were Australia, France, Germany, Italy, Japan, Korea, the United Kingdom, and the United States. The results show that both similarities and differences in key leadership abilities exist among countries. The ability to articulate a tangible vision, values, and strategy was considered the most important leadership characteristic in every country except Italy, where being flexible and a catalyst for cultural change were most important. The other critical leadership capabilities listed in most of the countries were being a catalyst for strategic change, being results oriented, empowering others to do their best, being a catalyst for cultural change, and exhibiting a strong customer orientation, although the relative importance of these capabilities did vary between countries. While these results indicate a remarkably high level of consistency, some differences are also significant. For example, the French managers listed the ability to manage internal and external networks higher than most other countries' managers. Japanese managers emphasized the ability to empower others, and the Americans emphasized the ability to get results and to design a management strategy to get action more than most other countries. Also, Japanese and Korean managers ranked the ability to be a catalyst for cultural change much lower than their Australian, French, and Italian counterparts.

A study comparing leadership styles in the United States and Germany found lower levels of transformational leadership styles among German employees (Kuchinke, 1999). The primary difference between the two countries is that charismatic and inspirational leadership are more likely to be used in the United States than in Germany. There were no differences between the countries in the level of transactional leadership. The findings indicate that cultural values have an effect on leadership styles, but the researchers note that other variables, such as job type and organizational position, may be more important and that culture might not be the most critical predictor of leadership behavior. The other finding of interest is that while differences in leadership style exist between cultures, there is very little difference across organizational levels within a culture.

Leadership can also be considered from the perspective of upward and downward influence of managers. Looking at leadership from this perspective, a comparison of managers in the United States and Hong Kong yielded differences between the countries in the way managers approach superiors and subordinates. The Hong Kong managers preferred to be assertive, whereas the Americans preferred to rely on rational arguments, ingratiation, and the exchange of favors (Schermerhorn and Bond, 1991). Along the same lines, strategies used by leaders to influence followers to behave in desired ways were investigated in a study of managers from the United States, the United Kingdom, Australia, Japan (but working in Taiwan), and Taiwan, which also included data from an earlier study conducted in the United States (Schmidt and Yeh, 1992). The specific leader-influence strategies measured were reasoning, bargaining, higher authority, sanctions, friendliness, assertiveness, and coalition. The researchers concluded that managers often used combinations of influence strategies and that bargaining was preferred in the United States, reasoned friendliness was preferred in Australia, assertive reasoning was preferred in Japan, sanctions were preferred in Taiwan, and the British sample relied more on formal authority and position power. The results indicated the prevalence of the same leader-influence strategies across the four countries, but there were differences in their relative importance and frequency of use.

Leadership in Chinese Cultures

Most of the attempts to understand Chinese leadership behavior have used American or Western theories that are then tested on Chinese samples. When attempting to apply American theories to Chinese cultures, it is important to take into consideration the fact that America is a more individualist culture than are the various Chinese cultures, all of which tend to be collectivist. Numerous studies have been conducted looking specifically at Chinese work organizations, and the majority of this research has focused on companies in Hong Kong (e.g., Redding and Wong, 1986). The results of one detailed study reporting on successful overseas Chinese, mostly from Hong Kong and Taiwan, led to the conclusion that Chinese organizations are based on filial piety, collectivism, and a strong work ethic, implying that authoritarian leadership and paternalism is the norm (Redding, 1990). Paternalism implies that the leader acts like and is treated like a father by employees.

A comparison of managers in the United States and Chinese and American managers working in Hong Kong was completed, using numerous scales that had been developed in the United States to measure different aspects of management. When the researchers checked the relationship between the performance evaluations of the managers and their leadership scores, they found that performance and leadership were correlated on eight of the twelve measures of leadership in the American managers in the United States. However, for American managers in Hong Kong, there was only one positive correlation. Further, for the Chinese managers in Hong Kong, there were no positive correlations. These results suggest that the dimensions of leadership that Americans view as important are different from those viewed as important by Chinese (Black and Porter, 1991). Clearly, there is a need to develop additional scales for use specifically in Chinese and other cultures.

These findings are reinforced by a study designed to identify effective leadership styles in Taiwan (Bond and Hwang, 1986). Effective leaders were found to be those who were highly ranked on both the task and interpersonal aspects of their leadership role. In addition, strengthening and exploiting *guanxi,* the granting of favors based on personal relationships, was also seen as an important component of leadership. *Guanxi* is of major importance in determining leadership effectiveness within Chinese cultures. Hong Kong managers also believed that the preservation of "face" is important for leaders, and they reported that they worked hard at maintaining face for themselves, their clients, and their subordinates. Failure to preserve face was seen as a failure of leadership (Redding and Ng, 1982). In a study conducted in three collectivist and emerging economies (China, India, and Kenya), transformational leadership appeared to be effective in all three cultures (Walumbwa and Lawler, 2002).

Another study looked specifically at Chinese leadership styles from a purely Chinese perspective using the PM leadership theory of J. Misumi (1985). Misumi reconceptualized the two dimensions of leadership discussed earlier by relabeling the task dimension *performance* (P) and the social dimension *maintenance* (M). His initial research showed that Japanese managers were considered to be effective leaders if they scored high on both maintenance and performance behaviors. The Chinese study was conducted in Beijing and looked at the perception of a manager's leadership ability from the subordinate's perspective. Based on the results from a cluster analysis, it was concluded that when considering leadership in a Chinese population, a third additional factor needed to be added to the performance and maintenance factors. This additional factor, labeled the *character* (C) dimension, concerns the moral integrity of the leader and includes concepts such as honesty, integrity, and willingness to listen, as well as an organizational commitment to the work team and the Communist Party (Xu, 1989). This is also an important dimension for family organizations, which are prevalent in Chinese cultures outside mainland China (Smith and Wang, 1996).

The identification and study of the character or moral dimension identified by L. C. Xu (1989) is unique in research on management and is not typically considered in Western research. Other research on Chinese populations has identified similar concepts. For example, S. K. C. Chang (1985) found that Chinese managers in Taiwan believed that companies should contribute to the solutions for societal problems. Further, in their major research project, which considered whether results using an "Eastern" values-assessment instrument would correlate with those found using "Western" instruments, the Chinese Culture Connection (1987) identified a cluster of Chinese values that they called *moral discipline.* They initiated this research based on their perception of a lack of sensitivity to non-Western values in most research attempting to understand Chinese organizations and societies. These various dimensions of character appear to be a uniquely Chinese cultural variable and a key dimension of perceived leadership. Further, other research on leadership in Chinese culture (Hui and Tan, 1996) found that Chinese employees want their leaders to be considerate and benevolent. This indicates that in the Chinese culture a task emphasis is less important than a relationship emphasis.

Leadership in Mainland China

The current organizational-leadership patterns in mainland China (PRC) evolved from the "three-man leadership system" established in the 1930s. The PRC used a centralized decision-making process rooted in the Communist Party system rather than in the family structure found in other Chinese cultures (Wang, 1994). More recently, state enterprises have adopted a "management responsibility system" under which managers have greater authority to run their enterprises (Child, 1994). The PRC is a country where joint ventures have been favored over the past twenty-five years, as the country has attempted economic and business reforms. Joint ventures present a unique leadership challenge for managers and organizations (Li, Xin, and Tsui, 1999). Leadership behavior in teams that include people from different countries was investigated in the PRC and led to several suggested strategies for successful team leadership in international joint ventures. These strategies include ensuring that the team contains individuals who have the ability to work in cross-cultural settings and who do not have just technical business expertise, promoting greater interdependence among the team members, and fostering leaders with strong group-process skills and leadership ability (Li, Xin, and Tsui, 1999).

A study of implicit leadership theory in mainland China identified these four components of leadership: personal morality, goal effectiveness, interpersonal competence, and versatility. These factors were quite different from those identified by L. R. Offermann and colleagues (1994) in a U.S. sample, suggesting that Western theories of leadership are not very effective if applied to PRC samples and that the overemphasis in Western studies on overt behavior of leaders may be overlooking the implicit aspects of leadership, with possible negative consequences (Ling, Chia, and Fang, 2000).

Leadership in Other Asian Countries

In general, Asian leadership expectations are based on "paternal authoritativeness" (Hui, 1990), where leaders are expected to behave much like concerned fathers. In Chinese cultures, the importance of filial piety and the role of the father in many small businesses demonstrate the centrality of this concept (Punnett, 1995). The paternalistic approach can include both authoritarian and nurturing elements. When the leader places emphasis on task and duty, paternalism is considered authoritarian, whereas when the leader emphasizes loyalty and shows genuine concern for employees, paternalism is considered to be nurturing. Basing his observations on Korean leadership behaviors, U. M. Kim (1994) characterized these two forms of paternalism as authoritarian and benevolent and concluded that Korean organizational leaders tend to prefer an authoritarian paternalistic approach.

While research on leadership in India is limited, some studies have concluded that the nurturant-task leadership model is generally always effective, while the participative and authoritarian models of leadership are not. However, if the subordinates are well trained and efficient, the participative model is effective, and if the situation is stressful, the authoritarian leadership model is effective (Sinha, 1980, 1990, 1995). Similar results have been found in Brazil (Farris and Butterfield, 1972) and Iran (Ayman and Chemers, 1983). A study comparing Indian and American salespeople found that the two groups were similar on the dimensions of consideration, role ambiguity, role conflict, and organizational commitment but differed on the dimension of initiation-of-structure behavior (Agarwal, DeCarlo, and Vyas, 1999). Structure-type leadership did not reduce role ambiguity and conflict in the Indian sample, whereas it did for the American sample. Also, the impact of Indian culture on leadership was shown to still exist, despite the extensive exposure to Western theories and practices that has occurred in recent years. The leader in India is often seen as autocratic but, at the same, is the recipient of significant idealization from key followers, which unfortunately limits the amount of feedback the leader receives from followers, reducing the leader's ability to adapt and grow (Kakar, Kets de Vries, Kakar, and Vrignaud, 2002).

In Japan, the research mentioned earlier conducted by Misumi (Misumi and Peterson, 1985) over a thirty-year period found that a combination of performance- and maintenance-oriented behaviors (PM) provided the most effective leadership behavior. Japanese managers were found to be similar to American managers on dimensions such as assertiveness, sanctions, and appeals to higher authority, but the Japanese also use socializing and personal development, whereas American managers do not (Rao, Hashimoto, and Rao (1997).

Leadership in Arab Countries

There is very little leadership research available from Arab cultures in the Middle East. Research in Arab cultures has been categorized in three ways: Westernized, Arabized, and Islamicized (Ali, 1990). Some studies test Western theories, while others attempt to understand the culture with either a general Arabic viewpoint or a view that is rooted in Islam. Several countries in the Middle East have adopted a more prescribed view of Arab culture by integrating aspects of Islam into everyday behaviors, including those within organizations. For example, M. Badawy (1980) tested a Western perspective and was able to identify some organizational and personal factors that influence leadership. While A. J. Ali (1988) attempted to analyze managerial practices and concepts in Arab culture, I. Sharfuddin (1987) advocated using Islamic principles as the foundation for management practices and values. The prophetic-caliphal model of leadership developed by B. Khadra (1990) focuses on the antecedents of two distinct types of leadership. There is a strong disposition toward the "great or prophetic leader," perceived by followers as a worker of miracles. In contrast, the "ordinary or caliphal" leader rules by coercion and fear (Dorfman, 1996). Since these distinctions are similar to those found in the transformational-charismatic leadership theory, this theory appears to be salient in the Arab world.

In the Islamic world, management practices are influenced by tribal traditions, and a manager is expected to act as a father figure, viewing his role in "a highly personalized manner characterized by providing and caring for employees and favoring individuals within the family and tribe over outsiders" (Dorfman, 1996, p. 307). Arab nations in the Gulf region endorse collective values and practices such as personalized relationships, in-group cooperation, and out-group avoidance (Abdalla and Al-Homoud, 2001). In a study of mid-level managers from Kuwait and Qatar, the results indicate that there is an Arab Gulf culturally endorsed implicit leadership theory, for which the most desirable dimensions are charismatic-value based, self-protection, and consideration (Abdalla and Al-Homoud, 2001). The sample from Kuwait ranked vision, strategic planning, and future orientation as the most important characteristics of an outstanding leader, while the Qatar sample ranked inspirational, motivational, and directional skills as the most important. Overall, there was a high degree of consistency in the listings for both countries in terms of the top-ten valued traits. This study emphasized desirable traits of leaders as opposed to the actual traits of leaders as perceived by followers. The researchers note that the findings from earlier research on actual traits of leaders (e.g., Badawy, 1980) differ from those of research that considered the desired traits of leaders. Desirable leaders were seen as future oriented and visionary, whereas actual leaders were seen as unlikely to possess or embrace these two traits.

A study of Iranian business leaders found that they embraced the concept of empowerment, which has a strong emotional impact on employees and facilitates a loyal work force (Javidan, 1996). In other research, Iranian leaders scored high on the visionary and high-commitment concepts of leadership (Dastmalchian and Javidan, 1998). More recently, some Project GLOBE data for Iran was reported (Dastmalchian, Javidan, and Alam, 2001) that isolated seven dimensions of leadership: supportive, dictatorial, planner, familial, humble, faithful, and receptive. These findings suggest creating two foundations for leadership characteristics. One is based on historical and cultural factors and includes familial, faithful, and humble dimensions, and the unique characteristics of the Iranian culture. The supportive and dictatorial dimensions constitute the second foundation, which leans more toward affirming a universal view of leadership that could be considered to be culture free.

Leadership in Turkey

Turkey is an interesting country to consider in terms of cultural differences since it has roots in both the Western and the Middle Eastern cultures. Collectivism is the dominant cultural and organizational value in Turkey. There is a predominance of leader behaviors that are considered paternalistic-considerate and laissez-faire. Leaders prefer a benevolent paternalism style. This preference is attributed to the fact that followers tend to accept sharing responsibility and that leaders are seen as having "granted authority" based on the large power distance found in the Turkish culture (Pasa, Kabasakal, and Bodur, 2001). Ideal leaders are often considered to be team-oriented individuals who encourage participation. The ideal leader in Turkey is decisive, ambitious, and assertive, with a hands-on approach. These characteristics are most often found in countries, such as Turkey, with high power distance. The results from research indicate that Turkish leaders play a paternalistic role, treating employees like a member of the family, and use a team approach to make employees feel they belong. Leaders operate in very hierarchical organizations that have centralized decision making, have strong leadership, and tend to be considered family-type organizations (Trompenaars and Hampden-Turner, 1998). Similarly, Turkish managers have been found to stress the autocratic style of leadership more and the consensus style of leadership less than American managers. Interestingly, Turkish respondents saw being concerned with the personal problems of employees as a characteristic of effective leaders (Marcoulides, Yavas, and Bilgin, 1998). Similar findings were seen with workers and managers in Russia (Silverthorne, 1992).

A study of how people from different cultures perceive charismatic leadership, testing leadership perceptions based on two alternative processes, compared subjects from Turkey and the United States. Inference-based perceptions involve making attributions of leadership characteristics based on outcomes ascribed to a leader (Ensari, 2001). For example, a leader is perceived as charismatic when the company is successful (Shamir, 1992). The second perception process, called *recognized-based,* depends on the person connecting actual or perceived leadership characteristics with how they think a person should behave as a particular type of leader (den Hartog et al., 1999). People from individualist cultures (such as the United States) and collectivist cultures (such as Turkey) make attributions about the leader's behavior differently. People in an individualist culture rely more on perceived characteristics of leaders, while the people in a collectivistic culture rely more on performance outcomes (Ensari, 2001). The results of this study suggest that the way people perceive leadership behavior varies in different cultures and that these differences will influence how leaders can both affect culture and be constrained by it. In other words, the leader's behavior may not be critical in terms of effectiveness. Rather, it is how followers perceive the leader's behavior that is important. In Western culture, public praise is common in organizations. For example, people are often given rewards or identified as "employee of the month." This is considered both appropriate and motivating. However, to draw attention to an Indian employee in the same way would be embarrassing to them, would be seen as not appropriate, and would almost certainly not be motivating. The leader's behavior is the same in both of these cases, but the perception of his or her behavior by employees from the United States and from India would be significantly different.

Leadership in Africa

Africa has received very limited attention from researchers. As mentioned earlier, Project GLOBE has generated some information for the five countries in the sub-Saharan cluster, but many other African countries were not included. A study looking at The Gambia provides some insights into leadership styles in that and neighboring African countries (Banutu-Gomez, 2003). Traditional African leadership practices have been passed down from generation to generation. The chief of the tribe was generally appointed on the advice and consent of the village elders and with the participation of village members, leading to decisions based on consensus. This tradition continues today. Decisions are made in discussions involving everyone, and open communication is an important aspect of traditional African leadership practices.

In The Gambia, five sets of leadership practices were identified. Traditional African leadership practices include the passing down of customs, information, and beliefs from one generation to the next. This creates a communal decision that is often very time consuming, as advisement, consultation, collaboration, and good communication skills are involved in the decision-making process. Families are valued, and the older generation is respected and influential in the decision-making process. Leadership is also based on a shared vision, accountability, patriotism, and willingness and openness to change. These findings suggest that The Gambia prefers a participative style of leadership under the Project GLOBE classification system, which is quite different from the results for Namibia, Zambia, Zimbabwe, Nigeria, and black South Africa. These findings also suggest that other African countries not yet studied should not be classified on the basis of current information and that more detailed studies of leadership in African countries should be undertaken.

Organizational Justice and Leadership

Organizational justice plays an important role in leadership. An increase in subordinates' opportunity to express opinions has been shown to heighten their perceptions of fairness and their evaluations of supervisors' leadership capabilities, especially when subordinates have low decision control (Tyler, 1989). In the literature on organizational justice, a two-part conceptualization of justice is generally accepted: procedural justice is concerned with fairness of procedures, and distributive justice is concerned with fairness of outcomes. Transformational leadership has been found to be related to procedural justice, which in turn influences employees' trust and job satisfaction. The underlying social-exchange process that characterizes transformational relationships may be influential in the linkage between transformational leadership and procedural justice. Thus, although the underlying mechanisms may be different, there is a possibility of a strong link between transformational leadership and procedural justice across cultures (Pillai and Williams, 1996). A follow-up study surveyed subjects in the United States, Australia, India, Colombia, Saudi Arabia, and Jordan. It found further support for the relationship between leadership and organizational justice and job satisfaction in the U.S. and Australian samples, and it found support for a link between aspects of organizational leadership and LMX in all the countries surveyed except India. The researchers conclude that there are more commonalities than differences in the leadership process across cultures (Pillai, Scandura, and Williams, 1999).

Leadership and Entrepreneurship

Certain leadership styles are probably better suited to encouraging or reflecting entrepreneurship than others are. Entrepreneurship is a growing phenomenon throughout the world and generally grows out of small businesses. In an attempt to provide a conceptual framework for research, Gartner (1990) investigated the meaning that three groups of individuals (researchers, practitioners, and politicians) attached to the concept of entrepreneurship. His results led him to isolate eight themes, which according to his sample were considered to be important to the concept of entrepreneurship. In the United States, most new jobs are found in small businesses, and women and minorities, prevented from being promoted by the "glass ceiling," can be successful by opening their own businesses. The increase in entrepreneurial activity can also be seen in many other countries. For example, there has been a surge of entrepreneurial activity in the People's Republic of China (Chang and MacMillan, 1991). Taiwan has always been known as a country in which small businesses, based on entrepreneurial activities, are the norm rather than the exception. So, what are the leadership characteristics of an effective entrepreneur?

Researchers have investigated entrepreneurial capital, the growth stages of small businesses from start-up to maturity, the tendency of various ethnic minorities to focus on particular entrepreneurial activities and eschew others, the personality characteristics of successful and unsuccessful entrepreneurs, and, more recently, the setting in which successful entrepreneurship occurs. While some researchers restrict the term *entrepreneur* to the founder-owner of a small business, others attempt to distinguish entrepreneurs in some ways from small-business owners, and still others focus on certain personality characteristics of the entrepreneur, such as the need for achievement, which can be expressed in various ways. This last approach to entrepreneurship mirrors the early approaches to identifying effective leaders using traits.

F. L. Fry (1993) defines an entrepreneur as a person who begins or significantly improves a venture. He points to innovation as a key characteristic of the "entrepreneurial personality." This personality is defined as including the following traits: the desire for an internal locus of control (i.e., the individual is self- rather than outer-directed); a need for autonomy, or the desire to be free to act alone; a need for achievement; and a willingness to undertake moderate risk taking—with the word *moderate* being the key qualifier, clearly implying that too great a love for risk taking is dangerous to an entrepreneur who wishes to satisfy his or her drive for achievement. In fact, Fry believes that entrepreneurs need not fit the popular image of being risk takers. They are, however, willing to face risks that are sufficiently "moderate." There may be an intuitive attraction to this view, but the distinction between "seeking" and "facing" is not clearly stated, and it is possible that, in reality, a person can create a risk, which must then be faced in some way.

D. McClelland (1961) also emphasizes the importance of innovation in entrepreneurship. As McClelland uses the terms *entrepreneur* and *entrepreneurship,* they refer to managers working in organizations largely owned by other people but engaging in significant entrepreneurial activities. He developed a theoretical framework referred to as "achievement-power-affiliation." This theory argues that most people, including entrepreneurs, are primarily motivated by three basic needs: the need to be successful (N Achievement), the need to have power (N Power), and the need to belong (N Affiliation). Every individual has these needs, but not at the same level or relative importance. The entrepreneur particularly feels the need to succeed or achieve and therefore, presumably, has a higher need for achievement than for affiliation or power (McClelland, 1961).

The concepts of social motivation have also been used with some success in studies of leadership. Studies have investigated achievement motivation as it applies to the entrepreneur, and a review has been conducted of several psychological tests that have been used in entrepreneurial research to measure the need for achievement. While there does indeed seem to be a relationship between achievement-oriented motivation and entrepreneurship, it is difficult to say precisely just what this relationship is (Johnson, 1990).

Of particular interest here is a comparison of the leadership styles of entrepreneurs and those of other upper-level managers. Entrepreneurs and leaders are both seen as having "authority," which has also been defined in various ways. One text says that it is composed of the "rights inherent in a managerial position to give orders and expect the orders to be obeyed" (Robbins, 1998, p. 116). This is conventional enough, but it does not clearly distinguish between the concepts of entrepreneurship, management, and leadership. D. Sexton and N. Bowman (1985) think that there are significant differences between the psychological traits and characteristics of entrepreneurs and those of other corporate executives and managers. In general, they conclude that entrepreneurs are more tolerant of ambiguity, more likely to prefer autonomy, and more likely to resist conformity. Further, these individuals are more likely to be aloof but socially sensitive and skillful people who enjoy risk taking. They can maintain these characteristics because they are able to easily accept change and have a low need for support from others.

Another study examined the entrepreneurial orientation (EO) of a sample of independent business people, comparing people with high, medium, and low EO along a series of distinctive marketing-competency and organizational-performance measures. EO was found to be positively and significantly related to distinctive marketing competencies and organizational performance (Smart and Conant, 1994).

B. Cunningham and J. Lischeron (1991) identified six schools of entrepreneurial thought:

1. The "great person" school, which focuses on the supposed inborn intuitive ability of the entrepreneur, without which the entrepreneur would be just like everyone else.
2. The "psychological characteristics" school, which assumes that entrepreneurs have unique values, attitudes, and needs that drive them.
3. The "classical" school, which assumes that the central characteristic of entrepreneurial behavior is innovation.
4. The "management" school, which assume that entrepreneurs are organizers of economic ventures, people who organize, own, manage, and take on risks.
5. The "leadership" school, which assumes that entrepreneurs are leaders of other people and that they have the ability to adapt their style to the needs of people.

6. The "entrepreneurship" school, which assumes that entrepreneurial skills exist and can be useful to complex organizations. (p. 55)

Any study of leadership and entrepreneurship must include the question of the extent to which talent and success are products of individual psychology and the extent to which they are products of the socioeconomic environment. Is business success a function of the individual or of socioeconomic history and environment? Probably there is at least some truth that both the individual and the socioeconomic environment are important. In fact, the role of culture in entrepreneurial behavior suggests that entrepreneurship is more compatible with certain cultures than others. Cultures that are less tolerant of power distance, more willing to live with uncertainty, and that are more individualistic, masculine, and achievement oriented are more likely to have an entrepreneurial orientation (Lee and Peterson, 2000).

There are at least two viewpoints on the characteristics of the entrepreneur and the outcomes of the entrepreneur's actions. The first of these two viewpoints relates back to the theories discussed earlier that are built on the role of personality and individual differences, while the second focuses on outcomes of action rather than on the person. Since different cultures emphasize or prefer certain characteristics of individuals, there is a strong need to look at the impact of different cultures on the same phenomenon.

Little research on how entrepreneurs think across cultures has been undertaken. Such research is important to understanding whether the characteristics of entrepreneurs are universal or culture specific. A study of entrepreneurs in eleven countries attempted to address this issue (Mitchell et al., 2002). The countries studied included the United States, Canada, the United Kingdom, Germany, France, Italy, Japan, Australia, Chile, Mexico, and China. The results indicate that culture does matter in entrepreneurship in the areas of existence (the need for entrepreneurship), nature (what constitutes entrepreneurship), and the relative importance of specific characteristics. Universal aspects of entrepreneurship include arrangements (making mental maps about contacts) and ability and willingness (supporting the commitment and being willing to undertake a venture).

There has also been a movement toward privatization in many countries. The process of privatization is such that a public organization effectively becomes a private one. The selling off of state-owned enterprises has widespread implications for entrepreneurship, regulatory frameworks, financial institutions, foreign investment, and leadership. The support and development of small businesses will result in a strong entrepreneurial spirit developing and continuing. The role of government may well be to provide direction to businesses so that they will enter into new or promising areas within the changing global economy. In this way, government resources will be able to provide broad guidelines to the small business. The identification of entrepreneurs and leaders and the differences, if any, between them is a critical area for consideration as organizations change and grow (Doshi, 1994).

Some Further Thoughts on Leadership

The majority of the research conducted across cultures has focused on understanding how specific roles and approaches to leadership work in different cultures and how these approaches affect employee and subordinate or follower performance. While a large number of similarities have been found across cultures, studies have found different types of behavior in different contexts. For example, a study of Russian and American managers found that Russian managers spent more time on traditional managerial behaviors such as planning and coordinating, and American managers spent more time on networking both inside and outside the organization (Luthans, Welsh, and Rosenkrantz, 1993). Along the same lines, Chinese managers spent more time with their superiors and others within the organization than their American counterparts, who were more likely to spend time with their peers and people from outside their organization (Boisot and Liang, 1992).

It is also reasonable to believe that managers in different cultures face different challenges. A comparison of the challenges faced by managers in twenty-one countries found different patterns in countries previously labeled high or low on power distance (Peterson et al., 1995). Managers from countries with high power distance reported more problems with role overload, whereas managers from countries considered to have low power distance reported more problems with role ambiguity. The results from a seven-nation study reflected differences in the power distance of the country. When researchers asked managers to indicate how they would handle a variety of situations at work, Polish and Czech managers preferred an autocratic approach, while German, Austrian, and Swiss managers chose a participative approach. The approaches of managers from France and the United States fell somewhere between these two extremes (Jago, 1993). Similarly, a study of managers in fourteen countries found that managers from high-individualism cultures relied on personal experience and training to handle routine work tasks, whereas managers from high-power-distance cultures relied on formal rules and procedures (Smith, Peterson, et al., 1994).

In marketing and sales, leadership has been considered from the perspective of the impact of individualism and power distance. A study of leadership styles used to foster cooperation among marketing-channel members in auto dealerships led to inconsistent results between the United States, Finland, and Poland. The results suggest that using standardized approaches to leadership style in marketing across different cultures is probably unwise (Rajiv et al., 2001). Further, a study of organizational commitment as a function of leadership in American and Indian salespeople found that leadership that focused on initiation of structure reduced role stress of American but not Indian salespeople. On the other hand, leadership that emphasized consideration found a strong positive relationship with organizational commitment in both the American and Indian samples (Agarwal, DeCarlo, and Vyas, 1999).

These results suggest that leaders' effectiveness relates to how they handle the challenges they face. The challenges managers face differ from country to country based on issues embedded in their culture. In a recent survey of over one thousand CEOs from around the world, the respondents indicated that their three most critical tasks with regard to global competitiveness were to build a strong executive team, to set and communicate the vision, and to establish the right structure (Verespej, 1999). Having leadership talent at all levels was seen as critical by 57 percent of the CEOs, and improving leadership talent was seen as the area requiring the most attention by 54 percent of the CEOs. These findings did not differ significantly among the different countries of origin of the CEOs surveyed. This survey and the results of other research clearly indicate that leadership will remain a critical issue for companies in the global economy, especially in the near future. Add to this the concern that a significant percentage of the large baby-boomer population in the United States now in the work force will retire within the next ten or so years and that the selection of new leaders will rely on a smaller population, and the problems of finding good global leaders are staggering (Wellins and Byham, 2001). Other countries are also experiencing equivalent population size shifts that will affect their workplaces in similar ways. While one cannot develop global leaders until one knows what being a global leader means, it does appear that effective global leaders are able to see the world's challenges and opportunities, think from an international perspective, act with global-centric leadership behaviors, and lead world-class teams (Thaler-Carter, 2000).

Several suggestions that have been offered to leaders and managers who are working in developing countries are worth sharing here and can be useful for any cross-cultural assignment (Banutu-Gomez, 2002). The leader should accept, support, value, and maintain locally based organizations. To do this, the leader must be willing to use team building in the local community, group problem solving, task autonomy, accountability, and responsibility. Leaders must maintain a high standard of conduct and be willing to integrate local people, needs, and values into the organization's goals.

Summary

Leadership plays an important role in management and organizational success. The leader is typically the individual who, by working with the employees, moves the organization toward the goals it has established. The study of leadership has moved from the trait approach to the more-complex contingency models of a variety of researchers and theorists. These more-complex models, designed to explain leadership, have added to the ability to explain a range of human behaviors within organizational settings.

The research findings from the studies discussed here can help leaders operating in other countries better understand their own behavior and make reasonable accommodations to become more cross-culturally effective. Leaders need to understand the cultural expectations followers have of them. They need to continually check the employee perceptions of leadership, and they need to ensure that cultural issues are incorporated into choosing the best leadership style. While employees in many countries indicate that they favor a participative leadership style, what exactly participation involves can vary dramatically across cultures. It is not enough to understand differences in leadership styles because the perception and definition of leadership behavior also varies across cultures. In addition, training programs can be better informed about the needs of individuals preparing to lead across cultures, and consultants can better assist companies in their global expansion in the areas of human resources, management, and organizational structure.

7

Work Motivation

The impact of motivation on work performance has been of considerable interest to researchers for many years. Since the role of work in a society reflects the values of that society, work motivation is also presumably influenced by cultural issues. Managing across cultures requires motivating employees from various cultures, but finding a framework for motivating and managing behavior across cultures has proven difficult (Adler and Doktor, 1989). Overall, the evidence for the impact of culture on motivation is primarily experiential and anecdotal rather than research based.

What Is Motivation?

Theories of motivation can be categorized into two primary schools of thought: content and process. Theorists such as A. H. Maslow (1943), F. Herzberg (1966), and D. McClelland (1976) developed what are known as content theories, in that they emphasize *what* motivates an individual. In contrast, Vroom (1964) and Locke (1991) proposed theories that emphasize *how* an individual is motivated to behave. These are known as process theories.

In an attempt to pull together the different theories and approaches to work motivation, Locke (1991) noted that content and process theories are not necessarily different. Rather, they address different aspects of the motivational sequence. He proposed that motivation be looked at as having a motivation core and a motivation hub. The model begins as a need theory and then moves to values and motives, which are the core of the motivation. Need theories, as proposed by Maslow and others, start with the assumption that people have a variety of needs that have to be met and that motivation is driven by the desire to satisfy those needs. Values and motives, which fit into the theories of Vroom and others, shape how we attempt to meet our needs. The hub of motivation includes goals, intentions, and expectations. As the hub is fulfilled, rewards are gained and satisfaction is achieved.

Intrinsic and Extrinsic Motivation

The concepts of intrinsic and extrinsic rewards have been theorized for some time and are generally accepted in the field of organizational behavior. However, there has been disagreement on what exactly is meant by both extrinsic and intrinsic rewards and motivation. F. Herzberg first popularized the distinction between intrinsic and extrinsic work rewards (e.g., Herzberg, Mausner, and Snyderman, 1959). He proposed two basic classes of work rewards: (1) intrinsic or job-content factors such as achievement, recognition, and advancement, and (2) extrinsic or job-context factors such as pay, working conditions, and job security. Herzberg also believed that, while adequate extrinsic rewards are necessary, only intrinsic rewards truly motivate people.

Some people seem to be driven by a passionate interest in their work, a deeper level of enjoyment and involvement in what they do, while others seem to be motivated more by external inducements to work. Intrinsic motivation can be considered the "labor of love" aspect driving human behavior, which comes from inside the individual, based on their individual interests and involvement in work. This type of motivation occurs when individuals engage in work primarily for its own sake, because the work is engaging or in some ways satisfying. On the other hand, extrinsic motivation is to work primarily in response to something apart from the work itself, such as a reward, recognition, or the dictates of other people. Extrinsic motivation is thus based on the goal of achieving something other than the work itself (Amabile, 1997). The majority of research on work motivation has focused on intrinsic rather than extrinsic motivation.

Although the extrinsic-intrinsic dichotomy of rewards has been well established and accepted in the field of organizational psychology, there are still some major issues to be considered. The classification of types of reward is based on definitions and constructs that are difficult to establish consistently. Further, various researchers have used different definitions of intrinsic and extrinsic motivation, making comparison of the research findings difficult. For example, some researchers define an intrinsic reward as one that is self-administered and an extrinsic reward as one that comes from others (Kanungo and Hartwick, 1987).

Contemporary views of intrinsic motivation include both cognitive (thoughts and judgment) and affective (emotions or feelings) components. For example, cognitive-evaluation theory argues that self-determination and competence are the hallmarks of intrinsic motivation (Deci and Ryan, 1985). Intrinsic motivation has also been defined as the experience of gaining enjoyment from performing a work task without the performance being controlled by external contingencies (Thomas and Velthouse, 1990). The researchers who formulated this definition suggest that there are four dimensions of assessment or judgment that individuals use to evaluate their work environment and that these are part of the cognitive component of intrinsic motivation. These four dimensions are impact, competence, meaningfulness, and choice. Most employees will experience job satisfaction when given moderate challenges on the job, since individuals tend to prefer jobs that give them the opportunity to undertake mentally challenging work. Jobs that have too little challenge result in boredom, while jobs with too much challenge can lead to frustration, stress, and feelings of failure (Katzell, Thompson, and Guzzo, 1992). Affective components of intrinsic motivation include interest and excitement (Izzard, 1977), elation and the flow of deep task involvement (Csikszentmihalyi, 1997), or happiness and surprise (Reeve, Cole, and Olsen, 1986). Extrinsic rewards have been considered to be primarily cognitive in nature (Lepper and Greene, 1978).

While individuals may be motivated by either intrinsic or extrinsic motives, using a combination of the two types of motives is common (Amabile, Hill, Hennessey, and Tighe, 1994). But one type or the other is likely to be a primary motivator for a given person doing a specific task (Amabile, 1993). The prevailing psychological model of the interaction between intrinsic and extrinsic motivation suggests an inverse relationship between them, so that as extrinsic motivation for an activity increases, intrinsic motivation decreases (Amabile et al., 1996). Generally speaking, this theoretical approach means that the two types of motivation are expected to work against each other (Deci and Ryan, 1985). Thus, if people are rewarded with financial incentives (extrinsic motivation) for doing their job, then they are less likely to make an additional effort without the reward (intrinsic motivation). It is generally thought that intrinsic motivation occurs because people find self-initiated actions and behaviors rewarding and satisfying. If people are encouraged to do something by effectively being bribed, they will no longer want to do it for just the enjoyment of doing it. Rather, they will expect to be bribed every time they are asked to do something. The workplace situation is similar to the child who is given money for every A on his or her report card. Child psychologists worry that the child will not want to get an A for personal satisfaction, as an intrinsic reward, but will expect to be paid, or receive an extrinsic reward, to study hard. By offering money, we may be taking away or reducing the child's internal motivation and desire to do well.

However, the expected negative impact of extrinsic motivation on the effectiveness of intrinsic motivation has been challenged by the results of some field research studies. These results suggest that under certain conditions, intrinsic and extrinsic motivation may actually complement each other and enhance outcomes (Amabile, 1993). There are three important determinants of whether extrinsic motivators will work with intrinsic motivators in an additive way: the person's initial motivational state, the type of extrinsic motivator used, and the timing of the use of the extrinsic motivator (Amabile, 1993). The first of these determinants is the initial level of intrinsic motivation. For example, if a person is deeply involved in the task because it is interesting or personally challenging, intrinsic motivation may be relatively impervious to the undermining effects of extrinsic motivation. If intrinsic motivation is strong, extrinsic motivation tends to have an additive effect on behavior, and if intrinsic motivation is weak, then extrinsic motivation tends to have a negative effect (Amabile, 1993). If you enjoy working, then extra rewards and recognition can spur you on to even better performance, but if you have a job you do not like, being paid more does not provide additional motivation—though it may provide justification for you to stay in a boring job while maintaining the lowest permissible level of work performance. Of course, in work situations the removal of all extrinsic rewards probably means the elimination of your job, and many people do work in poor-paying jobs because they love their work. Certainly many people in the helping professions are poorly paid, but the satisfaction of knowing that they are helping others encourages them to keep their jobs despite the low levels of extrinsic reward.

The prominent view in education and psychology is that rewards decrease a person's intrinsic motivation. However, a meta-analysis of the research in this area concluded that rewards can be effectively used to enhance or maintain an individual's intrinsic motivation (Cameron and

Pierce, 1996). But this conclusion is not accepted by many researchers (e.g., Ryan and Deci, 1996), who maintain their belief that rewards reduce intrinsic motivation. Monetary rewards and supervision crowd out intrinsic work motivation under certain specific and identifiable conditions, so that work performance will decrease if the crowding effect dominates. Crowding theory, or the negative impact of multiple extrinsic rewards on intrinsic rewards, explains a variety of empirical and real-world findings within organizations (Frey, 1997). One important outcome of increasing employees' intrinsic motivation is a reduction in the need for giving extrinsic rewards and monitoring employees' task behavior (Poulton and Ng, 1988). A complete understanding of these apparently contradictory findings is essential if intrinsic and extrinsic rewards are to be used effectively in organizations.

The role of intrinsic motivation has been explored from a variety of perspectives, including its impact on work commitment, overall job satisfaction, and turnover intentions (Lynn, Cao, and Horn, 1996). In fact, differences in the work-attitude patterns of men and women as well as in the career stage of employees have an impact on their motivation and attitudes. Thus, gender and career stage play an important role in the effectiveness of different types of motivation. Additional research in these areas is necessary. It is interesting to note that E. B. Hollander and L. R. Offermann (1990) argue that the implementation of intrinsic-motivation concepts reflects a change from a leader-dominated situation to one where the follower plays an important role.

Cognitive-evaluation theory argues that when extrinsic rewards are used in organizations as payment for superior performance, the impact or value of intrinsic rewards may be reduced. Thus, the introduction of extrinsic rewards, such as pay, for work that had previously been considered responsive to intrinsic rewards tends to decrease the overall level of motivation (De Charms, 1968). If the cognitive-evaluation model is valid, it has major implications for managerial practices. While the applicability of the theory is still being debated, the research results obtained so far indicate that the relationship between intrinsic and extrinsic rewards is real (Miner, 1980). Subsequent development of the cognitive-evaluation theory focusing on a trait-oriented approach to motivation suggests that autonomy-oriented individuals are more likely to be intrinsically motivated and that control-oriented individuals will more often be extrinsically motivated.

In general, it appears that when rewards are offered contingent on the completion of a task or are delivered unexpectedly, intrinsic motivation is maintained. Rewards have a negative effect when they are not made contingent on the level of performance. While money itself may not be a motivator, people do need to perceive that the pay system and promotion procedures and practices are based on a fair and equitable set of standards (Witt and Nye, 1992). Research has indicated that people will consider working for less money if there are other benefits such as a short commute or more flexibility in their workday. The key factor is that people must perceive that pay and raises are fair. The reality is less important than the perception of reality. The implication is that organizations need to work at communicating openly about all aspects of pay, promotions, benefits, and raises (Witt and Nye, 1992). Extrinsic motivation needs to be considered in this context. It has also been argued that job satisfaction is enhanced by employee benefits that individuals see as beneficial (Barber, Dunham, and Formisano, 1992). Employee benefits include health insurance, retirement programs, educational support, and childcare.

Some researchers theorize that the type of extrinsic rewards available makes a difference. "Synergistic extrinsic motivators," including certain types of reward, recognition, and feedback, do not necessarily undermine intrinsic motivation. Some extrinsic motivators may, in fact, enhance some aspects of performance. On the other hand, constraints on how work can be done, as well as other types of reward, recognition, and feedback, will be detrimental to intrinsic motivation and performance. A particular extrinsic motivator may never work in a positive way with intrinsic motivators if it has the effect of undermining a person's sense of self-worth (Deci and Ryan, 1985).

In the United States, the benefits portion of the employee's salary package is a significant expense and may account for over a third of the employee's total cost to the employer. This is less true in other countries, but when the labor market is tight and changes in employment patterns occur, especially when people are increasingly reluctant to work in manufacturing jobs, benefits become a very important facet of employee satisfaction in many countries. One aspect of the benefits issue is that employees are often unaware of the employer's costs for benefits and may actually undervalue their benefits (Wilson, Norcraft, and Neale, 1985). Recent research has focused on the general issue of benefits and the more specific issue of benefits communication. A higher level of job satisfaction seems to occur when individuals have flexibility in deciding their benefits. This finding suggests that the development of a plan that communicates benefits information to employees will enhance employees' satisfaction with their compensation, and the overall job satisfaction of employees would also aid in improving morale (Rabin, 1994). A recent survey indicates that the best companies to work for in the United States maintain a high concern for employee motivation and retention, even in an environment that requires cutbacks and layoffs (*HR Focus,* 2003).

The investigation of individual differences in motivational orientation is important for organizational theory. Because of differences in individuals' motivational orientations, there is a substantial range of behaviors that results from the way individuals react in different social settings (Deci and Ryan, 1985). One survey exploring elements of job satisfaction found that workers were more satisfied with intrinsic aspects of the job than with extrinsic ones (Richardson, Trewatha, and Vaught, 1995). Other researchers have demonstrated the linkages between competence, autonomy, and intrinsic motivation (Deci and Ryan, 1991). While feelings of competence can directly and positively influence intrinsic motivation, individuals also need to seek support from their colleagues and the working environment if they are to be satisfied at work (Reeve and Deci, 1996). People work for a variety of reasons other than money, and for many employees the job serves to meet social and group-membership needs. Therefore, relationships with co-workers and the attitude of the boss play an important role in generating employee job satisfaction (Scarpello and Campbell, 1983). The employee's work environment is important since people tend to seek an environment that is not dangerous or uncomfortable. Employees also tend to like working close to home in jobs that have good equipment and nice offices (Scarpello and Campbell, 1983).

Intrinsic rewards are an important element of the relationship between an employee and the organization. Managers are now often required to involve employees in the decisions that effect them and to share critical information. The increase in employee rights, such as participating in important decisions, also has the effect of increasing employee responsibility for the health of the entire organization. These significant changes in the role of intrinsic rewards place a much greater responsibility on both the manager and the organization to provide more intrinsic rewards than extrinsic ones, since intrinsic rewards drive performance (Hitchcock,

1994). One strategy for increasing intrinsic motivation is to develop self-leadership in employees through training interventions (Scott, 1997).

A practical application of changing the relative balance between intrinsic and extrinsic rewards was undertaken by the U.S. government when it attempted to create a more entrepreneurial federal government through legislative action in 1978. The program was designed to implement recognition and pay-for-performance objectives. In evaluating this program, it was found that individuals who exhibited higher levels of extrinsic motivation were somewhat more successful. This occurred probably because of the moderate levels of intrinsic motivation and the low levels of extrinsic motivation that previously existed in government agencies (Daley, 1995). As pointed out earlier, if intrinsic motivation is strong, the addition of extrinsic rewards can have an additive effect. Further, neither intrinsic motivation nor job satisfaction seemed to enhance the transitional process from a bureaucratic to an entrepreneurial organizational structure.

Another issue that affects the impact of extrinsic motivation is timing. Synergistic motivators may be the most useful at those stages in the creative process when there is a low level of novelty attached to the task (Amabile, 1997). It may be best to reduce the use of all types of extrinsic motivators at those stages with the greatest novelty, since intrinsic motivation seems conducive to creativity while extrinsic motivation is generally detrimental to creativity unless the extrinsic motivation is informational or enabling, particularly if the initial levels of intrinsic motivation are high. Creativity is important in many organizations, and there is ample evidence to indicate that people will be the most creative when they are primarily intrinsically motivated, rather than when they are extrinsically motivated by expected evaluation, surveillance, competition with peers, dictates from supervisors, or the promise of rewards (Amabile, 1996). Research on children has supported the belief that, with training, extrinsic rewards can enhance intrinsic behavior, particularly with regard to creativity (Hennessey and Zbikowski, 1993). Other research in business has uncovered several extrinsic motivators that operate to support creativity: reward and recognition for creative ideas, clearly defined overall project goals, and frequent constructive feedback on the work (Dweck, 1986). The evidence for a connection between social environment, intrinsic motivation, and creativity comes from a series of controlled experiments (Amabile, 1996, 1997).

Research reports have documented striking differences in task performance between intrinsically and extrinsically motivated individuals. For example, extrinsically motivated individuals tend to behave creatively more often, but the level of creativity is lower on a number of tasks (Amabile, 1997), and they are more likely to show impatient, rigid behavior in task engagement (Deci and Ryan, 1985). However, most of the research on motivation has studied short-term or temporary motivational states only. This situation is quite different from the long-term, permanent states found in organizations. There is also the possibility that individuals will create self-fulfilling expectations. For example, those who see themselves as strongly intrinsically motivated may strive to select work assignments that allow them to develop new skills, exercise creativity, and become deeply involved in their work. On the other hand, individuals who see themselves as strongly extrinsically motivated might seek out tasks or jobs where extrinsic rewards are much more important to the position (e.g., commission sales). Thus, both intrinsically and extrinsically motivated individuals may seek work that meets their needs or expectations (Amabile, Hill, Hennessey, and Tighe, 1994).

Driven by various motivational theories, new managerial techniques have been designed to provide increased motivation for employees. Some of these include pay raises, bonuses based on performance, promotions, and increased fringe benefits. However, several alternate systemic approaches also exist. One such approach is job enrichment, which involves redesigning the job so that motivation is increased, such as increasing the employee's responsibility and decision-making power. Management by objectives allows employees to work with management on establishing mutually acceptable objectives or goals for the employee, and as a result, the employee becomes more accountable for his or her job outcomes at a level acceptable to the organization.

It has been suggested that responsiveness to intrinsic motivation is part of a person's personality (Amabile, Hill, Hennessey, and Tighe, 1994). This conclusion is based on the observation that some people are more strongly driven than others by the sense of challenge in their work. While personality issues are important, so is the social environment in which a person works. People enter different business sectors for different reasons, a factor which needs to be taken into account in determining appropriate managerial techniques (Perry and Wise, 1990). Employees with psychological ties to their workplace are likely to stay there. These ties are often linked to investments they have made in the workplace and/or feelings of commitment to an agency. Cultivating employee commitment through the agency's culture, socialization processes, and ability to fulfill employees' expectations about work can thus lead to a more stable work force (Romzek, 1990).

Performance Evaluation

Understanding motivation and its impact requires that performance on the job be effectively measured and then tied to employee motivation. While the data available on the affect of culture on performance is limited, there is ample evidence that culture will affect performance and performance evaluation. It has been suggested that performance evaluation can be considered in the context of the dimensions of culture discussed earlier. Specifically, traditional (Western) performance-evaluation approaches will work best in individualist cultures, while group or team evaluations will work best in collectivist cultures. High-power-distance cultures will be less likely to use or embrace feedback systems that involve others, particularly peers and subordinates. Direct performance feedback is more likely in cultures with a low tolerance for uncertainty. Feminine cultures will be more likely to emphasize relationships, while masculine cultures are more likely to emphasize achievements and accomplishments. Finally, cultures that have a long-term time orientation are more likely to emphasize behavioral change based on performance, while cultures with short-term time orientation are likely to emphasize relationships over performance (Davis, 1998). Sometimes evaluation systems include self-evaluations, but these can also be affected by cultural patterns. For example, Chinese workers in Taiwan gave themselves lower ratings than their supervisors gave them, while Americans gave themselves higher ratings than their supervisors. The Chinese were more modest, and if these ratings are misunderstood, they might leave an American supervisor, for example, with the belief that Chinese perform poorly at work, even though this is not the case (Farh, Dobbins, and Cheng, 1991).

Feedback is an important part of both the motivational and performance-evaluation process, but how feedback is given and received can vary in different cultures. In a study conducted in the United States, Japan, and China (PRC), individuals in the collectivist countries (Japan and China) preferred failure feedback, whereas those in the individualist culture (the United States) preferred success feedback (Bailey, Chen, and

Dou, 1997). The researchers conclude that culture affects "individual desire for, behavior toward, and perception of, performance feedback" (p. 621). Knowledge of preferred feedback styles is beneficial to managers working outside their home culture. The introduction of performance evaluation into an organization requires sensitivity to cultural issues.

The concept of the learning organization has received considerable attention recently (Garratt, 1995). A learning organization is one that has developed the continuous capacity to adapt and change. The key elements of this type of organization are that people play the key role in organizational learning, learning has both an intrinsic (personal development) and extrinsic (organizational change and development) value, and learning has to be a continuous process in organizations. People in a learning organization put aside their own needs and self-interests to achieve the organization's shared vision by working together. In addition, team building, designed to improve the functioning of teams, and quality circles, allowing employees to meet and discuss ways to improve the quality of their work, are two approaches involving group processes. All of these alternate approaches attempt to package the work itself into something that is more motivating for employees.

Work Motivation in Other Countries

Whether the preceding theses and claims are valid and applicable to employees in all countries is an important question. Most studies of motivation have been conducted in a single culture with managers from the same culture. The general assumption has been that the findings are valid in every sector of the economy, that is, that people tend to be motivated by the same things. It has been argued that all managers tend to employ four types of motivation, which can be modified to fit the culture (Erez, 1997). The four types of motivation are the differential distribution of rewards, with high performers receiving most rewards; allowing subordinates to participate in goal setting and decision making; modifying tasks or job design and reporting relationships; and focusing subordinates on strategic objectives to improve quality. Thus, in individualist cultures rewards are individual, and in collectivist cultures they are provided for teams or work units. In high-power-distance cultures, goal setting is done for employees, while in low-power-distance collectivist cultures, employees and work group or team set the goals. Motivating across cultures or within multicultural organizations requires different approaches for different people, and it increases the challenges associated with treating everyone equally but differently and ensuring rewards are seen as fair, just, and equitable.

There have been very few attempts to test assumptions about the universality of work motivation in cultures outside the United States. In both Eastern and Western societies, results have been equivocal (Goh, Hian, and Chan, 1991). The effectiveness of a manager is based on the values he or she holds and the ability to motivate employees. The values guide the selection and evaluation of managerial behaviors, including style of management and motivation (Terpstra and David, 1990). These values are influenced by both the nationality of the manager and the business environment within which the individual manages (Adler and Bartholomew, 1992). The role that culture plays in international development highlights the need to understand the relationship between cultural values, systems of governance, managerial behavior, and motivation (Pearson, 1991).

The degree of match between managerial style and motivation is crucial, since the motivators identified as important by managers are usually not the same as those perceived by employees. For example, in one study, managers were asked to rank a list of ten things they thought workers wanted from their jobs. Workers were then asked to rank the same list of items based on what they wanted from their jobs. This list included items such as job security, good wages, full appreciation for work done, and promotion and growth on the job. If managers were in tune with their workers' needs, these two lists should be the same. In fact, they were quite different, with managers ranking "good wages" the most important to employees, while the employees ranked this item fifth. Employees ranked "full appreciation of the work done" number one in importance, but managers ranked it only eighth. These large discrepancies demonstrate management's lack of understanding of employees' needs, and they show that a particular manager's style of management may not necessarily be the most appropriate one to motivate employees (Hersey and Blanchard, 1988).

It is reasonable to expect that these discrepancies might be exaggerated when studied across cultures. In a replication of this study, data was collected from managers and employees in the United States, Taiwan, and

Russia (Silverthorne, 1992). The data showed an apparent improvement since 1988 in the American sample in the accuracy of managers' perceptions of the factors that motivate employees. Perhaps American managers have become more in tune with their employees' needs over the past fifteen years, as many organizations have changed and adapted to the changing environment. The Russian sample reflected the earlier results obtained in the United States, with the Russian managers significantly misidentifying what employees say motivates them. The sample from Taiwan showed a strong positive relationship between manager and worker responses, indicating that the Taiwanese managers had a good sense of their employees' motivational needs. In 1991, the top-three motivational factors for the American sample of employees were appreciation, work that is interesting, and job security. In Russia, the top-three motivational factors for employees were promotion and growth, feeling in on things, and interesting work. Finally, for the Taiwan sample of employees, the top-three factors were job security, good wages, and promotion and growth. These results clearly demonstrate that there are significant differences among these three countries in the motivational needs of employees. One other interesting finding is that the Russian managers ranked "sympathetic help on personal problems" the number one issue for employees, even though employees ranked this item number eight. There are still indications of a mismatch between employee and organizational perceptions of needs.

In a recent but less-scientific survey, employees and human resource professionals in the United States were asked to rank five "very important job components." Job security was ranked number one for employees but was considered number four by the human resource professionals. For employees, job security was followed in order of importance by benefits, communication between employees and management, employee flexibility to balance work and life issues and pay. The human resource professionals perceived communication between employees and management as the employees' highest priority, followed by recognition by management, relationship with immediate supervisor, job security, and pay (*HR Focus*, 2003).

Similar information on the relative importance of various aspects of motivation has been collected for Dutch managers, indicating that the Dutch place more emphasis on working climate, environment, friendly colleagues, cooperative atmosphere, freedom, and challenge (Lawrence, 1991). Motivation for French managers is difficult because it is hard to get close to employees in France. Employees' reluctance to see themselves as an integral part of the organization means that French managers must rely more on formal authority and rank to get results. The British tend to emphasize extrinsic rewards such as pay, health insurance, and retirement plans. In Scandinavian countries, the governments tend to emphasize social programs, freeing organizations from providing insurance and retirement benefits independent of government programs, but there are between-country differences. The Danish emphasize teamwork and social integration. Swedish companies tend to provide relatively poor pay and, perhaps because Swedish workers are more intrinsically motivated, this is tolerated more than it might be in other countries. Motivation is based on interest, involvement in personal development, and the opportunity to shape growth and contributions. In Norway, motivation is seen as a key task for managers, with an emphasis on personal qualities and development (Lawrence and Edwards, 2000).

A cross-cultural study looked at rankings of preferred job characteristics in seven countries: Belgium, Israel, the United Kingdom, the United States, Japan, the Netherlands, and Germany. The results showed a lot of consistency in the responses, with interesting work ranked first in Belgium, the United Kingdom, the United States, and Israel and ranked second in the other three countries (Harpaz, 1990). In a similar earlier study of work-preference rankings, growth, achievement, and responsibility were ranked one through three in the United States, Canada, Australia, and Singapore (Popp, Davis, and Herbert, 1986).

An interesting and unusual historical study examined Danish and German bureaucrats' responses to the Nazi attempt to exterminate the Jews. While the German bureaucrats carried out orders, claiming that they had no option but to obey their leaders, the Danish bureaucrats went to exceptional lengths to protect Jewish people and their property. The study concluded that German bureaucrats were obsessed with individual career success, while Danish bureaucrats operated on the basis of a commitment to Denmark's democratic values and a love of all residents of the country. The study proposed "patriotism of benevolence" as a motivating force for civil servants and made several suggestions about how to introduce it into the American bureaucracy (Frederickson and Hart, 1985).

Motivation in Chinese Cultures

Reward-system and work-value research has focused on Western organizations, rarely addressing issues in other societies and ethnic groups (Tuch and Martin, 1991). More research is necessary to elucidate relationships among gender, job level, work values, and job satisfaction in non-Western societies such as Taiwan, because there is a paucity of published studies of Chinese people (Hui and Tan, 1996). Moreover, the countries in which the Chinese play a significant role in the business structure have many unique differences, so comparing Chinese people in Taiwan and the PRC may be problematic. Such research is of interest because the sociocultural context in Chinese cultures is sharply different from that in Western countries and therefore furnishes a crucial test for differences in dimensions of job satisfaction and work values, such as task (intrinsic reward), team (social reward), reward (tangible reward), and status (promotion), as well as job level.

In one study, I investigated motivational issues related to public- and private-sector managers and nonmanagers in Taiwan, with an emphasis on why people took their jobs, their preferred managerial styles, and their motives related to work. The focus on these issues was designed to indicate the differences underlying job satisfaction and, thus, to indicate the factors affecting motivation in the workplace in Taiwan's public and private sectors. A test of either the Theory X, Y, or Z approach to motivational behavior and managerial style was used. The Theory X and Y aspects were derived from the work of D. McGregor (1960), who argued that the management style a person uses is based on the person's attitudes and beliefs about subordinates. Managers who believe that subordinates will not work hard without close supervision will supervise them closely and use a Theory X approach. Managers who think that employees are self-motivating and directing will assume a Theory Y approach and give subordinates space and flexibility to work using their own initiative. Both Theory X and Theory Y tend to be self-fulfilling prophesies in that if the manager treats subordinates according to how they are expected to behave, then employees tend to behave as expected. Theory Z is an alternate third approach, based on Japanese practices, which assumes that long-term employment is the basis of effective organizations (Ouchi, 1981). Theory Z assumes that humans are basically rational, open to being controlled by reason, and driven by intellect and interdependent relationships.

A commercially available test was used to measure the level of as-sumptions based on the different theories managers hold about how their employees will behave. The public employees were more altruistic. Pub-lic-sector managers indicated that being given the chance to make a con-tribution to society motivates them. Managers in the private sector were more concerned with their personal life goals and "self-fulfilling" needs, and they can be motivated by being given the chance to attain career and job satisfaction. All of the Taiwanese managers tended to be Theory Z oriented (Silverthorne, 1992).

Chinese management style is also influenced by Confucian values (Bond, 1996). While all Chinese cultures share a common cultural and re-ligious tradition, Confucianism, the management systems in different countries have some marked differences. As mentioned earlier, Confu-cianism creates a belief in harmonious interpersonal relationships, the be-lief of hierarchy and order in society. The people in the PRC have been living under a socialist system in which Communists dominate and the economic system is centrally controlled. However, Chinese living in Tai-wan have enjoyed a version of free market and capitalist economic sys-tems. Different social systems will clearly affect the management systems (Chen, 1995). Some preliminary observations suggest that individual per-formance and short-term challenging goals should be deemphasized in the PRC, while seeking right and correct behavior should be considered more important. This implies that emphasis should be put on general, rather than short-term and specific, goals. Formally designated leaders will be accepted as long as they consider both tradition and the long-term implications of decisions. Further, rewards should be tied to position and proper behavior rather than individual performance. Rewards should also be general and directed toward the long-term outcomes (Punnett, 1995).

The emergence of market forces in the PRC economy, the creation of joint ventures with overseas organizations, and the increase in wholly foreign-owned subsidiaries have brought about a challenge to tradi-tional management values. As a result, dramatic changes are already oc-curring within Chinese organizations, particularly with regard to the role of the manager (Chen, 1988). These changes have brought into question the ability of many managers in the PRC to deal with compe-tition, uncertainty, ambiguity, and relative autonomy. The manager's role is changing from the previous concentration on people and process to a greater awareness of market forces, financial management, and strategic planning, as competition is being encouraged and the number of joint ventures increases. The changes have also created a need for large numbers of competent managers. Such managers do not currently exist in sufficient quantity. The skills managers need in a market-driven economy are not necessarily the same skills that were effective in a bureaucratic system. In addition, market-driven organizations are more likely to discard policies of guaranteed life-long employment and to seek to develop a flexible work force (Loong, 1994). These changes are having a profound effect on the motivational needs of employees in the PRC.

For example, compensation is often a key element of work motivation, and a comparison of American and Chinese managers yielded some interesting differences in the reasons given for using increased compensation as a reward (Zhou and Martocchio, 2001). Chinese managers place less emphasis on employees' work performance when making monetary-recognition decisions and more emphasis on employees' relationships with others when making nonmonetary-recognition decisions than American managers do. Also, Chinese managers are more likely to give monetary bonuses based on employees' personal needs, whereas the Americans never consider this element when making their decisions. American managers were found to be more performance oriented and Chinese managers were more need and relationship oriented. According to some research, the way to keep local talent in China is to provide money, promotions, and training. The ability of younger Chinese to speak English well has also meant that these employees can rapidly get promotions, which is creating a generational gap within China. The research suggests that hiring women in China (and other parts of Asia) is good business, since women tend to have the necessary English skills and are often more flexible than men (Johnson, 1998).

Motivation in Other Cultures

A few studies in other cultures have specifically targeted motivational issues. For example, in Turkey, a study of motivators indicated that having power and authority, a peaceful work environment, opportunity for career advancement, and pay were the most motivating factors. On the other hand, close supervision and guidance, praise from the supervisor, feedback on performance, and sense of belonging were the least motivating factors (Aycan and Fikret-Pasa, 2000).

One study of managers, in a culture rarely studied, looked at motivational needs in Papua New Guinea through a comparison of samples of managers from Australia and Papua New Guinea based on Maslow's need-classification system. The two samples responded in quite different ways. The results were interpreted to mean that cultural differences as well as differences in the stage of economic development affect the importance attached to each of the five need categories posited by Maslow. He argued that there is a hierarchy of needs and that the lower needs must be satisfied before the higher needs require attention. According to Maslow, the order of needs begins at the lowest level with the basic or physiological needs such as food, water, shelter, and sleep, followed by security, autonomy, self-esteem, and finally, self-actualization. The order of importance of the needs in the Australian sample was self-actualization, autonomy, security, social, and esteem. The needs in order of importance for the Papua New Guinea sample were self-actualization, security, autonomy, social, and esteem. While the rankings were similar in both samples, the raw scores indicated a large difference in the level of concern about job security; in the Papua New Guinea sample this need was more important (Onedo, 1991).

Although the concept of the Protestant work ethic originated in the West, the same strong values exist in Arab countries. The Islamic religion and Arabic cultures encourage workers to maintain a high level of cooperation and cohesion, rather than competition, in the work setting. Managers remain closely bound to their extended family, tribe, and kinship network, and they work for the collective welfare of the group. Moreover, group solidarity is probably the most important characteristic of Middle Eastern society. For employees in the Middle East, cooperation is stressed more strongly than individualism. Altruism is the best way to achieve recognition and good human relations, especially in large organizations, since helping others is the best way for employees to achieve their goals, based on the norm of reciprocity and social exchange (Konovsky and Pugh, 1994). Middle Eastern employees have long-term employment, and supervisors are concerned with most aspects of employee welfare. Hard-working Middle Eastern employees are particularly motivated to work for the collective welfare of the group (Ali and Al-Shakhis, 1987). In addition, the manager's self-esteem is considered the most important need (Ali and Al-Shakhis, 1987).

Managerial motivation of employees should result in greater organizational success, according to hierarchic-role motivation theory. This theory proposes that motivation to manage rises with job level and is higher in the private sector (Miner, 1965). These assumptions have been supported by research conducted primarily in the United States. The theory has also been tested in China (PRC), where hierarchy has been shown to play an important role (Miner, Chen, and Yu, 1991). While China has a history of hierarchical structure, it also has strong collective values within the culture, which may make the existence of effective organizational hierarchies debatable. Support was found for motivational patterns that are typical in hierarchical organizations, and weak support was found for higher levels of motivation to manage in the private sector, leading to the conclusion that there are more similarities than differences between the United States and China.

In the United States and other Western cultures, individuals tend to be rewarded for good performance and will often seek and accept responsibility as a way to improve their career opportunities. On the other hand, many PRC Chinese organizations create disincentives for assuming responsibility. While additional money may motivate Chinese employees, they will not generally demand raises directly. As members of a collectivist society, the Chinese are more likely to see success or failure as a group effort, leading to group recognition and raises rather than individual rewards. Because the Chinese believe that relationships generate results, they put much more effort into developing relationships both within and outside the organization. While Western managers are likely to believe that there should be a separation between their work and personal lives, the Chinese seek and expect friendships to develop between managers and workers (Beamer, 1998).

One interesting overview of motivational issues facing managers lists some of the critical differences in what motivates employees in different countries. Change, the sense of time, the use of communication, cooperation versus competition, and work orientation are all areas where cultures may respond differently. For example, in the United States employees generally see change as positive, but change is more likely to be seen as negative in countries such as France and India where stability and continuity are more highly valued. In the United States time is of the essence, whereas in many countries in Latin America, Africa, and the Middle East time is viewed more casually. In these cultures relationships tend to be more important, and since it takes time to develop a relationship, decision making, for example, is a slower process in these countries than Americans may like or desire. When motivating employees through recognition of accomplishments, Americans prefer public praise, Finnish and German workers prefer written recognition, the Japanese prefer to be privately recognized, and Latin American cultures value recognition of employees' contributions to building relationships. Another difference between cultures is that Americans tend to value competition, whereas in Sweden and Japan cooperation and teamwork are emphasized. Clearly, motivational success or failure will be influenced by the national culture in many countries, and the blanket application of what appears to motivate employees in the United States is not likely to succeed in other cultures (Nelson, 1998).

Empowerment

Empowerment has been proposed as another way to increase employee motivation (e.g., Bennis and Nanus, 1985), since a shared vision of a common purpose and objectives can strengthen cooperative goals. Recently, there has been an interest in the role that intrinsic motivation plays both in the concept of empowerment and in its successful application within organizations (Thomas and Velthouse, 1990). In their model, K. W. Thomas and B. A. Velthouse state that "intrinsic motivation involves those generic conditions by which an individual undertakes activities pertaining directly to the task that produces motivation and satisfaction" (p. 668). The application of this model requires that cognitions, called *task assessments,* be identified. Thus, intrinsic motivation is a key component of any successful application of empowerment, and a clear definition of intrinsic motivation is the foundation for any theoretical or practical model of empowerment. A study of managers in Hong Kong found that they have different levels of cooperative goals than managers in the United States. However, the Confucian values of the Chinese managers did not stop them from acting democratically and developing cooperative goals, and when this occurred, task progress and efficiency were improved (Tjosvold, Hui, and Law, 1998).

The effectiveness of empowerment as a motivational strategy in Russia has been found to be useful in some studies (Elenkov, 1998) and not useful in others (Welsh, Luthans, and Sommer, 1993). Some believe that if Russian employees are given adequate resources, training, and encouragement, empowerment can be successful and that the discrepancies among study results exist because empowerment options did not exist until recently. Russian managers can be more effective if they use motivational techniques that focus on group benefits and if individual motivational approaches are tied to the development and mastery of work-related skills. Another way that motivation can work in Russia is by using "hard currency" (i.e., U.S. dollars) to protect Russian workers from high inflation rates that currently exist in Russia and by emphasizing group productivity (Elenkov, 1998).

Locus of Control

Locus of control is a rather useful concept in motivation, which relates to a person's belief about the source of rewards received. People with an internal locus of control believe that they control such things as pay, promotion, job performance, and rewards because these things follow directly from their behavior. Individuals with an external locus of control believe that these same things are dependent on forces outside their control, including luck. A study of locus of control covering twenty-four countries included consideration of individualism and collectivism, in addition to well-being. Well-being includes job satisfaction and the absence of psychological and physical strain. In countries where there is a high tendency for internal locus of control, reports of the level of well-being were higher. In addition, although well-being is generally considered an individual-level concept, there may be national-level differences as well. In fact, such differences have been found in other studies. For example, Western nations (Germany, New Zealand, Sweden, and the United States) have better psychological health and higher job satisfaction than countries in Asia (Japan and Singapore), South America (Brazil), and the Middle East (Egypt) (McCormick and Cooper, 1988). Internal locus of control was highest in New Zealand, followed by the United States and South Africa, and lowest in the PRC and Bulgaria. Job satisfaction was highest in Canada and Sweden and lowest in

Japan and the United Kingdom. Psychological well-being was highest in India and Germany and lowest in Bulgaria and the United Kingdom. Physical well-being was highest in India and Israel and lowest in Hong Kong and the United Kingdom. Some countries reported consistently high or low scores across all variables, while other countries varied widely from factor to factor. Hong Kong and the United Kingdom scored low on all factors, while Germany, Israel, India, Sweden, and the United States tended to score relatively high on all factors (Spector et al., 2001).

Summary

Overall, the research evidence presents an interesting view of the role of intrinsic and extrinsic motivation. There are a limited number of studies that have been conducted in field situations, which raises questions about the generalizability of the findings and theories. In addition, there are relatively few research studies that have looked specifically at issues of intrinsic and extrinsic motivation outside the United States. Future research in non-Western cultures would add significantly to the general field of knowledge about the role of intrinsic and extrinsic behavior on organizational work performance in a global environment.

There are numerous theories of motivation. Some are based on need theories while others are driven by values and attitudes. Research in other cultures highlights the fact that if we accept that meeting or filling needs is the primary motivating force, then individuals in different cultures have different needs and will respond to different types of motivation. In the same way, if we accept that values and attitudes drive motivation, these will also vary across cultures. It seems clear that in most cultures employees respond to being involved in the decisions that affect them. Linking rewards to performance also seems to be an effective way to motivate across cultures, although defining appropriate rewards and performance standards may be culture specific. While it is likely that most people within a culture will respond to similar attempts to motivate, there are many individual and gender differences in the type of motivators to which people respond. It is important for managers and leaders to understand what matters to each employee and what will motivate them. The type of motivator that is effective in a culture is a good place to start when seeking to develop motivational strategies, but individual differences should play an important role as well. The key is to maintain equity even though people are motivated in different ways. The perception of being appropriately rewarded by the organization can enhance employees' intrinsic motivation and thus increase organizational commitment and citizenship behavior.

8

Managerial Values and Skills

Managerial effectiveness is based on shared values, the organizational culture, and the fit between them. While the role of managers is basically consistent across organizations and cultures, managerial styles can vary significantly. The evidence available from research on managerial styles across cultures is limited, but different social systems have been found to have a significant impact on management systems and this, in turn, influences managerial style.

In Europe, there is variability in approaches to management, between Western and Eastern Europe and between Northern and Southern Europe (Smith, 1997). It has also been suggested that there are five major approaches to business. Two of these are Western approaches, while the other three are rooted in the Asian cultures. Asian cultures have a tradition of keeping the organization together as a dynamic group. Since Asian organizations tend to be hierarchical and reflect the collective norms of Asian culture, the dynamic approach works well in these kinds of organizations (Redding, 1992). In addition, when individuals and organizations need to assess events in order to help decide what action to take, they frequently use values that are reflective of their culture. As a result, multinational managers face special problems when choosing, adopting, and using a particular managerial style. While some differences in preference for leadership styles across cultures have been identified, actual management behavior can vary a great deal (Hui, 1990).

Effective management in organizations has been studied by a number of major researchers. While all of the theorists suggest that there are general sets of rules, which, if followed, will result in more-effective management, managerial values seem to be strongly dependent on national culture (Ralston, Gustafson, Cheung, and Terpstra, 1993) and are also related to issues of gender (Oskamp and Costanzo, 1993). Further, in order to fully understand the organizational environment of a national culture, one also needs to consider important within-culture differences (Schneider and Barsoux, 1997) and to examine the potential changes in managerial values across generations. Value differences between generations are due to a variety of factors, with the most important being changing societal objectives (Inglehart and Carballo, 1997).

Managerial values can be defined as concepts or beliefs about desirable behaviors. Values guide the selection and evaluation of managerial behaviors and the way such issues as employee motivation and conflict are resolved or handled (Terpstra and David, 1990). Therefore, values held by the managers in an organization are important to employee and organizational performance. One way to gauge a society's cultural values is by looking at how it uses metaphors. For example, in America we say that "the squeaky wheel gets the grease," while the Japanese say "the nail that stands out gets pounded down." These metaphors represent two opposite sets of values, but both reflect how each culture expects employees to behave. Clearly values are influenced by both the nationality of the managers and the business environment within which they manage (Adler and Bartholomew, 1992). There is, however, a tendency to assume that management systems in organizations evolve to reflect the values of the local society rather than the parent organization's values (Adler and Doktor, 1989).

Measuring Managerial Values

As might be expected, researchers measuring managerial values have used a variety of approaches and measurement scales and techniques. For example, D. A. Ralston, D. J. Gustafson, F. M. Cheung, and R. H. Terpstra (1993) examined managerial values by measuring personality traits (Machiavellianism, dogmatism, locus of control, and intolerance of ambiguity). B. Z. Posner and W. H. Schmidt (1992) had managers rate the importance of various organizational goals, whereas D. R. Cressey and C. A. Moore (1983) examined organization conduct codes for policy statements pertaining to social responsibility. W. C. Frederick and J. Weber (1987) measured the relative importance of terminal values (e.g., family security and friendship) versus instrumental values (e.g., honesty and responsibility) among corporate executives, union members, and community activists.

By pulling together the results from a number of studies, R. B. Peterson and J. George-Falvy (1993) identified the dominant American managerial values: achievement and success, hard work, efficiency and pragmatism, optimism, puritanism, scientific orientation, impersonality in interpersonal work relationships, equality of opportunity, and an acceptance of competition as a fact of life. However, we need to assess whether managerial work values such as these are either universal or culturally unique. For example, a study comparing the relative importance of ten work values in the United States, Australia, Canada, and Singapore found similarities among the countries (Popp, Davis, and Herbert, 1986). A similar study comparing managers in the United States, Colombia, Peru, and Chile also found that the countries shared similar work values (Peters and Lippitt, 1978). The results of these two studies show that good pay, opportunity for growth, and a feeling that the job is important are universally valued. However, other studies have found that differences in values among cultures exist (e.g., Hofstede, 1984).

Corporate-citizenship values and cultural differences are also related. This connection is most apparent in multinational firms, where it is important to maintain effective relationships. Values and cultural practices in the host nation may differ from those of management's home country (Rondinelli and Berry, 2000). When corporate-citizenship behavior was compared among the United States, Mexico, Japan, and China in order to create a framework to help managers anticipate citizenship issues in different countries, the researchers found that managers emphasized consumerism and environmental concerns in the United States while Mexican managers expressed a concern for the environment along with a high concern for economic development and local issues. The Japanese are more likely to have businesses take care of consumer issues than to rely on consumer activism, and the Chinese are more likely to rely on friends and show nationalistic tendencies when making consumer decisions (Katz, Swanson, and Nelson, 2001). Even in large Chinese organizations, an individual's loyalty to the manager and the organization, as well as the manager's loyalty to a subordinate, tends to be more significant. All of these findings suggest that corporate citizenship will be manifested differently in various cultures; if multinational companies are to be accepted and effective within the host culture, the organization and managers need to understand these differences.

Convergence and Divergence of Cultures

The role that culture plays in international development highlights the need to understand the relationship between cultural values, systems of governance, and managerial behavior (Pearson, 1991). In general, two polar-opposite theories have been proposed and evaluated to explain these relationships: convergence and divergence.

Convergence

Convergence implies that all countries' management systems will eventually converge to a model used in fully developed countries such as the United States. Bass (1990) theorizes that the increase in the number of multinational companies, electronic communication, and the rapid increase in the rate of internationalization will lead to convergence of values in the countries within the European, Japanese, and U.S. triad, where most worldwide economic activities currently take place. This will happen because industrialized countries will embrace common values with regard to economic activities and behavior at work. Since industrialized countries have typically embraced capitalism, convergence means adopting Western ideological values. This, in turn, would probably lead to an increased acceptance of individualistic work values. However, it should be noted that the exact nature of the model to which organizations are said to be converging is unknown.

Convergence of behaviors or managerial practices, however, may not mean that the cultural values are converging (Barkema and Vermeulen, 1997). One way to measure whether convergence in values is occurring is to compare equivalent data from the same population at two different time periods. A study designed to use this approach investigated Indonesian managerial practices, with an emphasis on the individualism-collectivism and power distance dimensions proposed by Hofstede (1984). The results for Indonesian and American samples at one particular point in time, 1996, were compared, and these results were also compared with similar data previously reported by Hofstede in 1991. The results for the Indonesian samples from the 1991 and 1996 data were equivalent. While the difference between the American and Indonesian scores in the 1996 study on the individualism-collectivism dimension remained statistically significant, it was much smaller than it had been five years earlier. However, for the power distance dimension, the difference that existed in 1991 between the two nations no longer existed in 1996. Since the data for the American samples from 1991 and 1996 remained at about the same levels, it can be concluded that the Indonesian sample changed to become more like the American sample. Thus, on the two Hofstede dimensions compared, convergence occurred, perhaps reinforced by the rapid growth in Indonesia's economy (Huer, Cummings, and Hutabarat, 1999).

Another view of convergence can be explored by considering the sociological concept of modernization. Modernization is a universal process whereby all societies work toward bettering the lives of citizens. However, Western culture does not define modernization, and modernization is not equivalent to Westernization. One way to answer the questions related to the effects of societal trends is to think about psychological characteristics as either functional or nonfunctional. A functional psychological characteristic is "an attitude, value or behavior that is helpful or instrumental in the adjustment of most individuals in a society to some aspects or features of the social life in that society. A nonfunctional psychological characteristic is an attitude, value or behavior that does not have such a function for adjustment and is purely stylistic, expressive, or terminal in nature" (Yang, 1988, p. 83). For example, in many organizations today, a willingness to accept and integrate technology into work life represents a functional psychological process, whereas rejection of technology does not. Functional characteristics are more likely to be affected by the modernization process. This approach implies that some psychological characteristics will converge while others diverge.

One study to test this hypothesis looked at locus of control (also discussed in the previous chapter) and gender roles as psychological characteristics, comparing Taiwanese and American students over a fifteen-year period (Chia et al., 1995). The Chinese emphasize attending to others, fitting in, and trying to achieve harmony, while Americans emphasize tending to the self and maintaining independence (Markus and Kitayama, 1991). Thus, the Chinese are more likely to have an external locus of control and Americans an internal one. Modernization is also tied to changes in gender roles and attitudes, and research has indicated that women may be more externally focused than men (De Brabander and Boone, 1990). Over a fifteen-year period, Americans maintained their internal locus of control while the Chinese sample became less externally and more internally focused over time. The results were interpreted as providing partial support for the modernization hypothesis for both locus of control and gender-role attitudes.

Divergence

The second theory developed to help to understand the role that culture plays in international development is based on the assumption that there are cultural norms in each country that are a powerful force for differentiation across borders. This approach is called the *comparative cultural* or *divergence* theory. Thus, the organization's values, which are shaped by the society, increase resistance to any change brought about by exposure to international differences. Divergence theory argues that individuals will retain their diverse, culture-based values regardless of the country's economic ideology. It also implies that management styles are independent of international influence, which is a dubious assumption in the countries of South East Asia, for example, whose success has been very much tied to effective global penetration.

Crossvergence

In reality, convergence and divergence both probably are appropriate theoretical approaches, and the question to be considered may well be not whether the convergence or comparative cultural (divergence) theory is correct, but rather which of the two approaches affects which particular aspect of management style. This question led to another conceptualization of these two views, called *crossvergence,* which provides an integration of cultural and ideological influences to produce a unique set of values that are influenced by both national culture and economic ideology. Economic ideology is the workplace philosophy that dominates organizations in a particular country. The two major economic ideologies are capitalism and socialism. National culture can take many forms, but the researchers who developed the concept of crossvergence considered that two possible all-encompassing dimensions of national culture are Eastern and Western. Thus, they think that an organization in an Eastern socialist country may well behave differently than one in a Western socialist country, since they see national culture and economic ideology as two independent variables.

Evidence of crossvergence has been found between the United States and Singapore but not between the United States and China (Tan, 2002). In addition, the Chinese in the PRC were less dogmatic than in Singapore and placed less emphasis on their cultural roots during the recent industrialization and modernization of Chinese society. The results of this particular study raise questions about the previously assumed transportability of Chinese values from China to countries whose populations are predominantly overseas Chinese such as Singapore. While crossvergence can be considered as lying somewhere on a continuum between convergence and divergence, it may in fact be quite different from any set of values directly affected by either national culture or economic ideology (Ralston, Holt, Terpstra, and Yu, 1997). One implication for resolving the contradictions between these two approaches is that support for a convergent theory would lead to multinational companies having a seamless organizational culture not significantly influenced by national culture. Further work is needed to understand if this will be possible at some time in the future.

Individual Effectiveness and Organizational Values

A study of the relationship between organizational values and individual effectiveness examined different models and techniques of predicting a relationship between the two. Using four different measures of organizational values, it tested the relationship between values and individual effectiveness and found some positive correlations. For example, innovation may well be a key variable for organizational success; how cultural behaviors are reflected in innovative strategies is important (Cheng, 1993). Champions of innovation, who advocate change despite personal risks, and how such change occurs in organizations have been studied in American organizations (Howell and Higgins, 1991) and in a broad cross-section of thirty other countries (Shane, Venkataraman, and MacMillan, 1995). Cultural values seem to be related to innovation-championing strategies. In collectivist societies, innovation champions seek support across the organization. In higher-uncertainty-acceptance countries, innovation champions are more likely to violate organizational norms and procedure. And in higher-power-distance countries, those in authority are sought out for support in overcoming resistance to innovative ideas. These findings suggest that learning culturally appropriate innovation-championing strategies is an important managerial skill needed in multicultural settings.

Effective Managerial Behavior in Other Countries

Even if it is concluded that management practices need to be adapted to different cultures, there is only limited research directed at finding out which should be adapted and how they should be adapted. One survey of middle managers in China, India, the Philippines, and the United States attempted to identify the important determinants of managerial performance in these countries. The survey results indicate that culture has a significant impact on managerial practices and successful job performance. The biggest differences were found between the United States and China, but differences between the Philippines, India, and China were also found, even though these three countries can all be classified as "Asian." In terms of communication skills, past experience, and leadership ability, the Chinese were different from the other nationalities studied and the most unique in their perceptions (Neelankavil, Mathur, and Zhang, 2000). In order to positively influence job performance, managers should evaluate their own cultural values against those of their subordinates and work to create an environment that is sensitive to both cultures.

A study comparing managerial-style differences and the relationship between managerial style and productivity was undertaken in five plants owned by a U.S.-based multinational corporation. The plants were in Mexico, Spain, England, Italy, and the United States. The data collected was based on equivalent production types and procedures. It led to the finding that the U.S. and British plants used significantly different management systems than did those in the other three countries. Specifically, the British and U.S. managers used more participation and a consultative system, whereas the plants in Mexico, Italy, and Spain employed a "benevolent authoritative" management system. These differences may reflect cultural and societal value differences, showing that management objectives can be achieved in many different ways (Pavett and Morris, 1995).

As mentioned earlier, the issue of national culture (East-West) and economic ideology (capitalist-socialist) and divergence was studied by comparing samples from the United States, Russia, Japan, and China (Ralston, Holt, Terpstra, and Yu, 1997). Three higher-order variables, individualism, openness to change, and self-enhancement, were considered. The results showed that the U.S. managers scored higher on individualism and openness to change than managers from the other three countries. In addition, on the self-enhancement dimension, the Russian and

American scores were similar, as were the scores of the Chinese and Japanese managers.

Value Congruence

Value consistency or congruence has been investigated in several countries. Value congruence occurs when an organization behaves in the same way as it says it will. Recent research studied the relationship between the value congruence of Brazilian executives and their leadership styles. The initial expectations that value congruence exists and that the values of Brazilian executives reflect the values of their organization were supported, and a small but positive relationship between values and leadership style was found (Preziosi and Gooden, 2001). A related study, conducted in Jamaica, looked at the relationship between value congruency and the presence of organizational sustainability factors. The study found a positive relationship between these two variables (Preziosi, 2000). Further, a study of the relationship between value congruence and total quality management (discussed in chapter 10) in Panama found that the greater the congruence of values, the greater the commitment to total quality management (Preziosi, 1999). Taken together, the results of these three studies in developing countries indicate that a strong value congruence will benefit organizations in a variety of ways and in a variety of cultures.

Managerial Values in Europe

Just as researchers have attempted to understand what makes someone an effective manager in America, others have attempted to answer the same question about European managers. For example, managers were compared from four European countries: Sweden, Belgium, Germany, and Spain. The effective managerial skills identified in Sweden included decision making and interpersonal relations, and the personality characteristics of leadership, achievement, and goal orientation were also valued. In Belgium, the respondents thought that the most effective managerial skills were planning and evaluation, decision making, and forecasting, in that order. Personality characteristics of effective leaders included being open-minded, practical, and energetic. These sets of characteristics describe a cautious, controlling type of management style. In Germany, decision making and pertinent technical knowledge were considered to be key managerial skills, and being self-confident, energetic, and competitive the key personality characteristics. Finally, in Spain, decision making, planning and evaluation, and management techniques were considered key managerial skills. Being businesslike, supportive, thoughtful, and intuitive were listed as the key personality characteristics. These findings show both similarities and differences between countries and indicate that formulating a single concept of a "European manager" is premature at best (Boldy, Jain, and Northey, 1993).

Often employment legislation and regulations affect managerial behavior. For example, in Sweden it is not possible to fire an employee. As a result, an employee who does not agree with a manager's request can simply ignore it, with little fear of serious negative sanctions. Thus, government regulations help shape how managers behave. Swedish managers rely more on consensus building than American managers do and are more likely to work to find mutual ground on which to create solutions. Conflict is therefore not the preferred problem-solving approach in Sweden. The Swedish also value honesty very highly and prefer not to discuss personal issues until after a close relationship has developed (Frazee, 1997).

The work values present in the fifteen countries that formed the European Union at the time were compared in 1999 using data from the European Values Study. The results revealed that the work value most often referred to as being important in the fifteen countries was "being well paid" (73 percent). The next most important values included "having a pleasant human environment," "having an interesting job," "having a safe job," and "fulfillment on the job." The work values least referred to as being important by the average of the European Union workers were "having a respectful work" (39 percent), "having a work that is useful for society," "promotion opportunities," "not being pressured," and finally, "having good holiday periods." However, the results showed that there are significant differences among the European Union countries and that work values are not classified as being important in the same way in the fifteen countries (Caetano, Tavares, and Reis, 2003).

Managerial Values in Russia

Russia is an interesting country to study, especially in terms of values, because of the rapid changes that have occurred within the culture in recent years. In addition, Russia has attracted the interest of many American organizations because of the market potential and developing free-market economy. I have worked with American, Asian, and Russian managers, and several differences were clearly apparent. For example, the first Russian group that I worked with about ten years ago had an interesting perspective on time. I concluded that the Russian managers looked at things from the perspective of "what can you do for me in the next ten seconds?" The Americans looked at things from the perspective of "what can you do for me today?" The Asian managers worked from the perspective of "what can you do for me over the next ten years?" As a management consultant, I found the Russian time perspective frustrating, and I always had the sense that what I had just done was not enough because the next activity always had to be under way right away. Others have taken a more scientific approach to studying the values of Russian managers. Their results indicated a sharp decline in the size of the power distance dimension over time, with power sharing replacing the historically prevalent approach of a "centralized democracy." The Russian managers' responses reflected no change on the individualism-collectivism dimension, with collectivism prevailing despite a rise in entrepreneurial behavior. The researchers conclude that the Russian manager today is a person "who is more willing to question any power distance in the management hierarchy, less ideologically oriented, more comfortable with less structure, willing to take risks and adapt to the demands of a free market, able to be a team player, and even more disposed to take the long view" (Veiga, Yanouzas, and Buchholtz, 1995, p. 22). They also found a significant generational gap in values on four of the six dimensions they studied, with the younger generation reflecting a more open approach to change. Research that tested the value of using performance-based management techniques and performance-based incentives in Russia (Welsh, Luthans, and Sommer, 1993) found support for these approaches, and a related study (Luthans, Welsh, and Rosenkrantz, 1993) found that paradigms describing managerial behavior could also be applied in Russia.

Some interesting insights into core Russian values and their relationship to core American values have come from a study that identified eight American values based on a review of the available literature and various research publications. When these eight core values were then compared for Russians and Americans, differences in the core values of the two countries were discovered. In America, achievement and success are highly valued and often are integrated into personal and organizational values. But in Russia, achievement and success are much more likely to be restricted to personal gain rather than to benefiting the organization. Materialism and progress are highly valued in the United States, but in Russia, the average person is more concerned with obtaining basic necessities than obtaining material goods. Americans tend to be optimistic about the future, while Russians tend to be pessimistic. Americans are very aware of time, and time often is considered equivalent to money, to be used wisely. For Russians, time is a process that is filled with boring work. The overall issue often becomes one of different ethical and moral business standards because of the Russian need to adapt to difficult circumstances. The researchers conclude that while core value change will occur in Russia, it will be a very slow process (Tongren, Hecht, and Kovach, 1995). The results of another study attempting to find out whether American management concepts will work in Russia led to the conclusion that certain American management concepts could be successfully implemented in Russia but that they would need to be implemented patiently and systematically. The areas where overlap is possible include a power-based but not participative leadership style, employee relation policies, gain sharing, appraisals based on work-team performance, and strategic alliances (Elenkov, 1998).

Managerial Values in Latin America

Latin America has become a major center of foreign investment, and Latin American countries have trade agreements with both North American and European trading partners. Despite the increase in investment in Latin American countries, few studies have explored managerial behaviors and values in these countries. In order to help remedy this lack of research, one project investigated managerial values in twelve Latin American countries: Argentina, Bolivia, Brazil, Chile, Ecuador, Mexico, Paraguay, Peru, Puerto Rico, Venezuela, and Uruguay. It measured different sets of values, which were combined into four value groupings: civility (how well people behave toward each other), self-direction (including imagination and independence), integrity (honesty and responsibility), and drive (ambition and courage). By combining the data for the twelve countries, the order of importance of the four value sets was integrity, civility, drive, and self-direction. In fact, all twelve countries ranked integrity as the most important, and eleven of the twelve countries considered civility the second most important value. Overall, while some differences exist among the countries, there is a lot of similarity at least in terms of the four value groupings measured here. While this was an exploratory study, it seems that social fit and social responsibility will tend to take precedence in Latin American countries over self-interests, but at the same time, between-country differences in self-direction and drive suggest that there are some underlying differences, which should not be ignored. In selecting managers to work in Latin American countries, selection based on ability to get along with others is probably a safe and important criterion to use (Lenartowicz and Johnson, 2002).

Managerial Values in Japan

Japanese management values have been described as being based on groupism (the emphasis on doing things in groups defines how jobs are defined and carried out), harmony, hierarchy, *amae* (encouraging a dependence by subordinates on the supervisor, which in turn, enhances the sense of responsibility of the supervisor for subordinates; or, more generally, depending on the kindness of others), *on* (favor, obligation, and a debt of gratitude) and *giri* (sense of duty and obligation between supervisor and subordinate, which leads to loyalty based on honor, decency, and courtesy) and *gambare* (tenacity, endurance, and attitude that one must keep going no matter what; or, more colloquially translated, to always try to be your best). In Japanese companies, transfer to a new department is often done with little warning or preparation. Training is most likely to be done "on the job," so the concept of *gambare* is critical. Management transfers and development can only work if managers have an attitude that they will always try to do their best regardless of their preparation or knowledge of the job (Taylor, 1993). A comprehensive review of studies that had been conducted on Japanese companies concluded that the organization of work in Japan reflects the social structure of the society and that the workplace is therefore a major source of an individual's identity (Smith, 1984).

A study of employee work attitudes and management practice, which compared American and Japanese employees (Lincoln, 1989), found that commitment to the organization was equivalent in the Japanese and American samples. However, job satisfaction scores were not equivalent, with the Americans scoring much higher than did the Japanese. It is important to note that high job satisfaction in America may not be a good thing if it reflects low expectations, and low job satisfaction in Japan may not be bad if it reflects a striving for perfection. Americans tend to put the best face on events, whereas the Japanese tend to describe things in a pessimistic way, using humility and understatement. It seems that Japanese management practices contribute to worker motivation in Japan and that the application of similar practices in the United States has produced similar results.

Differences between Japanese and Korean management styles were investigated, and it was observed that while organizations are not all alike, there are similarities within each country (Choe, Lee, and Roehl, 1995). In Japan, market share is important and leads to an emphasis on aggressive marketing and finding economies of scale (Aoki, 1994). The Japanese also place an emphasis on long-term supplier relationships, which reduce market options but increase the coordination of production and speed the development of new products (Kamath and Liker, 1994). The Japanese also value participation, consensus building, and group loyalty (Nonaka, 1988), and they scan both competitors and customers frequently to ensure good information flow between them. Because the foundation of modern Korean practices was established during thirty-five years of Japanese occupation, Korean management practices are similar to those of Japan, but there are several distinct differences. Both Korea and Japan advocate lifetime employment practices, but the implementation of this practice is much more flexible in Korea than it is in Japan. Korea is less participatory, with more decisions being made by top management than in Japan, and most large Korean firms are family owned and managed by the family of the founders (Alston, 1989). Koreans also tend to be more individualistic than the Japanese, and their organizations tend to be more hierarchical.

Study results indicate that there has been a convergence of management styles between Japan and Korea, driven by growth and internationalization in Korean firms. This finding supports the convergence model, although the convergence here is toward regional values rather than global ones. Perhaps convergence occurred because the Koreans imitated the success of the Japanese as they sought to enter some of the same markets, often directly competing with the Japanese. An internationalization strategy has historically been a strong force in both countries, which could also be the reason for convergence in this rather unique situation. When everyone competes in the same marketplace, it seems reasonable to assume that there will be pressure for the competitors to compete on the same issues, so that the customers can make rational comparisons among them; hence, a convergence strategy or outcome is useful. However, in terms of management style, the Japanese still prefer participation more than their Korean counterparts, indicating that cultural differences are still important and that some aspects of human resource management are difficult to change (Lachman, Nedd, and Hinings, 1994). Overall, the concept of convergence may have to be reconsidered or redefined as either regional or global convergence, especially in areas where the business practices that are being adopted have been successful. The existence of pressure for convergence of management styles between Japanese and Korean managers was found in a related study, which also noted that internationalization was a stronger force for convergence than growth was. Korea entered the international market later than Japan but has focused on competing industries such as automobile manufacturing, consumer electronics, and shipbuilding. It is not surprising that the pressure to enhance management systems has created convergence of Korean with Japanese management styles. Indeed, convergence is more likely to occur when organizations are competing internationally rather than domestically (Lee, Roehl, and Choe, 2000).

Another value-related issue is how employees behave in groups. Group-process effectiveness has been researched by looking at the relative impact of collectivist versus individualist cultures. The interaction effects of culture and time on group composition and process have been investigated using a sample in the United States, representing an individualist culture, and a sample from Korea, representing a collectivist culture. The results indicate that groups can be effective regardless of the type of culture but that the group process differs between the two cultures. The American sample tended to learn from each other, whereas the Korean sample invested more time in the social and interpersonal relationships (Sosik and Jung, 2002). The results suggest that managers working across cultures should be sensitive to how group characteristics vary between countries.

Managerial Values in Chinese Cultures

While much of the literature and research on Asian management has focused on Japanese companies and management systems, the economic successes in the Asian trading area are not limited to the Japanese. In fact, a large number of studies have been conducted that look specifically at Chinese work organizations. The majority of this research has looked at companies in Hong Kong (Redding and Wong, 1986). Hong Kong scholars have been very active in this area, so the available material on Chinese organizations reported in this chapter is disproportionately greater than research from other cultures. For example, a study of senior Chinese executives in Hong Kong, Taiwan, Singapore, and Indonesia found that the different countries had different managerial values. In addition, management practices in mainland China are different from those found in Taiwan and Hong Kong, because the culture in the PRC still typically relies on authority figures to establish order and resolve disputes. In studying the characteristics of successful overseas Chinese–owned organizations, mostly from Hong Kong and Taiwan, it was noted that these organizations operate based on the concepts and values of filial piety, collectivism, and a strong work ethic (Redding, 1990). In another study of the Chinese managerial values in Hong Kong, the dominant managerial values were found to include a commitment to the family within organizations, resulting in adaptiveness, flexibility, and cohesiveness; a view of time as cyclical rather than linear; a view of the self built on interpersonal relationships and connections; harmony; a sense of propriety (*li*); maintaining face; and participation (Kirkbride and Westwood, 1993).

Taiwan and the other "little dragons" have been economic success stories as well. The development and growth of three of the four little dragons (Adler, 1997) has been driven by the overseas Chinese business in East and Southeast Asia. The three little dragons driven by Chinese businesses practices are Hong Kong, Singapore, and Taiwan, and the one not influenced by Chinese businesses is Korea. The emergence of market forces in the PRC economy, the creation of joint ventures with overseas organizations, and the increase of wholly foreign-owned subsidiaries have brought about a challenge to the traditional management values in the PRC. More recently, Vietnam has entered the economic picture in a significant way. Each of these cultures has distinct management styles that have contributed to the economic process and organizational development (Chen, 1995). There is a need to identify successful strategies for measuring both managerial styles and values within different cultures, especially when the cultures speak the same language. The PRC is basically a bureaucratic, centrally managed, socialist business environment, whereas in Taiwan there is a predominantly Western-style business environment, and many managers in Taiwan completed their university education in the United States. The capitalist and market-driven forces that operate in Taiwan make it easier for managers to accept an American or Western management philosophy. Indeed, one study of Taiwanese managers who were assigned overseas found that managers felt more at home in company branches in the United States than they did in company branches in the PRC (Shieh, 1989).

There are four key features of Chinese management in Chinese cultures outside the PRC that are distinctive from Western management but present in most Chinese organizations. They are human-centeredness, family-centeredness, centralization of power, and small size. The human-centered management style emphasizes human relationships, with people the center of concern and particular attention paid to issues of emotion and trust. Management decisions have to take emotion into consideration (Warrington and McCall, 1983). Chinese see the business relationship as involving friendship, loyalty, and trustworthiness (Sheng 1979). Highly associated with concern for feelings and respect of relationships is the concept of "face," which is used as a mechanism for inculcating a strong sense of group responsibility and serves as a mediating force in social relationships (Redding and Ng, 1982). The Chinese "Five Relations"—sovereign-minister, parent-child, husband-wife, elder-younger brother, and friends—and the five corresponding virtues—loyalty, filial piety, faithfulness, care, and sincerity—represent the acceptable patterns of interpersonal relationships that characterize the very particular way the Chinese deal with others.

Family-centeredness is demonstrated by the extraordinarily important role that the family plays in Chinese culture. The family is the primary agent of socialization for Chinese culture, and as such, it has exerted the most significant influence on the individual's value system and role expectations. These personality features form the basis of cooperation and interaction with others. However, there is still a distinct power hierarchy within the organization. The impact of the family-centered approach to management is represented by the following two quotations from Chinese scholars: "Chinese have learned relationships with others almost exclusively from the family experience" (Hsu, 1984, p. 758), and "Relation among family members provided the human basis for the moral virtues of the Chinese" (Nakamura, 1964, p. 268). A Confucian saying advises, "Those who love their parents, dare not show rudeness to others" (quoted in Lin, 1935, p. 179). Since many Chinese organizations are family-run businesses, family relationships play a central role in these organizations, and even some larger organizations are run like a family. For example, the Chinese consider filial piety the first and ultimate of all virtues, so that parental authority has a strong impact on Chinese management. The boss-employee relationship at work follows the model of filial piety in the parent-child relationship at home. Obligation also plays an important role: workers feel obligated to be loyal and to obey the boss, and the boss feels obligated to be concerned with workers' welfare.

Two distinct layers usually characterize the centralized power structure in Chinese organizations: the power core controlled by the boss or a small number of people, usually family members; and employees, who fall into one of three categories: relatives, friends, or outsiders. The sense of obligation mentioned earlier ties the two layers together. However, power struggles can occur both between the older and younger generations and among the shareholders. The owner-father rarely delegates authority or management functions, and there is little participation in the decision-making process, even by other family members. Conflicts are usually avoided, due to "face consciousness" and a desire to maintain social harmony (Bond, 1991). Nepotism allows the maintenance of ownership and control within the family, and the Chinese ethic of respect toward and compliance with the father figure allows the maintenance of a centralized control system (Waley, 1938).

The fourth unique organizational characteristic that has a significant impact on Chinese management is the organization size. Most Chinese organizations are started with a small amount of capital, and the number of employees usually remains small. A small organization has the advantage of making possible closer interpersonal relationships, a shorter decision-making chain, active managerial involvement, and faster decision making. Financially coordinating a group of several small businesses, rather than developing and enlarging a single organization, to achieve expansion is preferred. While these four characteristics are by no means unique to Chinese organizations, when grouped together, they reinforce each other and make Chinese management unique (Ralston et al., 1996).

The emphasis on Confucianism has created a political economy in Taiwan that underlines the primacy of the harmony and order of society. As we have seen, the Confucian school of thought pervades Chinese culture. This value system requires individuals to develop themselves and serve others (Cheng, 1997). Taiwan has a culture based in the Confucian tradition (Bond and King, 1985) and has experienced rapid economic growth. In terms of the dimension of individualism versus collectivism, Taiwan's culture is different from that of the United States and most Western countries (Hofstede, 1984; Marsh, 1996). Its collectivism has a long history rooted in Confucianism, which Taiwan's government has endeavored to promote and reinforce (Ma and Smith, 1992).

Using in-depth interviews, a study of forty-three industrial firms in Taiwan investigated the organizational structure and the managerial assumptions, values, and other sociodemographic features of the senior managers. Based on their findings, the researchers argue that there are four primary types of managerial patterns in Taiwan. The "grass roots" management pattern is typical of organizations run by native Taiwanese over the age of fifty. The "mainlander" type of management is used by managers who originally came from mainland China, most of whom are over the age of sixty. The grass roots and mainlander types are considered to represent an approach characteristic of Chinese traditional value orientations, underpinned by the family, paternalistic authoritarianism, and a precedence placed on morality before capability and relationships. The "specialist" type of management is typical of enterprises whose leader is not the owner and is said to assimilate the Western logic of rationalism as its basic value. The "transitional" pattern of management is the second generation of family-owned businesses and is considered a hybrid based on traditional Chinese values, Japanese management style, and Western rationalism. Overall, an approach of "management by trust" seems reflective and supportive of contemporary Chinese values (Jou and Sung, 1990).

Guanxi (connections) is very important in Chinese society. Organizations and individuals emphasize relationships and social networking. A comparison of social networking in Chinese and Western societies found four strategies for building and maintaining *guanxi*: instrumentalism, trust, reciprocity, and longevity. The building of relationships is similar to the mentoring process in Western societies, and *guanxi* is a critical element in Chinese organizations and society (Yeung and Tung, 1996).

Conflict between joint-venture partners can have a negative impact on joint-venture performance. These conflicts can result from divergent objectives, the sharing of power, differences in organizational cultures and national cultures, and incompatible management styles and approaches (Kozan, 1992). A study of work goals of Taiwanese men and women managers who worked in numerous companies controlled by either Taiwanese, Japanese, or American investors supported this finding (Yeh and Granrose, 1993). The researchers found that when age, education, tenure, and position level were controlled, men believed that the work goals of contributing to company success, advancement, earnings, and task challenge were more important than did women. These results support the idea that Taiwanese cultural work goals remain the same regardless of the national culture of the parent company and that the national culture of the employees will be the dominant one (Adler, 1997). However, there is always a possibility that individuals will seek out particular companies and corporate cultures so that they will fit into the organizations. If this is true, it requires that applicants to a particular company have some advance idea of the corporate culture that they wish to work in. In addition, the company's selection procedure may take into account an applicant's characteristics when making a decision to hire them (Schneider, 1988).

The problems that Chinese organizations are facing in the modern competitive world, especially with the new challenges posed by multinational corporations, are worth considering in the context of the convergence/divergence question in organizational behavior. Organizations and management systems are reflections of the society in which they are created. People build organizations according to their values, and societies are composed of institutions and organizations that reflect the dominant values of the culture. The challenge of integrating Western styles of management with traditional styles is being confronted in many developing countries, such as Taiwan. Taiwan is a small country going through a process of Westernization and modernization. Therefore, it is inevitable that many managers in Taiwan will be exposed to Western management concepts. Studies have shown that most managers, especially those in the younger generation, are aware of differences between Western and Chinese management, and they often find themselves struggling to integrate the two (Kelley, Whatley, and Worthy, 1987). This is particularly the case given the large and increasing number of managers who have earned advanced degrees in the United States and other Western countries. While most of these managers recognize that neither approach to management is inherently good or bad, they also recognize that the social trend toward Westernization is moving the business culture away from reliance on family, friends, and personal relationships. The friction between traditional and Western management styles is manifested in the potentially conflicting perspectives held by different generations on how organizations should be managed, with the older generation being more traditional and the younger one being more Westernized (Lin, 1995).

As we have seen, family businesses are very important in Chinese cultures. Immediate family members usually fill the top management positions, and other key management positions are often occupied by relatives (Wong, 1985). This family orientation and perspective is also true for larger organizations, even those traded publicly on the stock market (Redding, 1986). The majority of businesses in Taiwan are privately owned, with up to 98 percent of the businesses having less than fifty employees (Hwang, 1989). The large number of small businesses is caused in part by the desire of many Chinese to be a boss. This desire is best demonstrated by the Chinese expression "It is better to be the head of a chicken than the tail of an ox" (Hwang, 1989). Chinese businesses tend to be centralized, implicitly structured, paternalistic, and reliant on nepotism both within the organization and externally through networks of contacts (Redding and Tam, 1985). While these observations were made about businesses in Taiwan, they also hold true for Hong Kong and other countries with a significant overseas Chinese population.

The Chinese family business has certain inherent strengths and weaknesses. The dominance of the family members in an organization makes it difficult for non–family members to develop loyalty and commitment to the organization. As a result, turnover rates of employees who are not part of the extended family can be as high as 50 percent, which creates significant financial and organizational costs for the organization (Hall and Xu, 1991). The autocratic leadership style tends to repress professional talent, and talented individuals who are not members of the immediate family will often be underutilized. The level of involvement of external, very talented individuals generally only changes if the skills they possess are unique and critical to the organization's operations or if the individuals marry into the family (Hsu, 1985).

Another weakness in the Chinese family business is the lack of succession planning. After an owner's death, the company often passes down to the next generation of sons. As a result, power must be shared and fragmentation of the company begins. This process is exaggerated after the expansion created by the next generation. Power struggles often result, and the organization can fall apart. This is a primary reason that Chinese family organizations rarely last more than a hundred years and rarely expand beyond the family. The limitations of this type of organizational setting are that the family structure imposes limitations on the growth and size of the organization (Redding, 1986). As a Chinese organization grows, the dependence on family members often proves to be a stumbling block to further growth, since the need for managers often exceeds the supply of competent or available family members. As a consequence, the organization frequently faces a crisis of growth that is hard to resolve.

On the positive side of the equation, Chinese family organizations have been very successful and contributed greatly to the economic miracle in Taiwan and other cultures where overseas Chinese play an important role in the economy. The organizational structure creates high internal efficiency and consistency of operations. The balance among the various organizational factors produces small but effective organizations (Redding and Wong, 1986). The family orientation in Chinese businesses may make managing easier because the internal environment of the organization is easier to master, but there is also evidence that a closed management system can create special problems. The most frequent pattern of organization development in Chinese organizations is for the organization to remain small with the father as the owner. Rather than expand, many Chinese organizations encourage sons and other relatives to leave and set up their own businesses. This process perpetuates the large number of small businesses in Chinese cultures (Lassere, 1988). In addition, Chinese family businesses have the advantage of developing networks, which can be used to create favorable purchasing and distribution relationships. Further, they are successful when flexibility is necessary and when deal-making skills are crucial to seizing business opportunities (Redding, 1990).

In many Chinese businesses, the owner-father is allowed to exert fatherlike authority over the business. As a result, the organizational leadership is autocratic, paternalistic, and highly personalized (Wang, 1992). Although the father has authority over the business, the assets belong to the family. As the owner of the business, the father has a responsibility to maintain the family's interests. The emphasis on the family has resulted in difficulties related to personnel planning, particularly in management, and a lack of loyalty from non–family members. When ideas for change are introduced into a Chinese organization, the owner-father must accept or possibly even originate the idea. If he opposes the change, it is very difficult for the other members of the family, even though they may be key members of the organization, to prevail. Decisions of the father must be respected. It can therefore be very difficult for organizations to change and grow within the Chinese family structure. Filial piety has served as a guiding principle governing general Chinese patterns of socialization. It justifies absolute parental authority over children and, by extension, those with generational rank over younger individuals. Of all human relationships, the one between father and son is the most important in the Confucian social fabric (Tu, 1985). A strong power core exercised by the proprietors characterizes Chinese management and is accepted by employees. However, the Chinese ethic of respect and compliance with the father figure has still remained strong. Although many of the younger generation in family-owned companies have been exposed to Western education and want to Westernize their organizations, they still accept their obligation to their father and the organization for which they work (Yang and Bond, 1990).

Other researchers have suggested that Confucian family-centered values guide small businesses but not other types of businesses in Taiwan. While family-owned businesses scored lower on such values as resorting to legal actions, when compared to private enterprises or American-run companies in Taiwan, as organizations move away from Confucian values such as paternalism, personalism, and filial piety, they become more effective (Hwang, 1990). Chinese family businesses and enterprises that are not family owned were compared in Taiwan, and the results indicate that the perceived clarity and reasonableness of both types of organization is very high and that Chinese organizations seem to become more effective only as they move away from structures reliant on Confucian values. Confucian values create a restrictive environment that is responsive to the internal environment of the organization but is less able to be flexible and responsive to the external environment. Further, the lack of interaction and feedback between leaders and followers, because of respect driven by filial piety, prevents the development of a learning organization (Hwang, 1991). The importance of individualism, collectivism, and Confucianism as societal values in Taiwan, as well as their being indicators of the struggle between modernization and traditional values, has been established (Boisot and Child, 1996; Bond, 1991; Redding, 1990). Generation (age) is one obvious variable that represents the potential conflict between the traditional and modern approaches to values in Taiwan. However, there are five additional factors—gender, education, position level, company size, and industry—that also have an impact on individual values (Child and Stewart, 1997).

There is some evidence to suggest that traditional filial piety is on the decline in Taiwan and that, as a result, there is now more intergenerational tension and conflict. Typically, a son, who has been exposed to more education and other cultures, is in conflict with the father, who still relies on his traditional beliefs in understanding the relationship (Ho, 1987). The increase in people's educational level, the changing values in Taiwanese society, the rise in capitalism, and changes in the demands on business are all contributing to these changes. The Taiwanese government's policies have historically encouraged small businesses. Now, as Taiwan moves to become a full economic partner in world trade, the emphasis is shifting toward larger and more-flexible organizations that can compete with multinational companies. This trend is also breaking down the role of traditional values within Taiwanese society (Hwang, 1991). Traditional Chinese management is embedded in a collectivist society in which individuals can expect their relatives, clan, or other in-group to look after them in exchange for unquestioning loyalty. In moving toward a more individualist society, in which a loosely knit social framework is preferred and in which interpersonal commitment and responsibility are perceived to be less important, the continued use of a traditional Chinese management style is being threatened. Younger managers are now placing more emphasis on expertise, reward performance, individual achievement, and professional relationships. As a result, the decision to hire a staff person is becoming more likely to be based on merit rather than the traditional reliance on a relationship with the owners.

Traditional Chinese management does not emphasize formal rules, written plans, organizational objectives, fixed times for meetings, or fixed criteria for performance evaluation, while attributes such as modesty, caring for the weak, and interest in the quality of life are valued highly (Chinese Culture Connection, 1987). However, the younger generation is demanding structure, standardization, and ritualization. Many Chinese organizations have started implementing monthly meetings, planning sales strategies and budgets, setting recruitment criteria, and producing reports. In addition, performance and career are being emphasized more, and competition among young managers is evident. In the wake of these changes, the traditional obligations of "the old taking care of the young" and "the senior taking care of the junior" will be difficult to maintain.

Managerial Values in the PRC

In the People's Republic of China (PRC), managerial values and organizational structures differ from those found in other countries with a large overseas Chinese population. The PRC focused the economic development of the country on large and medium-sized Chinese state enterprises. These organizations make up 50 percent of China's total industrial value and over two-thirds of the tax revenue (Wu, 1992). Historically these organizations were very inefficient. This inefficiency was caused in part by the influence of two different, and competing, government entities. The central government provided one set of leadership directives while the local government institutions provided a second set. This ambiguity in administration created a large bureaucracy, low levels of efficiency, and a lack of accountability (Pan, 1988). Since 1979, the Chinese government has moved to reduce the central government's role and given the state enterprises more control and decision-making authority (Gao, 1992).

The change in organizational emphasis has permitted more responsiveness to the marketplace, a significant change from past practices (Jackson, 1992). This and other changes have also influenced management styles and values, although there is little research evidence to indicate the nature of all these changes (Gao, 1992). The PRC also suffers from a shortage of quality academic institutions to train managers to function in the new business environment. This lack of ability to develop managerial resources is a potential barrier to both managerial and organizational development. A wider managerial training and development strategy will be required to meet the economic growth that is projected for the PRC in the coming years (Borgonjon and Vanhonacker, 1994).

Many Chinese managers, especially the younger generation, find Chinese management to be a very illogical, unscientific, and paternalistic practice and do not like certain facets of the culture. They may, consequently, attempt to implement change. However, they often fail to realize that they cannot produce such change simply by adopting the management style of another culture (Ralston, Gustafson, Cheung, and Terpstra, 1993). Younger Chinese managers need to understand the Chinese culture and the managerial paradigms that it has created.

In the PRC, the persistence of pre-industrial-era attitudes and behaviors means that hierarchical structures remain well established and results in both the acceptance of a paternalistic system and a socialist state. The Communist system preserved the Chinese cultural values that were consistent with socialist values while suppressing those values that ran counter to socialist principles (Child and Markoczy, 1993). The result of this approach was a centralized planned economy. Political ideology ran counter to both material incentives and market forces, resulting in significant inefficiency, inertia, and waste (Kerr, 1983). In one study, the PRC respondents perceived status to be more often ascribed than achieved and were less willing to adapt to various situations, believing that fate played an important role in organizational behavior (Trompenaars, 1993). In addition, relationships were seen in a more global and diffuse manner by mainland Chinese than by overseas Chinese. Dramatic changes are already occurring within mainland Chinese organizations, particularly as they affect the role of the manager (Chen, 1988). These changes have brought into question the ability of many managers in the PRC to deal with competition, uncertainty, ambiguity, and relative autonomy. The manager's role is changing from the previous concentration on people and process to a greater awareness of market forces, financial management, and strategic planning, as competition is being encouraged and the number of joint ventures increases.

It has been stated that the management procedures in the PRC today are characterized by a clear and defined knowledge base rooted in quantitative and operational methods (Warner, 1993). Management training focuses on the traditional quantitative, numbers-oriented (or hard) approach rather than the people-oriented and humanistic (or soft) approaches. The management style in the PRC can be characterized as emphasizing the quantitative rather than qualitative aspects of management. Professional background, ideology, and tradition dictate a distinct interpretation of the theory and practice of management in mainland China (Warner, 1993). There is also a growing sense of Chinese-style individualism, and younger managers are beginning to adopt Western procedures and management styles (Ralston, Gustafson, Terpstra, and Holt, 1995).

A comparative study of managers in Hong Kong, the United States, and mainland China attempted to measure whether the managers in Hong Kong were being influenced by American management practices and what impact, if any, this might have (Ralston et al., 1992). The researchers used measures that had been designed in the West as well as those designed on the basis of traditional Chinese values (Chinese Culture Connection, 1987). They found that there was a stronger relationship in management approaches between the PRC and the Hong Kong samples than with the American sample, indicating that Chinese cultural roots remain strong. The Western measures used were Machiavellianism, dogmatism, locus of control, and tolerance for ambiguity; the Eastern (or Chinese) values used were Confucian work dynamism, human-heartedness, integration, and moral discipline. Significant differences were found among managerial values in the three countries on all the values except the Eastern value of moral discipline. The biggest differences were between the managers from the United States and the PRC. The values of the managers from Hong Kong fell somewhere between the two extreme positions (Ralston, Gustafson, Cheung, and Terpstra, 1993). The conclusion was that both the national culture and the business environment can create a unique set of managerial values in any particular country. Chinese managers operate within the context of relatively high collectivism and high power distance, regardless of the particular country studied.

Other Comparisons in Different Cultures

Singaporean Chinese represent the largest ethnic group in Singapore, and this group has also been influenced by Western management trends. A comparison of work-related values of Singaporean Chinese with those of Japanese expatriate managers was undertaken. One of the major findings was that the constructs of individualism, masculinity, power distance, and uncertainty avoidance received only weak support in the Singaporean sample, which led the authors to suggest that the Japanese and Singaporean Chinese had different interpretations of the value constructs. In particular, they noted that the Singaporean Chinese interpreted collectivism as loyalty toward family whereas the Japanese interpreted collectivism as a higher allegiance to the workplace. So, even if two cultures are both considered collectivist, how the concept is interpreted and manifested can vary. Some other differences were found, leading the researchers to question the applicability of Hofstede's constructs in Singapore. However, it should be noted that Hofstede compared people across cultures using groups from within each culture, whereas in this study, Japanese expatriates were used as the comparison group. Perhaps expatriate managers are different from typical managers or behave differently from managers operating in their own country (Chew and Putti, 1995).

The culture and traditions that differentiate management styles in China and Europe have been investigated using personal experiences. The result was a proposal for a training model for both Chinese and Western managers that emphasizes cross-cultural negotiations and management differences. Specifically, it was argued that training should include skills and knowledge that help a manager develop a sense of belonging, understand cultural and religious differences and management analysis, and develop language skills related to management (Liu and Mackinnon, 2002). Another comparison of Chinese and European organizations found that the members of the lower levels of Chinese organizations had less influence than equivalent employees in European countries but that this difference did not exist within top management. The influence differences between the top and lower management levels in China were significant (Laaksonen, 1992).

Managerial Values in Vietnam

A series of articles explored the differences between Vietnamese and American managerial and worker behaviors. While Vietnamese and other Asians use the idea of "trying to save face" to mean that people avoid conflict and confrontation, the Vietnamese also consider whether any potential confrontation is with someone within or outside their group. Loss of face occurs when someone outside the group expresses negative feedback, but when the feedback comes from someone within the group, it is seen as evidence of caring about the other person. This dual notion of saving face is also reflected by the fact that two people will maintain distance early in a relationship, but once they move beyond the acquaintance level, they become more direct and open. Once they reach this level of closeness, they can become more frank and open with each other than Americans are. Feedback to improve performance is necessary and appropriate in Vietnam, but praise for a job well done is seen as leading to complacency and conceit. While Vietnam is a collectivist country, this does not necessarily mean that teams will be effective. Indeed, the concepts of teams and team building are interpreted quite differently in America and Vietnam. The Vietnamese tend to interpret collectivism as teams working together but not necessarily toward a common goal, whereas working toward a common goal is the key purpose of teams from an American management perspective. The result is that the Vietnamese understand very well what it means to be part of a group but not what it is like to be part of a team. Americans think of themselves as individuals first and as part of a group second, whereas the Vietnamese are likely to see themselves as part of a group first and as individuals second. To Americans, a team means taking individuals and putting them into a group; to the Vietnamese, it means taking them from one group and putting them in a new one. American teams tend to come together quickly and solve problems, but Vietnamese teams are more likely to work independently and seek additional information from their manager, making the team process slow and continually dependent on seeking more information from outside the team (Risher and Stopper, 2000a, 2000b, 2000c).

How things get done also differs between the United States and Vietnam. The United States is more likely to depend on contracts, and the Vietnamese to rely on relationships. However, even this is more complicated, since the Vietnamese tend to see relationships as one of two types, either friendships or calculative relationships. Understanding the difference is not always easy, and Vietnamese will sometimes sacrifice a business goal in order to maintain a friendship. Overall, the Vietnamese are likely to move much more slowly than Americans in almost every aspect of business and relationships, but at the same time, the business and political environment is so chaotic that the Vietnamese have learned to be comfortable with taking risks and experimenting as a way of coping.

Managerial Values in Africa

There is little organizational research published on Africa, even though there are numerous potentially large consumer markets with low labor costs. One study compared Nigerian and British managers by looking at managerial competence (Erondu, 2002). Managerial competence is of particular interest in a cross-cultural setting, but because multiple definitions about what defines competence abound in the literature, any comparison needs to be based on a consistent set of measurable concepts and variables (McAuley, 1994). Using a broad definition of managerial competency based on several different factors to measure individual, supervisory, line-management, and strategic management skills, Nigerian human resource directors reported that the manager had skill levels that were below average importance for current competent management practice but above average importance for future competent management practice. In the British sample, the skills measured were considered to be of average importance for current competent management practice and higher than average importance for future competent management practice

(Erondu, 2002). The conclusion was that current managers in Nigeria do not need a high level of managerial skills to be considered competent, but in Britain they do. Interestingly, both groups considered the need for future managerial competency to be higher than average. It is important to note that the researcher in this study had serious concerns about the results and whether they were really culturally or methodologically based (Erondu, 2002). The study is of interest, however, because it highlights definitional issues in cross-cultural research and also because it is one of a limited number of studies conducted in Africa.

Summary

Managerial values differ across countries, and they influence many areas of organizational, managerial, and employee behavior. These differences are particularly important for managers working in cultures other than their home culture, where large differences within cultures exist, and where generational differences are large. American and Western values include achievement, hard work, individualism, optimism, and competition. Asian or Eastern values include hard work, collectivism, fatalism, and cooperation. Given that different values exist in different cultures, a key question is whether, over time, these differences will remain the same, grow greater or diverge, or become more similar or converge. Research on convergence and divergence of values has provided some evidence to support the idea that values are converging across cultures and that the dominant values are Western ones. However, the evidence for drawing this conclusion is limited in scope and indicates that convergence may only apply to some, rather than all, values. To successfully understand the effects of convergence and divergence of cultural values, a more detailed analysis of the differential effects on various managerial and cultural values needs to be undertaken.

Numerous research studies have found differences between cultures and within cultures on a variety of values. Different government regulations regarding employment, the environment, and social issues can also have a significant impact on managerial behavior. Also, differences occur because of different dominant organizational structures within cultures. For example, the small family business is the dominant Chinese organizational structure, and this leads to business relationships built on trust, parental respect, and personal relationships, and company size tends to remain small.

The majority of research in non-Western cultures has been conducted in the various predominantly Chinese cultures. As a result, the knowledge of the use and impact of managerial values in other countries and types of cultures is rather limited, and the opportunities for advances in research and theory in understudied cultures are significant.

9

The Impact of Cultural Values on Problem Solving, Teams, Gender, Stress, and Ethics

Cultural values have an impact on a variety of aspects of organizational and managerial behavior. Cooperation between and within organizations, which has a profound impact on approaches to and outcomes from these behaviors, is influenced by culture, personal preferences, and relationship history. This chapter will explore these issues.

Problem Solving and Decision Making

The impact of cultural values on several other areas of managerial behaviors and values is important to consider. For example, managerial behavior includes problem solving and decision making, and cross-cultural differences play a role here as well. A comparison of employee beliefs and behaviors about different problem-solving approaches and their effectiveness was completed, with samples from seven countries: Australia, Fiji, France, New Zealand, Papua New Guinea, South Korea, and the United States (Van Deusen, Mueller, Jones, and Friedman, 2002). The researchers concluded that national culture plays an important role and leads to differences in how problems are solved and in the quality of the solutions. Specifically, organizations in more-individualist countries are moving toward using more-collectivist approaches to problem solving. Based on problem recurrence as a measure of the quality of an initial solution, the United States performed the worst while South Korea performed the best.

Culture also affects the way problems are introduced for resolution. Chinese employees are more likely to delay informing a manager about a problem until the manager sees the problem on his or her own. The employees are also likely to minimize the seriousness of the problem. In Western cultures, managers are more likely to appreciate and give credit to an employee who draws attention to a problem, and therefore, problems are more rapidly identified and brought to the attention of management. The result is that Western managers are more likely to speak directly about a problem, whereas Chinese managers will avoid talking about the problem, since they think to do so would be inappropriate.

Western managers also tend to break down problems into smaller pieces and work backward from the problem to a solution. This is a linear process that generally works well. However, the Chinese tend to work in a nonlinear way, preferring to look for patterns that are similar to earlier events, and they place greater emphasis on the relationship aspects of any solution than their Western counterparts. At the same time, Chinese managers are more likely to be pragmatic and find solutions that work around, rather than strictly follow, regulations.

Another aspect of decision making is the level in the organization at which decisions are made. This is generally based on specific practices rather than values, particularly in Europe. Labor-union practices and other issues such as the social charter that governs a wide variety of organizational and employee issues within the European Union also have a significant impact on some organizational decisions.

Decision-making strategies are also influenced by cultural variables. For example, in collectivist cultures, decision making is more likely to rely on consensus (Triandis, 1995). A survey of managers in sixteen countries led to the conclusion that managers from individualist and low-power-distance countries rely more on their own experience and training when making decisions than do managers from collectivist and high-power-distance countries (Smith, Peterson, et al., 1994). A comparison of Japanese and Australian students found that Australians prefer a decision-making style based on having a selection of choices that require careful individual thought, whereas the Japanese prefer styles that require more reference to other people (Radford, Mann, Ohta, and Nakane, 1991). Most Chinese and East Asian managers reported more confidence that their decisions were correct than did mangers from the United States. However, the Japanese reported less confidence in the correctness of their decisions (Yates, Lee, and Shinotsuka, 1996).

All decisions involve an element of risk, but some cultures are more open to greater levels of risk-taking behavior than others. Decision making was evaluated in several countries based on subjects evaluating the relative level of risk of a series of decisions and indicating which decision they would make. The results of one study indicated that the Chinese were more willing to invest in financial deals that Americans considered too risky. And in a second study, the Chinese were willing to invest the most money in financially risky ventures, while Americans were willing to invest the least. In this latter study, samples were included from Germany and Poland, and these two groups fell somewhere between the Chinese and the Americans in their willingness to take risks. One possible explanation for these findings is that Chinese cultures are collectivist and so provide a lot of support and networks to cushion any failures. Finally, the Japanese were found to be more like Americans in their relatively low tolerance for risk, indicating that not all Asian cultures act the same way (Azar, 1999). These results point to differences in the way that cultures approach decision making and problems. These differences need to be considered, especially in cross-cultural negotiations and communication.

One unique aspect of decision making is how managers handle past decisions that become problematic. In some cases, managers will immediately inform others and withdraw support from the decision or rescind it. On the other hand, there is a tendency for some managers to increase commitment to projects that are in trouble. A comparison of Mexican and American managers yielded several differences. Mexican managers were much more likely to increase their commitment to a failing project than their American counterparts. The Mexican managers were reluctant to report bad news. The researchers argue that this reaction is based on cultural differences and suggest that joint ventures between the United States and Mexico should include safeguards and procedures that will discourage Mexican managers from escalating their commitment to poor decisions (Greer and Stephens, 2001).

When decisions are made in groups, there is a risk that if the level of consensus is too high, groupthink will occur. The term *groupthink* describes group decisions that include a kind of pathology that leads to bad decisions because dissent has been stifled to the point where rationality disappears. The Bay of Pigs fiasco and the first space shuttle disaster are frequently used as examples of groupthink in that, had the individuals involved in the decisions been challenged or able to review issues objectively, a different, more appropriate decision would probably have been reached and disaster avoided. Groupthink is not an exclusively American phenomenon, and a few research studies have explored the concept in other cultures. For example, in the Netherlands the groupthink phenomenon was replicated and was found to increase when the group was more homogeneous, sharing similar backgrounds, values, and gender (Kroon, Van Kreveid, and Rabbie, 1992). A comparison of Australian and American groups found that Australians were more pluralistic, while Americans were more elitist and, thus, more likely to engage in groupthink than their Australian counterparts (Bovasso, 1992).

Team Behavior and Effectiveness

There are many different types of teams within organizations, and the number and prevalence of different types varies by culture. Many organizations use teams made up of members from different cultures, and the differences among the cultural values of team members can influence team performance and processes (Unsworth and West, 2000). For example, different cultures have different perceptions of time, with Asian cultures having a long-term orientation while many Western and American cultures have a short-term time perspective. The result is that approaches to decision making, goal setting, deadlines, and scheduling will vary significantly (Waller, Conte, Gibson, and Carpenter, 2001). Even such simple things as coming to meetings late rather than on time can be seen in a different light, with workers in Brazil seeing it as a positive behavior and Americans seeing it as a negative behavior (Levine, 1997).

In general, individualist cultures such as the United States are less comfortable with using teams or embracing them if they are introduced, whereas teams in collectivist cultures are more likely to be well accepted. For example, in Japan, individuals are likely to measure their personal success by the success of their team and organization. It is not unusual for Japanese employees to begin the day singing the company song and to wear company colors to show their loyalty (Levine, 1997). A longitudinal study specifically considered the impact of culture, either individualist or collectivist, on several areas of work-group performance. The study measured functional heterogeneity, or the group members' perceptions about the diversity of the other members' skills and experiences; group potency, or how effective members think the group will be; and outcome expectations, or how effective the group believes it will be in achieving the goals for the group. Several differences were found between the two types of cultures. Individualist cultures, such as the United States, reported higher levels of functional heterogeneity, group potency, and outcome expectation. In the collectivist culture, Korea, outcome expectations were high during the initial stages of the group but decreased over time. The researchers concluded that work groups are effective in individualist cultures, despite the common belief that work groups are more effective in collectivist cultures (Sosik and Jung, 2002). Clearly, cultural issues in teams and groups present organizations with both challenges and opportunities, and organizations need to be aware of how group characteristics and behaviors differ across cultures.

Quality circles are teams of individuals who meet regularly to generate ideas that will lead to greater productivity and quality. This approach was developed in Japan, where it remains popular. It was introduced into the United States when Japanese management systems were popular, although they have declined in popularity in the United States lately, partly because it is hard to sustain continuous improvements after the initial substantive improvement (Gibson and Tesone, 2001).

Managerial values are also integral to approaches to teamwork, which, as we have seen, also has different definitions in different cultures. Teams are widely used in American companies, and there is every indication that their use will continue to increase (Lawler, Ledford, and Mohrman, 1995). At the same time, American companies have attempted to implement teams in subsidiaries in other countries, with mixed success (Manz and Sims, 1993). In order to understand the influence of national culture on work teams, J. Tata (2000) proposed a model of the relationship between national culture and the level of team autonomy. She thought that, in national cultures with low power distance and low uncertainty, teams with a high level of team autonomy could likely be successful, whereas in countries with high power distance and uncertainty avoidance, teams with a low level of autonomy are more likely to be successful. If companies are to use teams effectively, Tata believes that they need to be proactive. She proposes a four-step model for implementing teams in other countries. First the company needs to conduct a cultural diagnosis to understand how values and beliefs are influenced by the national culture. Based on the outcome of the diagnosis, a determination of the fit between the culture and the level of autonomy is made. If it is decided after the first two stages have been completed that teams will still be implemented, then the organization has to carefully develop an implementation plan and design how the change will be put in place. Finally, the company needs to decide how to implement the change so that resistance is minimized. Top-management support for team implementation is critical, and the key to success is effectively aligning the level of team autonomy to the cultural values of both the society and the organization.

A conceptual model of national and organizational culture and their impact on teamwork has been proposed, which compares how five different types of metaphors (military, sports, community, family, and associates) are used to describe teamwork in different cultures. Interviews about how teams work were conducted in four different countries—France, Puerto Rico, the Philippines, and the United States—and in several different multinational companies. The researchers analyzed the interview content to look for distinct ways that people described teamwork. For example, if a culture tended to use military metaphors to describe the team process, managers would use expressions such as "in the trenches" to describe team behavior. If the culture used such phrases as "our star quarterback," then they were using more sports metaphors. Using this approach, it became clear that people in different cultures use different metaphors when talking about teams, indicating that they also hold different views of teamwork both organizationally and nationally. In cultures where there is tight control over teams, military and family metaphors are more likely to be used. In highly individualist cultures, sports metaphors are more likely to be used (Gibson and Zellmer-Bruhn, 2001). The researchers suggest that an awareness of how metaphors are used in a particular culture or organization will enhance teamwork and improve team effectiveness. Teams that are managed in a way that is compatible with the external cultural norms are more profitable than teams that are not (Newman and Nollen, 1996).

Teams are defined differently in different cultures because of the variance in aspects of team behavior such as the scope of the project, the make-up of the team and roles of team members, and the reasons that teams typically are formed (Cohen and Bailey, 1997). For example, team leaders need to be more sensitive to group norms in Iran and Mexico than in the United States, because in Iran and Mexico clear role definitions are seen as an important aspect of the group process whereas in the United States they are not (Ayman and Chemers, 1983). Further, teams in collectivist cultures behave more cooperatively, have less conflict, and use fewer competitive tactics than teams in individualist cultures (Oetzel, 1998). The assessment of what makes an effective work team is also different in different countries. Supervisors rated teams as more effective in Japan if team members showed more reliance on peers, more effective in the United States if team members showed more reference to superiors, and more effective in the United Kingdom if the team members showed more self-reliance (Smith, Peterson, et al., 1994).

One approach to coping with the increase in technological change, product and service innovation, and global competition has been the use of fluid work teams. This type of team can have changing membership and leadership in order to be more flexible and innovative (Livinthal and March, 1993). The national-culture dimensions of individualism-collectivism and power distance were used to look at the adaptability of fluid work teams in Australia and Taiwan (Harrison, McKinnon, Wu, and Chow, 2000). The results indicate that Taiwanese employees tend to have greater difficulty adapting to fluid work teams than Australians. The authors conclude that this is consistent with the role of high power distance and collectivism in Chinese society and low power distance and individualism in Australian society. They point out that these findings should only be considered in terms of fluid work teams, rather than teams in general, but that culture does seem to play an important role in how effective fluid work teams will be.

More American and multinational companies are turning to using self-managed work teams (SMWT) as a way to remain competitive (Osterman, 1994). Self-managed work teams typically have five components: (1) they manage themselves, (2) they decide work assignments, (3) they plan and schedule the work, (4) they have decision-making responsibility, and (5) they solve problems (Wellins et al., 1990). Cultural values directly affect a variety of managerial issues including team effectiveness (Adler, 1997), and the success of SMWTs in other cultures and multicultural SMWTs requires careful attention to culture-based resistance (Kirkman and Shapiro, 1997). Teams need to become globalized, as opposed to being just multicultural, if they are to be truly effective.

Global or transnational teams are becoming more common and have the advantage of providing international expertise and perspective to problem solving. These teams are composed of multinational members with varying responsibilities in different countries. While there are many similarities to traditional teams, cultural differences and logistics related to team meetings introduce new challenges. The primary reason for the failure of this type of group is a lack of trust between members, exaggerated by differences in language, geography, and culture. The team should also be able to communicate in the same language despite differences in the members' native languages.

The role of the team leader is especially important to achieve success. Choosing the right leader will help ensure that the person is flexible, supportive of the team process, understanding of cultural differences, and able to listen and communicate with the team members (Solomon, 1995). Effective global teams need be able to handle issues of national, professional, and organizational culture. Given the large distances involved, a communication system that allows geographically dispersed team members to communicate with one another is critical to success and information sharing.

Gender

If we compare countries' cultural values, one of the most readily apparent differences relates to the role of gender, and particularly the role of women, in society. Because significant changes in the role of women in society and at work have occurred in recent years, it is important to understand how issues related to gender are treated in various cultures. The role of women in management has been considered from two perspectives (Adler and Izraeli, 1988). The first is the equity approach, which assumes similarity between males and females and works to assess performance and contributions of the two genders in an equitable and normative way. The other approach is the complementary-contribution approach, which assumes differences in the contributions of each gender and attempts to recognize the value of these differences.

Research on gender differences in management has been concentrated in Western countries and in the United States in particular. Further, most of the research on women managers was conducted in the 1970s and 1980s; there has been relatively little recent research. Research in Eastern cultures has been very limited because of the continued emphasis on the role of the woman as daughter-mother-wife, and only recently has this stereotype begun to change (Li, 1992). One reason for the change is that the economy in Asia was booming in the 1990s, creating a greater demand for women in the work force, and a greater percentage of women have filled management positions. In addition, the educational level of women has been steadily increasing, giving them the education necessary to advance in many organizations (Adler and Izraeli, 1988).

Implicit in gender issues is the role the family plays in the culture, the organization, and the employee's life. Organizations in the United States have only just begun to realize the importance of family-friendly work environments as a motivational tool. Elsewhere, some cultures have always viewed the family as very important. For example, in Singapore, maintaining family structure and values is seen as linked to economic success, and in Latin America, the Middle East, and Africa, issues facing families often take precedence over work (Nelson, 1998). Conflict between work and family has been studied in the United States and Hong Kong to see how societal issues affect employees in the two countries (Aryee, Fields, and Luk, 1999). The research examined work-family conflict (how work problems affect the family) and family-work conflict (how the family affects work). Work problems are more likely to cause conflict in the family in Hong Kong, whereas in the United States family problems are more likely to cause problems at work. These findings suggest that the family is relatively more important than work in Hong Kong, and work is relatively more important than family in the United States, although work and family concerns were more balanced in the United States. Stress generated by family responsibilities can lead to absenteeism, high turnover, and reduced productivity (Grover and Crooker, 1995). Developing family-responsive work policies benefits many organizations but is especially essential in cultures where the family has a primary position of importance.

The role of women in work and management is changing rapidly throughout the world. For example, in the United States, statistics indicate that about 45 percent of the work force is female, and many are in management (Pedigo, 1991). In France, the United Kingdom, and Spain, there has been a steady increase in the number of women in the work force and, in most cases, in the percentage of women in traditionally male jobs and occupations. While equal-opportunity legislation protects women in most European countries, there are still cultural differences that influence attitudes toward women working. For example, Italy has the lowest percentage of women in the work force, with only about 30 percent of the women working and only 3 percent in upper management. This low rate has been attributed to the strong role played by the Catholic Church in Italian society and to the encouragement of families to have children (Davidson and Cooper, 1993). In Hong Kong, data collected between 1981 and 1991 showed an increase of almost 600 percent in the number of women managers in organizations (Hong Kong census data, 1991). Similar changes have occurred in the PRC, Taiwan, and Thailand. For example, while attitudes toward women are still rooted in cultural expectations, the rapid economic growth in the PRC has resulted in the percentage of women in the management work force increasing to almost 30 percent (Korabik, 1993). This is a dramatic increase, especially given cultural expectations (Zhang, 1993). It is also true that even in some countries where women are not generally promoted to managers, multinationals operating in the country have been willing to promote more women (Lansing and Ready, 1988).

In other countries, the role of women is more clearly prescribed by the culture, and change is much slower or even nonexistent. For example, in Japan, women are still expected to take primary responsibility for domestic issues while the men take responsibility for work. Even female college graduates who work are not taken as seriously as their male counterparts, and they are often given positions in which they are expected to be pleasant, cheerful, and helpful rather than leaders or major contributors to the organization. In Saudi Arabia, women, both Arab and expatriate, are not allowed to drive, work with men, or work with non-Muslim foreigners (Mayer and Cava, 1993).

Not only has the majority of the research conducted up to now been centered in Western countries and particularly the United States, but the majority of this research has also centered on the managerial behavior of women and how it differs from that of male managers (Coates, Jarrat, and Mahaffie, 1990). In addition, any discussion of the impact of gender in management has focused on the role of women rather than looking at the role of men or, even, conducting comparisons. One review of the literature looked at 130 studies related to women in organizations (Terborg, 1977). This study concentrated on the entry level for women, which tends to be lower than that for men, and the socialization process for women in organizations. In considering leadership behavior, it seems that women in America are more likely than men to be charismatic leaders and are more likely to temper criticism with positive feedback (Bass, 1990). Women are also more likely to use more democratic and participative leadership styles, while males are more likely to use a more autocratic or directive style of leadership (Eagly and Johnson, 1990). While women are likely to be more caring in their managerial approach, they are also very concerned about doing a good job. Just like their male counterparts, they have a desire for independence and a drive to achieve career advancement. In other words, while women managers care about their subordinates, they still have a strong need to perform well on the job and, through their work, to attain economic security (Kagan, 1983).

One study of gender and culture influence on leadership was conducted in four countries: Norway, Sweden, Australia, and the United States (Gibson, 1995). In each of the countries, the results show that men are more likely to place greater emphasis on setting goals, while women are more likely to place greater emphasis on facilitating interaction. However, no other gender differences were found. In terms of country differences, the Australians place less emphasis on the laissez-faire style of leadership and significantly more emphasis on the benevolent-autocratic style. Interestingly, the results indicated little difference between the Norwegian, Swedish, and American samples in preferred leadership styles. However, since much of the other research has tended to focus on one country at a time, a comparative analysis is often difficult or inappropriate (Adler and Izraeli, 1994).

It is likely that managers' techniques of obtaining the cooperation of employees will be affected by both their culture and their organization. A study explored these two issues as they affect Chinese women managers in four cultures: China, Hong Kong, Taiwan, and Thailand. The study involved only Chinese women, even though they were from different countries (Chow and Luk, 1996). In this way, the cultural basis of all managers was rooted in Confucianism, but the national culture in which they work was different. This approach permits an excellent comparison of national differences, rather than just cultural differences based on ethnic background. Chinese managers predominate in Hong Kong, Taiwan, and the PRC but are not as prevalent in Thailand, although overseas Chinese do form a significant part of the managerial work force there. The women reported that their top-five job motivators included "recognition for good work," "having a good relationship with superiors and colleagues," and "a good chance for promotion." However, the other two items in the top five were different. The PRC sample included "good pay" and "working in a prestigious company" as the other two motivators. The sample from Hong Kong included "challenging and interesting work" and "a job that enables me to use my skills and abilities" as the other two motivators. Further, the PRC sample indicated that the most important managerial skill is directing, while the Hong Kong group indicated that planning is the most important.

Gender differences were considered in relationship to job satisfaction and work values for a sample of employees in Taiwan (Cheung and Scherling, 1999). The researchers found that male employees had higher job satisfaction and job levels than female employees but that there was no difference in the work values held by male and female employees. Male employees were favored in Taiwan and scored significantly higher on task satisfaction, team satisfaction, status satisfaction, and rank. By controlling for extraneous variables, such as educational level, the researchers felt confident that the results could be attributed to gender differences. In addition, the researchers concluded that, while Taiwan has become more individualist and egalitarian, gender differences remain.

Such research is of interest because the sociocultural context of Asian culture is very different from that of Western countries and, therefore, can provide a crucial test for the effect of gender differences in the areas of job satisfaction and work values. This is particularly true in relation to task (intrinsic reward), team (social reward), reward (tangible reward), and status (promotion), as well as to job level, which appear to be important factors of job satisfaction identified by studies in the West. For example, when women's managerial behavior in the Philippines was studied, female managers were found to be more interested in people than male managers and more likely to build personal relationships with employees, even mixing business with personal issues, whereas men in managerial positions were less likely to do this (Licuanan, 1993).

The plight of women's labor-market position is well documented by economists, sociologists, psychologists, and other social scientists. They have shown that women's investments in human capital generally have a lower rate of return than those of men (i.e., wage discrimination exists), that labor-market segregation (both horizontal and vertical) often hinders women in their choice of employment and in their advancement opportunities, and finally, that violence at work primarily affects women. It is thus paradoxical that women should have higher levels of job satisfaction in Western countries than men (Blanchflower and Oswald, 2004; Clark, 1997). Very few studies have made an explicit attempt to explain this paradox. Using data from the 1991 British Household Panel Survey, it was suggested that the satisfaction differential might be explained by the possibility that women's labor-market-related expectations are being met or exceeded (Clark, 1997). A further characteristic of job-satisfaction research is that it has primarily been based on a very small number of nations (Veenhoven, 1991) and heavily weighted toward Europe and the United States (e.g., Blanchflower and Oswald, 2004).

There is one significant study of job satisfaction and gender differences across countries (Sousa-Poza and Sousa-Poza, 2002). The results show that, in countries where women are much more satisfied than men (i.e., a job-satisfaction differential of over 5 percent), work-role outputs tend to be higher for women than for men. This is especially the case for women in the United Kingdom, who have much higher levels than men of (self-perceived) job security, jobs that are useful to society or that help other people, and good relations with management and colleagues. Similar results were found for the United States. The researchers also found that, in most countries, no significant gender difference in job satisfaction exists when jobs and responsibility differences are controlled. In only three countries, the United Kingdom, the United States, and Switzerland, did they find that women are still (i.e., after taking the different work-role inputs and outputs into consideration) more satisfied than men. What is evident from their analysis is that large job-satisfaction differentials in women's favor are predominantly encountered in the United Kingdom and the United States. Furthermore, these differentials cannot be entirely explained by different work-role inputs and outputs, so that there is no obvious explanation as to why the gender effect applies primarily to these two Western countries. However, women managers surveyed in the United Kingdom report that the characteristics their organizations value most in a manager are competitiveness, cooperation, and decisiveness, and those they value least are emotionalism, manipulativeness, and forcefulness (Traves, Brockbank, and Tomlinson, 1997). These characteristics cut across styles that are typically identified as masculine or feminine. It seems that, in practice, management styles are evolving toward valuing a mixture of the so-called masculine and feminine characteristics.

Stress

Stress on the job has been generally accepted as a universal phenomenon that follows a physiological pattern. However, there are individual differences in how people react physically and psychologically to the same event and how or why individuals perceive a particular event to be a job stressor. It is reasonable to assume that cultural differences will also play a role either independently or by interacting with individual characteristics. Generally, stress is created by role ambiguity or conflict, workload, lack of perceived control over events affecting a person's life, job security, and the demands of the job.

There is support for the generalized impact of stress in various countries. A study in the Netherlands found that postal workers reported lack of control over their jobs was a significant source of stress (Carayon, 1995). A Swedish study found that employees most likely to die of a heart attack were those who had the least control over their job (Siegrist, 2001). In China, increased job pressure and job insecurity resulted in higher levels of stress, as measured by higher blood pressure and cholesterol levels (Siegrist, 1996). Also, job monotony has been found to be related to stress in Finland and Israel.

All aspects of stress can be affected by national culture and government policies. For example, government policies on family leave, work hours, and vacation days vary greatly from country to country. There are some reports of particular stress issues in different countries. For example, the Paris police department reported an unusually high suicide rate among its members. In 1995, sixty police officers committed suicide, which is twice the rate found in New York City. The cause was attributed to staff cutbacks, lack of control over working conditions, poor pay in a high-priced city, and a lack of social and emotional support. The lack of employee-assistance programs in France, along with a general lack of concern for dealing with psychological issues such as stress, reflects national-culture priorities and social norms (Simon, 1996).

In Japan, it has been reported that 59 percent of Japanese workers reported feeling "markedly fatigued" from work. Only between 15 and 30 percent of Americans reported similar feelings, even though American and Japanese workers work an equivalent amount of time—the most working hours in the world. Along the same lines, stress or *karoshi* in Japan is reported to claim up to ten thousand lives a year, whereas in the United States few deaths are attributed directly to stress. These differences are attributed to cultural factors such as the extreme work ethic in Japan and a cultural bias against seeking help. The rates of depression, anxiety, and suicide in middle-aged men are increasing. Since Japan is still a male-dominated business environment, the effects of stress are most frequently seen in men, or the "business Samurais," and little data is available for female stress-related incidents (Segall, 2000).

One cross-cultural study, including twenty-one countries, found work overload and stress were greater in non-Western countries such as India, Indonesia, Korea, and Nigeria than in Western countries (Peterson et al., 1995). Another study, issued by the United Nations, focused on stress and mental health in the United Kingdom, the United States, Germany, Finland, and Poland. The results indicate that one in ten workers in the five countries are affected by work-related stress and that depression ranks as the second most common disabling illness after heart disease. Stress-related issues seem to be a global problem. There is evidence that stress at work is a major concern in Europe, and the European Union is spending about 4 percent of its gross national product in treating stress and mental illness generated by work (Cox and Rial-Gonzales, 2003). Organizations are being prompted to act and supported by government programs and policies.

New-Product Development and Creativity

Since a new product can be a substantial portion of a company's revenue, it is worth considering how national culture can play a role in new-product development. In countries with a high degree of individualism, successful new-product development is likely, given that new-product champions are often associated with successful new products. However, given the success of new-product development in Japan, collectivism may also be a positive force. Collectivism often involves teams, and the success of a team approach in Japan has been well documented (Kennard, 1991). Power distance has also been considered in new-product development, and since low power distance is often associated with decentralization, which in turn facilitates new-product development, indications are that countries with low power distance are more likely to be innovative. However, high power distance with centralized, top-management support can also facilitate new-product development (Nakata and Sivakumar, 1996). The same apparent contradictions have been found for the dimensions of masculinity-femininity and uncertainty avoidance, as both ends of these two continua also seem to support new-product development. One clear finding is that a positive level of Confucian dynamism facilitates innovation, while a negative level impedes innovation. The implication of these findings is that some cultures are better at the initiation stage of new-product development, while others are better at the implementation stage. Initiation-preference cultures tend to be high in individualism but low in power distance, masculinity, and uncertainty avoidance. Implementation-preference cultures tend to be low in individualism but high in power distance, uncertainty avoidance, and masculinity. Some ways to take advantage of these differences are to initiate in one culture and implement in another or to create multicultural teams with complementary strengths.

Finally, a three-country study looked at how the national environment affects new-venture performance. Data was collected from entrepreneurs in the United Kingdom, Norway, and New Zealand. The results indicate that the national environment does not seem to affect new-venture performance (Shane and Kolvereid, 1995). A study of entrepreneurial traits across cultures found that internal locus of control, moderate risk-taking propensity, and high energy level decrease as cultural distance from the United States increases. The trait of innovative orientation was consistent across the cultures studied (Thomas and Mueller, 2000).

Ethics

One key element of managerial values is rooted in the ethical system of a country. As companies do more and more business in other countries, it is inevitable that assumptions about what is and what is not ethical will be tested. According to F. Fukuyama (1995), "Culture is inherited ethical habit" (p. 34). Therefore, cultural values play an important role in ethical decision making. The United States has more laws relating to legislating ethical behavior of managers than any other country, which increases the probability that Americans will see what happens in other countries as unacceptable and not fitting American cultural expectations about what constitutes ethical behavior in organizations. For example, China is frequently criticized by people in the United States for using prison labor in manufacturing plants, but to the Chinese this is an appropriate use of criminals.

One investigation of the way managers structure their ethical decisions was undertaken in seven countries: Japan, Korea, Hong Kong, the United States, Australia, Russia, and Poland. Cross-cultural differences for both the structure and content of managers' ethical judgments were found. Specifically, American managers tend to use consequential criteria when making ethical decisions, Australian managers tend to use relativistic criteria and take the best interests of the company into consideration, and the Japanese and Korean managers tend to use a combination of both the consequential and relativistic criteria. Hong Kong managers look at the consequences of a decision but also consider their sense of obligation and what is acceptable to colleagues. The Russian and Polish managers use mainly deontological (right action and moral obligation) criteria and utilitarian considerations (Jackson et al., 2000).

Another study attempted to develop a model of ethical decision making based on data from ten nations. It used the cultural dimensions of individualism-collectivism and uncertainty avoidance to explain national-cultural differences in judgments of whether decisions are considered ethical. The countries included in the study were the United States, Australia, and the United Kingdom (high individualism, low uncertainty avoidance); France, Germany, and Switzerland (moderate individualism, high uncertainty avoidance); Spain and the PRC (moderate to high collectivism, high uncertainty avoidance); and India and Hong Kong (moderate to high collectivism, low uncertainty avoidance). The results confirm that ethical attitudes differ among national groups. Interestingly, one consistent finding in all cultures was that all the managers tended to see others as less ethical than they saw themselves. Other specific findings were that the British, American, and Australian managers thought relationships with external stakeholders require a higher level of ethical consideration, whereas the managers from Germany and Switzerland considered the ethical relationships with external stakeholders to be of little importance. The findings suggest that individualism-collectivism and uncertainty avoidance can be used to frame differences in the relative importance of ethical issues in various situations, particularly since judgments of what are "good" or "bad" ethics are not necessarily the same in different countries (Jackson, 2001).

When cross-cultural ethical conflicts occur, organizations can respond along a continuum from complete adaptation to the host country's ethical standards at one end to maintaining the home country's standards at the other end (Buller and McEvoy, 1999). There are seven strategies available to managers when attempting to resolve ethical conflicts: avoiding, forcing, education-persuasion, infiltration, negotiation-compromise, accommodation, and collaboration—problem solving. All of these strategies have value, and which approach should be used depends on the issue involved and the circumstances surrounding it. In order to choose the appropriate strategy, managers need to consider how much ability they have to control the situation (power), the urgency of the situation, the centrality of the issue in terms of importance to human life, and whether the values are universal and common or rarely seen and unusual.

When ethical-reasoning levels for auditors in China and Australia were compared to see if cultural differences influenced ethical reasoning, the results indicated that Australians had higher ethical-reasoning scores than the Chinese (Tsui and Windsor, 2001). Also, research in Korea found that Korean managers are more morally idealistic than American managers (Lee and Sirgy, 1999) and that Koreans tend to avoid uncertainty by building relationships rather than by making precise legal commitments (De Mente, 1998).

To illustrate the ethical complexities of doing business in other countries, the question of how to maintain an organization's ethical values while operating in a country with an ethically challenging environment was investigated in Burma. The results provide a provocative discussion of the issues, especially since, thanks to current information technology, multinational companies can no longer hide operations in other countries from public scrutiny (Schermerhorn, 1999). Because multinational companies operate in a context of diverse and conflicting values and norms, sensitivity to cross-cultural ethical differences is important.

The wide range of legally defined ethical behaviors in various countries compounds ethical-behavior and decision-making concerns. For example, the Foreign Corrupt Practices Act in the United States prohibits American companies from paying bribes to officials in other countries. However, Danish and German companies, for example, are allowed to pay bribes to officials in other countries, and these bribes are even tax-deductible. Therefore, companies need to become ethically aware and design strategies and human resource management in ethical ways that create a balance when cross-cultural differences are considered.

Summary

Differences in values are also manifested in the way cultures approach teamwork and group work, gender, and ethical standards. Of particular note is the role of women in cultures, since women are often treated differently than men, are generally paid less, have fewer opportunities for advancement, and are more likely to experience violence in the workplace, while at the same time reporting higher levels of job satisfaction in Western cultures. Any exploration of value differences needs to understand core differences in approaches and attitudes toward women and the use of teams and how differences in ethical standards based on different cultural expectations affect employee and managerial behavior.

10

Job Satisfaction and Organizational Commitment

Motivation and performance are influenced by the emotions we experience both at work and in our personal lives. How our attitudes and emotions affect our behavior is explored in this chapter.

Job Satisfaction

The very extensive literature concerning job satisfaction indicates that, across a variety of work settings, job satisfaction is an important workplace construct that is of concern for effective management. Job satisfaction is defined as "a pleasurable or positive emotional state resulting from the appraisal of one's job" (including various facets of that job). Job satisfaction can be broken down into three general areas: the values that an individual has or wants, the perception of how the organization meets these values, and their relative importance to the individual (Locke, 1976). Job satisfaction has been linked to positive workplace outcomes such as increased organizational commitment, with workers having high levels of job satisfaction being more likely to be committed to the organization (Brown and Peterson, 1994). Furthermore, individuals with higher levels of job satisfaction are less likely to seek out a different job (Sager, 1994) or to leave the organization (Boles, Johnson, and Hair, 1997). Employee job satisfaction is also a function of intrinsic and extrinsic rewards offered by a job (Tuch and Martin, 1991), status associated with job level (Cox and Nkomo, 1991), and work values (Drummond and Stoddard, 1991). Furthermore, task, status, monetary reward, and social relationships (or a team dimension) are four essential aspects of job satisfaction (Neil and Snizek, 1987) and are also important dimensions of work values (Shuka, Sarna, and Nigam, 1989). They are the basis of the reward thesis, which explains higher job satisfaction by the intrinsic and extrinsic rewards obtained from a promotion (Wright, Bengtsson, and Frankenberg, 1994). As mentioned earlier, turnover is a major issue for many organizations and is very important to control because of the costs associated with hiring and training new personnel, as well as the costs associated with not having that individual contributing his or her work efforts toward organizational goals. Creating and maintaining a high level of job satisfaction is one of the most important attitudinal issues faced by managers in the workplace.

One measure of performance is absenteeism. It has been demonstrated that there is a clear and consistent, though small, negative relationship between absenteeism and job satisfaction. The finding that the relationship is weak may be because most attempts to look at the relationship have been done at the individual, rather than the organizational, level. As a result, individual differences may mask the overall effect on the organization.

Another factor that is consistently and negatively correlated to job satisfaction is turnover (Carsten and Spector, 1987). It is not surprising that if people do not like their job, they will seek out alternate employment. However, finding another job is complicated by external environmental factors such as the level of unemployment in society and length of time on the job (Spencer and Steers, 1981). Another complicating factor is that high performers tend to be rewarded and, hence, derive satisfaction from the job, while low performers tend to be ignored or even encouraged to leave the organization. Consequently, job satisfaction is more important in influencing poor performers than top performers to stay with the organization (Judge, 1993). There is some indication that job satisfaction may be a very individual phenomenon, so the belief that it is possible to satisfy everyone's needs at the same time and in the same way may be optimistic at best.

Several studies have explored the affect of intrinsic and extrinsic motivation on job satisfaction in professional groups. For public child-welfare supervisors, five factors accounted for almost half of the effectiveness of reward systems. These factors were the length of time in their current position, emotional exhaustion, race, the amount of time spent collaborating with other professionals, and organizational climate (Silver, Poulin, and Manning, 1997). In the field of education, university teachers who are intrinsically motivated to learn are more likely to have students who respond to intrinsic rewards (Csikszentmihalyi, 1997). And while teaching in medical school, doctors tend to appreciate more the intangible rewards, such as the intrinsic rewards of teaching and professional support. While monetary rewards are important, they appear to be secondary in importance to intrinsic rewards (Sickler, Buschmann, and Seim, 1996).

Another approach looks at the relationship between situational factors and job satisfaction. Even though someone may have an excellent job in terms of salary, benefits, and security, he or she still may have a low level of job satisfaction. Moreover, two individuals doing the same job, or the same individual over a period of time, may experience quite different levels of job satisfaction. Job satisfaction can be predicted from both situational characteristics and occurrences, but situational occurrences are more likely to predict job satisfaction. Individual needs, while important, can be influenced by situational factors independent of individual differences. The level of job satisfaction has also been linked to productivity. Greater productivity implies that many nonmaterial costs will remain the same while output will increase. Greater output while maintaining or lowering most fixed costs should result in greater profits (Quarstein, McAffee, and Glassman, 1992).

Some researchers have explained the difference in job satisfaction based on gender by referring to intrinsic and extrinsic rewards, work values, and job level. A number of researchers have suggested that such intrinsic rewards as autonomy (Hodson, 1989), such extrinsic rewards as compensation (Lambert, 1991) and promotion (Hodson, 1989), work values (Lambert, 1991), and job level (Mottaz and Potts, 1986) are the primary variables that differ by gender in job satisfaction.

Some scholars have proposed three categories of variables that "substitute" for leadership in providing job satisfaction. The use of substitutes means that the leader's behavior may be redundant. The three categories of substitutes for hierarchical leadership are the personal characteristics of the individual subordinate, the task to be done by the subordinate, and the organizational characteristics. The characteristics-of-subordinate substitutes include the subordinate's abilities, experience, training, and knowledge, as well as the subordinate's need for independence, professional orientation, and indifference toward organizational rewards. Task characteristics include routine tasks, methodological-invariant tasks, intrinsically satisfying tasks, and task feedback. Organizational characteristics refer to organization formalization, inflexibility of rules, workgroup cohesiveness, amount of staff and advisory support, organizational rewards not controlled by the manager, and the degree of spatial distance between supervisors and their subordinates. A manager's behavior or style can influence the subordinate's job satisfaction (Kerr and Jermier, 1978).

Organizational research has identified a variety of work-related perceptions and attitudes that may affect job satisfaction. For example, supportive supervision is related to increased job satisfaction, and other supportive aspects of the work environment may also result in higher levels of job satisfaction (Babin and Boles, 1998). Role stress, on the other hand, is negatively related to job satisfaction (Noor, 2002). In fact, role conflict, role ambiguity, and how managers handle the conflicts may be the most important predictors of job satisfaction in many work settings.

Job Satisfaction in Other Cultures

Workers in different countries have different levels of job satisfaction. The International Social Survey program recently reported the results for twenty-one countries, most of which are in Europe with the exception of New Zealand, the United States, Israel, and Japan. Employees in Denmark were the most satisfied, followed by employees from Cyprus, Switzerland, and Israel. The employees with the lowest level of job satisfaction were from Hungary, with Russia and Japan close behind. The United States ranked seventh out of twenty-one, New Zealand ranked eighth, and the United Kingdom ranked fourteenth (Sousa-Poza and Sousa-Poza, 2000).

Job satisfaction, intent to stay, and evaluation of the supervisor are aspects of motivation that can be influenced by employee judgments about distributive justice (the perceived degree of fairness in distributing organizational rewards and resources) and procedural justice (the degree of fairness of the procedures used for distribution) (Spector, 1997). Intrinsic job rewards have been shown to affect job satisfaction both at the national level and when intracultural differences are taken into consideration, leading the researchers of this study to conclude that consensus on values and the values themselves are the keys to effectiveness and high job satisfaction in multinational organizations (Huang and Van de Vliert, 2002).

Employees' perceptions of organizational justice have a strong effect on their evaluation of the organization and authority within that organization. Differences in the effects of distributive and procedural justice were found between samples from Hong Kong and the United States (Fields, Pang, and Chiu, 2000). For Americans, procedural justice has been found to affect the relationship of distributive justice with evaluation of supervision but not with job satisfaction or intent to stay. The opposite was found in the Hong Kong sample, with procedural justice influencing the effects of distributive justice on job satisfaction and intent to stay but not on the evaluation of supervision. Paying more attention to fairness in the treatment of employees in Hong Kong would thus probably increase job loyalty and employee satisfaction. However, in the United States, fairness in reward allocation (distributive justice) has the most positive effect on employees.

Distributive-justice values have important implications for the perception of the legitimacy of reward systems. In transitional economies and societies, such as Russia and China (PRC), that are moving toward a free-market economy, the effective modification of pay and other reward practices may be essential to a successful conversion. In a comparison of American, Russian, and Chinese managers' distributive-justice values, Russian managers reported similar values to American managers whereas the Chinese managers did not. In addition, the research compared the responses of managers in either joint ventures or state-owned enterprises and found that the Russian managers in the two types of organizations had different values and that in the joint ventures the Russians demonstrated values closer to American values. Differences between Chinese managers in the two types of organizations were small. The results suggest that in China culture has a dominating influence on distributive-justice values, whereas in Russia managerial values are more influenced by exposure to joint-venture values (Giacobbe-Miller, Miller, Zhang, and Victorov, 2003). The researchers also suggest that Russians may be more receptive to change than the Chinese.

The national culture can determine gender inequality and, thereby, gender differences in job satisfaction. The Confucian heritage has favored the man at the expense of the woman, who is expected to take a subservient role (Zhu, 1991). As a result, Taiwanese students are more approving of patriarchal values than are American students (Szalay, Strohl, Fu, and Lao, 1994). A consideration of the impact of women-friendly polices in Hong Kong notes that while such policies are unusual in Hong Kong, where they exist they have a positive effect on the organizational commitment of both men and women (Chiu and Ng, 1999).

Organizational Commitment

Organizational commitment is closely related to job satisfaction. While there are several ways to define organizational commitment, all of the definitions include the attachment of the individual to the organization. A meta-analysis of numerous studies of organizational commitment suggests that it may in fact be a collection of elements that need to be studied in a broader context (Eby, Freeman, Rush, and Lance, 1999). However, organizational commitment is generally considered to include three broad components: an acceptance of the organization's goals, a willingness to work hard for the organization, and a desire to remain with the organization (Steers and Porter, 1979). The Organizational Commitment Questionnaire (OCQ), devised by L. W. Porter, R. M. Steers, R. T. Mowbay, and P. V. Boulian (1974), is the primary instrument used in the research on organizational commitment. It is considered a valid and reliable instrument and has helped to ensure equivalency of measures of the concept of organizational commitment in a wide variety of situations. In addition, the instrument has been translated into Japanese, and research conducted with it has produced results supporting its cross-cultural applicability, at least to Japan (White, Parks, McLean, and Gallagher, 1995).

Organizational citizenship, as a component of commitment, may result from employees' perceptions of their obligations to organizations and the degree to which those obligations are reciprocated, rather than resulting from attachment, loyalty, or satisfaction. Obligations and their fulfillment may underlie organizational commitment. Managers could, therefore, usefully pay more attention to managing beliefs regarding mutual obligations and endeavor to understand employees' perceptions of mutual obligations (Robinson, Kraatz, and Rousseau, 1994). Related to the concept of obligations is the issue of loyalty (James and Cropanzano, 1994). Group loyalty seems to be predictive of involvement in group-based activities, positiveness in attitudes toward an organization, and an inclination to perform behaviors for the benefit of one's own organization.

The issues of job involvement and organizational commitment have also been examined from the perspective of financial need (Gould and Werbel, 1983). The burden of meeting financial needs in single-wage-earner families usually rests with the wage earner, whereas among dual-career couples it is usually shared by both partners. Because financial rewards are obtained through greater job involvement and organizational commitment, it is reasonable to expect that the added pressure leads the single wage earner to experience a higher degree of job involvement and higher levels of organizational commitment than individuals in dual-wage-earner families.

A study involving undergraduates participating in a production-like setting examined group members' commitment levels in relation to conflict of interest and to equity and norms in groups. In evaluating contribution of effort to individual and group tasks, the researchers found that individual contributions (i.e., the level of commitment) to the group task increased over time and that free riders increased their contributions to the group task on receiving feedback from group members about their contribution levels. In fact, mean resource contributions to the group task in the study increased some 27 percent over the course of the resource-contribution trials. These findings suggest that norms of equity can develop in groups and that these norms can serve to enhance overall organizational performance. Credible commitment among team members can be enhanced by incentive structures that appropriately reward group, instead of individual, efforts. In this way, individuals in a team are more likely to develop mutual expectations and norms that facilitate cooperation within the team. Accordingly, "Given the importance of work groups for productivity in organizations, the need to have employees expend time and effort on group work is evident" (Sniezek and May, 1990, p. 1150).

The increase in two-earner families has meant that families have had to change their priorities and make accommodations to the reality of their personal situation. Accommodation refers to an individual's conscious decision to subordinate work demands to family demands. Accommodation is, thus, inversely related to work involvement and organizational commitment. A person who is highly involved in his or her job and is highly committed to the organization is likely to be low in accommodation. Likewise, a person who gives a higher priority to the family than to the job is likely to be high in accommodation (Schein, 1978). Accommodation has been identified as an important variable in the process of adjustment for dual-wage-earner couples who desire to maintain a satisfying quality of life (Bailyn, 1970). Consequently, a dual-career family, in which responsibilities are more likely to be shared, may have a greater tendency to accommodation than a single-income family, in which household responsibilities usually are fulfilled by the non-wage-earning spouse.

Similarly, dual-wage-earner families are likely to have lower job involvement and organizational commitment than single-wage-earner families.

Dual-career couples also experience increased levels of internal conflict. In one study, 34 percent of employed husbands and 37 percent of employed wives reported that their jobs and families interfered with each other. Having children in the home generates added pressure on dual-income families to share parenting responsibilities because the time required to provide child care must be added to both work schedules. This situation is less of a problem in single-income families, in which primary child-care responsibilities are usually vested in the non-income-producing spouse. Consequently, another aspect that warrants examination is the family status of the dual-wage-earner couple (i.e., whether they have children), because the demands for accommodation are presumably greater for couples with children than for those without (Pleck, Staines, and Lang, 1980). We would expect childless couples to have higher levels of job involvement and organizational commitment than couples with children.

Organizational-Commitment Research in Other Cultures

National culture and values may also play a role in the level of organizational commitment. A study conducted in Thailand that looked at issues of customer satisfaction (Tansuhaj, Wong, and McCullough, 1987) raises some interesting questions about how national culture affects organizations. While not a direct study of organizational commitment, this study did look at organizational issues that influence employees' behavior and how that behavior affects customer service. Organizations with better internal marketing practices, which satisfy the employees, also receive higher ratings of customer satisfaction. The researchers contrast the performance of domestic and foreign-owned banks, noting that cultural differences do affect performance and job satisfaction.

A study of Japanese employees in manufacturing firms found that the concept of organizational commitment could be viewed as a multidimensional construct that applied in Japan as well as in the United States. Annual "quit" rates were used as a measure of commitment and compared with two components of organizational commitment, attachment and identification, in Japanese and American plants (Lincoln and Kalleberg, 1996). The results of the study yielded several distinct differences between the American and Japanese samples. For example, quality circles in the United States, but not in Japan, were more likely to lead to greater commitment attitudes for both attachment and identification. On the other hand, on-the-job training had a positive effect on commitment in Japan but a negative effect on commitment in the United States.

Low organizational commitment is a major problem in the PRC, since turnover rates are very high and organizational commitment is very low. This has many implications for managing employees in the PRC, particularly for organizations owned by non-Chinese companies and joint ventures. The shortage of middle-level managers has meant that well-trained and competent managers are often aggressively recruited by other companies. Production-level workers attracted from rural areas to enterprise zones often return to their families after they have acquired reasonable savings. In Chinese samples from the PRC and Hong Kong, job satisfaction does not predict organizational commitment, as it does in Western organizations. In fact, the reverse is true for Chinese workers. That is, organizational commitment is more likely to predict job satisfaction and turnover intention (Wong, Hui, Wong, and Law, 2001). The researchers of this study believe that these effects are caused by the traditional cultural value of loyalty and that organizations operating in Chinese societies need to build positive long-term relationships with their employees.

A test of organizational commitment (Meyer and Allen, 1991) was conducted in South Korea to specifically test the applicability and value of the model in a non-Western country (Lee, Allen, Meyer, and Rhee, 2001). However, there were difficulties in applying instruments developed in the United States to Korea, and questionnaire items did not generalize across cultures. This finding is reinforced by the results of studies conducted in Belgium (Vandenberghe, 1996) and in Turkey (Wasti, 1999). Despite problems with ensuring the effective measurement of organizational commitment, the three organizational-commitment constructs, affective, continuance, and normative commitment, appear to be conceptually and functionally similar in both the United States and Korea.

Job and work involvement are two distinct constructs and, therefore, should be measured with different instruments (Kanungo, 1982). The relationship between job involvement, single- or dual-career status, and family status of an Australian sample population was examined in a study that incorporated these distinctions. The results were mixed. Research participants from dual-career families were found to be less involved in their jobs than participants from single-career families, but no relationship was found between job involvement and family status (Elloy and Suseno, 1987).

Organizational Citizenship Behavior

For the past several decades, other highly related constructs including organizational citizenship behavior (OCB) have been investigated by organizational researchers (e.g., Bateman and Organ, 1983). Specifically, motivation levels of employees can be measured indirectly by considering the concept of OCB. OCB has many similar characteristics to intrinsic motivation (Smith, Organ, and Near, 1983), and interest in the concept is on the rise (Farh, Podsakoff, and Organ, 1990). There are two distinct types of OCB. One is called *altruism,* which includes helping behaviors aimed directly at specific people (MacKenzie, Podsakoff, and Fetter, 1991). The other is *generalized compliance (conscientiousness),* which is defined by a more impersonal sort of conscientiousness and by doing things that are right and appropriate for the sake of the system rather than people. Thus, OCB has an impact on the perceptions of managers and subordinates about their job roles (Onedo, 1991).

OCB holds great promise for organizational-behavior research and should be explored in other cultures, since OCB and intrinsic motivation may be culture specific. OCB "represents individual behavior that is discretionary, not directly or explicitly recognized by the formal reward system, and in the aggregate promotes the efficient and effective functioning of the organization" (Organ, 1988, p. 4). The practical importance of OCB is that behaviors improve efficiency and effectiveness in both public and private organizations.

One study investigated how OCB affects managerial perspectives from the point of view of both supervisors and subordinates in the United States, Japan, Australia, and Hong Kong. As might be expected, employees from different countries tend to view the emic (culturally specific) aspects of OCB differently but view the etic (universal) aspects of OCB similarly. The study concludes that some performance norms transcend cultural values while others reflect cultural norms. Subjects from Hong Kong and Japan were more likely to see the courtesy and sportsmanship categories of OCB as part of their job than subjects sampled in the United States and Australia (Lam, Hui, and Law, 1999).

An unusual cross-cultural, public-sector research project compared samples from the United States and the Middle East. Looking at OCB and intrinsic and extrinsic motivation, the researchers found that organization-based self-esteem predicted altruism and compliance in both samples, whereas individual self-esteem only predicted altruism and compliance in the Middle Eastern sample. It was concluded that organization-based self-esteem is correlated with OCB. Further, intrinsic job satisfaction was positively related and extrinsic job satisfaction was negatively related to altruism. In addition, the employees in the American sample appeared to see their jobs as more challenging and interesting and had a lower work ethic and higher individual self-esteem than their Middle Eastern counterparts (Tang and Ibrahim, 1998).

Counterproductive Behaviors

Several factors have been identified that have an impact on employee withdrawal and result in counterproductive behaviors. They include the perception of fairness or organizational justice, absenteeism, turnover, and other behaviors such as aggression and sabotage. Trust between the employee and the organization is also important to employee behavior and how the organization's behaviors are perceived. For example, low-trust employees are more likely to question the fairness of organizational actions. The impact of these counterproductive behaviors and some strategies to offset that impact is discussed next.

Organizational Justice

An area of research that is closely related to organizational commitment and one that can affect the level of counterproductive behaviors is organizational justice. Organizational justice is made up of three components: distributive justice (fair decision outcomes), procedural justice (fair formal decision-making procedures), and interactional justice (fair interpersonal treatment by decision makers) (Colquitt et al., 2001). A study was conducted comparing employees from the United States and Bangladesh, on the basis of both organizational justice and organization-directed reactions (Rahim, Magner, Antonioni, and Rahman, 2001). The organization-directed reactions studied were organizational commitment and turnover intention. The results indicate that the organization-directed reactions are related to all three types of organizational justice, so that a positive perception of organizational justice results in higher organizational commitment and lower turnover intentions.

Absenteeism

Poor motivation can be manifested as high absenteeism rates, since if workers are not motivated, they are more likely to miss work and leave their jobs. In the United States, the latest figures indicate that between 1.7 and 2.1 percent of workers are absent from work on any given day, at a cost to employers of $789 per employee each year (Reed, 2003). Measures of absenteeism and sick days taken in other countries are difficult to use in a comparative way because not all countries give their workers the same number of sick days, family leave days, or vacation days. In the United States, workers use an average of 6.2 sick days out of an allowable 7.6 sick days (Commerce Clearing House, 2002). The typical worker in the United Kingdom misses an average of 7.8 days; in Canada, an average of 8 days; in Ireland, an average of 8.7 days; in Sweden, an average of 32 days; and in the Netherlands and Norway, an average of 20 days (Karaian, 2002). In the United States, the majority of sick days (67 percent) are taken for reasons other than employee illness. These reasons include employee stress, personal needs, family issues, a sense of entitlement, or for other reasons such as bad weather or transportation problems (Commerce Clearing House, 2002). Family issues may not be as important in countries where family-leave policies are very generous. For example, the Family Medical Leave Act in the United States permits a minimum of 12 weeks unpaid leave to attend to a variety of family matters. However, legally mandated unpaid-leave allowances under similar circumstances are 15 weeks in Belgium, 120 days in Brazil, between 17 and 70 weeks in Canada, depending on the province where you work, and 12 weeks in Mexico. Other countries are even more generous, such as the United Kingdom, where workers with less than 26 weeks on the job get 18 weeks of unpaid leave; with 26 to 52 weeks on the job, they get 18 weeks of paid leave; and if they have been on the job for more than a year, they are entitled to 40 weeks of leave. Most member countries in the European Union receive 14 weeks of paid leave. These divergent policies will obviously have an impact on both planned and unplanned absenteeism rates. Managers need to be aware that cultural values, personnel policies, and even weather will affect differences in absenteeism rates in different cultures.

Organizational Socialization

Organizations can develop better employees if steps are taken to socialize them to the values and goals of the organization, in much the same way as children need to learn socialization skills as they grew up in order to function better in society. These steps typically include orientations and discussions about responsibilities, duties, and expectations about the job. They may also include an orientation to the organization's culture and, for multinational companies, an orientation to the appropriate national-culture issues and values. Effective ways to implement the socialization process include paying attention to the person-organization fit and mentoring.

Person-Organization Fit

Given that the major expense for most organizations is labor costs, any steps that can be taken to reduce these costs will generally be beneficial to the company. While downsizing and automation can reduce labor costs, these approaches have their own new expenses, which can result in no overall net savings. Often, cost savings can be achieved by working with what already exists within the organization. For example, increasing productivity and/or a reduction in employee turnover will result in lower costs. Research has indicated that the quality of the fit between an individual and the organization is related to both productivity and employee turnover. The most recent empirical study I am aware of, conducted in the United States over twenty years ago, found that the costs of employee turnover ranged from the lowest amount, for a clerical employee, of in excess of $2,500. The highest amount, for a pilot, was in excess of $100,000 (Mobley, 1982). Given the rate of inflation in the United States between 1982 and today, it is not unreasonable to estimate that these costs now range from a low end of $7,000 to a high end of around $300,000. In fact, more recently, the Knight Ridder/Tribune News Service reported the results of an employee and customer survey conducted by the Hay Consulting Group (Stafford, 2001), which concluded that the average attrition costs are eighteen months' worth of salary for each manager or professional who leaves and six months' pay for each hourly worker who departs. So, if an organization has five thousand employees earning an average of $35,000 and standard annual attrition rates (14 percent for clerical workers, 12.5 percent for professionals, and 5.5 percent for managers), costs will be more than $20 million per year. In some occupations, turnover costs can be even higher. For example, the Meta Consulting Group found information-technology recruiting costs, interview and training investment, lost salaries, benefits, and tax payments can easily cost a company $100,000 per senior IT employee who leaves within 180 days of joining the company (Brown, 2000). While these estimates are for typical employee salaries and responsibilities averaged across organizations, the loss of key employees has even greater financial costs. The larger the organization, the greater the number of employees and the greater the potential costs from employee turnover will be. Clearly the costs related to turnover are significant and are often underestimated or ignored within organizations. Ensuring that the person-organization (P-O) fit is good will help to reduce turnover and increase employee productivity.

An organization needs to develop its human potential because employees are often the biggest investment and resource in an organization. Employees have needs that they want the organization to satisfy. At the same time, the organization has goals and needs that have to be met if it is to function effectively and prosper. In an effective organization, the needs of employees are successfully meshed with the organization's goals (Reilly, 1974). Being able to identify the individual and organizational needs and the relationship between them is a key issue for organizations. Several definitions of P-O fit exist, but they can be considered to fall into one of two general categories (O'Reilly, Chatman, and Caldwell, 1991). One approach is to look at the level at which the organization satisfies employees' needs and preferences (Cable and Judge, 1994). The other approach compares individual characteristics, such as personality and values, with organizational characteristics, such as culture and climate (Turban and Keon, 1993). Personality characteristics in particular may play an important role in long-term employment decisions (Cable and Judge, 1994).

The concept of the psychological contract has been proposed to explain how the organizational and individual needs mesh. The psychological contract, a set of unwritten rules that are generally understood by both management and employees, is based on creating a good fit between the person and the organization. It sets out the mutual expectations of the management (representing the organization) and the employees. The contract establishes how every individual within the organization is expected to behave (Reilly, 1974).

The concept of the psychological contract is both perceptual and individual (Rousseau and Parks, 1992). The individual nature of the psychological contract and the fact that it is based more on perceptions of reality than the actual reality make it different from all other forms of contracts, and the ambiguous and unwritten nature of the psychological contract makes any evaluation of it difficult. The psychological contract extends the concept of loyalty and commitment to the organization and uniquely focuses on both the employee and the employer (Rousseau and Parks, 1992), and it forms the basis of the P-O fit. The organization's corporate culture provides the framework within which the psychological contract must be implemented (Robinson, Kraatz, and Rousseau, 1994). A failure by either the individual or the organization to behave as the other party expects results in negative consequences for both the organization and the employee by negatively affecting morale, performance, and organizational productivity.

Both the employer and the employee share in the responsibility for successful implementation of the contract. In this way, the contract emphasizes the reciprocal and interdependent nature of the relationship between organization and employee. However, if middle managers are more concerned with their own needs than with honoring the psychological contract, an adverse impact on lower-level employees will occur (Hallier and James, 1997).

A recent paper included a model to help explain why problems occur in the fit between individuals and organizations. Usually, individuals feel betrayed and angry when they come to believe that the organization has not met one or more of the obligations that were expected of them. A previously good fit can become broken for a variety of reasons including a change in leadership, downsizing, and mergers and acquisitions. Given the changing work environment, the fit between the person and the organization may be less permanent than earlier researchers have believed (Morrison and Robinson, 1997). The relationship between organizational values and individual effectiveness has been investigated, using four different measures, and some relationships were found. The primary goal of this research was to look at different models and techniques of predicting a relationship between organizational values and individual effectiveness. The results found positive relationships between organizational values and individual effectiveness (Cheng, 1993).

The changing work environment has led to a move toward more employee independence and a redefinition of the psychological contract (Hall and Moss, 1998). A rapidly changing work environment requires adjustments in both the implementation of the psychological contract and human resource management (McBain, 1997). A comprehensive diagnosis of the organization is important if the organization is to understand why employees leave. Individual characteristics and an assessment of the manager responsible for any new employee are critical in adequately measuring the degree of fit between the applicant and the organization (Levinson, 1994). Possible strategies include improving selection procedures to ensure that new employees are appropriate for the organization, building organizational structures that integrate issues related to individual needs, ensuring that management is in tune with the needs of employees, and ensuring that employees are aware of the organization's needs. All this must be done in the context of the organizational culture. Therefore, greater awareness of the organizational culture by all members of the organization may be essential if the benefits of the P-O fit are to be maximized.

An organization is not a passive or stable institution. It evolves and grows but does so in the internal environment of the organizational culture. The process by which an individual learns to perform in an organization has been called *socialization* and involves individuals coming to appreciate the values, the expected behaviors, and social knowledge that are essential for assuming an organizational role and performing in the organization (Schein, 1980). Since the organizational culture serves many purposes including establishing the norms for employees' behavior, it can be expected that the culture will have an impact on the P-O fit. In trying to improve the effectiveness of the organization, companies look to engage the employees more in the organization. This can be done in one of at least two ways (Hawk, 1995). The organization can change the reward system or change the organizational culture. Companies often debate between these two approaches, since they are seen as independent of each other. The company may think it can only do one or the other, though studies have suggested that it is necessary for companies to change both the reward system and the organizational culture at the same time. As discussed earlier, the idea of organizational or corporate culture has been identified as an important aspect in the study of organizational behavior and has recently become more prominent as a concept that is useful in helping to understand how organizations function (O'Reilly, 1989). In addition, organizational culture may be an important factor in determining how well an individual fits within a particular organization (Kilmann, Saxton, and Serpa, 1985).

Tests of the Person-Organization Fit Concept in Other Cultures

While the application of the ideas discussed so far has been limited primarily to Western and, in particular, American organizations, there is some work that has looked at other cultures. Since organizational culture is developed through an interaction of national culture and ideology, it is reasonable to believe that there is theoretical and practical support for considering P-O fit in an international context (Valentine, 2000). One study examined organizational cultures across several national cultures. The researchers found that individuals' values and organizational practices needed to be integrated. Moreover, demographic variables, such as age and gender, could affect the P-O fit (Hofstede, Bond, and Luk, 1993). When the relative importance of work values was examined and the structure in eight different countries was analyzed, there were some cultural differences in the ratings of some values. But, overall, it was concluded that these differences were actually relatively small in the context of organizational-structure differences (Elizur, Borg, Hunt, and Beck, 1991).

One test of issues related to P-O fit in the PRC focused on assessing the attractiveness of firms to potential employees based on factors such as type of ownership, nationality of the supervisor, and firm familiarity (Turban et al., 2001). The switch to allowing a more free-market system and the increase in foreign-invested enterprises in the PRC has meant that employees, particularly recent university graduates, now have much more choice in the job they choose (Ding, Fields, and Akhtar, 1997). In fact, P-O fit has been found to influence job-search decisions, and pay and other rewards play an important role in helping employees to assess their fit with the organization (Judge and Cable, 1997). The type of company ownership influences perceptions of working conditions, so that foreign firms tend to be preferred to state-owned companies. However, individual differences occur when aversion to risk is considered, so that individuals with a low aversion to risk prefer foreign-owned companies

and individuals with a high aversion to risk prefer state-owned companies. Firms that are more familiar to the employee are also found to be
more enticing. People are attracted to familiar and foreign-owned companies because they perceive the P-O fit to be a good one, especially for
those willing to take a risk. Turnover in these types of business is high, so
perhaps the initial perception of a good fit does not work in the day-to-
day reality (Goodall and Burgers, 1998). Foreign firms might usefully attempt to become more familiar to potential Chinese employees by generating more contact with them and using strategies such as on-campus recruiting to achieve this. Overall, it seems that the concept of P-O fit can
be successfully used in a non-Western setting such as the PRC.

The same is true in Japan, based on the results of a comprehensive review of studies conducted in Japanese companies. The organization of
work in Japan reflects the social structure of the society, and, therefore,
the workplace is a major source of an individual's identity, making the P-
O fit very important (Smith, 1984). Certainly, Japanese companies have
been reluctant to hire non-Japanese nationals at the highest executive levels, resulting in an ethnocentric approach to management. This has
caused problems for such organizations, particularly in the United States
where affirmative-action laws are enforced (Beamish and Inkpen, 1998).

A study of senior Chinese executives in Hong Kong, Taiwan, Singapore, and Indonesia found that the cultures had different managerial values. Management practices in mainland China are different from those
found in Taiwan and Hong Kong because the culture in the PRC still relies on authority figures to establish order and resolve disputes (Redding,
1990). The emphasis on individual standing, respect from others, and
building close relationships in Chinese cultures means that Chinese employees prefer an organizational environment that encourages professional relationships and recognition (Sergeant and Frenkel, 1998).

The P-O fit and its impact on job satisfaction and organizational culture and commitment have been studied in Taiwan (Silverthorne, 2003a).
The results indicate that the P-O fit is a key element in both the level of
job satisfaction that employees experience and in their level of organizational commitment, as either directly measured or as reflected in employee turnover, regardless of the organizational culture. The better the
fit, the higher the level of organizational commitment and job satisfaction
reported by employees.

In Mexico, the preservation of respect is important, which in turn
influences how managers manage (Moran and Abbott, 1994). In addi-

tion, the allocentric or other-centered nature of Mexican culture means that individuals in Mexico tend to be less risk taking, individualistic, and competitive than many other cultures.

Poles tend to be fatalistic and avoid or diminish the value of various deterministic management practices such as total quality management, which is a philosophy of management driven by the goal of attaining continuous improvement of all organizational practices in order to ensure high levels of customer satisfaction (Roney, 1997). As a result, Poles lack the motivation and goal orientation to be entrepreneurial, resulting in a negative impact on business development and entrepreneurship (Sood and Mroczkowski, 1994).

The P-O fit is clearly influenced by the national culture of an organization, and a better understanding of the impact of cultures on fit is necessary as organizations move into new and different cultures. This is an area where additional research is urgently needed.

Mentoring

In general, the research on mentoring has shown a broad range of positive outcomes, and the value for both the mentor and the protégé has been established. One additional benefit for the organization is that a person who had been mentored or who had been someone else's protégé is more likely to become a mentor later in his or her career (Ragins and Cotton, 1993). Some research has found that all types of past mentoring experiences (as a protégé, mentor, or both) are positively related to a willingness to mentor others (Allen, Poteet, Russell, and Dobbins, 1997). Other research has suggested that current mentors are more willing to serve as mentors in the future, whereas current protégés are less willing to become mentors. Mentoring has both long- and short-term positive benefits for both the organization and the individuals involved (Olian, Carroll, and Giannantonio, 1993). Mentoring also enhances work effectiveness (Kram, 1985) and job success (Fagenson, 1989). However, there have been very few empirical studies that have looked at the relationship between mentoring and career mobility and outcomes, particularly in multinational companies.

Two dimensions of the mentoring process that affect careers are vocational (career coaching) and psychosocial (social support) (Kram, 1985). Very little empirical research currently exists in which career outcomes and mentoring experiences are linked. Most research has focused on the nature of the mentoring process. This research has found that mentors provide multiple forms of career and psychological support. Career functions include providing the protégé with coaching, protection, challenging assignments, exposure and visibility, and direct forms of sponsorship. Psychosocial functions include serving as a role model, friend, and counselor, and providing positive regard and acceptance (Kram and Isabella, 1985). The mentoring system provides a special form of entry into social networks. Social networks in organizations are part of the informal communication system of an organization and represent a source of valuable information and resources that may not be generally available. Entry into social networks allows individuals to develop alliances and coalitions by being visible to the upper-level decision makers. Based on research findings, there is ample evidence to indicate that successful mentoring relationships in organizations are beneficial both to the organization and those individuals who are involved in the mentoring process as either mentors or protégés.

One situational factor that has received some attention, as it relates to mentoring, is the role of the organizational reward system. "A reward system that emphasizes bottom-line results and does not place a high priority on human resource development objectives creates conditions to discourage mentoring" (Kram, 1985, p. 16). If experienced managers are to take on a mentoring role, they should be reinforced or rewarded for doing so. Employee development should be linked to the performance-appraisal system, and mentoring should be rewarded as part of this process (Posner, Hall, and Harder, 1986). In job satisfaction and related variables, mentoring has also been shown to have a positive effect. Organizational satisfaction (Chao, Walz, and Gardner, 1992), career commitment (Bachman and Gregory, 1993), and turnover intentions (Scandura and Viator, 1994) were all positively affected by a good mentoring relationship in organizations. The evidence suggests that mentoring enhances work effectiveness (Kram, 1985) and job success (Fagenson, 1989). In addition, mentoring can be very beneficial to expatriate managers both before and during overseas assignments.

While mentoring might be considered a very Western approach to supporting younger and newer employees, in other cultures mentoring also occurs but may be labeled differently. The Western mentoring process almost implies a specific and official system. In Eastern and Arabic cultures, the father-figure role is common, and mentoring can in fact evolve from this organizational framework in a much more subtle and unofficial way.

The number of research studies that look at mentoring across cultures is limited. One of the exceptions is a study of early-career-stage mentoring of Hong Kong Chinese employees (Aryee, Lo, and Kang, 1999). The researchers compared the relationship between personality, situational characteristics, and protégé-initiated mentoring. Specifically, the personality characteristics of extraversion and Type A personality influenced protégé-initiated mentoring. In other words, ambitious or driven individuals were more likely to seek support from more senior members of the organization. Other results from this study supported the notion that the developmental nature of the organization influences the willingness of experienced managers to undertake a mentoring role and that a strong individual and developmental organizational culture is most likely to foster mentoring behavior. In a study of Singaporean managerial motivation to mentor, the personality characteristics of altruism and positive affectivity (a positive outlook on life), as well as the organizational characteristics of an employee-development-linked reward system and the opportunity to interact with others, were all found to be positively associated with a willingness to mentor others (Aryee, Chay, and Chew, 1996). However, the results of these two studies appear to offer limited insight into any specific cultural differences or similarities in mentoring behavior.

Summary

High job satisfaction and organizational commitment will generally lead to higher productivity and better employee performance. Research in the United States and in other cultures suggests that this effect is universal but that there may be cultural differences in the things that help ensure higher job satisfaction and commitment. Since job satisfaction is closely related to motivation and individual needs, it is not surprising that individuals in different cultures have different need priorities, resulting in different responses to the organization's desire to provide job satisfaction.

One way to integrate potential differences between individual and organizational needs is to use strategies that maximize the person-organization fit. A better fit between the organization and the individual will result in higher levels of job satisfaction and lower levels of employee stress and turnover. This is not a one-way process, however. While the recruitment and selection process can find people that best fit the needs of the organization and the needs of the individual, the organization should also be open to change. Failure to change may result in not being able to hire the best people, and for multinational companies, it may imply a lack of sensitivity to local concerns.

Mentoring of employees is important within many American organizations. The same is not true in other countries, and the values associated with helping newer or younger employees vary across cultures. However, while mentoring tends to be formalized in the United States, it may exist in more-subtle forms in other cultures. For example, the role of the father figure in Eastern and Arabic cultures serves many of the same functions but in a less formal way.

11

Conflict and Power

Conflict

Breakdowns in communication are a leading cause of conflict, and good communication skills are important to effective conflict resolution and negotiations. Whether or not conflict within an organization is viewed as desirable, the fact is that conflict exists and is endemic. As human beings interact in organizations, differing values and situations create tension. When conflict is recognized, acknowledged, and managed in a proper manner, personal and organizational benefits will result. A caring, effective manager uses conflict as an opportunity for growth both for segments of the organization and for the individuals involved. Effective managers use conflict creatively to stimulate personal development, to address apparent problems, to increase critical vigilance and self-appraisal, and to examine conflicting values when making decisions (Rahim, 2001). Conflict management recognizes that while conflict does have associated costs, it can also bring with it great benefits. Even though some managers see conflict as something that should be avoided at all costs, others see conflict as presenting exciting possibilities if managed in a positive, constructive fashion (Darling and Fogliasso, 1999). Today's effective manager seeks not to avoid but to manage conflict within the organization (Rahim, Antonioni, and Psenicka, 2001).

Conflict means there are differences of opinion, and so alternatives need to be considered and opposing points of view studied. When conflict signals these activities, it is often seen as a sign of a very good organization (Hellriegel, Slocum, and Woodman, 1995). If the organization develops the coping skills necessary to survive in its environment, it will change and thrive. Adaptation, accommodation, and flexibility are the keys to organizational survival in such a situation. Conflict can lead to change, change can lead to adaptation, and adaptation can lead to survival and even prosperity (Walton, 1987).

While managers have historically seen their role as being to keep the peace at all costs, more-enlightened managers see conflict as an indication that something needs their attention (Rahim, Magner, and Shapiro, 2000). Just as an individual's physical discomfort may signal a more serious medical problem that needs attention, conflict may signal a potentially serious (or developing) situation for the organization. The challenge of dealing positively with conflict is also the challenge of using effective teamwork, and team leadership is critical for successful conflict resolution. Organizations expect their employees to be productive. Organizational goals based on specific outcomes that focus on employees' behavior are associated with a concern for meeting production goals, because they represent what to do, what decisions to make, where to go, how to allocate resources, and so forth (Wilmot and Hocker, 2001). As a result, conflict based on the production process is focused on how effective, rather than how appropriate, the process is. In general, U.S. firms appear to experience substantial conflict within and between functional areas (Hall, 1991). Also, cultural differences within and between organizations can create conflict, and failure to respond effectively will usually result in even more conflict.

What Is Conflict?

It is important to begin an exploration of conflict management by examining the concept of conflict. Some definitions suggest that conflict exists where there are real or perceived differences that arise in specific circumstances and that engender emotion (Kolb and Putnam, 1992). Others have focused more narrowly on the phenomena associated with competitive intentions, such as the deliberate interference with the goals of others (Thomas, 1992). Conflict in the workplace can be normal and healthy. A workplace devoid of tensions is ultimately dull and stagnant and unlikely to foster creativity and growth.

Conflict occurs due to a variety of factors. Individual differences in goals, expectations, values, proposed courses of action, and suggestions about how to best handle a situation are unavoidable. When we add to these differences concerns about changes in the business's internal and external environments, conflict often increases (Bolman and Deal, 1997). Changes in technology, global shifting of power, political unrest, and financial uncertainties all contribute to the creation of conflict.

Currently no one definition of conflict predominates (Van de Vliert and Kabanoff, 1990). However, conflict is generally defined as a disagreement regarding interests or ideas, whether it is within oneself, between two people, or within an organization. Generally conflict is seen as negative and may also be interpreted as an indication of a lack of support for the decisions of management. Unfortunately, managers often behave as though serious interpersonal confrontations are the result of personality defects. They label people who are frequently involved in conflicts "troublemakers" or "bad apples." Yet, while conflict can be viewed as negative, it also has the potential for increasing the effectiveness of an organization's work performance.

R. R. Blake and J. Mouton (1964) presented a conceptual scheme for classifying the modes (styles) for handling interpersonal conflicts into five types based on two broad dimensions. The first dimension explains the degree (high to low) to which a person attempts to satisfy his or her own concerns. The second dimension explains the degree (high to low) to which a person wants to satisfy the concerns of others (Rahim and Bonoma, 1979). Various combinations of the two dimensions result in five specific styles of handling interpersonal conflict: problem solving, smoothing, forcing, withdrawal, and sharing. Blake and Mouton's (1978) two-dimensional model for handling interpersonal conflict has given rise to several theoretical approaches dealing with modes or styles of conflict management (Rahim, 2001), as well as empirical research designed to evaluate these styles (Van de Vliert, 1997).

Generally, when analyzing styles of conflict resolution in organizations, researchers tend to consider the various styles separately. This analytic approach, comparing the different styles one by one, treats them as if they are independent of each other. A more recent approach has adopted an all-embracing perspective labeled *conglomerated conflict behavior,* which implies the need to consider the interactions between conflict styles as well as considering the conflict style as an independent process (Van de Vliert, 1997). People generally combine several different behaviors when handling a disagreement with an opponent, and the term *conglomerated conflict behavior* refers to "such an aggregation of various degrees of several modes of conflict handling" (Van de Vliert, Euwema, and Huismans, 1995, p. 279).

E. Van de Vliert and his colleagues investigated the patterns of styles in conflict management and the relationships between them found in previous studies. They reviewed studies that assessed the five generally accepted styles of conflict management: dominating, avoiding, compromising, integrating, and obliging. Based on the data from these studies, the researchers generated statistical measures of the relationship between the various combinations of the five styles of conflict management. They found positive and significant correlations among three of sixteen pairs of styles: compromising and integrating, compromising and obliging, and avoiding and obliging. These correlations mean that during conflict, individuals show high frequencies in the combined use of the compromising and obliging styles, integrative and compromising styles, and avoiding and obliging styles. In addition, the researchers found that the avoiding and integrating styles are incompatible. Further, the large number of negative and statistically significant correlations led to the conclusion that highly integrative individuals do not avoid conflict. The finding of an important relationship between the integrating and compromising styles also supports this conclusion. In addition, the dominating and obliging styles are also incompatible. The total number of statistically significant correlations found was not large, and the number of negative correlations was much greater than that of positive correlations. Based on these findings, it seems that highly assertive individuals (i.e., those employing integrating and dominating styles) tend to maintain and protect their own interests. Because the more-cooperative conflict-handling styles have generally been found to produce more-constructive conflict management, these results have important implications for organizations and their management.

Interestingly, the fact that an unusually high number of correlations exist between variables in the dual-concern model has led some authors to question whether the five constructs are really theoretically independent or whether strong linkages exist between them (Weider-Hatfield and Hatfield, 1995). Furthermore, some have suggested that the existence of these correlations means that there are probably fewer than five different styles of conflict management, although what they are has yet to be determined.

As an alternate theoretical approach to a discrete taxonomy of conflict styles, some theorists believe that individuals normally use a combination of conflict strategies. Further, it has been suggested that the literature on conflict-handling styles has propagated the implicit and inaccurate assumption that individuals adhere to one style of conflict management for the duration of a single conflict event, even though evidence exists that an individual's conflict style often changes from one style to another during the same interaction (Conrad, 1991).

The understanding and management of conflict plays a central role in organizations. From the viewpoint that visible conflict is a sign that a team is learning (Senge, 1990) to R. T. Pascale's (1990) notion of the need for "creative tension," conflict can be seen as an accepted and important part of organizational life and a necessary part of change and development for organizational learning, as well as for individual learning (Brown and Duguid, 2001). Managers are often expected to embrace and foster conflict as an important development tool. In fact, one responsibility of the organization is to create a climate of altruistic self-interest by ensuring that individual needs and corporate goals are aligned. This outcome can be enhanced by actively enabling employees to resolve conflicts. Too often organizations let conflicts between individuals or departments fester or escalate until terminating or reassigning employees seems the only solution. More typically, people find their own way of maneuvering themselves within the organization so that they avoid their antagonists, or they find ways of marginalizing or excluding them. Such conflicts may even become institutionalized, so that disparate departments end up working to achieve their own goals and rarely communicating with each other. These behaviors can be very destructive to an organization.

One of the more classical and foundational reviews on conflict as an organizational phenomenon suggests that the research on conflict can be categorized into either a process or a structural model (Thomas, 1976). The process model views conflict between two or more parties in terms of the internal dynamics of the conflict. It includes five sequentially ordered events. The first is frustration, where one party perceives the other as interfering with the satisfaction of one's needs, wants, objectives, and such. Next, conceptualization occurs, which is where each party defines the conflict situation, the salient alternatives available, and people's behavior. Then the behavior that results from the perception of conflict and the parties' strategic objectives is observed. Interaction between the two parties then occurs, and this is when the conflict will either escalate or deescalate. Finally, there is the outcome of the conflict, where we see the results, which can range from agreement to long-term hostility. Research results have generally supported the five-step-process model, but some researchers have argued that the last two stages, interaction and outcome, can be combined into a single stage (Robbins, 1998).

The structural model, unlike the process model, identifies the parameters that shape the conflict episode. There are four such parameters: behavioral predisposition, social pressure, incentive structure, and rules and procedures. Behavioral predisposition includes the motives, abilities, and personalities of the people involved. Social pressure arises both from the employee's group and from cultural values, organization work-group norms, and public interest. Incentive structure addresses the objective reality that gives rise to conflict, for example, the stakes, the relationship between parties, conflict of interest in competitive issues, and common problems. Rules and procedures include the decision-making machinery, that is, decision rules and negotiation and arbitration procedures, which constrain and shape the behavior of conflicting parties. The structural model suggests that conflict can be defined as an interpersonal dynamic that is shaped by the internal and external environments of the parties involved, and this dynamic is manifested in a process that affects group performance either functionally or dysfunctionally (Thomas, 1976).

A similar approach to understanding conflict is rooted in the typology of R. H. Miles and C. S. Snow (1978), which ties strategy, structure, and process together, describing the relationship between strategy and conflict in detail. This approach is one of the most popular classifications of business-level strategies (Zahra and Pearce, 1990). According to this typology, there are four strategic types of organizations: prospectors, defenders, analyzers, and reactors. Prospectors move quickly to seize opportunities in the marketplace by creating new products, new markets, and new technologies. Defenders find and keep secure niches in a stable product or service area, not looking beyond their current product domain. Analyzers mix a new-product and aggressive-new-domain approach in one business with a stable approach in a second business. Reactors, who lack a true strategic perspective, are buffeted by environmental elements and are generally considered to be dysfunctional. Prospectors and defenders represent two polar positions, while analyzers and reactors pursue a mixture of the two polar positions, though for different reasons. Because reactors fail to implement a coherent strategy, they tend to perform the least effectively.

Furthermore, each strategic type uses a distinctive approach to handling conflict. Specifically, prospectors are characterized as decentralized organizations, so that the relationships between the smaller diverse parts of the organization tend to generate frequent and varied types of conflict in response to complexity and uncertainty within the organizational structure. Prospector organizations need to employ personnel to coordinate interfunctional processes and handle conflict. Defenders engage in a narrow range of repetitive, routinized, and sequential tasks that result in relatively few conflicts. Because standardization, scheduling, and hierarchical authority exist, it is easy to provide inexpensive and fast conflict resolution when needed. Analyzers exhibit qualities of both prospectors and defenders because they maintain a stable core while simultaneously seeking new market opportunities. Thus, prospectors will have the highest level of conflict, followed by analyzers and then defenders. Because reactors lack a coherent strategy, their level of conflict can be quite high, if there is a battle over strategy, or quite low, if the lack of a plan leaves the organization unaware that problems exist.

Managerial conflict styles have also been investigated using these same four categories. Prospector managers have to engage in high levels of interaction in response to frequent cross-functional contact, they place an emphasis on engaging in multiple functions and cooperative behavior, and they have a high level of interest in both themselves and others. As a result, they use an integrative approach to conflict. Defender managers interact infrequently and in a routine way, seeking timely and simple conflict resolution and using a nonintegrative approach. Defenders tend to use either a forcing or avoiding approach to conflict handling. Analyzer managers handle conflict that occurs in their core business in the same way as defenders. However, they behave more like prospectors when being entrepreneurial. The approach to conflict of reactors is unclear because the type of conflict that these managers are required to resolve varies significantly, resulting in no single preferred approach to conflict resolution.

Justice (or fairness) in organizational decision making has been shown to be a central concern of employees (Sheppard, Lewicki, and Minton, 1992). While subordinates often identify justice-related issues (e.g., inequitable administration of rewards, unfair evaluation) as sources of conflict between them and their supervisors, I am not aware of any study that has directly assessed the relationship between employees' perceptions of organizational justice and the styles they choose to manage existing conflict with their supervisors. Nevertheless, several studies have indicated that positive perceptions of organizational justice lead to the use of cooperative behavior. For example, employees who perceive the existence of a greater level of justice generally engage in more organizational-citizenship behavior (Moorman, 1991). Similarly, greater frequencies of integrative (win-win) behaviors and concessions have been observed when negotiators perceive the other side to have acted in a trustworthy or fair manner (Shapiro and Bies, 1994). When managing conflict with their supervisors, employees who perceive that organizational justice exists are more likely to use cooperative styles (e.g., integrating, obliging, compromising) rather than less-cooperative styles (e.g., dominating, avoiding). This expectation follows from the consistent finding in the organizational-justice literature that greater levels of perceived justice are generally related to more-positive work attitudes and behaviors and, thus, more-positive conflict-management behaviors (Lind and Tyler, 1988).

Researchers in social psychology and organizational behavior have proposed models that divide the approaches of negotiators and managers into several basic styles. Early models of strategy in conflict (Deutsch, 1973) followed the intuitive notion that styles can be arrayed on a single dimension ranging from selfishness (concern about one's own outcomes) to cooperativeness (concern about the other party's outcomes). However, a limitation of single-dimension models is that they fail to encompass styles that involve a high concern for both self and others and, likewise, styles that involve a low concern for both self and others.

Subsequent theorists have drawn on R. R. Blake, H. Shepard, and J. Mouton's (1964) taxonomy of managerial styles to model conflict styles within a framework of two motivational dimensions, a self-oriented and an other-oriented concern (Pruitt and Rubin, 1986). Within this framework, K. W. Thomas and R. H. Kilmann (1974) developed an instrument for measuring an individual's dispositions toward each of five discrete styles. The five conflict styles that emerge from various combinations of the dimensions of concern for self and concern for others are (1) integrating, high concern for both self and others, (2) dominating, high concern for self and low concern for others, (3) obliging, low concern for self and high concern for others, (4) avoiding, low concern for both self and others, and (5) compromising, moderate levels of concern for both self and others. However, low concern for the opponent can lead to two quite different styles: passively avoiding the discussion of conflict, as opposed to actively collaborating, and competing, as opposed to accommodating, seem to be approaches that are particularly likely to generate conflict in working relationships.

Research findings show mixed support for the appropriateness of a five-fold taxonomy to describe conflict behaviors (Jehn and Weldon,

1997). On theoretical grounds, D. G. Pruitt and J. Z. Rubin (1986) have argued that modeling conflict style in terms of five dispositions is redundant. Nevertheless, the Thomas and Kilmann scales for tapping particular conflict styles, such as avoiding and competing, compare favorably to other methods in terms of validity and reliability (Brown, Yelsma, and Keller, 1981).

To understand the roots of cultural differences in avoiding and competing in conflicts, we need to be able to measure underlying values. The extent to which a way of handling conflict is effective depends on the requirements of the specific situation and the skill with which that method is used. In any given situation, one particular way of handling conflict may be more suitable than others. In fact, conflict styles probably reflect strategic (large-scale, enduring), rather than tactical (small-scale, episodic), intentions. If this is true, then multiple behaviors proportional to the strength of an intention are necessary (Thomas, 1992). This effect has been largely ignored despite evidence that individuals in conflict can alter their behavior over time (Bergman and Volkema, 1989). There are a number of different ways to deal with conflict, and each of these can be useful under different sets of circumstances, so that not all conflict is best resolved by searching for a win-win situation.

A review of styles of interpersonal conflict is crucial to a comprehensive understanding of organizational conflict management. Information about the appropriateness and effectiveness of each style as it relates to specific situations is necessary (Canary and Spitzberg, 1987). While researchers have largely ignored the relationship between the amount of conflict and conflict style, the causes and implications of organizational conflict are important to understand (Rahim, 1986b).

Variables associated with important organizational outcomes can be identified using several basic models of organizational effectiveness. According to M. A. Rahim (1986a) there are six sources of organizational conflict: affective conflict (conflict based on emotional issues), conflict of interest, conflict of values, cognitive conflict (conflict based on different ways of thinking about something), goal conflict, and substantive conflict (genuine conflict based on real differences). Using a two-dimensional model of behavior (concern for self and concern for others), Rahim (1986a) identified five styles of handling conflict that are similar to those discussed already: integrating, obliging, dominating, avoiding, and compromising. It was Rahim's contention that "organizational participants must learn the five styles of handling conflict to deal with different conflict situations effectively" (1986a, p. 30).

There are three levels of organizational conflict: intrapersonal, intragroup, and intergroup. Intrapersonal conflict occurs when a member of an organization is required to perform certain tasks, activities, or roles that do not match his or her expertise, interests, goals, or values. Intragroup conflict occurs as a result of disagreements or inconsistencies among the members of a group or between subgroups within a group. Intergroup conflict refers to disagreements or inconsistencies between the members, or their representatives or leaders, of two or more groups. The amount of conflict at each of these levels may vary, but some research findings indicate that a moderate amount of conflict at each level is necessary for optimal job performance (Rahim, 1986a). Other researchers (Knapp, Putnam, and Davis, 1988) have attributed organizational conflict to "heterogeneity of the work force, environmental changes, differences in goals, diverse economic interests, differential role structures, conflict group loyalties, and value discrepancies in organizations" (p. 423). Still others have verified the following causes of intraorganizational conflict: differences in knowledge, beliefs, or basic values; competition for a position, for power, or for recognition; a need to release tension; drive for autonomy; personal dislike; and differing perceptions or attitudes generated by the structure of the organization (Renwick, 1975).

Research results indicate that more-cooperative conflict-management styles (in which a meaningful amount of concern is shown for the other party, particularly problem-solving styles such as integrating) are likely to produce positive individual and organizational outcomes, while less-cooperative styles (in which little concern is shown for the other party) frequently result in escalation of conflict and negative outcomes (Ohbuchi and Takahashi, 1994). The problem-solving conflict-management style is generally preferred by employees (De Dreu et al., 2001).

Conflict and Culture

There are several general characteristics of culture that affect conflict-resolution strategies. One such variable is cultural similarity. When we see other people's or group's perceptual and behavioral patterns as similar to ours, we also see them as culturally similar (Kim, 1991). Since cultural similarity and nationality are two distinct concepts, people from different countries may perceive each other to be similar attitudinally and behaviorally when a common or intermediate set of values and norms exist between them (Parkhe, 1991). In terms of conflict-resolution strategies, similarity encourages participants to adopt a more cooperative, integrative approach (Campbell, Graham, Jolibert, and Meissner, 1988). Similarity also facilities a problem-solving strategy because people will presume they share similar approaches to how problems should be solved and will be more tolerant of similar people's approaches to conflict management (Johnson, Cullen, Sakano, and Takenouchi, 1996). Conversely, people may hesitate to openly communicate and exchange information if they believe that the other person holds dissimilar views to them. If this is the case, their frames of reference for interpreting, understanding, and communicating are presumed to be different (Geringer, 1988). If cultural similarity is thought to exist, a problem-solving approach, rather than a legalistic strategy, is more likely. In fact, the lack of perceived cultural similarity is a significant factor in explaining why people and organizations rely on a legalistic strategy in social interactions. As a result of this increased dependence on formal institutions, trust tends to break down (Zucker, 1986). When two organizations work together but view each other as culturally dissimilar, the perception that they do not share common values leads to a higher degree of behavioral uncertainty. The result is a greater reliance on legal and written documents and the use of legal mechanisms for resolving conflicts.

A second general characteristic of cultural differences is relative power, or the level of one person's ability to influence another person's decisions. Relative power is derived from the resources that each person brings to the situation. These resources include capital (i.e., equity share) and labor (e.g., management, technical know-how) (Gray and Yan, 1997). Relative power can be used as an effective mechanism to coordinate and integrate the activities of two business partners. However, if an unbalanced power relationship exists, less-integrative behavior is used to resolve conflicts. In general, power imbalances lead the more-powerful partner to engage in more-demanding and coercive behavior (i.e., forcing) and in less-forthright communication (Dwyer and Walker, 1981). The more powerful one partner is, the more likely it is that a lengthy problem-solving process can be avoided, especially during the formative stage of a relationship, and the more likely it is for the partners to avoid compromise (Friedmann and Beguin, 1971). With the strong position of the powerful partner comes leverage, which can be used effectively because of the expectation that his or her goals will be accepted (Schaan and Beamish, 1988).

The third characteristic that plays a role in the cultural impact on conflict resolution is relationship age. In general, the longer the relationship, the greater the opportunity for both parties to interact and gain mutual understanding (Pruitt, 1981). Relationship duration correlates with communication frequency and information exchange between business partners, which in turn facilitates an open problem-solving approach to resolving conflicts (Hallen, Johanson, and Seyed-Mohamed, 1991). Compromise is more likely in ongoing relationships, since long-term partners often understand better that short-term imbalances in bargaining outcomes are likely to balance out over time (Dwyer, Schurr, and Oh, 1987). In a long-term relationship, partners are more likely to be concerned with the other party's interests and less likely to force a particular resolution of a conflict. Uncertainties regarding the other party's competence, reliability, and other qualities tend to decrease over time, and trust tends to increase over time. Longer-term relationships are less likely to rely on legal mechanisms. Cooperation reduces the probability of opportunistic behavior and, consequently, lowers the need for legal safeguards (Parkhe, 1993).

Conflict in Other Cultures

As organizations adjust to globalization, frequent shifts in strategy and general management practices occur worldwide, and conflict during strategy implementation is increasing (Beechler and Zhuang Yang, 1994). Too much conflict can slow down and impede successful communication and strategy implementation (Hall, 1991). Preferred conflict-resolution approaches are changing. If convergence theory is correct, then Eastern and Western management techniques will converge, resulting in a realignment of cooperative and individualistic behavior (Misawa, 1987). This realignment affects the way individuals and collective groups within the organization accept or challenge strategic goals (Triandis et al., 1988). Thus, strategy implementation will suffer if managers do not clearly understand how employees handle conflict. The increasing international diversity of personnel within companies, although potentially positive, will increase implementation challenges due to complications in decision making and problems in communication (Tse, Lee, Vertinsky, and

Wehrung, 1988). Such cultural differences can introduce extraneous conflict, as well as situationally inappropriate ways of handling conflict, that damage the strategy-implementation process (Abramson, Lane, Nagai, and Takagi, 1993). Consequently, businesses need to make the right changes in their strategy-implementation processes, even though the changes often create conflict rather than cooperation (Hutt, Walker, and Frankwick, 1995).

Research into organizations across cultures has found that cultures construe conflict in different ways (Gelfand, Nishi, Ohbuchi, and Fukuno, 2001). The conflict climate of the organization influences the perception of positive outcomes directly and overall performance indirectly. Two important performance measures are successful cross-functional relationships characterized by trust, commitment, and satisfaction, and relative firm success, or the multiple dimensions of financial performance. More-collaborative styles of conflict-handling behavior are associated with high-performance firms. The collective nature of Japanese firms and their drive for harmony, influenced by Confucian, Shinto, and Buddhist beliefs, suggests the likelihood of success in cross-functional endeavors (Jun and Muto, 1995). For example, Japanese tend to perceive conflicts as more compromise focused than Americans do, so identical conflict episodes may be viewed differently in the two cultures. One cross-national study of U.S. and Japanese firms examined the relationship of strategy to conflict-resolution approaches (Dyer and Song, 1997). The researchers used the typology of Miles and Snow (1978) discussed earlier and found that it could be successfully applied in Japan and used to compare American and Japanese managerial practices. They also found that conflict management was markedly different between the proactive and reactive strategy firms, as defined by Miles and Snow, in both the U.S. and Japanese samples. Strategic position had a greater impact on conflict management and perceived success in the Japanese sample than in the American sample, suggesting a major difference in how strategy is handled in Japanese and U.S. firms.

The evidence clearly suggests that not all highly collectivist cultures share a tendency to rely on an avoidance conflict-resolution strategy (Graham, 1985). A study comparing conflict styles of Japanese and U.S. students found that twice as many Japanese than American students reported reliance on avoidance in their most recent conflict (Ohbuchi and Takahashi, 1994). One of the most important reasons given by the Japanese students for avoiding explicit discussion of the conflict was the desire to preserve their personal relationships. Interestingly, though both Japanese and U.S. respondents agreed that avoidance is the least effective strategy for resolving conflict, it was the preferred style for the Japanese, because they have competing values and place a higher value on maintaining existing relationships. Adjusting to a stable social structure, which includes relationships, organizations, and institutions, is a virtue in Confucian tradition.

Role-appropriate behavior is a central theme in Chinese culture and is also influential in Japanese culture (Su et al., 1999). Confucian ethics lays out certain "rules of propriety" that structure interpersonal relationships, and adhering to these rules is highly valued. This Confucian virtue has been a critical variable in studies of Chinese values and was labeled *moral discipline* by the Chinese Culture Connection (1987). A comparison of the endorsement of Chinese values and conflict-management styles of U.S. and Hong Kong Chinese participants showed that Chinese respondents scored higher on both the moral discipline and conflict avoidance scales (Chiu and Kosinski, 1994).

Although the competitive nature of Japanese society and organizations implies the potential for high conflict levels, the management literature on Japanese business usually characterizes it as highly cooperative (Parry and Song, 1993). Cooperation occurs because of several factors, including the collective nature of Japanese culture, cross-training in Japanese firms, and the widespread use of cooperative total quality management techniques (Yang, 1984). Many authors believe that total quality management has succeeded in Japan because of the collective ethic of firms, whereas such efforts frequently have failed in U.S. firms due to the highly individualistic and competitive behavior favored in Western cultures (Hofstede, 1984). Although a variety of pressures are forcing Japanese firms to incorporate more individualism into their processes, any change in a cultural value such as collectivism is likely to be slow. The Confucian value of harmony in Japanese society suggests that integrating and avoiding behaviors in handling conflict are likely to be encouraged in organizations, while a forcing or confrontational approach is discouraged (Jun and Muto, 1995).

Organizations can use the formalization and centralization structural methods to reduce the chance of conflict and to facilitate resolution (Dyer and Song, 1995). Evidence suggests that Japanese firms operate in a very formalized fashion. For example, in building consensus, lower management creates a *ringisho,* or formal written recommendation, that circulates to relevant personnel to gather support before being sent to top management for final approval (Yang, 1984). This process also demonstrates that Japanese firms operate hierarchically, reflecting the Japanese social structure.

There is adequate evidence to conclude that conflict-management behavior differs as a function of cultural values. For example, Chinese managers prefer an avoiding style while American managers prefer a competing style. These different approaches are rooted in differences in value orientations (Morris et al., 1998). Conformity and tradition are social-conservatism values, which underlie the Chinese preference of avoiding workplace conflicts (Bond and Wang, 1983). On the other hand, Americans have an orientation toward self-enhancement, and achievement in particular, which encourages a more competitive approach. Other researchers argue that it is the values rooted in the Chinese preference for long-term relationships that discourage direct and assertive ways to deal with conflict. A number of theorists have suggested that Chinese culture promotes an indirect, avoiding style of handling conflicts (Chow and Ding, 2001), that conflict is usually considered a "bad thing," and that Chinese people try to avoid or ignore it (Tse, Francis, and Walls, 1994).

Chinese values do not necessarily discourage constructive conflict. In particular, confirming social face and using persuasion rather than coercion help both the relationship and conflict resolution. Several studies demonstrate that the use of cooperative conflict, rather than avoiding or competing conflict, helps overcome a variety of problems between Chinese organizations (Wong, Tjosvold, Wong, and Liu, 1999), with Chinese customers (Tjosvold, 1999), or between Chinese and Japanese employees in Japanese companies (Tjosvold, Sasaki, and Moy, 1998).

In conflict management among the Chinese and other East Asians, the role of social face is critical (Tjosvold and Sun, 2000). Indeed, collectivist societies tend to seek harmony and to communicate respect between the managers and workers. As a result, individuals in these societies tend to avoid aggressive acts that might be interpreted as a direct challenge to the "face" of others, since direct disagreement can be interpreted as communicating a lack of respect. This, in turn, can affect a variety of interactions including negotiation styles and approaches (Tse, Francis, and Walls, 1994). Social-face concerns play a critical role in managing conflict in

China. Conflict is seen as acceptable and potentially productive by the Chinese as long as they feel that they are personally accepted as competent and that social face is not challenged (Tjosvold and Sun, 2000).

Chinese organizations may restrict the opportunity for debate and, therefore, the potential for creativity and innovation. This situation may be compounded by the nature of local management and society itself. These values can be found in other Asian countries—for example, in Japanese society, with its concept of *tate mai,* keeping up the appearance of socially approved behavior and consensus; in Indonesian society, with its emphasis on avoiding conflict or making others feel *malu* (shame/anger); and in Thailand, with the concept of *mai pen rai,* the desire to keep things on an even keel. Therefore, it is useful to study managers in other Asian cultures that, while highly collectivist, have cultural heritages that lead us to expect differing conflict-resolution styles. For example, observers have argued that Indian managerial conflict-resolution tendencies reflect Hindu norms of seeking a solution that pleases everyone, as well as British norms of active, mutual problem solving (Moran and Stripp, 1991). Indian managers tend to have a style less inclined toward competing than U.S. managers have, but not the avoidance style found in Chinese cultures.

Similarly, in the Philippines, where the historical influence of Chinese culture has been moderated by the more-recent influence of Spanish and U.S. cultures, managers avoid overt competing in conflicts with colleagues, but not through avoidance of addressing the issues. Rather, the tendency is to express a point of view indirectly or to soften statements so as to preserve smooth relationships (Gouchenour, 1990).

Studies have measured participants' choices between competitive and cooperative strategies in conflict games. For example, U.S. children relied on competitive strategies to a greater extent than did matched samples of children in Hong Kong and Taiwan (Li, Cheung, and Kau, 1979). In one study of cultural differences, competitive styles of handling conflict were explored in dispute-resolution procedures. Whereas North Americans preferred competitive adversarial procedures, less-competitive procedures, such as mediation, are preferred in many other countries, such as Hong Kong and Spain (Leung and Lind, 1986). In another study, preferred conflict-resolution strategies in two individualist cultures, the Netherlands and Canada, were compared to those in collectivist cultures, Spain and Japan. Negotiation and compliance were more preferred and accusing less preferred in the collectivist cultures (Leung, Au, Fernandez-

Dols, and Iwawaki, 1992). Also, the preferred conflict-resolution strategies of Nigerians and Canadians were compared. While both groups preferred negotiation, Nigerians were also more likely to use threats and to
believe that threats would reduce the level of conflict than were the Canadians (Gire and Carment, 1993). Israelis preferred arbitration but were
more likely to make threats than Hong Kong Chinese (Bond, Leung, and
Schwartz, 1992). Finally, a study of Germans and Lebanese Arabs, as well
as Turkish Kurds seeking asylum in Germany, found that the Germans
preferred legal solutions to conflicts while the Lebanese and Kurds preferred more-informal solutions based on tradition or morality (Bierbrauer, 1994).

A study of Turkish organizations and employees looked at the role of
subculture, rather than national culture, in conflict management, based
on the argument that intranational variations may be as or more important than cross-national differences, particularly in countries such as
Turkey where marked subcultural differences exist. The results indicate
that both organizational and subcultural issues have an effect on conflict-
management styles. The choice of styles is affected by organizational hierarchy and whether the organization is publicly or privately owned.
There is a strong general preference for the problem-solving style, while
other preferences varied according to subculture membership (Kozan,
2002).

The Role of Individualism and Collectivism

Most researchers studying culture and conflict styles have emphasized the
importance of the individualism-collectivism dimension. S. Ting-Toomey
(1985) and colleagues (Ting-Toomey et al., 1991) believe that country
differences in communication style can be accounted for in terms of the
individualism-collectivism dimension. Specifically, collectivism is associated with indirect communication, such as the avoiding style of handling
conflict, whereas individualism is associated with direct modes of expression, such as the competing style of handling conflict. Two predictions
follow from an individualism-collectivism framework. First, measures of
avoiding and competing behaviors should be dramatically different for
U.S. and Asian managers. Moreover, Asian patterns should resemble
those in other highly collectivist societies, such as Middle Eastern and
Latin American societies. The general prediction of similarity across all

highly collectivist cultures has been disconfirmed by careful comparative studies of conflict style (Graham, 1985), leading to the conclusion that predicting the conflict strategies that are preferred or used in different cultures may not be possible based solely on the level of individualism or collectivism.

A second argument is that differences in preferred conflict style between countries will be affected by individual differences on measures of individualism-collectivism. But once again, the existing data is not encouraging. Researchers who have correlated participants' scores on individualism-collectivism scales with conflict behaviors have found no statistically significant relationships (Leung, 1988). The problem may be that the individualism-collectivism construct includes a number of distinct values and attitudes, and so relationships between specific values and social behaviors are hard to find. The reliability of individualism-collectivism scales is quite low, and in recent years some of its supporters have shifted from the position that individualism versus collectivism is a unitary dimension of values. Similarly, cross-cultural differences in conflict-management style cannot be based on a single value dimension running from individualism to collectivism alone (Morris and Leung, 1999).

Conflict Resolution in Joint Ventures

In Western societies, organizational conflict is considered normal and even healthy. However, management's inability to resolve disputes effectively or prevent serious conflicts can be counterproductive. Although cultural differences present a challenge in a one-time formal negotiation, the problem of cultural differences is even more serious in joint ventures, where managers need to resolve everyday conflicts with co-workers from other cultures (Baird, Lyles, Ji, and Wharton, 1990). Two types of misunderstanding in conflicts frequently occur in joint ventures between U.S. and Asian firms. First, U.S. managers make the error of reading silence from their Asian counterpart as an indication of consent and, as a result, fail to pick up on the indirectly expressed objections of Asian colleagues. Second, Asian managers make the error of reading a U.S. colleague's direct adversarial arguments as indicating unreasonableness and lack of respect (Graham and Sano, 1984).

Conflict-resolution strategies may also affect international joint venture (IJV) performance. Open problem-solving and compromising strategies not only enable participants to escape from "deadlock" situations, but they also lead to long-term IJV success (Friedmann and Beguin, 1971). Conflict between joint-venture partners can have an important impact on joint-venture performance. These conflicts can occur from divergent objectives, the sharing of power, differences in organizational cultures and national cultures, and incompatible management styles and approaches (Kozan, 1992). High-performance international alliances are often characterized by constructive communications and regular information exchanges in dealing with day-to-day managerial and operational issues (Olson and Singsuwan, 1997).

A problem-solving approach tends to lead to satisfying relationships, since its goal is to achieve positive outcomes for both partners (Campbell, Graham, Jolibert, Meissner, 1988). When information is openly exchanged, partners tend to see things in a positive way, and a positive attitude toward working together is created (Boyle and Dwyer, 1995). Quite often, there are situations in which both IJV partners need to adopt a "give-and-take" attitude in resolving disagreements (Schaan, 1988). If a balance is sought between the needs and concerns of both parties, overall performance is likely to be evaluated in a positive way (Ganesan, 1993). While IJVs are more likely to be successful when partners see themselves as culturally similar, clear conflict-resolution strategies can offset problems caused by dissimilar cultures (Lin and Germain, 1998).

A forcing or legalistic conflict-resolution strategy may negatively affect performance since both strategies have a win-lose orientation. When one IJV partner attempts to dominate the conflict-resolution process, the other partner becomes frustrated and more rigid, reducing the chance of eliminating the underlying cause of the conflict and also increasing the likelihood of future conflict (Cadotte and Stern, 1979). If voting (majority rules) is used to force a resolution of an IJV conflict, the goodwill of the minority partner may be damaged, requiring significant time for repair (Schaan, 1988). The use of forcing behavior implies an inherently weak ongoing relationship, and a legalistic approach is likely to aggravate, rather than solve, the problem (Pfeffer, 1994). Interviews with IJV managers show that frequent reference to legal contracts is viewed as coercive by the other partner and damages a potentially trusting environment (Frazier and Summers, 1984).

Power

Power is defined as "the ability of one party to change or control the be-havior, attitudes, opinions, objectives, needs, and values of another party" (Rahim, 1989, p. 545). This definition implies that research on power should be limited to the influence of one individual (leader) over another individual (follower). However, power can be looked at from at least two different perspectives in cross-cultural settings. First, in order to understand power issues as they effect organizations in other countries, it is worth considering one theoretical perspective that explains how orga-nizations differ in their approaches to coping with the political forces of host governments. Bargaining power of a multinational company (MNC) is affected by different levels of government involvement and the ability to influence governments. The MNCs with the most bargaining power will probably obtain the most favorable terms in negotiations with host governments and are less likely to face interventions generated by the host government.

There are three types of measures of bargaining outcomes: categorical measures (Hill, 1995), intervention-experience measures (Kim, 1987), and the ownership-level measure (Lecraw, 1984). Categorical measures focus on incidents of government intervention, such as red tape, domes-tic content requirements, and expropriation. Categorical measures are simple to collect and objective but do not adequately differentiate be-tween the various types and levels of intervention.

Intervention-experience measures focus on strategies such as export in-centives, protectionism, and import taxes. These measures have the ad-vantage that the organizational structure and characteristics provide a basis from which estimates of possible and actual changes can be made. However, this approach has been criticized because any government in-tervention in one area can significantly affect other areas. Another draw-back of the intervention-experience measure is that it is subjective and usually based on managerial judgments. Sometimes changes are initiated to reduce political risk in anticipation of a host-government intervention, and these changes can provide a measure of the difference between gov-ernment policies, pressures for change, and the actual change required.

Another aspect affecting power in an MNC is ownership level, or "the percentage of MNC's equity ownership struck from the negotiation be-tween an MNC and a host government" (Lecraw, 1984, p. 30). This is an important indicator of relative bargaining-power positions (i.e., a higher ownership percentage typically represents higher bargaining power). Ownership split has the advantage of being an objective and documented measure of bargaining outcomes (Gomes-Casseres, 1989), but it assumes that MNCs always prefer full ownership to partial ownership and that the goal is to have a high ownership level. However, ownership-level preference will vary depending on (1) the nature and type of transactions involved (Hennart, 1991); (2) the cultural distance between home and host countries (Kogut and Singh, 1988); and (3) the strategic benefits sought, such as acquisition of technological and marketing capabilities (Gomes-Casseres, 1989). In addition, using the level of ownership when an MNC is established to assess relative power implies a stable and permanent MNC–host government relationship (Lecraw, 1984), even though power levels can change over time with such changes as the industrialization and technological development of the host country. Because the percentage of ownership and the relative amount of control are not necessarily the same (Lecraw, 1984), it is better to bargain for greater control over the things that are critical to the success of the venture rather than just an increased percentage of ownership (Poynter, 1985).

The source of MNC bargaining power includes size, technology, advertising, resource sources, export intensity, staffing patterns, product diversity, ownership, and political behavior. Research results indicate that larger subsidiaries have a weak bargaining-power position if they risk greater host-government interventions because of their greater economic significance and high visibility (Hill, 1995). On the other hand, large subsidiaries may be ignored because they are too difficult to take over, manage, and compensate (Ghoshal and Bartlett, 1990), plus they bring significant financial resources to a developing country (Fagre and Wells, 1982). Subsidiary size, as measured by the number of employees, is positively related to intervention level (Poynter, 1985), and expropriation rate is positively correlated with subsidiary asset size (Hill, 1995). But if subsidiary size is based on assets, then it has a positive relationship to such bargaining outcomes as actual ownership, bargaining success, and control over the subsidiary (Lecraw, 1984), and both subsidiary sales and assets are positively related to the level of actual ownership held by MNCs (Fagre and Wells, 1982).

MNC political behavior includes social responsiveness to various local needs such as local employment and job-related education for host nationals (Borys and Jemison, 1989), though research suggests that political behavior alone cannot substantially reduce government interventions

(Kim, 1987). Generally, governments are more likely to intervene if the political benefits to the host government of intervening exceed the economic benefits of not intervening.

A second aspect of power is the use of social power within organizations. Little research has considered how social power works, even though power and conflict are two major areas of study in organizational psychology and management. Further, little has been done to investigate the relationship between power, negotiating, and conflict and their effects on job performance and other measures of organizational effectiveness.

J. R. French and B. Raven (1959) proposed the following typology of social power that is still widely accepted:

1. Coercive power is based on subordinates' perception that a superior has the ability to punish them if they fail to conform to his or her influence attempt.
2. Reward power is based on subordinates' perception that a superior can reward them for desired behavior.
3. Legitimate power is based on subordinates' belief that a superior has the right to prescribe and control their behavior.
4. Expert power is based on subordinates' belief that a superior has job experience and special knowledge or expertise in a given area.
5. Referent power is based on subordinates' interpersonal attraction to and identification with a superior because of their admiration or personal affection for the superior.

It is generally agreed that coercive, reward, and legitimate power bases can be reclassified as position power bases and that expert and referent power bases can be reclassified as personal power bases. A statistical analysis of data from a group of managers and employees provides evidence of these two basic dimensions (Rahim, 1988). There are significant intercorrelations among the five power bases. These interrelationships need to be understood so that managers can acquire and use the appropriate power base to improve subordinates' performance.

The manager's or leader's preference for the use of a particular base or bases of power can have a significant effect on an employee's behavior. In an attempt to understand the applicability and usefulness of the power typology in other cultures, I compared the preferences of managers in the United States and Taiwan (Silverthorne, 2003b). Since Taiwan is a more hierarchical and paternalistic culture than the United States, it was anticipated that the differences in culture would be reflected in the preference for power-base use. However, the results indicate that both cultures prefer the use of referent power and prefer not to use reward or coercive power. It would appear that paternalism in Chinese culture is manifested as respect rather than reward or coercive power and, thus, has a bigger influence over power strategies than anticipated.

Summary

Conflict can arise for a variety of reasons including communication problems. Conflict may or may not be valued in different cultures, and the preferred style of conflict resolution also varies across cultures. Regardless of the cultural preferences, the successful management of conflict will benefit the organization. There are many sources of conflict both within and outside an organization, and several distinct styles of handling conflict have been identified. While different theorists use different classifications of conflict resolution, there are five generally accepted approaches: dominating, avoiding, compromising, integrating, and obliging. In general, individuals, organizations, and cultures prefer specific types of conflict-resolution style, but there is evidence that people can and do change approaches to conflict even as they seek to resolve a specific incident.

Within organizations, six sources of conflict have been identified: affective, conflict of interest, conflict of values, cognitive conflict, goal conflict, and substantive conflict. In order to handle conflict successfully, managers need to understand the source of the conflict and then choose the appropriate style of conflict in order to resolve it. In general, cooperative conflict-management styles will be more successful than competitive conflict-management styles, with employees preferring a problem-solving approach.

Conflict-resolution strategies are affected by the amount of cultural similarity between the conflicting parties, the relative power that exists between them, and the length of the relationship. The impact of these factors is most obvious in international joint ventures, where cultural differences can be significant. Research on this type of organization indicates that a problem-solving approach based on openness and compromise is the most effective approach. When the parties resort to a legalistic approach to resolving conflicts, they are more likely to encounter long-term or unsolvable problems, often leading to the failure of the joint venture. It is clear that flexibility, adaptability, and a willingness to compromise and solve problems are necessary for successful conflict resolution and effective organizational relationships.

Power plays a role in the communication process and in the choice of conflict and negotiating styles. There has been a lot of research on the role of power both in international joint ventures and in the establishment and running of subsidiaries of multinational companies in different countries. Specifically, power can be based on such factors as the percentage of ownership of the subsidiary, the importance of the output or products, the level of industrialization of a country, and the level of technological development. In addition, power affects the level and type of host-country government interventions into how the subsidiary conducts business and even possibly whether the government may take over the subsidiary.

Social power operates within all organizations, and in one study the use of referent power was preferred in the two cultures studied. However, the role of social power across cultures has received little attention.

The impact of conflict, conflict-resolution style and processes, and power on organizations is significant. In each of these areas, the manager has an important role to play, so a good understanding of cultural differences and expectations in these areas will assist organizations and managers to become more effective when managing across cultures.

12

Communication and Negotiation

Problems in communication can have a direct impact on key organizational issues such as production quality, decision making, planning, conflict, and power. So effective communication is very important to an organization's success, especially when the communication is between international business partners and subsidiaries. Communication affects the quality of the exchange of information and, consequently, work relationships and performance. It has been suggested that it serves four different but equally important functions: control, motivation, emotional expression, and information (Scott and Mitchell, 1976). While it is important to share organizational information and to provide the opportunity for emotional expression within the organization, the two key issues facing managers are motivation and control.

Given differences in culturally accepted behavior, groups from different cultures are likely to communicate in different ways. In fact, in international relationships, communication effectiveness is influenced by the fit between the national and organizational cultures and by the cultural diversity of the employees (Li, 1999). Communication obstacles will be experienced when national-cultural inconsistencies exist in communication strategies. Further, as discussed in chapter 3, organizational culture has a direct effect on communication patterns. And when two different organizational cultures come into direct contact, miscommunication will result, damaging the relationship between them.

A central factor in the success or failure of intercultural encounters in management is the quality of interpersonal communication. One way to improve communication between individuals from different cultures is to provide training for managers on how to manage across cultures. G. L. Lippitt and D. S. Hoopes (1978) created several guidelines for effective cross-cultural training, which, even though they are more than twenty-five years old, still have relevance today. Specifically Lippitt and Hoopes proposed that managers should

> be aware of values that are inherent in the host culture;
>
> become familiar with the significant unique characteristics of the culture;
>
> take considerable interest in what people in the culture do;
>
> be able to greet people in their language and know certain key phrases;
>
> ask the individuals to indicate cultural and technical pitfalls, expectations, and potential problems a manager might experience before the assignment;
>
> ask clear open-ended questions; and
>
> develop the attitude that the host organizational system is "not problem people" but "people with a problem." (p. 28)

The better a manager understands a worker, the better he or she will be able to understand what the worker is trying to communicate, whether it is between diverse groups in the United States or multinational companies operating in various countries. The barriers to effective cross-cultural communication can be overcome if people are aware of several important issues. Sensitivity to the existence of cross-cultural barriers is a good first step. Once we are aware that the barriers exist, we will be able to explore them and reach a better understanding of why people from different cultures act as they do. The key is to look for understanding, rather than acceptance, of what you are trying to say. Everyone needs to believe that he or she is being treated with respect, and this is especially true when dealing with people from other cultures. Respecting customs, dress, and habits is one way to show respect to the individual and his or her culture, although I must admit it was hard for me to get used to spittoons outside offices when I visited companies in China. When dealing with people from another culture, generally English will not be their first language. Communication is enhanced when you speak slowly and clearly and use straightforward language. When I teach students from Taiwan, I am very cognizant that many of the words I could use with American students are relatively unusual in everyday speech and that, therefore, since English is their second language, the Taiwanese students are less likely to have encountered these words before. So I always try to be aware of the words I am using and either substitute more-common words or use several different words to say the same thing.

Different cultures also have different rules for behavior, or etiquette. Being aware of a culture's rules of behavior will help ensure better communication. For example, many Eastern cultures respect age and seniority much more than in the United States. So how a person is addressed in another culture will often reflect age, seniority, or position, and the use of first names, popular in Western countries, is frowned on in Eastern cultures. I have worked closely with a Chinese colleague and friend for about twenty-five years, yet he still insists on calling me "Dr. Silverthorne," and I likewise call him "Dr." But this would never happen with any of my American or British colleagues. A German colleague always asks that students call him "Professor" rather than "Dr." He always tells them during the first class of the semester that his father always wanted his son to be a professor so he was given the first name Professor, and that the students should feel free to call him by that name. The Chinese also like to give their professors small gifts as a token of their respect. These must be accepted or the students will feel insulted. Being a guest at a Chinese banquet always means that you sit facing the door and your host (i.e., the person paying the bill) will have his or her back to the door. These examples of etiquette need to be understood because they represent cultural values that differ from those found in other countries. Understanding these differences helps ensure better communication by saving face and showing appropriate respect to others.

Decision making in groups, in particular, involves different communication patterns. One especially troubling outcome of group decision making occurs with the groupthink phenomenon. *Groupthink,* discussed more fully in chapter 9, is the result of a great desire among group members to get along and agree, at the expensive of effective group processes. The consequences are often poor or even disastrous decisions, since critical evaluative comments are not introduced or discussed in the group. In a study based in Austria, numerous groups composed of students from different countries completed a groupthink exercise (Auer-Rizzi, 2000). Most of the subjects were from Sweden, Finland, or Austria and participated in groups with either homogeneous or heterogeneous membership. In general, when a group included several members from one culture, the other group members tended to treat them as a single unit and as if they had a single opinion. The inclusion of a person from another national

culture in a group dominated by one culture led to a better group decision if the minority group member was familiar with and understood the
majority group's culture.

Communication issues cannot be assumed to be consistent across cultures. There are potential differences in communication issues such as
feelings about talking to the boss. For example, Swedish and Finnish subjects talked to the boss only when they had well-thought-out opinions
and questions, whereas the Austrian subjects were more likely to talk to
the boss within the hierarchical framework of the organization. This implies that different cultural frameworks can result in different "interpretations" of the situation being considered, such as when and how to talk
to the boss.

Communication across Cultures

When I arrived in America from England and was visiting the graduate
psychology department for the first time, a woman came up to me and
asked if I could tell her where the rest room was. I immediately assumed
that either she was about to collapse and needed medical attention or that
this was quite a department if it provided a room where people could rest!
Now if she had asked for the loo, I would have understood immediately.
Needless to say, I rapidly developed a new vocabulary, even though I was
still speaking "English," and became aware of the importance and
difficulties of communication across cultures.

In an expanding global economy, many managers are assigned to overseas positions, raising special management concerns. Specifically, expatriate managers face cultural and language barriers in communicating with
local staff, so that the multiplicity of languages used and the diversity of
cultures have a constraining influence on communication in multinational corporations. Yet, although the failure rate of expatriate managers,
especially Americans, has been extremely high (Tung, 1987, 1988a),
some individuals have been able to overcome cultural and language constraints and develop effective and efficient communication strategies. It
would certainly be of value to be able to identify why some people can
communicate effectively across cultures while others cannot. However,
there has been little content-specific management-level organizational-
communication research in multinational corporations. This deficiency
can be attributed to research difficulties in doing international and com-

parative studies, especially the complexities relating to distance, language, and managerial policies (Teboul, Chen, and Fritz, 1994).

Workers and managers from different cultures working together face a variety of cultural issues because of communication differences. However, some strategies to resolve cross-cultural communication problems have been developed. For example, one theorist proposes four rules to follow in order to reduce cross-cultural communication problems. First, managers should start out assuming differences, rather than similarities, in communication styles and patterns. Most managers believe that other people are more similar to them than they really are. This false expectation creates an immediate potential for communication problems. Assuming that the other person is different is more likely to reduce communication problems across cultural groups. Managers should emphasize descriptive explanations rather than an interpretative or evaluative approach. Focusing on describing or evaluating a behavior, rather than the individual, will make the person less defensive, and this will facilitate allowing the manager to take the time to really understand the issues being discussed. In addition, the manager should practice empathy and try to understand the event or issues from the perspective of the worker. The better a manager understands the worker's viewpoint, the better he or she will be able to understand what the employee or colleague is trying to communicate. Finally, managers should treat any interpretation of a communication as a working hypothesis rather than assume that their interpretation is accurate (Adler, 1997). The manager should consider the initial interpretation as just one alternative that needs to be considered and tested as more information is being obtained. The manager should not be hesitant to seek additional information from others who can validate or correct his or her interpretation. In other words, cross-cultural communication requires that managers remain even more open to listening than usual and that they play an even more active role in the communication process than they would when communicating within a single, or their own, culture.

Several distinctive communication differences between cultures have been identified. For example, Americans tend to prefer an open, direct form of communication and confrontation, whereas in Sweden, where direct communication is also valued, heated disagreements and confrontation is unusual. Swedish culture strongly favors compromise, while Asian managers tend to be sensitive to employees' feelings and needs (Nelson, 1998). In Sweden, communication is based on building consensus and rapport among team members. Relationships, while important, take time to build, and Swedes avoid sharing personal information until the people know each other well (Frazee, 1997).

One way to summarize cultural differences in communication is to categorize differences on the basis of cultural context. Cultural context is the cultural information that surrounds a communication incident. While context is always important in understanding the meaning of communication, context is more important in some cultures and languages than in others (Klopf, 1995). I was recently talking to a Chinese American colleague who related a time when he asked someone to translate something he had been told in Cantonese. The person replied that he needed to know what was being talked about (context) before he could translate because intonations in the way things are said have a very strong influence on the meaning. Asian and Arab cultures tend to be high-context cultures, where more meaning is derived from the context in which the message is sent. This means that literal interpretations are often in error. So if a Japanese executive says "that may be a problem," an American would probably respond by trying to solve the problem, whereas the Japanese executive actually meant that the outcome was not possible at all. Low-context cultures, such as Germany, Switzerland, Scandinavia, and the United States, communicate in a more literal way; what is being said is probably what is meant. These differences affect the communication process between cultures. People in high-context cultures are more likely to want to know about you and your company in some detail, are more likely to be sensitive to age and rank since they·are highly valued, tend to be slow to get to the point, tend to take longer to negotiate, and place less emphasis on legal strategies and contracts. People from low-context cultures tend to want to get to the point quickly, focus on the message so that age and rank are less important, and tend to rely less on nonverbal communication cues than people in high-context cultures.

Other research has explored communication differences between specific countries. For example, a comparison between Japanese and Americans found that the Japanese felt uncomfortable with the Americans' tendency to speak while lacking intuitive understanding, as well as their tendencies for hasty decision making and informality. The Americans, on the other hand, felt frustrated by the lack of verbal clarity and specificity shown by the Japanese (Kim and Paulk, 1994). Japanese and American communication protocols were found to be opposite, with Americans preferring public argumentativeness; majority decision making, rather than consensus; formalized and downward communication patterns; reliance on written or electronic, rather than face-to-face, communication; and a preference for task-oriented, rather than relationship-oriented, goals (Goldman, 1994).

In an extensive study of management differences in various European countries, it was noted that several differences in patterns of communication can be presumed to exist. British managers are effective communicators, and they are self-aware without being self-conscious and enjoy responding to open-ended questions. People in most Scandinavian countries communicate in a way that reflects the egalitarian nature of the culture, as well as a general desire to avoid conflict. In Spanish organizations almost all communication is oral, whereas in France it is more likely to be written, despite the high level of linguistic ability in France. In Italy, communication is formal but, at the same time, may be marked by immediacy and intimacy. In Swiss organizations, communication tends to be low-key and relaxed. Organizations there tend to be small and decentralized, with few barriers to communication. Oral communication is preferred to written communication, and people tend not to talk about their personal lives at work. Turkish managers place significant emphasis on communicating and achieving a shared definition of quality at work (Lawrence and Edwards, 2000).

The amount of verbal communication varies between Americans and Mexicans. Americans tend to be brief and to the point with little unnecessary communication between people. But compared to Americans, Mexicans tend to have a linguistic style that is very elaborate. It is also important for Mexicans to develop a positive personal relationship in order to have a good business relationship. Mexicans also place a greater emphasis on harmony than Americans, who prefer a good argument as a way to open up communication between partners (Heydenfeldt, 2000).

Although there has been little reported research on communication in multinational corporations, cultural and language studies do provide the basis for theorizing on the nature of intercultural and organizational communication. This connection is possible because such studies establish the link that culture has with language and communication practices and processes (Triandis and Albert, 1987). The identified cultural variables include power distance, masculinity-femininity, individualism-collectivism, uncertainty avoidance, and long-term or short-term orientation (Hofstede, 1984, 1997), as well as contextuality (Hall, 1976). Contextuality implies that the actual use of language in different cultures varies. In high-context cultures, a lot of the meaning is implicit and what is said will be more indirect and incomplete. In low-context cultures, language is more explicit and the message is complete and clear. Comparative studies have found differences between specific cultures. For example, one study points out that Chinese individuals make extensive use of intermediaries in delicate communication transactions, whereas Westerners do not (Bond, Wan, Leung, and Giocalone, 1985). Collectivists (such as the Chinese) organize topics interdependently, aware that ideas and problems often overlap, whereas individualists (such as many Western cultures) organize topics independently (Yamada, 1990). In addition, language studies find that second-language speakers adopt a variety of strategies that either change and simplify the content or ignore difficult-to-express subjects (Corder, 1983).

Cultural and language studies have unfortunately been treated as two separate areas of inquiry, rather than taking their mutual interaction into consideration. In particular, intercultural research has ignored language competency, even though language studies point out that people at different competency levels communicate very differently. Low-proficiency second-language speakers contribute fewer ideas than fluent second-language speakers or first-language speakers (Hamzah-Sendut, Madsen, and Thong, 1989). It is difficult to communicate in meetings, especially those that are fast paced and free flowing, if you do not understand what is being said. I have a deaf cousin who was a manager in a British aerospace company. He was very competent and received several promotions, and although he could read lips, he could not function in higher-level management because in meetings he had no way of knowing who was talking and, by the time he looked at the right person, he had missed a lot of the communication. In much the same way, people with a poor command of the language spoken in a meeting have a hard time keeping up with translating and understanding what is being said. Taken together, these language and cultural studies provide a framework for understanding intercultural organizational communication in the multinational corporation. They do not, however, provide specific illustrations of effective intercultural communication in multinational corporations.

One area that has been studied in several within-country research projects is the impact of communication-relationship satisfaction on organizational commitment. A study conducted in Singapore found that communication satisfaction improved organizational commitment, particularly as it related to communication from top managers and supervisors

(Putti, Aryee, and Phua, 1990). Similar results were found in the United States (Potvin, 1991), Australia (Downs, 1991), and Guatemala (Varona, 1996).

Cross-cultural communication is a key component of effective international joint ventures. In interviews, managers in the PRC reported that communication style differences created problems, particularly in the start-up phase of the operations, and often could explain why the joint venture failed. There are several key issues that contribute to communication problems between PRC and Western managers. For example, what appears to be a problem in one culture may not be perceived as a problem in another culture. All of these issues suggest a need for cross-cultural communication training, selection of managers who are experienced with and sensitive to cultural differences, and ongoing training around issues that have been found to generate conflict and misunderstandings between people from different cultures (Beamer, 1998).

Because communication is so important in international organizational relationships, D. A. Griffith (2002) conducted a series of interviews with managers and executives from China, Canada, Japan, and the United States in order to create a model for international communication effectiveness. The model suggests that managers need to have three broad and interrelated communication competencies. First, cognitive competence relates to the manager's ability to understand the meaning behind verbal and nonverbal language by effectively adjusting to communication differences in very different environments. By adapting to their partners' communication patterns, managers are able to develop better relationships with others and a more effective communication environment. Second, affective competence relates to emotionality in communications and includes the manager's tolerance for ambiguity and ability to accept and respond to different and unique communications. The third communication competence is behavioral competence, which includes behavioral flexibility, communication authenticity, and the ability to interact with another person in a genuine way.

The second aspect of the model involves the communication environment. Every company has norms for communicating within relationships. Effective communication interaction occurs when two organizations develop a common set of norms and patterns. The communication environment also includes cultural interaction because the national culture dictates certain communication behaviors such as time orientation and relationship norms. The third aspect of the model is the quality of the relationship, which includes the level of trust, commitment, and satisfaction with the relationship.

A strategy for implementing the model and, thus, improving communication between international partners is also proposed. Organizations should assess the communication competence of their managers and then match a manager's competencies with both those of the partner organization and those of the manager's counterparts in the other organization with whom most of the between-organization communications will occur. Once the relationship is established, it should be monitored by the parent organization to ensure that it remains effective and is building a strong relational quality. Finally, the organization should develop an appropriate communication strategy and evaluate communication performance. Multifirm committees can both evaluate and provide guidance for improving the communication process.

Cultural Differences When Giving Presentations

When working in other cultures, it is often necessary to communicate ideas, goals, and training using presentations. Generally, before giving a presentation in another culture, it is best to ask your host or other key people what your audience will expect. For example, before beginning a presentation, speakers may be expected to recognize and pay respect to people in the audience or spend some time giving the audience background information about themselves or their company. Also, Americans tend to use presentations to present a problem and then outline one or more solutions. However, people in some cultures may take the problem personally and not be responsive to the presentation or the solutions, and presenting a recommendation or suggestion may be seen as being too direct and rude. Also the use of slides and PowerPoint presentations in American companies signifies preparation and expertise, but some cultures prefer not to use visual aids because they have a negative impact on the relationship being built between the speaker and the audience. Finally, the use of humor and what people see as funny vary from culture to culture; what one person sees as funny another may find offensive, so carefully consider your humor before using it with audiences from different cultures (Bell, 1992).

Negotiation

One area where communication plays a very important role is in negotiations. Negotiations between cultures take place at many levels, and cultural groups develop different negotiating strategies to be consistent with their shared cultural values. Successful negotiations require respect and understanding of the other side's position. In international negotiations, it is also necessary to understand, accept, and respect the other side's cultural beliefs and norms. Globalization of economic and organizational activities across national borders has increased the significance of cross-cultural differences in managing organizations (Redpath and Nielsen, 1997). Companies with foreign interests need to understand how to conduct effective negotiations as they consider expansions, mergers, acquisitions, and joint ventures in other countries (Hendon and Hendon, 1990). It is reasonable to assume that culture also plays a role in any decisions for which negotiation influence strategy is used. Certainly trust is basic to forming alliances (Gulati, 1995). Research on alliances has focused on trust as a consequence of repeated transactions, with trust emerging after partners have successfully completed deals in the past, complied with norms of equity, and forsaken opportunistic tendencies (Gulati, 1995). Trust prior to alliance negotiations appears to determine its role in the behavior of negotiators (Tung, 1988b). Trust works to reduce the perception of opportunistic behavior, limits transaction costs, and encourages openness and a willingness to use soft tactics, such as providing favors (Tung, 1988b).

Negotiations can be viewed through the subjective reality of the negotiators, rather than considering the norms or rules of the negotiation process, which may or may not be used (Rubin and Zartman, 1995). Unfortunately, the majority of research on negotiating has relied on laboratory experiments (e.g., Francis, 1991), which are often not realistic or generalizable to real-world situations. Negotiation is persuasive communication implemented by individual negotiators, so both the organizational and individual aspects of negotiation should be considered. Negotiator behavior is tactical, so negotiators attempt to achieve goals by gaining compliance through influence.

The three metacategories of hard, soft, and rational negotiation strategies provide a useful classification for describing negotiator influence tactics. Hard tactics involve threats, demands, and sanctions and can work if the other party faces high costs for noncompliance, which facilitates compliance with the demands (Kipnis and Schmidt, 1983). In contrast, soft tactics emphasize friendliness because the option of noncompliance is considered to have little cost. Soft tactics create interpersonal affection and build a sense of obligation and reciprocity as the means to get compliance (Kipnis and Schmidt, 1983). Indirect tactics, such as mobilizing the support of suppliers or trade unions, are also soft tactics. Rational influence tactics include the use of logic, data, information, and nonemotional arguments to gain compliance and is best used when compliance is not expected or is taken for granted (Kipnis and Schmidt, 1983). In negotiation experiments, negotiators who believe that they have a power advantage tend to use hard tactics, whereas negotiators perceiving themselves to be in a relatively low power position (dependent), such that they possess few valued resources or few alternative partners, tend to use soft and rational tactics, including information exchange, forming coalitions with secondary parties, or friendliness (Rubin and Zartman, 1995). Negotiators may set deadlines, demand concessions, act in an assertive or forceful manner, and threaten to terminate negotiations.

Hofstede's five-dimension framework has been applied to cross-cultural negotiations between Chinese (PRC) and American negotiators (Chang, 2003). Power distance is high in China, which means that Chinese are less likely to be willing to negotiate with someone from a lower rank. So it is important that any negotiator from another country has equal status. In terms of uncertainty avoidance, both the Chinese and Japanese cultures attempt to limit risk and uncertainty by using policies, procedures, and rules to govern actions. The result is that the Chinese are more likely to take their time in negotiating, requiring patience on the part of negotiators, especially if they are American. On the individualism-collectivism dimension, the Chinese are collectivist and prefer to work and reach decisions on negotiating positions in teams, rather than to work alone, when negotiating with other countries. At the same time, they will judge the other negotiator's sincerity based on the number of negotiators, so sending a single negotiator is not a good idea. China is also a masculine culture in terms of Hofstede's dimensions and, as a result, will be more focused on performance and justice than on trust and compassion. Asian men in general are more likely to prefer to negotiate with other men, whereas in American society women are also likely to be active in negotiations. This is changing, however, and gender-difference effects between negotiators in other cultures are shrinking (Chang, 2003).

Also, cultures that identify with the dimension of Confucian dynamism value qualities such as loyalty, reciprocal obligations, and honesty. Therefore, honesty and politeness are important to building long-term business relationships, which the Chinese with their long-term orientation expect (Buttery and Leung, 1998). The Chinese value a win-win situation, and this is best established by being honest about your intentions, goals, and interests. Having a good understanding of the other culture will help negotiators gain a better outcome (Chang, 2003). In fact, successful negotiation strategies used by Chinese negotiators focus primarily on rational professional approaches, whereas Western negotiators focus on coping with Chinese societal values (Sheer and Chen, 2003).

Negotiation is a mutual communication exchange and includes both verbal and nonverbal communication. Negotiators from different countries can easily misread a message or send an unintended message. However, research on negotiation has tended to ignore culture as an important variable while proposing theories of negotiation that can be applied universally (Pruitt and Carnevale, 1993). In addition, some research results suggest that U.S. negotiators struggle with crossed signals when negotiating not only with people from completely unfamiliar cultures, but also with people from cultures with which they have some familiarity, such as Japan (Graham and Sano, 1984) and China (Pye, 1982). Successful negotiations are based on understanding that the other party's strategies, conduct, attitudes, and cultural values play an important role in the negotiation process.

Negotiating across Cultures

Negotiations between people from different countries have been increasing as global business arrangements increase, whether through direct trade, joint ventures, or licensing and distribution agreements. So understanding cultural variables in the negotiation process is important to successful trade and organizational negotiations as well as conflict resolution. Indeed, nationality is an important determinant of most negotiators' attitudes. For example, American negotiators tend to be more trusting, more willing to take risks, and more believing in self-determination than negotiators from Central Europe, Greece, Japan, Scandinavia, South Africa, Spain, and Thailand (Harnett and Cummings, 1980).

It is unlikely that results from studying negotiation patterns of managers within a country will apply when the same managers negotiate with managers from outside their country (Adler and Graham, 1989). This means that domestic negotiating styles do not necessarily predict international negotiating styles. In a comparison of the behavior of American, Canadian Anglophone, Canadian Francophone, and Japanese businesspeople in a negotiation simulation, subjects were assigned to either same-culture pairs or different-culture pairs. The researchers conclude that negotiators do adapt their negotiation behaviors in cross-cultural negotiations. However, the researchers also note that Americans were the least likely to respond to their partner's behavior and, as a consequence, rarely adapted their own behavior. On the other hand, the Japanese were the most likely to adapt.

Accountability in negotiations is affected by cultural expectations, especially on the individualism-collectivism dimension. In individualist societies, such as the United States, there is an emphasis on autonomy and related traits, which tends to minimize the effects of accountability in negotiations. On the other hand, in collectivist societies, such as those in Asia, the emphasis on belongingness, conformity, and related traits tends to increase accountability. In fact, negotiations produce different outcomes depending on the negotiators' level of collectivism and on the situation (Gelfand and Realo, 1999).

Sweden is one of the most collectivist societies in Europe, and the cultural value of sharing responsibility for the support of all members of society is strong (Frazee, 1997). In Sweden, negotiations seem to take longer because the Swedes have a desire to avoid conflict and focus on consensus building. However, once a deal is made, a handshake will ensure that the deal will be kept, since honesty is another core national value (Frazee, 1997).

A comparison of American, Arab, and Russian negotiating styles, responses to arguments, concessions, and deadlines shows that Americans think deadlines are very important, rely on facts and logic in their attempts to persuade and counteract opponents' arguments, and make small concessions early in order to help build a relationship with the other side in the negotiations. On the other hand, Arabs are more likely to use an appeal to emotion as their persuasion strategy, to use subjective feelings to counter arguments, to not take deadlines seriously, and to use concessions continually as a bargaining strategy. Finally, the Russians base their arguments on asserted ideals, make few concessions because making concessions is a sign of weakness, and tend to ignore deadlines (Glen, Witmeyer, and Stevenson, 1977).

Negotiating conflict strategies is one particular aspect of negotiating, which was studied in a research project that compared negotiators in the United States, Japan, and Germany (Tinsley, 2001). If the culture values individualism and egalitarianism, then negotiators are more likely to use interest strategies, which focus on resolving the underlying concerns that generated the conflict in order to ensure that there is more benefit gained when there is a successful resolution. On the other hand, negotiators are more likely to use regulation strategies if the culture values contracts and regulations. Finally, if the culture values collectivism, hierarchy, and few regulations, negotiators are likely to use power strategies. Thus, the Japanese use more power strategies than the Germans, who, in turn, use more power strategies than Americans. Americans and Germans use more interest strategies than the Japanese, and Germans use more regulation strategies than either Americans or Japanese. Since the French tend to like conflict, negotiations tend to take a long time, especially since they appear not to care whether their opponents like or dislike them (Schmidt, 1987).

The ability of the Chinese to develop excellent deal-making skills has been the inspiration for some interesting studies (Engardio, 1991). Chinese businesspeople do not separate marketing and financing as a Western businessperson might (Limlingan, 1986), and as a result, they are able to take advantage of financial situations and concentrate on the cash outcomes to a much greater extent. The Chinese have also been the focus of several studies on negotiation style differences. For example, one study compared Chinese (from both the PRC and Taiwan) and Americans to see if there is a preferred negotiating style based on culture. The results indicate that if culture is the only factor considered, then both groups are equally competitive, collaborative, and accommodating in their negotiation approach. However, the Chinese subjects were more likely to use the withdrawal negotiation style. In addition, other differences in negotiating style were found if the conflict was about a business situation rather than with a close friend or if it involved the individualism-collectivism dimension. If cultural differences affect negotiations, the impact of the situation and the role of individualism-collectivism on style need to be simultaneously considered.

In an investigation of negotiating practices between China and the United States, as well as between various Chinese countries, researchers concluded that the Chinese prefer to do business with "known quantities." Because of this, they prefer to negotiate with companies or individuals with whom they have had a solid history. The Chinese also view relationships as structured and hierarchical, whereas Americans tend to see relationships as more informal and based on equality among the participants. A variety of strategies for use at different stages of the negotiation process have been proposed, which stress that when working with the Chinese, discussion of personal issues is not appropriate and a polite, formal relationship should be maintained (Shenkar and Ronen, 1987).

Another study of Chinese negotiating styles compared Hong Kong Chinese and American samples using a negotiation simulation (Tinsley and Pillutla, 1998). The results indicate that Americans are more likely to express higher levels of self-interest and joint problem-solving norms, while the Hong Kong Chinese are more likely to express norms of equality. The expected differences in the levels of expressed altruism and competitive norms between the groups were not found. There were also cultural differences in the way that the subjects in this research interpreted negotiating instructions. The Americans interpreted a direction to cooperate as meaning that they should strive for maximizing the joint outcome. On the other hand, the Chinese interpreted this instruction as ensuring that the parties have equal outcomes. This is a subtle but potentially significant difference in negotiating outcomes. Finally, the results also showed that there were culturally different reactions to the negotiations, which were manifested in different levels of negotiator satisfaction with the process and outcome. Americans felt more satisfaction when they maximized joint gain, whereas the Hong Kong Chinese expressed more satisfaction when the results created parity for the two parties.

Organizational power, power dynamics, and negotiation strategies between managers and employees are affected by whether cooperative or competitive goals are being pursued. A comparison of samples from Canada and the United States found that cooperative goals induce higher expectations of helping behavior, more actual help, greater support, and more trust than do competitive goals (Tjosvold, 1985). A replication of an earlier study was undertaken in a Chinese setting to test whether similar results would be found in the non-Western setting, since the Chinese preference for diffusing open conflict and avoiding face-to-face confrontations has been well established (Bond, Wan, Leung, and Giacalone, 1985). The Chinese from Hong Kong behaved in a similar way to Americans in reacting to cooperative goals but were less likely to allow competitive goals to interfere with their interactions and pursuit of individual goals (Tjosvold, Hui, and Law, 1998).

It has been suggested that people categorize themselves into psychological groups based on obvious characteristics such as culture (Triandis, 1976). When cultural distance between two groups is small, as with U.S. and British negotiators, then negotiators see the other team as part of their own psychological group. On the other hand, the cultural distance between U.S. and Chinese negotiators is large and, as a result, in negotiations the Chinese are seen as different, difficult to understand, less trustworthy, and less cooperative (Harrigan, 1988).

Negotiation is a critical component of the process of establishing joint ventures and other international business alliances. A study looking at the behavioral aspects of negotiations and real-world behavior, rather than the more-typical use of laboratory research, used interviews with American negotiators who had recently been involved in international negotiations. Even though previous research has indicated that perceived relative power plays a role in negotiating style, this finding was not replicated for the American sample. Rather, the American negotiators used perceived absolute power to guide their negotiating strategy. And by assuming that their partners could negotiate with others, the Americans adopted a soft negotiating style. The results also suggest that when the level of trust is low, soft tactics are effective. However, once trust is established, more-aggressive and open tactics are more effective (Rao and Schmidt, 1998). There is no question that negotiating styles, strategies, and tactics are influenced by culture.

Summary

Effective organizational behavior by managers and executives across cultures requires that they be able recognize the importance of cultural differences. In order to overcome cross-cultural communication barriers, you need to be sensitive to their existence; respect cultural differences; speak slowly, clearly, and in simple, nonjargon English; and listen for understanding rather than agreement. Of course, it is best to learn other languages and not fall back on the arrogance of expecting everyone else to speak your language. But unfortunately, many Americans avoid learning, or are not given the opportunity to learn, other languages.

Communication between cultures is difficult and rife with the potential for problems. In organizational settings, communication patterns affect a wide variety of organizational behaviors including decision making, motivation, teamwork, and the relationship between manager and employee. Cultural and language barriers can have a strong impact on relationships and influence in multinational companies, and expatriate managers need to be prepared for assignments with both language and cultural training, as well as be expected to have the appropriate attitudes and expectations about subordinates from another country. Styles of communicating also vary among cultures, with some cultures, such as the United States, preferring an open, direct form of communication and other cultures preferring a more indirect form. Since good cross-cultural communication is a key component of effective international joint ventures, organizations need to pay attention to the communication competence of managers and monitor the communication between key employees to ensure appropriate communication is occurring where it is most critical to the success of the venture.

One place that communication breaks down frequently is during the negotiation process. Successful negotiations require mutual respect and understanding on the part of both parties. Negotiators enter the process with a subjective view of the other party's values and goals that may or may not be accurate. Negotiators can use a variety of tactics to influence the outcome, and these tactics can be classified as hard, soft, or rational. Negotiators who think they have the power advantage will tend to use hard tactics, while soft tactics are used when interpersonal affection and a sense of obligation and reciprocity are present. Rational approaches use nonemotional arguments to gain acceptance when there is some doubt that achieving acceptance is possible. Different cultures use different negotiating strategies, and it is important that these differences are understood and integrated into the negotiating process by both sides. Differences in negotiating style and values can be seen in differences in the speed of negotiations, use or avoidance of conflict, and level of commitment to the outcome.

13

Personnel Psychology and
Human Resource Management

In a global economy with growing competition, flat organizational structures, and share- and stakeholder orientation, there is increasing pressure to perform in all types of organizations. Organizations and their managers need to find new efficient ways of operating and to use technology and resources, especially personnel, to their fullest capacity. Personnel issues generally include staffing and recruitment, training and development, compensation, labor-management relations (unions), and the nature of the labor market. While research on these topics in international or cross-cultural settings has been growing, there are still areas that have been understudied. The majority of the research to date has focused on managers, particularly those who are assigned to overseas positions. As companies expand globally, managers are often sent overseas to manage in joint ventures or subsidiaries, and a large proportion of international joint ventures fail because of problems based on cultural factors (Park, Gowan, and Hwang, 2002).

World-class organizations need a new breed of managers who have the intangible assets of concepts, competence, and connections (Kanter, 1995). Without world-class managers being available within the organization, many multinational companies will not be effective and competitive (Harvey, 1997). Managers who are willing to work as expatriates are major corporate assets (Brett, Stroh, and Reilly, 1993). This chapter will explore personnel selection and some of the issues related to both overseas assignments and the impact of returning home, as well as related human resource issues.

Personnel Selection

Over the past few decades, American literature on personnel selection has emphasized the role of science in the development of sound psychological-testing selection practices that are valid, reliable, and legally defensible. The goal of increasing the psychometric rigor of selection practices has been driven by the American human resource management (HRM) paradigm, which states that selecting the best-qualified candidates on the basis of job-related knowledge, skills, and abilities is the means by which organizations can achieve a competitive advantage. The assumption that the most qualified candidate is the best candidate for any position exemplifies the American cultural value orientation toward independence and individual achievement. This assumption fails to recognize the diversity of cultural values and norms that exists outside America. It is not surprising, therefore, that HRM practices that are instrumental to organizational productivity and effectiveness in America fail to be as useful or effective when implemented in other cultures (Brewster, 2002).

There is evidence to support the belief that organizations in different cultures make staffing decisions in different ways and utilize different types of information. A survey of fourteen countries found that job descriptions are used fairly universally, as are educational qualifications, application forms, references, and interviews. However, collectivist cultures are more likely to prefer objective measures, while individualist cultures are more likely to use a more personal approach that emphasizes and values the unique characteristics of job applicants (Nyfield and Baron, 2000).

Other Selection and Human Resource Issues

One of the questions facing organizations that hire workers from other countries is to what extent differences between people are a function of the culture or are simply individual differences (Arvey, Bhagat, and Salas, 1991). If individual differences are more important than cultural differences, this affects the selection and recruitment process. The answer to this question is unclear, and the question is a perplexing one for organizations. Hopefully, future research in this area will provide the kind of answers that will facilitate successful hiring.

In general, American selection processes involve relatively objective criteria based on merit and qualifications. In some respects, the legal requirements of hiring in the United States, such as equal employment opportunity legislation, create and require a more legalistic approach to hiring practices. In addition, companies in the United States are more likely to use psychological testing and assessment centers when selecting managers and executives than European companies, but European companies are more likely to rely on individuals being nominated for a position and to seek out key industry individuals and encourage them to switch companies (Derr, 1987).

The process of selecting and recruiting employees varies from culture to culture. Western selection techniques include interviews, application forms, references, and psychological testing. However, even within Western countries there are variations in the selection approaches used. Interviews are the most commonly used selection procedures in Belgium, France, Italy, Spain, Germany, and the United Kingdom. Germany and the United Kingdom are most likely to use application forms and references to complement the use of interviews, whereas France and Belgium are more likely to use personality and cognitive testing. Interestingly, the French and French-speaking companies also use handwriting analysis between 12 and 17 percent of the time as a supporting tool in personnel selection (Shackleton and Newell, 1994). The British are also more likely to use interview panels, rather than individual interviews, and intelligence tests, whereas the French prefer individual interviews and rely on a measure of rapport between interviewer and interviewee when making decisions. Interviews are rarely used in Taiwan or China, where the preferred selection process is more likely to include consideration of the college a person attended and its prestige (Huo and von Glinow, 1995) or recommendations from current senior managers based on family relationships (Child, 1994).

There are also differences in the basic philosophy to choosing managers. In the United Kingdom, it is generally accepted that generalists make the best managers. A good manager has the appropriate personality, social skills, leadership qualities, and ability to get along with others. Americans take a similar approach but place emphasis on drive, ambition, energy, and social competence. While the French also have a generalist view of management, managerial universalism is based on intellect and an educated mind. The educational specialty of the managerial candidate is less important than the perception that the candidate is intellectually and educationally superior. On the other hand, the Germans and Swiss take a specialist view of management, so managers are recruited and selected based on their expertise and knowledge (Lawrence and Edwards, 2000). These differences in perceptions of what makes an effective manager will obviously influence managerial selection procedures, outcomes, and even performance.

In mainland China, while the opening of the Chinese economy to multinational companies and joint ventures is encouraging hiring based on merit, the government still assigns many employees to jobs (Li, Xin, and Tsui, 1999). In most other Chinese cultures, jobs are still filled by family and friends (Redding and Hsiao, 1990). A similar finding has been reported for Mexico, where trustworthiness and loyalty are valued and best achieved by favoring relatives and friends of other employees, especially since this helps ensure that the person "fits" with the group (Kras, 1988). In Japan, the national testing of students and the hierarchy of high schools and universities translate into educational history being very important in recruitment and selection. As in France, in Japan this is determined in part by the stature of various universities, with the University of Tokyo being the most prestigious. Organizations use informal and subjective selection procedures including multiple interviews and participation in social events. Organizations will also contact friends and family members to gather further information on candidates (Tung, 1984).

One final area of difference in selection, and especially promotion, is how cultures handle seniority. In Asian cultures, age is respected so that seniority plays a very important role, but it is less important in the United States, where ability is preferred over seniority and seniority tends to have a moderating rather than direct effect. For example, for me as a faculty member operating in a union setting, only two issues are prescribed as being driven by seniority: parking and office assignments. At the same time, seniority is considered but not prescribed in a variety of other areas such as class assignments and general influence in departmental affairs. In Europe, seniority is very important in France, Switzerland, and Italy for pay and promotions, and in Germany seniority plays a major role in how knowledge and expertise are perceived and received by others.

Cultural Approaches to Training

Training is seen as important in many countries as a way to ensure that new hires can do the job, current employees can learn new skills, and managers can develop. However, once again there are cultural differences in attitudes about, approaches to, and who is responsible for training. European countries have fewer universities per capita than does the United States, but more technical and vocational training programs. Many European countries still use apprenticeships rather than formal education to train people for specific occupations. This is particularly true with regard to, but not limited to, learning a trade. So plumbers and carpenters always serve apprenticeships. In addition, while an accountant is trained in a university in America, in many European countries, such as the United Kingdom, accountants are "articled" and learn their trade through being apprenticed to other accountants. And only after they have passed a series of standardized tests are they considered to have met the requirements for different skill and knowledge levels, until they are finally allowed to call themselves accountants. As a result of this different approach to training, accountants need less on-the-job training once hired in Europe than they do in the United States, especially since many accountants remain in the companies that offered them their apprenticeship.

The Swiss and Germans take training very seriously, and both countries provide an abundance of training opportunities. In the United Kingdom, a lack of management and post-hire training had been the norm, but this has been changing in recent years as organizations are beginning to give a priority to management development, which is now seen as a strategic commitment to organizational development (Thomson, 1997). The British also see the line manager as responsible for employee development, whereas the Germans see development as the responsibility of staff-development specialists. While the Dutch value training, they see it as a major networking mechanism and a way to get exposure to upper-management personnel and, thus, to potentially have their abilities recognized and rewarded (Lawrence and Edwards, 2000).

Expatriate Assignments

Inadequate assessment and selection of the skills needed to adapt to an expatriate assignment is one of the main reasons cited for high failure rates among expatriates. Selection for overseas duties seems to be determined by informal judgments of potential adjustment and effectiveness, as well as the willingness to relocate (Ones and Viswesvaran, 1997).

Given the high costs of failed expatriate assignments, sometimes estimated to exceed a million dollars each, there is a strong incentive to improve the selection process. Even if an assignment is successful, it has been estimated that the cost of sending a manager overseas is at least three times the manager's base salary. Given the potentially limited return on this major investment, corporate leadership is beginning to realize the valuable contribution of and need for globally competent managers (Wederspahn, 1992).

There are three types of expatriate assignments: (1) joining another part of the company to provide expertise to an underdeveloped area of the organization; (2) working on a specific project, typically the largest number of assignments, with the intention of transferring these functions in the future; and (3) a developmental assignment, which is used to further the skills or career development of the expatriate. The selection criteria can change depending on the type of assignment. For example, if the assignment is developmental, then the person may need to gather information about the procedures, strengths, weaknesses, and so forth associated with the assignment location. Research indicates that failure to adjust to the foreign environment, rather than a lack of appropriate abilities, is the major reason for failure in overseas placements. The adjustment process begins with effective recruiting, selection, and training. While the two most important factors in the selection process that are likely to lead to successful placements are previous international assignment and experience and knowledge of the language, other selection criteria including an openness to the experience and the ability to learn from other people are also important (Andreason, 2003).

A distinction has been made between expatriate and global managers (Pucik and Saba, 1998). The international or expatriate manager is linked to an assignment in a specific location. This person is an executive who can provide leadership in international assignments. The global manager is an individual with cross-border responsibilities. This individual has extensive knowledge of international business and is able to effectively work with a global perspective across cultures. The key is that the global manager can balance the simultaneous demands of global integration and national responsiveness (Bartlett and Ghoshal, 1992). Successful globally competing organizations require both types of managers.

The global manager requires a mind-set that reflects the global perspective, and the competencies needed are more complex and dynamic than those needed by an expatriate manager (Pucik and Saba, 1998).

Global competence can be defined in terms of knowledge, skills, abilities, and other characteristics (Caligiuri, 2000). Several scholars have identified dimensions of global competence. For example, one approach is based on the measurement of three dimensions of cross-cultural skills: self, relationship, and perception. The self dimension refers to skills needed to maintain one's mental health, effectively reduce stress, and promote feelings of self-confidence. The relationship dimension refers primarily to skills needed to foster relationships with host nationals. The perception dimension refers to cognitive skills that promote an accurate perception of the host environment and its social systems (Black and Mendenhall, 1990).

Two major issues related to overseas postings and the success or failure of expatriates have emerged. The first has to do with how well a person will adapt to the new temporary-home culture. The process of adaptation includes acculturation and can take the form of integration, assimilation, separation/segregation, or marginalization (Tung, 1998). Integration is the most functional level of acculturation, and marginalization is the most dysfunctional. An investigation of expatriates' perceptions relative to international assignments included American expatriates who were or who had been assigned overseas to numerous countries. The assignment experiences were generally seen as very positive. There seems to be a trend toward more women and employees with families being assigned to overseas assignments, leading to the conclusion that the American expatriates were able to perform effectively wherever they were assigned. While many individuals in the sample were bilingual or multilingual and had had previous living or working experience overseas, the availability of a diverse and well-qualified pool of individuals was also seen as a positive trend (Tung, 1998). Having a favorable attitude toward accepting an overseas assignment, being single, having prior international experience, and having a strong commitment to the organization were all found to have a positive impact on the success of an overseas assignment (Borstoff, Field, and Stanley, 1997).

American expatriates tended to perceive international assignments as beneficial to their career development and advancement even though the majority of those studied worked for an organization that did not guarantee promotions, or in some cases even a job, upon their return home. This finding leads to the second expatriate concern, which has to do with the process of repatriation upon the return home. Recent research has suggested organizations should be concerned about what happens when managers return to the parent company, since turnover rates are very high in this group (Stroh, Gregersen, and Black, 1998). One approach to reducing the impact of repatriation is to ensure that the gap between expectations and reality is minimized for expatriates (Stroh, Gregersen, and Black, 1998). After several years abroad, managers often return to the parent company expecting an easy transition, but the reality is often quite different. For example, managers may return to a changed parent organization and a changed social environment. As a result, between 20 and 50 percent of expatriates resign shortly after returning to their home base. This is a much higher rate than that of normal turnover for managers and executives (Black and Gregersen, 1998). However, it should be noted that after conducting a meta-analysis of published literature, A. W. K. Harzing (1995) concluded that it is in fact a myth that American turnover rates are very high. Nonetheless, the implications of a high degree of turnover for both the manager and the organization are serious. A large percentage of expatriates have also reported experiencing burnout, low motivation, and stress during completed assignments, and the negative impact of these experiences may be potentially more costly to the individual and the organization than failure in an assignment. The major cause of these types of problems is a lack of cultural preparedness and training, as well as poor or inappropriate selection procedures (McGrath-Champ and Yang, 2002).

Mergers and acquisitions between companies from different cultures create problems, and acculturation between two different cultures may be difficult to achieve. In fact, pre-merger cultural attributes play a major role in determining post-merger acculturation (Cartwright and Cooper, 1993). Using a form of meta-analysis based on case studies of Swedish and American companies, researchers found socialization activities involving employee participation to be the best strategy for achieving acculturation, as long as the new organization was autonomous. If, however, there is less autonomy, which is common when the prime organization tries to maintain control, additional control mechanisms may be necessary. These mechanisms can include transition teams, senior-management involvement, and temporary personnel exchange or rotation. The key finding from this study was that social controls were the best mechanism for creating acculturation and that mandated changes were never successful, regardless of the initial nature of the merged companies. Thus, cross-cultural acculturation is possible as long as the informal integration processes are not ignored (Larsson and Lubatkin, 2001). The creation of cohesive managerial teams in international joint ventures is made more difficult by the low level of organizational commitment and trust that often results from combining managers from both the host and parent countries (Park, Gowan, and Hwang, 2002).

There has been a continuing increase in the number of managers assigned to international markets and operations. Because it is expensive and difficult to relocate managers, only the higher-level and key managers tend to be assigned. Even so, 25 to 40 percent of managers posted overseas return early, and if the posting is to a developing country, the early-return rate can be as high as 70 percent (Black, Gregersen, Mendenhall, and Stroh, 1999). Given that these assignments usually involve critical positions, appropriate and effective preparation for these assignments is essential. In a study of managers' perceptions of the organization's strategy in sending them abroad, the predeparture preparations and orientation process, and the career outcomes, researchers found that the majority of the managers felt that they were not adequately prepared for their assignments and that there is a need to include career-development counseling as a component of any decision to offer or accept an assignment overseas. This led to the suggestion that it is helpful to develop a mentoring program that uses expatriate networks to assist in problem solving in the unique situations that can occur overseas and to provide practical, moral, and psychological support when dealing with culture shock (Dunbar and Ehrlich, 1993). Intracultural differences need to be taken into consideration because they can have an even bigger impact on organizational behavior than national norms. Expatriates will have a harder time adjusting to cultures that show large rather than small intracultural variation, and as a result, expatriate managers should be given more-sophisticated adaptation training in high-intracultural-variation countries (Au, 2000).

Culture shock contributes to expatriate turnover and includes homesickness, irritability, hostility toward host nationals, and the loss of ability to work effectively (Cascio, 2003). Research has focused on three components of expatriate success and ways to help overcome culture shock: cross-cultural adjustment, completion of the global assignment, and performance in the global assignment (Caligiuri, 1997). Cross-cultural adjustment is very much an individual characteristic and is the degree to which expatriates feel comfortable working away from their home country. An exploration of how contact by American expatriates with host nationals affects cross-cultural adjustment found that while contact was an important variable, it was positively affected by the personality characteristics of openness and sociability of the expatriate. Further, contact alone was not enough to ensure cross-cultural adaptation, and the availability of compatriot friends plays an equally important role. Another study looked at these issues from the perspective of a German multinational company with operations in Britain and Spain (Matthias, 2001). The parent company's national business system had the greatest influence on the organization's behavior, and this influence was often subtle. American expatriates living in other countries learned about their host country through reflective learning, or learning from their real-life experiences, suggesting that training programs designed to prepare managers for work abroad should reflect actual needs and real-world situations. Expatriates were helped by having previous cross-cultural experience, knowledge of the language, relationships with people from the host country, and information about the host country from several sources (Shim and Paprock, 2002).

Successful cultural adaptation has been found to be critical to levels of organizational commitment (Jun, Lee, and Gentry, 1997) and to how much the organization values overseas assignments as part of a career path (Feldman and Tompson, 1993). Failure to adjust successfully may lead to a variety of negative psychological consequences. Adaptation to the host marketplace has been associated with successful cultural adaptation for Korean expatriates in numerous countries. The consumer behavior of the expatriates and their families is an important nonwork variable affecting cultural adjustment. Also, managers in multinational companies need to develop managerial networks within the organization to encourage the exchange of information and learning (Nohria and Ghoshal, 1997). And management should promote communication across diverse groups of managers since, although managers can develop relationships across cultures, they rely on managers with similar backgrounds for their social relationships (Manev and Stevenson, 2001).

Intercultural sensitivity is of value to all members of an organization, not just managers who are being assigned overseas. In the United States, there is a great deal of diversity in the workplace, and this includes a growing number of new immigrants and temporary-visa employees from other countries. Being able to interpret particular events the same way as people from other cultures will be of great value to all employees and organizations. Intercultural sensitivity has been defined as including comfort with other cultures, positive evaluation of other cultures, an understanding of cultural differences, empathy for people from other cultures, open-mindedness, the sharing of cultural differences with others, adaptability, and a willingness to seek feedback on how a particular behavior is received in other cultures (Dunbar, 1996).

One valuable area of research on overseas assignments and expatriate behavior has looked at issues that affect Chinese managers working in offshore factories. This is important because the number of Chinese managers from Taiwan currently employed in the PRC is significant and has the advantage of providing a large database for researchers. To some extent, there are also controls over some of the cultural differences normally found between countries, since all the managers have a similar cultural background and typically can speak the same language. Taiwan has been moving from a manufacturing to a service business environment. As a consequence, the majority of the work force is being attracted to service businesses and away from manufacturing. The reasons for this include the fact that the Taiwan population is becoming more educated and therefore prefers to work in jobs that they perceive to match their educational level, the pay in the service sector tends to be higher, the working conditions are much more pleasant, and there is a higher social status attached to these jobs. The basic manufacturing-industry worker has and requires a minimal level of education, receives low wages, and works in an environment that is often both noisy and dirty. In addition to the move into the service sector, Taiwan is a major manufacturer and exporter of technology. Working in this sector also pays well and provides greater incentives to workers. The consequence of these changes in the Taiwanese business environment is a shortage of labor for many types of manufacturers. As a result of the labor shortage and relatively high labor costs, an increasing number of companies from Taiwan are moving overseas, first to the PRC, then to Indonesia and, more recently, Vietnam. These moves are seen as necessary to counter increasing labor costs and country-specific import quotas.

The Republic of China (Taiwan) has opened up trade and economic links with the PRC in recent years, despite the political differences and ideological posturing between the two countries. As a result, there is a growing economic dependency between the two countries. Entrepreneurs from Taiwan have invested significantly in the PRC, and the PRC has become a significant destination for Taiwanese businesses relocating out of Taiwan in search of lower labor costs and favorable business environments. This move by Taiwanese companies to open joint ventures, branches, factories, and stores in the PRC has not always been easy. Problems have been encountered and issues have had to be resolved. Plus, all of this business expansion has occurred in a difficult political environment. Despite the risks and problems facing Taiwanese businesses as a result of political uncertainty, both in the PRC and between Taiwan and the PRC, the move offshore has continued. Since many of these offshore organizations are using Taiwanese citizens as managers at factories within the PRC, there is significant potential for a conflict of managerial styles and values between the two cultures, with which the expatriate managers will have to cope. Any understanding of these issues can only benefit everyone involved and hopefully create a more successful business environment for Taiwanese entrepreneurs in the PRC, as well as offer insights into broader issues of identifying critical expatriate behaviors.

The Japanese have invested heavily in the United States and have used managers from Japan to oversee their investments and manage their employees in North America and elsewhere. Intercultural influence was studied in Taiwan, and the strategies of American and Japanese expatriate managers in influencing their Taiwanese subordinates were compared (Yeh, 1995). Japanese managers were more likely to use bargaining, assertiveness, and upward appeal than the Americans. Likewise, the use of influence strategies by Japanese expatriates in Canada was compared for Canadian and Japanese subordinates (Hashimoto and Rao, 1996). The results indicate that the Japanese expatriates use more influence strategies with their Canadian subordinates than with their Japanese subordinates. The Japanese feel that it is not necessary to use direct communication and influence with Japanese subordinates because, culturally, employees are expected to accept and understand decisions and not to speak out if they have differing opinions. However, with Canadian subordinates, Japanese managers explain the reasons for requests more and support their positions with data, documentation, and logic.

In selecting managers to work overseas, a variety of human resource issues come into play. It is critical to the success of a multinational organization that it selects, attracts, and retains employees who can operate successfully away from their home culture (Stroh and Caligiuri, 1998). The number of employees sent overseas has been increasing dramatically in the past ten years. Since expatriate managers are often involved in high-level negotiations, managing the subsidiary and perhaps even new-product development, any managerial failure will have significant effects on both the offshore company and future global business ventures. In fact, the cost of training, relocation, and compensation for each expatriate assignment was estimated to be around $80,000 in 1996 (Ones and Viswesvaran, 1997).

It has been suggested that there are five essential components to creating competent managers in overseas assignments: language training, cultural and business orientation, family consultation, mentoring on site (in the overseas placement, by a seasoned expatriate or appropriate host national), and a career approach to expatriation (Dunbar and Katcher, 1990).

Training for Cross-Cultural Assignments

Cross-cultural training is a valuable tool for employees and managers, particularly those being assigned overseas. The goal of this training is to develop an understanding of basic differences in values, styles of communicating, and customs. The cultural assimilator is one approach to cross-cultural training that has been well researched and found to be valid in a variety of situations. It is a computer-based program that uses a series of scenarios describing challenging cross-cultural incidents. The person then makes his or her choice from one of several behavioral objectives and receives feedback on the cultural implications of that choice (Harrison, 1992).

In preparing expatriates, training is a critical factor in their success. Several recent reviews of research on cross-cultural training indicate that it is valuable because it has a positive impact on job performance, situational and cross-cultural adjustment, and individual skills (e.g., Morris and Robbie, 2001). However, questions have been raised as to whether training works for everyone and whether it is possible to design training to provide all the necessary competencies for success (Kealey, 1996). There are indications from the reactions of people in other countries that Americans need more intercultural training before being posted overseas. For example, Arabs report that Americans and other Westerners act superior, are unwilling to share credit with others, are unwilling or unable to adjust to local customs, prefer solutions developed in their home culture, ignore local-culture channels and procedures, and tend to be too autocratic and imposing (Harris and Moran, 1996). While *Forbes* magazine reported a survey of eleven countries in 1999 that indicated Americans were generally viewed negatively on several behavioral dimensions,

Americans were admired for their optimism, industrialism, inventiveness, decisiveness, enthusiasm, and friendliness. In addition, non-U.S. expatriates are also seen as having a variety of negative characteristics. Specifically, the Dutch are seen as blunt, Germans as inflexible, Japanese as vague and indirect, and managers from Latin America are seen as unable or unwilling to keep to deadlines (Wederspahn, 2002).

There is also evidence that cross-cultural training can benefit managers and make them more effective during their assignments (Black and Mendenhall, 1990). While training and development issues play an important role in preparing managers for overseas placements, they also play an integral role in many American organizations. However, American organizations are less likely to provide training than European and Japanese multinational companies before sending managers overseas (Black, Gregersen, Mendenhall, and Stroh, 1999). In America, this type of training program tends to be short, not to involve spouses or other family members, and to emphasize language and cultural basics. By contrast, training programs in Japan and Europe tend to be more extensive and rigorous. In addition, special programs are designed and offered for spouses and family members.

Successful expatriates seem to require self-maintenance competencies including self-efficacy, stress-management skills, cultural knowledge, conflict-resolution skills, and emotional stability. While most of these skills can be taught at a theoretical level, not all managers can effectively apply what they have learned. Other variables such as extraversion and agreeableness are personality characteristics that are hard to develop through training. There is still a need for extensive research to identify all the issues that can or need to be addressed in any cross-cultural-competencies training program (Leiba-O'Sullivan, 1999). A. Rosenbaum (1999) reports the results of one approach using the "Triangle Test," which is used to assess how and where executives from one culture may conflict with those of another. The test "measures" three sets of concepts that are designed to display fundamental cultural differences: behaviors, bedrock (cultural and social values), and work systems. While the results are mostly anecdotal and the test is not designed to be scientific, it does seem valuable in raising executive and organizational awareness of the issues involved in cross-cultural assignments.

Human Resource Management

Human resource management (HRM) has become increasingly important in organizations, but it takes on special importance in a global environment. Attaining the appropriate balance between local and global approaches is the key to success. In order to achieve this balance, it has been suggested that, rather than maximizing a particular approach such as decentralization, organizations should set minimum levels of desirable attributes (Evans and Doz, 1989). Therefore, in order to develop relevant HRM practices in MNCs, it is helpful to know how human resources are managed in other parts of the world. Several cross-national studies have attempted to identify the similarities and differences in practices. Different legal and cultural issues in various countries have resulted in research that has concentrated on comparing selection procedures, recruitment, training, and performance appraisal. For example, selection practices were considered in a twenty-two-country study, and the results supported earlier findings that staffing strategies differ by country and culture (Ryan, McFarland, and Baron, 1999).

Human resource practices in various countries are often driven by government regulations. These practices in some countries can be summarized as follows. In the Netherlands, laws make it hard to fire employees once they complete any probationary period, require hiring of the disabled as a percentage of the work force, prohibit most occupations from working on a Saturday or Sunday, and require management and worker representatives to consult on major decisions. More interestingly, the Dutch are attempting to make HRM the responsibility of line managers rather than treating it as a staff-departmental function (Hoogendoorn, 1992). This is also true in Denmark (Arkin, 1992). Germany has a very regulated work environment, so that employees can only be dismissed after a worker council approves the termination. These elected councils also have significant influence over working hours and conditions. Trade unions are active in all segments of industry, and the vast majority of employees belong to a union. This means that it is hard to terminate employees and that promotions tend to be internal (Arkin, 1992). In Italy and France, labor relations are highly regulated with active trade unions and worker councils. But in Italy there are several large state-owned holding companies and a few large private companies, but small family-owned businesses make up a large part of the economy. Italy is unusual in that a high number of managers are also part of a union. France has successfully assigned most HRM functions to line managers, with HRM managers serving as advisers who provide consulting help rather than staffing services. The large increase in the number of foreign firms in Ireland has led to significant changes in HRM policies and practices in recent years. Specifically, union membership has decreased, organizations are emphasizing efficiency, and the government is attempting to create a pro-business regulatory environment. In fact, Ireland is probably the best economic success story in Europe (Hannaway, 1992).

One way to consider the impact of culture on HRM practices is to look at the effectiveness of HRM practices of American companies operating overseas. American companies operating in other cultures must frequently balance the use of American HRM practices with the needs of the local business environment (Bartlett and Ghoshal, 1995). This balance requires organizations to seek consistency in the way they manage employees while, at the same time, adapting to the business practices and expectations of the country or region in which they are operating (Martinez and Jarillo, 1991). On the other hand, it may be appropriate or necessary to use different human resource strategies in different countries. Over half the MNCs surveyed adopted this strategy.

The pressures for globalization and the worldwide deployment of employees encourage uniform human resource strategies. Environmental forces that encourage local and situational factors lead to more-localized business practices. To some extent, human resources must be culture bound, and failure to acknowledge cultural differences is a mistake. In fact, cultural differences should be built on rather than ignored (Adler, 1986). Indeed, other companies will be operating in the same environment, and they will exert some influence over subsidiaries toward localization in such areas as wage rates and market competitiveness (Wright and McMahan, 1992). The dilemma faced by MNCs is that the global nature of a business requires more standardization and consistency, but diverse cultural environments demand differentiation. However, the more dependent a subsidiary is on the parent company's resources, the more likely it is that the parent company will push for standardization (Martinez and Ricks, 1989). At the same time, many countries have regulations governing business that will have an impact on human resource practices. For example, the United States has equal employment opportunity and minimum-wage regulations, and many European countries have regulations regarding termination of employees that make it either very expensive or very difficult to fire them.

One study that looked at this balance between the two sets of values compared HRM practices of American firms operating in Europe. Specifically, Ireland, the United Kingdom, and Scandinavia (Norway and Denmark) were included in the study (Gooderham, Nordhaug, and Ringdal, 1999). The results indicated that being an American subsidiary had a strong influence on HRM practices, although the company policies also reflected local influences, particularly in the Scandinavian countries. Other researchers have found similar results, supporting the idea that there is a strong link between the national home country of a company and the way the company manages and implements HRM practices (Harzing, 1999). To test this idea further, one study looked at German MNCs and the various HRM practices from the German and host-country perspectives. The results confirmed the importance of the parent country's HRM practices (in this case Germany). At the same time, local issues influenced the application of some HRM practices. The researchers also suggest that the process is an evolving one and that local practices will often need to be used to modify the home-country practices of some MNCs (Ferner, Quintanilla, and Varul, 2001).

Multinational companies face other special problems as they attempt to establish HRM practices in different countries and cultures (Shuler, Dowling, and De Cieri, 1993). For example, the need to measure the performance of a subsidiary is important to the parent company. One performance measure is performance management, which includes performance appraisal, communication of company strategy, links to training and development planning, and compensation. A study of subsidiaries of a European MNC located in China, Thailand, India, the United Kingdom, Germany, and the United States, in which the company had attempted to adopt a uniform performance-management system in all the business units no matter where in the world they were located, showed that the communication of subsidiary goals and the setting of job objectives, along with fair and frequent performance feedback, were important predictors of increased job satisfaction. The personal-development aspect of performance management also influenced job satisfaction in all countries. The universal nature of the findings, while important, should also be considered in the context of host-country adaptation, which was not necessarily identified in this particular survey process. However, with appropriate modifications, a consistent performance-management system can be of value to organizations operating in many countries (Lindholm, 1999).

Personality issues are also considered important in successful overseas placement. The basic question for the organization is whether certain types of people will be more comfortable and effective in overseas assignments. Identifying critical personality types is one way to ensure a good match between an employee and the assignment. For example, attitudes toward risk and work loyalty were compared for expatriate and indigenous managers in the United Arab Emirates (Ali, Krishman, and Azim, 1997). These two components of managerial behavior have been linked to absenteeism, organizational commitment, and motivation. The results indicated that foreign expatriates displayed less organizational loyalty but more personal loyalty than the Arab managers. Both Arab expatriates and indigenous employees were highly committed to organizational loyalty. Foreign expatriates indicated a higher willingness to take risks. The authors point out that, since accepting an overseas position already involves significant risk, maybe anyone willing to become an expatriate already enjoys risk-taking behavior. So any conclusion based on cause and effect needs to be interpreted with some degree of caution.

Role conflict and ambiguity may be quite different in international organizations than in uninational organizations. Chief executive officers in international joint ventures are likely to experience considerable role conflict and ambiguity as they balance the competing needs of the local operation with those of the parent company. Using in-depth interviews and a specially designed questionnaire, role conflict was found to be significantly lower for CEOs with more years of experience, and role ambiguity was significantly lower for CEOs with more education. Role conflict was positively correlated with differences in ownership, size, and objectives and negatively correlated with autonomy. Role ambiguity was positively correlated with power distance, masculinity-femininity, and autonomy and negatively correlated with individualism-collectivism and uncertainty avoidance. The findings suggest that cultural distance also needs to be taken into account when choosing a country within which to establish joint ventures (Shenkar and Zeira, 1992).

In Turkey, HRM is still a developing field, but the business environment in Turkey has been changing in recent years. Indeed, there is evidence that the results reported by Hofstede in 1980 are no longer valid today. For example, more-recent research indicates that Turkey has become less collectivist and less hierarchical (Aycan et al., 2000). In addition, Turkey tends to be very paternalistic, and in terms of HRM practices, scored high on job enrichment and empowering supervision but low on performance-reward contingency. It is also important to note that Turkey has a young, educated population (about 57 percent under the age of thirty) and that women are playing an increasingly important role in business (Aycan, 2001).

Summary

Industrial/organizational psychology has a long history of involvement in personnel selection. The biggest challenge facing organizations is the selection of personnel in a changing work force, both within the United States and in multinational organizations. As more managers are assigned overseas, the selection, training, and repatriation of managers is becoming more and more important. New types of organizations need new types of managers with unique and often intangible assets. Because of the intangible nature of the qualifications, skills, and abilities of successful managers and the wide range of cultural values and norms that exist outside the United States, current human resource practices are not always successful in selecting the best and most appropriate managers and staff for overseas assignments. The failure of expatriate mangers and the high probability that they will leave their organization upon their return is a major financial and asset drain for many organizations.

The distinction has also been made between expatriate managers, who are assigned to a specific country and position for a specified time period, and global managers, who have a global view and are able to easily and successfully work across cultures. The benefit of the presence of global managers within organizations outweighs that of expatriate managers, suggesting that organizations wishing to operate across cultures should seek and develop global managers at critical executive and upper-level management positions.

Psychologists have looked at both adaptation to a new culture and adaptation upon returning to the home culture. Individuals who have previous experience in other cultures, who are bi- or multilingual, who have a positive attitude toward accepting an overseas assignment, and who come from a large pool of possible candidates are most likely to succeed. In general, overseas assignments are viewed positively by American expatriates, who also believe such assignments will help their careers. However, this is not necessarily true, and adjustment upon returning home can be very difficult.

Mergers and acquisitions across cultures have raised issues related to the blending of the cultures. While these issues can also arise with mergers and acquisitions within a single culture, cross-cultural mergers pose a special personnel challenge.

In human resource management, the relationship between cultural and individual differences needs to be taken into consideration. Reliance on objective-criteria-based procedures works well in the United States but may not transfer to other cultures that rely on friendships and relationships to a much greater extent. Human resource practices that are illegal in the United States may be the cultural norm in other cultures. Even the use of interviews and application procedures varies among countries, and individuals may volunteer for a position in one country but be assigned to a position in another.

Training and development are important tools in preparing individuals for overseas assignments, although American companies have not attached the same level of importance or resources to this type of training as companies in other countries have.

Personnel issues have begun to be investigated in cross-cultural settings. Their relevance, use, relative importance, and effectiveness need further exploration. The emphasis on American higher-level-management overseas assignments has meant that interest in the selection and use of workers in other cultures has received little attention, even though hiring foreign workers is a common practice in many countries in Asia and Europe.

14

Some Final Thoughts

There is no doubt that the world is changing and relationships between countries are evolving in different ways. Business has led this process, as the global economy has taken shape and organizations such the World Trade Organization have added members and increased their influence. Cross-cultural industrial/organizational psychology researchers have begun to address the issues facing managers and organizations in this new and evolving organizational environment. During the past thirty years or so, there has been an increasing interest in country-based similarities and differences in leadership, managerial style, organizational practices, values, training, and selection. Government policies and regional and global trade treaties have also served to drive how organizations behave. International management issues will play an increasingly important role in organizations and organizational practices.

However, theory development and research endeavors have not yet reached a level that allows for most of the cultural similarities and differences to be identified accurately, analyzed, and applied effectively. It still remains true that most theory development has occurred in the United States and other Western countries. As a result, a significant portion of the research conducted to date has relied on American theories to drive the hypotheses being tested, and the examination of theories developed for the United States in non-Western cultures predominates. It is also true that the majority of publications that disseminate the research findings are American and European, and that English is the primary language used to report the research results. If research has been undertaken in other countries, it is either not easy to find or it is unlikely that the results have been shared outside the country where the research was conducted.

Having said that, there are numerous trends that suggest that the future is bright for conducting research in other countries and that this research will assist in providing both new theoretical frameworks for understanding various aspects of organizational psychology and valuable information for applying these theories and research results in other countries. The number of international conferences, such as the International Congress of Applied Psychology and the European Association of Work and Organizational Psychology conference, is increasing, so that the opportunities to share information outside traditional publication areas are also increasing, as are research collaborations by researchers from different countries. Also, there is an increase in the scope, size, and number of national psychology organizations with divisions committed to organizational psychology. For example, in Turkey the number of universities involved in industrial/organizational research has increased to fifteen, and graduate programs in industrial/organizational psychology are also on the increase. The current primary emphasis of the research and teaching programs is in the personnel issues related to human resources and employee and managerial selection instruments (Sinangil, 2002/2003). There is every reason to believe that similar movements are under way in other underdeveloped or newly developing countries.

One thing that became apparent when I attended a recent European conference is that the issues facing organizations and the research priorities in other countries are not necessarily the same as issues facing organizations and explored in research studies in the United States, if the number of research papers on a topic can be used as a guide. For example, there were more papers at the European conference on "bullying" in organizations than any other topic, while in the United States I have seen very few papers on this topic.

Social conflicts at work are a daily phenomenon. They have their origin in the social relationships between colleagues, supervisors, subordinates, and other members of the organization. Daily social conflicts at work are often the starting point of workplace bullying, which is used to systematically harass a person for a long time. In the context of stress theory, bullying is a severe form of social stressor at work, whereas in terms of conflict theory, bullying signifies an unsolved social conflict, which has reached a high level of escalation and has increased the imbalance of power because of its duration, frequency, and intensity. Bullying may also include constantly criticizing or undermining, threatening, shouting at, or excluding employees. More-subtle forms may include treating employees differently, overburdening them with work, setting unrealistic goals or deadlines, taking credit for their work, and monitoring them excessively.

Much of the leading research into workplace bullying originates in Europe, and the European psychology conferences have been instrumental in disseminating knowledge and helping to coordinate international research in the field, including research studies from Australia. Workplace bullying is reported as a major problem in Australia, where laws have been implemented in an attempt to reduce the problem. The laws have generated many claims, and the State of Victoria, for example, reported claims from bullying of A$57 million (approximately US$40 million) in 2001–2. In the United States, the United Kingdom, and Australia more than two-thirds of workplace bullies are supervisors and managers. For example, about 10 percent of employees surveyed in the United Kingdom reported that they had been bullied by supervisors (Willmott, 2002), and one in six American workers has reported that ongoing exploitive or abusive interactions with supervisors is a major source of stress (Namie and Namie, 2003). Although it has been suggested that even higher levels of bullying exist in American companies, there has been little research conducted in the United States either to identify the existence of bullying or, if shown to exist, to develop strategies to eliminate or correct it (Glendinning, 2001). It appears that bullying is just as common in the United States as in other countries, but surprisingly, bullying has only received significant attention from researchers in countries other than the United States. Whereas bullying at work has mainly been a subject of interest to psychologists in Northern Europe, whistle blowing has mainly been an American research topic of interest to lawyers, social scientists, and sociologists. So far, bullying and whistle blowing have been constituted into rather separate research areas that are rarely integrated or influenced by each other. It is clear, however, that many of the employees who take action with the intention of stopping illegal practices or wrongdoing at their workplace risk severe negative sanctions from colleagues or superiors, sanctions that may escalate into a situation where actual bullying occurs.

As discussed in chapter 2, the conceptualization and operationalization of culture remains problematic. Many researchers were enthusiastic about the work of Hofstede because he generated the promise of a theoretical framework around which theories could be developed and tested. However, serious questions have been raised about his interpretation of his research results, and this, in turn, may mean that subsequent results based on his theory need to be viewed with caution and, perhaps, explored and analyzed further to see if alternate explanations have merit. One of the basic questions facing researchers and theorists is whether a theoretical framework defining culture is necessary or possible. A conceptualization of a set of constructs, such as those developed by Hofstede, has been useful in generating research, but if the conceptualization is incorrect or too broad, its value is lessened or nullified. It may be that culture is much more complex and that the expanded list of categories used in the Project GLOBE research is better fitted to the reality and complexities of cultures. Even though the situation remains unclear, there is no doubt that culture affects behavior in many areas and that culture is an important variable in organizational psychology.

Leadership has generated the most research, based on the number of publications in this area, and a significant number of cross-cultural studies are continuing or have been completed. In looking at the research results, there is a lot of similarity across cultures in the preferred way of leading and being led. The participative style seems to be almost universally preferred as the first or second choice of managers in many countries. Having said that, it is also clear that the meaning of participation in one culture is quite different from its meaning in another. In Asian cultures, for example, participation may mean that you will be asked what you think but that your response will need to be framed within very specific culturally prescribed limits. In the United States, participation is more likely to mean group discussions with relatively open norms for individual behavior. In the same way, in Japan and Hong Kong a manager is thought to be considerate if he or she talks about a worker's problem with co-workers when the worker is not there, but the same behavior is seen as inconsiderate in the United States and the United Kingdom (Smith and Bond, 1999). Given equivalent responses by managers from different cultures to questions or surveys, but differences in what they mean by these responses, we should be careful not to interpret research results too literally or without at least some understanding of different cultural definitions for our standard organizational-psychology concepts.

One of the most important elements of work behavior is motivation, yet this is one of the least researched areas across cultures. While intrinsic motivation seems to be the generally preferred and most effective approach, in less-developed countries extrinsic rewards are more critical. F. Herzberg (1966) proposed that the factors that effect motivation could be broadly classified as being either satisfiers or motivators. Satisfiers, such as wages and job security, need to be met to a significant level if they are to truly work as motivators. The intrinsic motivators will not be as effective if basic needs, such as a decent salary, are not met. Obviously, different countries are at different levels of development, and people in many countries still fail to have their basic and security needs met through work. As a result, different types of motivation are effective in different countries, and the level of development of the culture and other societal issues play an important role. For example, in the PRC there is currently a lot of managerial turnover as people seek more money. This is only possible because the high demand for competent managers and the shortage of appropriately qualified employees provide the opportunities. The dramatic societal changes that are occurring within China are directly affecting motivational issues. Understanding motivation and its impact on employee behavior in various cultures requires a significant increase in research, especially given the relatively limited number of studies published to date.

Within cultures, values play an important role in how people behave in daily life. Values also play an important role in organizational behavior. In cross-cultural settings, differences in values can be a serious issue in management, turnover, organizational commitment, and conflict. The rapid expansion in the number of multinational companies has generated the need for negotiations between individuals from different cultures. Differences in negotiating and communication styles can cause serious problems and have a significant impact on whether a multinational company, merger, or joint venture succeeds across cultures. If cultural differences are mismanaged, the consequences are potentially disastrous, and previously effective managers and organizations can become ineffective and frustrated with overseas and multinational ventures. On the other hand, the successful management of cultural differences can create a competitive advantage, innovative business practices, and organizational learning.

Finally, the relative importance and effectiveness of global versus local standards for human resource procedures is open to debate. Based on the evidence available, local rules, norms, and regulations will affect this area of personnel psychology in significant ways. For example, different countries prefer different selection procedures. The utilization and procedures for the evaluation and appraisal of employees also differ from country to country. Some adaptation to local customs is probably necessary and may even be required by law, but this does raise concerns for multinational companies. For example, if relationships are key within an organization or between organizations, can an expatriate manger make effective decisions that should be based on relationships if they have been in a country for such a short time that they have yet to develop any? If the answer is no, then can they or do they have to delegate a potentially critical function to others?

So questions to be answered include, How can we use the information available to us to prepare managers to be effective in many cultures? and How can we use cultural differences effectively to enhance the organization's competitive advantage in the global arena? R. Rosen (2000) explores some of these issues in his study of global leadership. He suggests that every executive and manager must practice leadership universals that he calls "global literacies." He also concludes that as economic borders come down, cultural barriers go up. To be an effective executive or manager in today's environment, Rosen argues that managers must be globally literate. As such, these leaders need to have four distinct competencies, which Rosen identifies as personal literacy (understanding and valuing oneself), social literacy (engaging and challenging other people), business literacy (focusing and mobilizing one's organization), and cultural literacy (valuing and leveraging cultural differences). Culture will effect how these literacies are expressed because, according to Rosen, culture influences our purpose, plans, networks, skills, and results.

M. Javidan and R. J. House (2001) provide an interesting framework to help "global managers." Using the data they collected in Project GLOBE, information is available for each of the nine dimensions they studied from sixty-four countries (see chapter 3 for more details). For example, they point out that in the United States, a high-performance-oriented country, aggressiveness and directness are valued, but in Sweden such behavior would not be appreciated and in Greece discussion and exploration of issues is preferred over a commitment to explicit results. An understanding of the relative importance of these nine dimensions within a country will certainly assist managers in understanding which leadership or managerial behaviors are acceptable and effective and where the need for adaptation or compromise is most acute.

Of course, research and theory cannot prepare managers for every possibility. For example, when my brother was negotiating a contract with a government in French West Africa, the first set of complications was that the he represented a British subsidiary of an American company, which was negotiating in French in an African country that is strongly influenced by culture rooted in the country's French-colonial history. At least four cultural influences were in play during the negotiations. The second set of complications arose because he represented private industry but was negotiating with the national government, and private and public organizations generally have different agendas. The third complication was that during negotiations, there was an attempted military coup. The negotiating team was trapped for three days in a conference room with little food and no shower or change of clothes. The coup was defeated and the negotiations were successful, but no research or training could have prepared my brother for all aspects of the experience.

The research reported in this book relies heavily on published research in American and other Western journals. In all probability, research and information has been published in country-specific journals that are not readily available in the United States. There is a great need to expand the sharing of data across cultures, particularly from those countries under-represented by past research. Even so, it is clear that Western psychologists are actively pursuing research plans that broaden our understanding of organizational issues and concerns. What may be surprising to some is the relatively large number of research studies and publications in Chinese societies. The presence of a large and dedicated group of researchers in Hong Kong in particular has driven the research. Also, because of the widespread use of English in the former British colony, the majority of the research has been published in American and British journals. Chinese cultures have also provided a fertile area for understanding change and allowing for a level of equivalency of samples not always possible in cross-cultural research. The fact that Hong Kong, Taiwan, and the PRC (and Singapore, to a lesser extent) all share the same languages and core Chinese culture is helpful. At the same time, all three countries have experienced significant political, social, and economic change in the past ten years or so. Interestingly, studies on Japan, so prevalent in the 1970s as American organizations woke up to the Japanese success and incursion into American core businesses, have decreased in recent years.

Some areas of the world are receiving an increasing level of attention. In particular, Turkey, some parts of the Middle East, and Russia have been the focus of more and more researchers. However, in reviewing the research and findings in this book, it should be clear that many areas of the world remain unstudied or understudied. The amount of research on Latin American countries is very limited despite the rapid growth of trade between the United States, Mexico, and Canada following the adoption of NAFTA and the discussions currently underway to expand NAFTA to include other Latin American and Caribbean countries. There are also very few studies on countries in South America, and some of the published studies involving these countries have treated them as part of a Latin American cluster, which may or may not be an appropriate strategy. African countries are also significantly underrepresented.

As the research reported in this book demonstrates, a multidisciplinary approach has value in theory development because of the complex nature of organizational psychology, especially when looked at through a cultural lens. Future cross-cultural research needs to expand the breadth and depth of organizational research (Hui and Luk, 1997). The favorite topics in cross-cultural industrial/organizational research, reflected in the chapters in this book, include leadership, values, motivation, conflict, expatriation, and teamwork. Even in these broad areas, there are major gaps in coverage and in the knowledge available from the research. However, other areas such as work performance and evaluation, selection and recruitment, and quality of work life have received even less attention (Aycan, 2000). Still other areas such as stress, which is extensively studied in the United States, and bullying behavior, which is extensively studied in Europe, have not been systematically studied in other parts of the world.

The development of research programs such as Project GLOBE demonstrates the feasibility and value of multinational teams in addressing the challenges faced by researchers. The field of cross-cultural research in industrial/organizational psychology is a challenging and promising one, and the need for rigorous research exists. I hope the researchers whose work inspired this book will also inspire you to follow in their footsteps to build theories, conduct research, and expand the contributions of psychology to the global work environment.

There is ample evidence to indicate that, while current theories provide a useful framework, their application across cultures should be undertaken very carefully. Interest in research and analysis may never come to an end, as the interest shifts to what country and regional differences and similarities exist and, more importantly, why they exist. Most research has focused on highlighting differences, but even where differences exist, it is often a difference of relative emphasis rather than the presence or absence of a specific approach.

Particular attention needs to be paid to the fact that while people may say the same thing and use the same words to describe something, their conceptualization of an idea and how they transfer it into action may be quite different. Today's managers are living in a rapidly changing environment, and as companies expand across national borders, these managers will need to think globally in order to be successful. There will clearly be some convergence in the ways that organizations conduct business, but it also seems that a country's societal and cultural values will continue to play an important role, so managers need to act in line with local cultural needs and expectations. In other words, they need to think globally but act locally.

References

Abdalla, I. and Al-Homoud, M. A., (2001). Exploring the implicit leadership theory in the Arab Gulf states. *Applied Psychology: An International Review,* 50(4), 506–531.

Abramson, N. R., Lane, H. W., Nagai, H., and Takagi, H., (1993). A comparison of Canadian and Japanese cognitive styles: Implications for management interaction. *Journal of International Business Studies,* 24(3), 575–587.

Adler, N. J. (1997). *International dimensions of organizational behavior* (3d ed.). Boston: PWS-Kent Publishing.

Adler, N. J. (1986). Do MBAs want international careers? *International Journal of Intercultural Relations, 10,* 277–300.

Adler, N. J. (1984). Understanding the ways of understanding: Cross-cultural management reviewed. In R. N. Farmer (ed.), *Advances in international comparative management,* 1:31–67. Greenwich, CT: JAI Press.

Adler, N. J., and Bartholomew, S. (1992). Managing globally competent people. *Academy of Management Executive,* 6(3), 52–65.

Adler, N. J., and Doktor, R. (1989). From the Atlantic to the Pacific century: Cross-cultural management reviewed. In C. Osigweh (ed.), *Organizational science abroad: Constraints and perspectives.* New York: Plenum.

Adler, N. J., and Graham, J. L. (1989). Cross-cultural interaction: The international comparison fallacy? *Journal of International Business Studies,* 20(3), 515–537.

Adler, N. J., and Izraeli, D. N. (1994). *Competitive factors: Women managers in a global economy.* Oxford, UK: Blackwell.

Adler, N. J., and Izraeli, D. N. (1988). *Women in management worldwide.* Armonk, NY: M. E. Sharpe.

Adler, N. J., and Jelinek, M. (1986). Is "organization culture" culture bound? *Human Resource Management,* 25(1), 73–90.

Agarwal, S. (1994). Socio-cultural distance and the choice of joint ventures: A contingency perspective. *Journal of International Marketing,* 2(2), 63–80.

Agarwal, S., DeCarlo, T. E., and Vyas, S. B. (1999). Leadership behavior and organizational commitment: A comparative study of American and Indian salespersons. *Journal of International Business Studies,* 30(4), 727–743.

Ali, A. J. (1990). Management theory in a transitional society: The Arab's experience. *International Studies of Management and Organization,* 20(3), 7–35.

Ali, A. J. (1988). A cross-national perspective on managerial work value systems. In R. Farmer and E. McGoun (eds.), *Advances in international comparative management.* Greenwich, CT: JAI Press.

Ali, A. J., Krishman, K., and Azim, A. (1997). Expatriate and indigenous managers' work loyalty and attitude towards risk. *Journal of Psychology, 131,* 260–270.

Ali, A. J., and Al-Shakhis, M. (1987). Hierarchy of needs among school administrators in Saudi Arabia. *Journal of Social Psychology, 127,* 183–189.

Allen, N., and Meyer, J. (1990). The measurement and antecedents of affective, continuance and normative commitment to an organization. *Journal of Occupational Psychology, 63,* 19–31.

Allen, T. D., Poteet, M. L., Russell, J. E., and Dobbins, G. H. (1997). A field study of factors related to supervisors' willingness to mentor others. *Journal of Vocational Behavior, 50,* 1–22.

Alston, J. P. (1989). Wa, guanxi, and inhwa: Managerial principles in Japan, China, Korea. *Business Horizons,* March–April, 26–31.

Amabile, T. M. (1997). Motivating creativity in organizations. *California Management Review,* 40(1), 39–58.

Amabile, T. M. (1996). *Creativity in context: Update to the social psychology of creativity.* Boulder, CO: Westview Press.

Amabile, T. M. (1993). Motivational synergy: Toward a new conceptualization of intrinsic and extrinsic motivation in the workplace. *Human Resource Management Review, 3,* 185–201.

Amabile, T. M., Conti, R., Coon, H., Lazenby, J., and Herron, M. (1996). Assessing the work environment for creativity. *Academy of Management Journal, 39,* 1154–1184.

Amabile, T. M., Hill, K. G., Hennessey, B. A., and Tighe, E. (1994). The work preference inventory: Assessing intrinsic and extrinsic motivational orientations. *Journal of Personality and Social Psychology, 66,* 950–967.

Anderson, T. D. (1992). *Transforming leadership: New skills for an extraordinary future.* Amherst, MA: Human Resources Development Press.

Andreason, A. W. (2003). Expatriate adjustment to foreign assignments. *International Journal of Commerce and Management, 13*(1), 42–61.

Aoki, M. (1994). The Japanese firm as a system of attributes: A survey and research agenda. In M. Aoki and R. Dore (eds.), *The Japanese firm: Sources of competitive strength.* New York: Oxford University Press.

Arkin, A. (1992). The land of social welfare. *Personnel Management, 24*(3), 33–35.

Arvey, R. D., Bhagat, R. S., and Salas, E. (1991). Cross-cultural and cross-national issues in personnel and human resources training. *Research in Personnel and Human Resources Management, 9, 376–407.*

Aryee, S., Chay, Y., and Chew, J. (1996). The motivation to mentor among managerial employees. *Group and Organization Management, 21*(3), 261–277.

Aryee, S., Fields, D. and Luk, V. (1999). A cross-cultural test of a model of the work-family interface. *Journal of Management, 25*(4), 491–511.

Aryee, S., Lo, S. and Kang, I. L. (1999). Antecedents of early career stage mentoring among Chinese employees. *Journal of Organizational Behavior, 20,* 563–576.

Ashkanasy, N. M., and Jackson, C. R. (2001). Organizational climate and culture. In N. Anderson, D. Ones, H. Sinangil, and C. Viswesvaran (eds.), *Handbook of industrial, work and organizational psychology, 332–345.* London: Sage.

Ashkanasy, N. M., Trevor-Roberts, E., and Earnshaw, L. (2002). The Anglo cluster: The legacy of the British Empire. *Journal of World Business, 37*(1), 28–39.

Atwater, L. E., and Wright, W. J. (1996). Power and transformational and transactional leadership in public and private organizations. *International Journal of Public Administration, 19*(6), 963–989.

Au, K. Y. (2000). Intra-cultural variation as another construct of international management: A study based on secondary data of 42 countries. *Journal of International Management, 6,* 217–238.

Auer-Rizzi, W. (2000). Business vs. cultural frames of reference in group decision-making: Interactions among Austrian, Finnish, and Swedish business students. *Journal of Business Communication, 37*(3), 264–292.

Aycan, Z. (2001). Human resource management in Turkey: Current issues and future challenges. *International Journal of Manpower, 22*(3), 252–258.

Aycan, Z. (2000). Cross-cultural industrial and organizational psychology: Contributions, past developments, and future directions. *Journal of Cross-Cultural Psychology, 31*(1), 110–128.

Aycan, Z., and Fikret-Pasa, S. (2000). Leadership preferences, career choices and work motivation in Turkey: A national profile and regional differences. Paper presented at the 15th International Congress of the International Association for Cross-Cultural Psychology, Pultusk, Poland, July.

Aycan, Z., Kanungo, R. N., Mendonca, M., Yu, K., Deller, J., Stahl, G., and Khursid, A. (2000). Impact of culture on human resource management practices: A ten-country comparison. *Applied Psychology: An International Review, 49*(1), 192–220.

Ayman, R., and Chemers, M. M. (1983). Relationship of supervisory behavior ratings to work group effectiveness and subordinate satisfaction among Iranian managers. *Journal of Applied Psychology, 68,* 338–341.

Ayman, R., Chemers, M. M., and Fiedler, F. E. (1995). The contingency model of leadership effectiveness: Its level of analysis. *Leadership Quarterly, 6*(2), 147–167.

Azar, B. (1999). How do cultures weigh the same decision? *APA Monitor, 30*(5), 12–14.

Babin, B. J., and Boles, J. S. (1998). Employee behavior in a service environment: A model and test of potential differences between men and women. *Journal of Marketing, 62*(4), 77–91.

Bachman, S. I., and Gregory, K. (1993). Mentor and protégé gender: Effects on mentoring roles and outcomes. *Group and Organization Management, 18,* 29–39.

Badawy, M. (1980). Styles of Mid-eastern managers. *California Management Review, 22*(2), 51–58.

Bailey, J. R., Chen, C. C., and Dou, S. G. (1997). Conceptions of self and performance-related feedback in the U.S., Japan and China. *Journal of International Business Studies, 28*(3), 605–625.

Bailyn, L. (1970). Career and family orientations of husbands and wives in relation to marital happiness. *Human Relations, 23,* 97–113.

Baird, I. S., Lyles, M., Ji, S., and Wharton, R. (1990). Joint venture success: A Sino-U.S. Perspective. *International Studies of Management and Organization, 20*(1), 125–134.

Bakacsi, G., Sandor, T., Andras, K., and Viktor, I. (2002). Eastern European cluster: Tradition and translation. *Journal of World Business, 37*(1), 69–80.

Banutu-Gomez, M. B. (2003). Leadership in government of The Gambia: Traditional African leadership practice, shared vision, accountability and willingness and openness to change. *Journal of the American Academy of Business, 2*(2), 349–359.

Banutu-Gomez, M. B. (2002). Leading and managing in developing countries: Challenge, growth and opportunities for twenty-first-century organizations. *Cross-Cultural Management, 9*(4), 29–41.

Barber, A. E., Dunham, R. B., and Formisano, R. A. (1992). The impact of flexible benefits on employee satisfaction: A field study. *Personnel Psychology, 45,* 55–75.

Barkema, H. G., and Vermeulen, F. (1997). What differences in the cultural backgrounds of partners are detrimental for international joint ventures? *Journal of International Business Studies, 28*(4), 845–864.

Bartlett, C. A., and Ghoshal, S. (1995). *Transnational management* (2d ed.). Chicago: Irwin.

Bartlett, C. A., and Ghoshal, S. (1992). What is a global manager? *Harvard Business Review,* September–October, 124–132.

Bass, B. M. (1997). Does the transactional-transformational leadership paradigm transcend organizational and national boundaries? *American Psychologist, 52*(2), 130–139.

Bass, B. M. (1990). *Bass and Stodgill's handbook of leadership: theory, research and managerial applications* (3d ed.). New York: Free Press.

Bass, B. M., and Avolio, B. J. (1993). Transformational leadership: A response to critiques. In M. M. Chemers and R. Ayman (eds.), *Leadership theory and research: Perspectives and directions,* 49–80. San Diego: Academic Press.

Bateman, T. S., and Organ, D. W. (1983). Job satisfaction and the good soldier: The relationship between affect and employee citizenship. *Academy of Management Journal, 26,* 587–595.

Beamer, L. (1998). Bridging business cultures. *China Business Review, 25*(3), 54–57.

Beamish, P. W., and Inkpen, A. C. (1998). Japanese firms and the decline of the Japanese expatriate. *Journal of World Business, 33,* 35–50.

Beechler, S., and Zhuang Yang, J. (1994). The transfer of Japanese-style management to American subsidiaries: Contingencies, constraints, and competencies. *Journal of International Business Studies, 25*(3), 467–91.

Bell, A. H. (1992). *Business communication: Toward 2000.* Cincinnati: South-Western Press.

Bennis, W. (1996). Leadership for tomorrow. *Executive Excellence,* April, 3–4.

Bennis, W., and Nanus, B. (1985). *Leaders: The strategies for taking charge.* New York: Harper Row.

Bergman, T. J., and Volkema, R. J. (1989). Understanding and managing interpersonal conflict at work: Its issues, interactive processes, and consequences. In M. A. Rahim (ed.), *Managing conflict: An interdisciplinary approach,* 7–19. New York: Praeger.

Bierbrauer, G. (1994). Toward an understanding of legal culture: Variations in individualism and collectivism between Kurds, Lebanese and Germans. *Law and Society Review, 28,* 243–264.

Black, J. S., and Gregersen, H. B. (1998). *So you're going overseas: A handbook for personal and professional success.* San Diego: Global Business Publishers.

Black, J. S., Gregersen, H. B., Mendenhall, M., and Stroh, L. K. (1999). *Globalizing people though international assignments.* Reading, MA: Addison-Wesley.

Black, J. S., and Mendenhall, M. (1990). Cross-cultural training effectiveness: A review and a theoretical framework for future research. *Academy of Management Review, 15,* 113–136.

Black, J. S., and Porter, L. W. (1991). Managerial behaviors and job performance: A successful manager in Los Angeles may not succeed in Hong Kong. *Journal of International Business Studies, 22,* 99–113.

Blake, R. R., and Mouton, J. (1978). *Modern approaches to understanding and managing organizations.* San Francisco: Jossey-Bass.

Blake, R. R., and Mouton, J. (1964). *The managerial grid*. Houston: Gulf Publishing.

Blake, R. R., Shepard, H., and Mouton, J. (1964). *Managing inter-group conflict in industry*. Houston: Gulf Publishing.

Blanchflower, D., and Oswald, A. (2004). Well-being over time in Britain and the USA. *Journal of Public Economics, 88*(7/8), 135–163.

Blank, W., Weitzel, J., and Green, S. (1990). Situational leadership theory. *Personnel Psychology, 6*, 579–597.

Boisot, M., and Child, J. (1996). From fiefs to clans and network capitalism: Explaining China's emerging economic order. *Administrative Science Quarterly, 41*, 600–628.

Boisot, M., and Liang, X. G. (1992). The nature of managerial work in the Chinese enterprise reforms: A study of six directors. *Organizational Studies, 13*, 161–184.

Boldy, D., Jain, S., and Northey, K. (1993). What makes an effective European manager? A case study of Sweden, Belgium, Germany and Spain. *Management International Review, 33*(2), 157–169.

Boles, J., Johnson, M., and Hair, J. (1997). Role stress, work-family conflict, and emotional exhaustion: Interrelationships and effects on some work-related consequences. *Journal of Personal Selling and Sales Management, 17*, 17–28.

Bolman, L. G., and Deal, T. E. (1997). *Reframing organizations: Artistry, choice, and leadership*. San Francisco: Jossey-Bass.

Bond, M. H. (1996). Chinese values. In M. H. Bond (ed.), *Chinese Psychology*. Hong Kong: Oxford University Press.

Bond, M. H. (1991). *Beyond the Chinese face: Insights from psychology*. Hong Kong: Oxford University Press.

Bond, M. H. (1988). Finding universal dimensions of individual variation in multi-cultural studies of values: The Rokeach and Chinese value surveys. *Journal of Personality and Social Psychology, 55*, 1009–1015.

Bond, M. H., and Hwang, K. K. (1986). The social psychology of Chinese people. In M. H. Bond (ed.), *The psychology of Chinese people*, 213–266. Hong Kong: Oxford University Press.

Bond, M. H., and King, A. Y. C. (1985). Coping with the threat of westernization in Hong Kong. *International Journal of Intercultural Relations, 9*, 351–364.

Bond, M. H., Leung, K., and Schwartz, S. H. (1992). Explaining choices of procedural and distributive justice across cultures. *International Journal of Psychology, 27*, 211–225.

Bond, M. H., Wan, K., Leung, K., and Giacalone, R. (1985). How are the responses to verbal insults related to cultural collectivism and power distance? *Journal of Cross-Cultural Psychology, 16*, 111–127.

Bond, M. H., and Wang, S. H. (1983). Aggressive behavior in Chinese society: The problem of maintaining order and harmony. In A. P. Goldstein and M. Segall (eds.), *Global perspectives on aggression*. New York: Pergamon.

Booysen, L. (2003). Understanding the duality in the dominant management paradigm in South Africa. Paper presented at the European Association of Work and Organizational Psychology, Lisbon, Portugal, May.

Borgonjon, J., and Vanhonacker, W. R. (1994). Management training in the People's Republic of China. *International Journal of Human Resource Management*, 5(2), 327–356.

Borstoff, P. C., Field, H. S., and Stanley, G. (1997). Who'll go? A review of factors associated with employee willingness to work overseas. *Human Resource Planning*, 20(3), 29–40.

Borys, B., and Jemison, D. B. (1989). Hybrid arrangements as strategic alliances: Theoretical issues in organizational combinations. *Academy of Management Review*, 14, 234–249.

Bovasso, G. (1992). Social structure in two national political subcultures. *Social Psychology Quarterly*, 55, 292–299.

Boyle, B., and Dwyer, F. R. (1995). Power, bureaucracy, influence, and performance: Their relationships in industrial distribution channels. *Journal of Business Research*, 32, 189–200.

Brett, J. M., Stroh, L. K., and Reilly, A. H. (1993). Pulling up roots in the 1990s: Who's willing to relocate. *Journal of Organizational Behavior*, 14, 49–60.

Brewster, C. (2002). Human resource practices in multinational companies. In M. J. Gannon and K. L. Newman (eds.), *The Blackwell handbook of cross-cultural management*. Oxford, UK: Blackwell.

Brislin, R., Lonner, W., and Thorndike, R. (1973). *Cross-cultural research methods*. New York: Wiley.

Brodbeck, F. C., et al. (2000). Cultural variation of leadership prototypes across 22 European countries. *Journal of Occupational and Organizational Psychology*, 73, 1–29.

Broome, B. (1996). *Exploring the Greek mosaic: A guide to intercultural communication in Greece*. London: Intercultural Press.

Brown, C. T., Yelsma, P., and Keller, P. W. (1981). Communication-conflict predisposition: Development of a theory and an instrument. *Human Relations*, 34(12), 1103–1117.

Brown, J. S. (2000). Employee turnover costs billions annually: A recent survey shows demand for executive talent will increase, while supply will decline. *Computing Canada*, 26(26), 25.

Brown, J. S., and Duguid, P. (2001). Creativity versus structure: A useful tension. *Sloan Management Review*, 42(4), 93–94.

Brown, L. D. (1983). *Managing conflict at organizational interfaces*. Reading, MA: Addison-Wesley.

Brown, S. P., and Peterson, R. A. (1994). The effect of effort on sales performance and job satisfaction. *Journal of Marketing, 58*(2), 70–80.

Brown, S. P., and Peterson, R. A. (1993). Antecedents and consequences of salesperson job satisfaction: Meta-analysis and assessment of causal effects. *Journal of Marketing Research, 30,* 63–77.

Bryman, A. (1992). *Charisma and leadership in organizations.* London: Sage.

Buda, R., and Elsayed-Elkhouly, S. M. (1998). Cultural differences between Arabs and Americans: Individualism-collectivism revisited. *Journal of Cross-Cultural Psychology, 29*(3), 487–492.

Buller, P. F., and McEvoy, G. M. (1999). Creating and sustaining ethical capability in the multi-national corporation. *Journal of World Business, 34*(4), 326–343.

Burns, J. M. (1978). *Leadership.* New York: Harper Row.

Buttery, E. A., and Leung, T. K. P. (1998). The difference between Chinese and Western negotiations. *European Journal of Marketing, 32,* 132–146.

Cable, D. M., and Judge, T. A. (1994). Pay preferences and job search decisions: A P-O fit perspective. *Personnel Psychology, 47,* 317–348.

Cadotte, E. R., and Stern, L. (1979). A process model of interorganizational relations in marketing channels. In Jagdish Sheth (ed.), *Research in marketing,* vol. 2, 127–158. Greenwich, CT: JAI Press.

Caetano, A., Tavares, S., and Reis, R. (2003). Work values in the European Union. Paper presented at the European Association of Work and Organizational Psychology, Lisbon, Portugal, May.

Caligiuri, P. M. (2000). Selecting expatriates for personality characteristics: A moderating effect of personality on the relationship between host national contact and cross-cultural adjustment. *Management International Review, 40*(1), 61–80.

Caligiuri, P. M. (1997). Assessing expatriate success: Beyond just being there. In Z. Aycan (ed.), *Expatriate management: Theory and practice,* 17–140. Greenwich, CT: JAI Press.

Calori, R., and Sarnin, P. (1991). Corporate culture and economic performance: A French study. *Organization Studies, 12*(10), 49–74.

Cameron, J., and Pierce, W. D. (1996). The debate about rewards and intrinsic motivation: Protests and accusations do not alter the results. *Review of Educational Research, 66*(1), 39–51.

Campbell, N. C., Graham, J., Jolibert, A., and Meissner, H. (1988). Marketing negotiations in France, Germany, the United Kingdom, and the United States. *Journal of Marketing, 52,* 49–62.

Canary, D. J., and Spitzberg, B. H. (1987). Appropriateness and effectiveness perceptions of conflict strategies. *Human Communication Research, 14,* 93–118.

Cao, Z. H. (1991). Establishing and perfecting a new type socialist economic operational system. *Liberation Daily,* September.

Carayon, P. (1995). Chronic effect of job control, supervisor social support, and work pressure on office worker stress. In S. L. Sauter and R. L. Murphy (eds.), *Organizational risk factors for job stress*, 357–370. Washington, DC: American Psychological Association.

Carless, S. A. (1998). Gender differences in transformational leadership: An examination of superior, leader, and subordinate perspectives. *Sex Roles, 39,* 887–904.

Carsten, J. M., and Spector, P. E. (1987). Unemployment, job satisfaction and employee turnover: A meta-analytic test of the Murchinsky model. *Journal of Applied Psychology, 8,* 374–381.

Cartwright, S., and Cooper, C. L. (1993). The role of culture compatibility in successful organizational marriage. *Academy of Management Executive,* 7(2), 57–70.

Cascio, W. F. (2003). *Managing human resources: Productivity, quality of work life, and profits* (6th ed.). New York: McGraw-Hill.

Chang, L.-C. (2003). An examination of cross-cultural negotiation: Using Hofestede's framework. *Journal of the American Academy of Business,* 2(2), 567–572.

Chang, L.-C. (2002). Cross-cultural differences in styles of negotiation between North American and Chinese. *Journal of the American Academy of Business,* 1(2), 179–187.

Chang, S. K. C. (1985). American and Chinese Managers in U.S. companies in Taiwan: A comparison. *California Management Review, 27,* 144–156.

Chang, W., and MacMillan, I. C. (1991). A review of entrepreneurial development in the People's Republic of China. *Journal of Business Venturing, 6,* 375–379.

Chao, G. T., Walz, P. M., and Gardner, P. D. (1992). Formal and informal mentorships: A comparison of mentoring functions and contrast with non-mentored counterparts. *Personnel Psychology, 45,* 619–636.

Chao, Y. T. (1990). Culture and work organizations: The Chinese case. Special issue: Social values and effective organizations. *International Journal of Psychology, 25*(5–6), 583–592.

Chatman, J. A., and Jehn, K. A. (1994). Assessing the relationship between industry characteristics and organizational culture. *Academy of Management Journal, 19*(3), 522–553.

Chen, C. C., and Van Velsor, E. (1996). New directions for research and practice in diversity leadership. *Leadership Quarterly, 7*(2), 285–302.

Chen, D. (1988). Chinese models for economic development and their implications for management training. *China Information, 3*(2), 38–50.

Chen, M. (1995). *Asian management systems: Chinese, Japanese, and Korean styles of business.* New York: Thunderbird/Routledge.

Cheng, B. (1993). The effects of organizational value on organizational commitment, organizational citizenship behavior and job performance: A comparison of weighting models and discrepancy models. *Chinese Journal of Psychology*, 35(1), 43–57.

Cheng, C. Y. (1997). *Modernized and universalized Chinese philosophy*. Taipei: Joint Economy Publication Enterprise Company. (In Chinese).

Cheung, C.-K., and Scherling, S. A. (1999). Job satisfaction, work values, and sex differences in Taiwan's organizations. *Journal of Psychology*, 133(5), 563–575.

Chew, I. K. H., and Putti, J. (1995). Relationship on work-related values of Singaporean and Japanese managers in Singapore. *Human Relations*, 48(10), 1149–1170.

Chia, R. C., Moore, J. L., Lam, K. N., Chuang, C. J., and Cheng, B. S. (1995). Locus of control and gender roles: A comparison of Taiwanese and American students. *Journal of Social Behavior and Personality*, 10(2), 379–393.

Child, J. (1994). *Management in China during the age of reform*. Cambridge, UK: Cambridge University Press.

Child, J., and Markoczy, L. (1993). Host country managerial behavior and learning in Chinese and Hungarian joint ventures. *Journal of Management Studies*, 30(4), 611–631.

Child, J., and Stewart, S. (1997). Regional differences in China and the implications for Sino-foreign joint ventures. *Journal of General Management*, 23(2), 65–68.

Chinese Culture Connection. (1987). Chinese values and the search for culture-free dimensions of culture. *Journal of Cross-Cultural Psychology*, 18(2), 143–164.

Chiu, R. K., and Kosinski, F., (1994). Is Chinese conflict-handling behavior influenced by Chinese values? *Social Behavior and Personality*, 22(1), 81–90.

Chiu, W. C. K., and Ng, C. W. (1999). Women-friendly HRM and organizational commitment: A study among women and men of organizations in Hong Kong. *Journal of Occupational and Organizational Psychology*, 72, 485–502.

Choe, S., Lee, J., and Roehl, T. (1995). What makes management style similar and distinct across borders? An examination of the influence of growth, international experience and national culture in Korea and Japanese firms. Paper presented at the Academy of International Business Conference, Seoul, Korea, November.

Chow, C., Harrison, G. L., MacKinnon, J. L., and Wu, A. (2002). The organizational culture of public accounting firms: Evidence from Taiwanese local and U.S. affiliated firms. *Accounting, Organizations, and Society*, 24(4–5), 347–360.

Chow, I. H. S., and Ding, D. Z. Q. (2001). Moral judgment and conflict handling styles among Chinese in Hong Kong and PRC. *Journal of Management Development,* 2(9/10), 666–679.

Chow, W. S., and Luk, V. W. M. (1996). Management in the 1990s: A comparative study of women managers in China and Hong Kong. *Journal of Managerial Psychology,* 11(1), 24–36.

Church, A. H., and Waclawski, J. (1999). The impact of leadership styles on global management practices. *Journal of Applied Social Psychology,* 29(7), 1416–1443.

Clark, A. E. (1997). Job satisfaction and gender: Why are women so happy at work? *Labour Economics,* 4, 341–372.

Clark, T. (1990). International marketing and national character: A review and proposal for an integrative theory. *Journal of Marketing,* 54(4), 66–79.

Coates, J. R., Jarrat, J., and Mahaffie, J. B. (1990). *Future work.* San Francisco: Jossey-Bass.

Cohen, S. G., and Bailey, D. E. (1997). What makes teams work: Group effectiveness research from the shop floor to the executive suite. *Journal of Management,* 23, 239–290.

Colquitt, J. A., Conlon, D. E., Wesson, M. J., Porter, C. O., and Ng, K. Y. (2001). Justice at the millennium: A meta-analytic review of 25 years of organizational justice research. *Journal of Applied Psychology,* 86, 425–445.

Commerce Clearing House. (2002). *2002 unscheduled absenteeism survey.* Riverwoods, IL.

Conrad, C. (1991). Communication in conflict: Style-strategy relationships. *Communication Monographs,* 58, 135–155.

Corder, S. (1983). Strategies of communication. In C. Faerch and G. Kasper (eds.), *Strategies in interlanguage communication,* 15–19. London: Longman.

Cox, T. H., and Nkomo, S. M. (1991). A race and gender group analysis of the early career experience of MBAs. *Work and Occupations,* 18, 431–466.

Cox, T. H., and Rial-Gonzales, E. (2003). Work-related stress: The European picture. *European Agency Topic Center on Good Practice.* Available at http://agency.osha.eu.int/publications/reports/stress.

Cressey, D. R., and Moore, C. A. (1983). Managerial values and corporate codes of ethics. *California Management Review,* 25(4), 53–77.

Csikszentmihalyi, M. (1997). Intrinsic motivation and teaching: A flow analysis. In J. L. Bass (ed.), *Teaching well and liking it: Motivating faculty to teaching effectively.* Baltimore: Johns Hopkins University Press.

Cunningham, B., and Lischeron, J. (1991). Defining entrepreneurship. *Journal of Small Business Management,* 29(1), 45–61.

Daley, D. M. (1995). Pay for performance and the senior executive service: Attitudes about the success of civil service reform. *American Journal of Public Administration,* 25(4), 355–372.

Darling, J. R., and Fogliasso, C. E. (1999). Conflict management across cultural boundaries: A case analysis from a multinational bank. *European Business Review, 99*(6), 383–396.

Dastmalchian, A., and Javidan, M. (1998). High commitment leadership: A study of Iranian executives. *Journal of Comparative Management, 1*(1), 23–27.

Dastmalchian, A., Javidan, M., and Alam, K. (2001). Effective leadership and culture in Iran: An empirical study. *Applied Psychology: An International Review, 50*(4), 532–558.

Davidson, J., and Cooper, C. (1993). *European women in business and management.* London: Paul Chapman.

Davis, D. D. (1998). International performance measurement and management. In J. W. Smither (ed.), *Performance appraisal: State of the art in practice,* 95–131. San Francisco: Jossey-Bass.

Deal, T. E., and Kennedy, A. (1982). *Corporate cultures: The rites and rituals of corporate life.* Reading, MA: Addison-Wesley.

De Brabander, B., and Boone, C. (1990). Sex differences in perceived locus of control. *Journal of Social Psychology, 130,* 271–272.

De Charms, R. (1968). *Personal causation: The internal affective determinants of behavior.* New York: Academic Press.

Deci, E. L., and Ryan, R. M. (1991). A motivational approach to self: Integration in personality. In R. Dienstbier (ed.), *Nebraska symposium on motivation,* vol. 38, *Perspectives on motivation,* 237–288. Lincoln: University of Nebraska Press.

Deci, E. L., and Ryan, R. M. (1985). *Intrinsic motivation and self-determination in human behavior.* New York: Plenum.

De Dreu, K. W., Evers, A. Beersma, B., Kluver, E. S., and Nauta, A. (2001). A theory-based measure of conflict management strategies in the workplace. *Journal of Organizational Behavior, 22*(6), 645–668.

De Mente, B. L. (1998). *NTC's cultural dictionary of Korea's business and cultural code words.* Lincolnwood, IL: NTC Publishing Group.

den Hartog, D., House, R. J., and Hanges, P. J., Ruiz-Quintanilla, S. A., and Dorfman, P. W. (1999). Culture specific and cross-culturally generalizable implicit leadership theories: Are attributes of charismatic/transformational leadership universally endorsed? *Leadership Quarterly, 10*(2), 219–256.

den Hartog, D., and Koopman, P. (2003). Gender differences in the perceived importance of leadership characteristics. Paper presented at the European Association of Work and Organizational Psychology, Lisbon, Portugal, May.

Derr, C. R. (1987). Managing high potentials in Europe: Some cross-cultural findings. *European Management Journal, 5,* 72–80.

Deutsch, M. (1973). *The resolution of conflict.* New Haven, CT: Yale University Press.

Ding, D. Z., Fields, D., and Akhtar, S. (1997). An empirical study of human resource management policies and practice in foreign-invested enterprises in China: The case of Shenzen special economic zone. *International Journal of Human Resource Management, 8,* 595–613.

Dorfman, P. (1996). International and cross-cultural leadership research. In B. J. Punnett and O. Shenkar (eds.), *Handbook for international management research,* 267–349. Cambridge, MA: Blackwell Publishers.

Dorfman, P., Howell, J. P., Hibino, S., Lee, J. K., Tate, U., and Bautista, A. (1997). Leadership in Western and Asian countries: Commonalities and differences in effective leadership processes across cultures. *Leadership Quarterly, 8*(3), 233–274.

Doshi, K. (1994). The rush to privatize the Asia-Pacific region. *Business Forum, 19*(1), 42–46.

Douglas, S. P., and Craig, C. S. (1984). Establishing equivalence in comparative consumer research. In E. Kaynak and R. Savitt (eds.), *Comparative Marketing Systems,* 93–113. New York: Praeger.

Dowling, P. J. (1989). Hot issues overseas. *Personnel Administrator, 34*(1), 66–72.

Downs, A. (1991). A case study of the relationship between communication satisfaction and organizational commitment in two Australian organizations. Master's thesis, University of Kansas, Lawrence.

Drummond, R. J., and Stoddard, A. (1991). Job satisfaction and work values. *Psychological Reports, 69,* 1116–1118.

Dunbar, E. (1996). Sociocultural and contextual challenges of organizational life in Eastern Europe. In D. Landis and R. S. Bhagat (eds.), *Handbook of intercultural training* (2d ed.), 349–365. Thousand Oaks, CA: Sage.

Dunbar, E., and Ehrlich, M. H. (1993). Preparation of the international employee: Career and consultation needs. *Consulting Psychology Journal: Practice and Research, 45*(1), 18–24.

Dunbar, E., and Katcher, A. (1990). Preparing managers for foreign assignments. *Training and Development Journal, 44*(9), 45–47.

Dweck, C. (1986). Motivational processes affecting learning. *American Psychologist, 41,* 1040–1048.

Dwyer, F. R., Schurr, P. H., and Oh, S. (1987). Developing buyer-seller relationships. *Journal of Marketing, 51* (April), 11–27.

Dwyer, F. R., and Walker, O. (1981). Bargaining in an asymmetrical power structure. *Journal of Marketing, 45*(4), 104–115.

Dyer, B., and Song, M. (1997). The impact of strategy on conflict: A cross-national comparative study of U.S. and Japanese firms. *Journal of International Business Studies, 28*(3), 467–493.

Dyer, B., and Song, M. (1995). The relationship between strategy and conflict management: A Japanese perspective. Developments in marketing science.

Proceedings of the Annual Conference of the Academy of Marketing Science,
18, 126–132.

Eagly, A. H., and Johnson, B. T. (1990). Gender and leadership style: A meta-analysis. *Psychological Bulletin, 108*(92), 233–257.

Early, P. C. (1989). Social loafing and collectivism: A comparison of the United States and the People's Republic of China. *Administrative Science Quarterly, 34,* 565–581.

Early, P. C., and Erez, M. (1997). *The transplanted executive.* New York: Oxford University Press,

Eby, L. T., Freeman, D. M., Rush, M. C., and Lance, C. E. (1999). Motivational bases of affective organizational commitment: A partial test of an integrative theoretical model. *Journal of Occupational and Organizational Psychology, 72,* 463–483.

Eisenhart, M. (1995). The fax, the jazz player, and the self-history teller: How do people organize culture? *Anthropology and Education Quarterly, 26*(1), 3–26.

Ekvall, G., and Arvonen, J. (1991). Change-centered leadership: An extension of the two-dimensional model. *Scandinavian Journal of Management, 7,* 17–26.

Elenkov, D. S. (1998). Can American management concepts work in Russia? A cross-cultural comparative study. *California Management Review, 40*(4), 133–156.

Elizur, D., Borg, I., Hunt, R., and Beck, I. M. (1991). The structure of work values: A cross-cultural comparison. *Journal of Organizational Behavior, 12*(1), 21–38.

Elloy, D. F., and Suseno, J. (1987). An examination of job involvement of dual wage earner and single wage earner families: An Australian study. *Proceedings Pan Pacifica Conference 4* (Taipei, Taiwan), 256–259.

Engardio, P. (1991). The Chinese deal makers of Southeast Asia. *Business Week,* November, 60–62.

Ensari, N. (2001). KLI research. *Illumine,* Fall, 3–6.

Erez, M. (1997). Culture based model of work motivation. In P. C. Early and M. Erez (eds.), *New perspectives on international and organizational psychology,* 193–242. San Francisco: New Lexington Press.

Erez, M. (1994). Toward a model of cross-cultural industrial and organizational psychology. In *Handbook of industrial and organizational psychology* (2d ed.). Palo Alto, CA: Consulting Psychological Press.

Erez, M., and Early, P. C. (1993). *Cultures, self-identity and work.* New York: Oxford University Press.

Erondu, E. (2002). Managerial competence in Nigerian firms: An empirical and comparative analysis. *Multinational Business Review, 10*(2), 129–137.

Evans, P., and Doz, Y. (1989). The dualistic organization. In P. Evans, Y. Doz, and A. Laurent (eds.), *Human Resource Management in the International Firms: Change, Globalization, Innovation*, 219–242. London: Macmillan.

Fagenson, E. A. (1989). The mentor advantage: Perceived career/job experiences of protégés versus no protégés. *Journal of Organizational Behavior, 10,* 309–320.

Fagre, N., and Wells, L. T. (1982). Bargaining power of multinationals and host governments. *Journal of International Business Studies,* Fall, 9–24.

Farh, J. L., Dobbins, G. H., and Cheng, B. S. (1991). Cultural relativity in action: A comparison of self-ratings made by Chinese and U.S. workers. *Personnel Psychology, 44,* 129–147.

Farh, J. L., Podsakoff, P. M., and Organ, D. W. (1990). Accounting for organizational citizenship behavior: Leader fairness and task scope versus satisfaction. *Journal of Management, 16*(4), 705–721.

Farris, G. F., and Butterfield, A. (1972). Control theory in Brazilian organizations. *Administrative Science Quarterly, 17,* 574–585.

Feldman, D. C., and Tompson, H. B. (1993). Expatriation, repatriation, and domestic geographical relocation: An empirical investigation of adjustment to new job assignments. *Journal of International Business Studies, 24,* 507–529.

Felfe, J., and Goihl, K. (2002). Transformational leadership and commitment. In J. Felfe (ed.), *Organizational development and leadership.* Frankfurt/Main: Verlag Peter Lang.

Ferner, A., Quintanilla, J., and Varul, M. Z. (2001). Country of origin effects, host country effects, and the management of HR in multinationals: German companies in Britain and Spain. *Journal of World Business, 36*(2), 107–127.

Fey, C. F., and Beamish, P. W. (2001). Organizational climate similarity and performance: International joint venture in Russia. *Organization Studies, 22,* 853–882.

Fields, D., Pang, M., and Chiu, C. (2000). Distributive and procedural justice as predictors of employee outcomes in Hong Kong. *Journal of Organizational Behavior, 21,* 547–562.

Fink, E., and Monge, P. (1985). An exploration of confirmatory factor analysis. *Progress in Communication Sciences, 6,* 167–197.

Francis, J. (1991). When in Rome? The effects of cultural adaptation on intercultural business negotiations. *Journal of International Business Negotiations, 22,* 408–423.

Franke, R. H., Hofstede, G., and Bond, M. H. (1991). Cultural roots of economic performance: A research note. *Strategic Management Journal, 18,* 165–173.

Frazee, V. (1998). Working with Indians. *Workforce, 77*(7), 10–11.

Frazee, V. (1997). Building relationships in Sweden. *Workforce, 76,* 19–20.

Frazier, G., and Summers, J. O. (1984). Interfirm influence strategies and their application within distribution channels. *Journal of Marketing, 48,* Summer, 43–55.

Frederick, W. C., and Weber, J. (1987). The values of corporate managers and their critics: An empirical description and normative implications. *Research in Corporate Social Performance and Policy, 9,* 131–152.

Frederickson, H. G., and Hart, D. K. (1985). The public service and the patriotism of benevolence. *Public Administration Review, 45,* 547–553.

French, J. R., and Raven, B. (1959). The bases of social power. In D. Cartwright (ed.), *Studies in social power,* 150–167. Ann Arbor: University of Michigan Press.

Frey, B. S. (1997). On the relationship between intrinsic and extrinsic work motivation. *International Journal of Industrial Organization, 15*(4), 427–439.

Friedmann, W. G., and Beguin, J. P. (1971). *Joint international business ventures in developing countries.* New York: Columbia University Press.

Fry, F. L. (1993). *Entrepreneurship: A planning approach.* Minneapolis/St. Paul: West.

Fukuyama, F. (1995). *Trust: The social virtues and the creation of prosperity.* New York: Free Press.

Ganesan, S. (1993). Negotiation strategies and the nature of channel relationships. *Journal of Marketing Research, 30,* 183–203.

Gannon, M. J., et al. (1994). *Understanding global cultures: Metaphorical journeys through 17 countries.* Thousand Oaks, CA: Sage.

Gao, S. (1992). New operating mechanisms. *Beijing Review,* June 15–21, pp. 18–24.

Gardenswartz, L., and Rowe, A. (2001). Cross-cultural awareness: Influences of culture in the workplace. *HRMagazine, 46*(3), 139–142.

Garratt, B. (1995). An old idea has come of age. *People Management, 1*(19), 25–28.

Gartner, W. B. (1990). What are we talking about when we talk about entrepreneurship? *Journal of Business Venturing, 5,* 15–18.

Gatley, S., and Lessem, R. (1995). Enhancing the competitive advantage of transcultural businesses. *European Journal of Industrial Training, 19,* 26–35.

Geier, J. G. (1967). A trait approach to the study of leadership in small groups. *Journal of Communication,* December, 316–323.

Gelfand, M. J., Nishi, L. H., Ohbuchi, K., and Fukuno, M. (2001). Cultural influences on cognitive representations of conflict episodes in the United States and Japan. *Journal of Applied Psychology, 86*(6), 1059–1074.

Gelfand, M. J., and Realo, A. (1999). Individualism-collectivism and accountability in inter-group negotiations. *Journal of Applied Psychology, 84*(5), 721–736.

Geringer, J. M. (1988). *Joint venture partner selection: Strategies for developed countries.* Westport, CT: Quorum Books.

Gerstner, C. R., and Day, D. V. (1994). Cross-cultural comparison of leadership prototypes. *Leadership Quarterly,* 5(2), 121–134.

Ghoshal, S., and Bartlett, C. A. (1990). The multinational corporation as an interorganizational network. *Academy of Management Review,* 15(4), 603–625.

Giacobbe-Miller, J. K., Miller, D. J., Zhang, W. and Victorov, V. I. (2003). Country and organizational level adaptation to foreign workplace ideologies: A comparative study of distributive justice values in China, Russia and the United States. *Journal of International Business Studies,* 34(4), 389–406.

Gibson, C. B., and Zellmer-Bruhn, M. E. (2001). Metaphors and meaning: An intercultural analysis of the concept of teamwork. *Administrative Science Quarterly,* 46(2), 274–303.

Gibson, C. R. (1995). An investigation of gender differences in leadership across four countries. *Journal of International Business Studies,* 26(2), 255–279.

Gibson, J. W., and Tesone, D. V. (2001). Management fads: Emergence, evolution, and implications for managers. *Academy of Management Executive,* 15, 122–133.

Gire, J. T., and Carment, D. W. (1993). Dealing with disputes: The influence of individualism-collectivism. *Journal of Social Psychology,* 133, 81–95.

Glen, E. S., Witmeyer, D., and Stevenson, K. A. (1977). Cultural styles of persuasion. *Journal of Intercultural Relations,* 2(3), 81–96.

Glendinning, P. (2001). Workplace bullying: Curing the cancer of the American workplace. *Public Personnel Management,* 30(3), 269–282.

Goh, C. T., Hian, C. K., and Chan, K. L. (1991). Gender effects on the job satisfaction of accountants in Singapore. *Work and Stress,* 5(4), 341–348.

Goldman, A. (1994). Communication in Japanese multinational organizations. In R. Wiseman and R. Shuter (eds.), *Communicating in multinational organizations,* 45–74. Thousand Oaks, CA: Sage.

Gomes-Casseres, B. (1989). Ownership structure of foreign subsidiaries: Theory and evidence. *Journal of Economic Behavior and Organizations,* 11, 1–25.

Goodall, K., and Burgers, W. (1998). Frequent fliers. *Chinese Business Review,* 25(3), 50–52.

Gooderham, P., Nordhaug, O., and Ringdal, K. (1999). When in Rome, do they do as the Romans? HRM practices of U.S. subsidiaries in Europe. *Management International Review,* 38(2), 47–64.

Goodson, J. R., McGee, J. W., and Cashman, J. F. (1989). Situational leadership theory. *Group and Organizational Studies,* 14(4), 446–461.

Gordon, G. C. (1991). Industry determinants of organization culture. *Academy of Management Review,* 16, 396–415.

Gouchenour, T. (1990). *Considering Filipinos.* Yarmouth, ME: Intercultural Press.

Gould, S., and Werbel, J. (1983). Work involvement: A comparison of dual wage earner and single wage earner families. *Journal of Applied Psychology, 68,* 313–319.

Graen, G. B., and Uhl-Bien, M. (1995). Relationship-based approach to leadership: Development of leader-member exchange (LMX) theory of leadership over 25 years: Applying a multi-level multi-domain perspective. *Leadership Quarterly, 6,* 219–247.

Graham, J. (1985). The influence of culture on business negotiations. *Journal of International Business Studies, 16*(1), 81–96.

Graham, J. (1983). Brazilian, Japanese and American business negotiations. *Journal of International Business Studies, 14*(1), 44–61.

Graham, J., and Sano, Y. (1984). *Smart bargaining: Doing business with the Japanese.* Cambridge, MA: Ballinger.

Gray, B., and Yan, A. (1997). Formation and evolution of international joint ventures: Examples from U.S.-Chinese partnerships. In P. W. Beamish and J. P. Killing (eds.), *Cooperative strategies: Asian Pacific perspectives,* 57–88. San Francisco: New Lexington Press.

Greer, C. R., and Stephens, G. K. (2001). Escalation of commitment: A comparison of differences between Mexican and U.S. decision makers. *Journal of Management, 27*(1), 51–78.

Grey, R. J., and Gelford, P. (1990). Corporate culture and Canada's international competitiveness. *Canadian Business Review, 17*(4), 21–25.

Griffith, D. A. (2002). The role of communication competencies in international business relationship development. *Journal of World Business, 37*(4), 256–265.

Grover, S. I., and Crooker, K. L. (1995). Who appreciates family-responsiveness human resource policies? The impact of family friendly policies on the organizational attachment of parents and non-parents. *Personnel Psychology, 48,* 271–288.

Groves, K. S. (2003). Gender and social/emotional communication skills: Are female organizational leaders predisposed to charismatic leadership? *Illume, 2,* 5–7.

Gulati, R. (1995). Does familiarity breed trust? The implications of repeated ties for contractual choice in alliances. *Academy of Management Journal, 38*(1), 85–112.

Gupta, V., Hanges, P. J., and Dorfman, P. (2002). Cultural clusters: Methodology and findings. *Journal of World Business, 37*(1), 11–15.

Gupta, V., Surie, G., and Javidan, M. (2002). Southern Asia cluster: Where old meets new? *Journal of World Business, 37*(1), 16–27.

Hall, D. T., and Moss, J. E. (1998). The new protean career contract: Helping organizations and employees adapt. *Organizational Dynamics, 26*(3), 22–37.

Hall, E. (1976). *Beyond culture.* Garden City, NY: Doubleday Anchor Books.

Hall, R. H. (1991). *Organizations: Structures, processes, and outcomes*. Engle-wood Cliffs, NJ: Prentice Hall.

Hall, R. H., and Xu, W. (1991). Run silent, run deep: Cultural influences on organizations in the Far East. *Organizational Studies, 11*(4), 569–576.

Hallen, L., Johanson, J., and Seyed-Mohamed, N. (1991). Inter-firm adaptation in business relationships. *Journal of Marketing, 55*, April, 29–37.

Hallier, J., and James, P. (1997). Middle managers and the employee psychological contract: Agency, protection and advancement. *Journal of Management Studies, 34*(5), 703–728.

Hambleton, R. L., and Gumpert, R. (1982). The validity of Hersey and Blanchard theory of leader effectiveness. *Group and Organizational Studies, 7*, 225–242.

Hamzah-Sendut, T., Madsen, D., and Thong, T. (1989). *Managing in a plural society*. Singapore: Longman.

Hannaway, C. (1992). Why Irish firms are smiling. *Personnel Management, 24*(5), 38–41.

Harnett, D. L., and Cummings, L. L. (1980). *Bargaining behavior: An international study*. Houston: Dome.

Harpaz, I. (1990). The importance of work goals: An international perspective. *Journal of International Business Studies, 21*(1), 75–93.

Harrigan, K. (1988). Joint ventures and competitive strategy. *Strategic Management Journal, 9*, 141–158.

Harris, P. R., and Moran, R. T. (1996). European leadership in globalization. *European Business Review, 96*(2), 32–41.

Harrison, G., McKinnon, J. L., Wu, A., and Chow, C. W. (2000). Cultural influences on adaptation to fluid workgroups and teams. *Journal of International Business Studies, 31*(3), 489–505.

Harrison, J. K. (1992). Individual and combined effects of behavior modeling and the cultural assimilator in cross-cultural management training. *Journal of Applied Psychology, 77*, 952–962.

Harvey, M. (1997). Dual-career expatriates: Expectations, adjustment and satisfaction with international relocation. *Journal of International Business Studies, 28*(3), 627–658.

Harzing, A. W. K. (1999). *Managing the multinationals: An international study of control mechanisms*. Cheltenham, UK: Edward Elgar.

Harzing, A. W. K. (1995). The persistent myth of high expatriate failure rates. *International Journal of Human Resource Management, 6*(2), 457–474.

Hashimoto, K., and Rao, A. (1996). Intercultural influence: A study of Japanese expatriates in Canada. *Journal of International Business Studies, 27*(3), 443–466.

Hater, J. J., and Bass, B. M. (1988). Superior's evaluations and subordinates' perceptions of transformational and transactional leadership. *Journal of Applied Psychology, 73,* 695–702.

Hawk, E. J. (1995). Culture and rewards. *Personnel Journal, 74*(4), April, 30–37.

Hellriegel, D., Slocum, J. W., and Woodman, R. W. (1995). *Organizational behavior* (7th ed.). Cincinnati: South-Western.

Hempel, P. S., and Chang, C. Y. D. (2002). Reconciling traditional Chinese management with high-tech Taiwan. *Human Resource Management Journal, 12*(1), 77–95.

Hemphill, J., and Coons, A. (1957). The leader and his group. *Journal of Educational Research, 28,* 225–246.

Hendon, D. W., and Hendon, R. A. (1990). *World class negotiations.* New York: Wiley.

Hennart, J. F. (1991). The transaction cost theory of joint ventures: An empirical study of Japanese subsidiaries in the U.S. *Management Science, 37,* 483–497.

Hennart, J. F., and Zeng, M. (2002). Cross-cultural differences and joint venture longevity. *Journal of International Business Studies, 33*(4), 699–716.

Hennessey, B., and Zbikowski, S. M. (1993). Immunizing children against the negative effects of reward: A further examination of intrinsic motivation techniques. *Creativity Research Journal, 6,* 297–308.

Herriot, P., Manning, W. E. G., and Kidd, J. M. (1997). The content of the psychological contract. *British Journal of Management, 8*(2), 151–159.

Hersey, P., and Blanchard, K. H. (1988). *Management of organizational behavior: Utilizing human resources* (5th ed.). Englewood Cliffs, NJ: Prentice Hall.

Hersey, P., and Blanchard, K. H. (1969). *Management of organizational behavior: Utilizing human resources.* Englewood Cliffs, NJ: Prentice Hall.

Hersey, P., Blanchard, K. H., and Johnson, D. E. (1996). *Management of organizational behavior: Utilizing human resources* (7th ed.). Englewood Cliffs, NJ: Prentice Hall.

Herzberg, F. (1966). *Work and the nature of man.* New York: World Publishing.

Herzberg, F., Mausner, B., and Snyderman, B. B. (1959). *Job attitudes: Review of research and opinion.* Pittsburgh: Psychological Service of Pittsburgh.

Heydenfeldt, J. A. (2000). The influence of individualism/collectivism on Mexican and U.S. business negotiations. *International Journal of Intercultural Relations, 24,* 383–407.

Hickson, D. J., Hinings, C. R., and McMillan, C. J. (1981). *Organization and nation: The Aston Programme IV.* Farnborough, UK: Gower.

Hill, C. W. L. (1995). National institutional structures, transaction cost economizing and competitive advantage. *Organization Science, 6*(1), 119–131.

Hill, R. C., and Levenhagen, M. (1995). Metaphors and mental models: Sensemaking and sensegiving in innovative and entrepreneurial activities. *Journal of Management, 21*(6), 1057–1074.

Hitchcock, D. (1994). Are you parents or partners with your employees? *Journal for Quality and Participation,* *17*(7), 6–10.

Ho, D. Y. F. (1987). Fatherhood in Chinese culture. In M. E. Lamb (ed.), *The father's role: Cross-cultural perspectives.* Hillsdale, NJ: Erlbaum.

Hodson, R. (1989). Gender differences in job satisfaction: Why aren't women more dissatisfied? *Sociological Quarterly,* *30*(3), 385–399.

Hofstede, G. (1997). *Cultures and organization: Software of the mind.* New York: McGraw-Hill.

Hofstede, G. (1993). Cultural constraints in management theories. *Academy of Management Executive,* *7*(1), 81–94.

Hofstede, G. (1984). *Culture's consequences: International differences in work-related values* (abridged ed.). Beverly Hills, CA: Sage.

Hofstede, G. (1980). Motivation, leadership and organization: Do American theories apply abroad? *Organizational Dynamics,* *7*(2), 42–63.

Hofstede, G., and Bond, M. H. (1988). Confucius and economic growth: New insights into culture's consequences. *Organizational Dynamics,* *15,* 5–21.

Hofstede, G., Bond, M. H., and Luk, C.-L. (1993). Individual perceptions of organizational cultures: A methodological treatise on levels of analysis. *Organizational Studies,* *14*(4), 483–503.

Hofstede, G., Kolman, L., Niclescu, O., and Pajumaa, I. (1996). Characteristics of the ideal job among students in eight countries. In H. Grad, A. Blanco, and J. Georgas (eds.), *Key issues in cross-cultural psychology.* Lisse, the Netherlands: Swets and Zeitlinger.

Hofstede, G., Neuijen, B., Ohayv, D. D., and Sanders, G. (1990). Measuring organizational cultures: A qualitative and quantitative study across twenty cases. *Administrative Science Quarterly,* *35,* 286–316.

Hogan, R., Curphy, G. J., and Hogan, J. (1994). What we know about leadership: effectiveness and personality. *American Psychologist,* *49*(6), 493–504.

Hollander, E. P., and Offermann, L. R. (1990). Power and leadership in organizations-relationships in transition. *American Psychologist,* *45,* 179–189.

Hoogendoorn, J. (1992). New priorities for Dutch HRM. *Personnel Management,* *24*(12), 42–48.

House, R. J. (1971). A path-goal theory of leader effectiveness. *Administrative Science Quarterly,* *16,* 19–31.

House, R. J., Hanges, P. J., Ruiz-Quintanilla, S. A., Dorfman, P. W., Javidan, M., Dickson, M. W., Gupta, V., et al. (1999). Cultural influences on leadership and organizations: Project GLOBE. In W. H. Mobley, M. J. Gessner, and V. Arnold (eds.), *Advances in global leadership,* 171–233. Greenwich, CT: JAI Press.

House, R. J., Javidan, M., and Dorfman, P. (2001). Project GLOBE: An introduction. *Applied Psychology,* *50*(4), 489–505.

House, R. J., and Wright, N. (1997). Cross-cultural research and organizational leadership: A critical analysis and a proposed theory. In P. C Early and M. Erez (eds.), *Frontiers of industrial and organizational psychology*. San Francisco: Jossey-Bass.

House, R. J., Wright, N., and Aditya, R. N. (1997). Cross-cultural research and organizational leadership: A critical analysis and a proposed theory. In P. C. Early and M. Erez (eds.), *New perspectives in international industrial organizational psychology*. San Francisco: New Lexington Press.

Howell, J. P., Dorfman, P. W., Hibino, S., Lee, J. K., and Tate, U. (1997). Leadership in Western and Asian countries: Commonalities and differences in effective leadership process across cultures. *Leadership Quarterly, 8*, 233–274.

Howell, J. P., and Higgins, C. (1991). Champions of change: Identifying, understanding, and supporting champions of technological innovations. *Organizational Dynamics, 18*(1), 40–55.

HR Focus. (2003). Motivation secrets of the 100 best employees. *80*(10), 1.

Hsu, F. L. K. (1985). The self in cross-cultural perspective. In G. DeVos, A. J. Marsella, and F. L. K. Hsu (eds.), *Culture and self*, 31–45. London: Tavistock.

Hsu, P. (1984). The influence of structure and values on business organizations in Oriental cultures: China and Japan. *Proceedings of the International Conference, Academy of International Business* (Singapore), 754–768.

Huang, X., and Van de Vliert, E. (2002). Intrinsic job rewards at country-level and individual-level codetermine job satisfaction. *Journal of International Business Studies, 33*(2), 385–394.

Huer, M., Cummings, J. L., and Hutabarat, W. (1999). Cultural stability or change among managers in Indonesia. *Journal of International Business Studies, 30*(3), 599–610.

Hui, C. H. (1990). Work attitudes, leadership style, and managerial behaviors in different cultures. In R. Breslin (ed.), *Applied cross-cultural psychology*, 186–208. Beverly Hills, CA: Sage.

Hui, C. H., and Luk, C. L. (1997). Management and organizational behavior. In J. W. Berry, M. H. Segall, and C. Kagitcibasi (eds.), *Handbook of cross-cultural psychology*, vol. 3, *Social behavior and applications* (rev. ed.), 371–412. Needham Heights, MA: Allyn and Bacon.

Hui, C. H., and Tan, C. K. (1996). Employee motivation and attitudes in the Chinese workforce. In M. H. Bond (ed.), *The handbook of Chinese psychology*, 364–378. Hong Kong: Oxford University Press.

Hui, C. H., and Triandis, H. C. (1989). Effects of culture and response format on extreme response style. *Journal of Cross-Cultural Psychology, 20*, 296–309.

Huo, Y. P., and von Glinow, M. A. (1995). On transplanting human resource practices to China: A culture driven approach. *International Journal of Manpower, 16*(9), 3–13.

Hutt, M. D., Walker, B. A., and Frankwick, G. L. (1995). Hurdle the cross-functional barriers to strategic change. *Sloan Management Review, 36,* Spring, 22–30.

Hwang, G. (1989). On the modernization of the Chinese family business. In Y. Jiang and J. Min (eds.), *Ancient management thinking and Chinese style management,* 121–134. Beijing: Economic Press.

Hwang, K. K. (1991). *The great way of the king.* Taipei: Students Bookstore. (In Chinese).

Hwang, K. K. (1990). Modernization of the Chinese family business. *International Journal of Psychology, 25,* 593–618.

Inglehart, R., and Carballo, M. (1997). Does Latin America exist? (And is there a Confucian culture?): A global analysis of cross-cultural differences. *Political Science and Politics, 30,* 34–46.

Izzard, C. (1977). *Human emotions.* New York: Plenum Press.

Jackson, S. (1992). *Chinese enterprise management.* New York: Walter de Gruyter.

Jackson, T. (2001). Cultural values and management ethics: A ten-nation study. *Human Relations, 54*(10), 1267–1302.

Jackson, T., et al. (2000). Making ethical judgments: A cross-cultural management study. *Asia Pacific Journal of Management, 17*(3), 443–472.

Jago, A. (1993). Culture's consequence? A seven-nation study of participation. *Proceedings of the 24th annual meeting of the Decision Sciences Institute.* Washington, DC: Decision Sciences Institute.

James, K., and Cropanzano, R. (1994). Dispositional group loyalty and individual action for the benefit of an in-group: Experimental and correlational evidence. *Organizational Behavior and Human Decision Processes, 60*(2), 179–205.

Javidan, M. (1996). Vision and inspiration: A study of Iranian executives. *Journal of Transnational Management Development, 2*(2), 69–85.

Javidan, M., and House, R. J. (2002). Leadership and cultures around the world: Findings from GLOBE: An introduction to the special issue. *Journal of World Business, 37*(1), 1–2.

Javidan, M., and House, R. J. (2001). Cultural acumen for the global manager: Lessons learned from Project GLOBE. *Organizational Dynamics, 29*(4), 289–305.

Jehn, K., and Weldon, E. (1997). Managerial attitudes toward conflict: Cross-cultural differences in resolution styles. *Journal of International Management, 34,* 102–124.

Jesuino, J. C. (2002). Latin Europe cluster: From south to north. *Journal of World Business, 37*(1), 81–89.

Johnson, B. R. (1990). Toward a multidimensional model of entrepreneurship: The case of achievement motivation and the entrepreneur. *Entrepreneurship Theory and Practice,* Spring, 39–54.

Johnson, J. P., Cullen, J. B., Sakano, T., and Takenouchi, H. (1996). Setting the stage for trust and strategic integration in Japanese-U.S. cooperative alliances. *Journal of International Business Studies, 27*(5), 981–1004.

Johnson, J. P., and Lenartowicz, T. (1998). Culture, freedom and economic growth: Do cultural values explain economic growth? *Journal of World Business, 33*(4), 332–356.

Johnson, M. (1998). Beyond pay: What rewards work best when doing business in China. *Compensation and Benefits Review, 30*(6), 51–56.

Joiner, T. A. (2001). The influence of national culture and organizational culture alignment on job stress and performance: Evidence from Greece. *Journal of Managerial Psychology, 16*(3), 229–242.

Jou, J. Y., and Sung, K. (1993). Chinese value system and managerial behavior. International symposium on social values and effective organizations. *International Journal of Psychology, 25*(5–6), 619–627.

Jou, J. Y., and Sung, K. (1990). Chinese value system and managerial behavior. *International Journal of Psychology, 23,* 619–627.

Judge, T. A. (1993). Does affective disposition moderate the relationship between job satisfaction and voluntary turnover? *Journal of Applied Psychology, 6,* 395–401.

Judge, T. A., and Cable, D. (1997). Applicant personality, organizational culture, and job choice decisions. *Personnel Psychology, 50,* 359–394.

Juhn, C., Murphy, K., and Pierce, B. (1993). Wage inequality and the rise in returns to skill. *Journal of Political Economy, 101*(3), 410–442.

Jun, J. S., and Muto, H. (1995). The hidden dimensions of Japanese administration: Culture and its impact. *Public Administration Review, 55*(2), 125–134.

Jun, S., Lee, S., and Gentry, J. W. (1997). The effects of acculturation on commitment to the parent company and the foreign operation. *International Business Review, 6,* 519–535.

Kabanoff, B. (1987). Predictive validity of the MODE conflict instrument. *Journal of Applied Psychology, 72*(1), 160–163.

Kabasakal, H., and Bodur, M. (2002). Arabic cluster: A bridge between East and West. *Journal of World Business, 37*(1), 40–54.

Kagan, J. (1983). Survey: Work in the 1980s and 1990s. *Working Woman,* June, 16–18.

Kagitcibasi, C. (1997). Individualism and collectivism. In J. W. Berry, M. H. Segall, and C. Kagitcibasi (eds.), *Handbook of cross-cultural psychology,* vol. 3, *Social behavior and applications,* 1–49. Boston: Allyn and Bacon.

Kakar, S., Kets de Vries, M. F. R., Kakar, S., and Vrignaud, P. (2002). Leadership in Indian organizations from a comparative perspective. *International Journal of Cross-Cultural Management, 2*(2), 239–250.

Kale, P., Singh, H., and Perlmutter, H. (2000). Learning and protection of proprietary assets in strategic alliances: Building relational capital. *Strategic Management Journal, 21*(3), 217–237.

Kamath, R. R., and Liker, J. K. (1994). A second look at Japanese product development. *Harvard Business Review, 72,* 4–14.

Kanter, R. B. (1995). *World class: Thriving locally in the global economy.* New York: Simon and Schuster.

Kanungo, R. N. (1982). Measurement of job and work involvement. *Journal of Applied Psychology, 67,* 341–349.

Kanungo, R. N., and Hartwick, J. (1987). An alternative to the intrinsic-extrinsic dichotomy of work rewards. *Journal of Management, 13*(4), 751–766.

Karaian, J. (2002). Sick of it. *CFO Europe,* December. (Available online at www.cfoeurope.com/200212i.html).

Katz, J. P., Swanson, D. L., and Nelson, L. K. (2001). Culture-based expectations of corporate citizenship: A prepositional framework and comparison of four cultures. *International Journal of Organizational Analysis, 9*(2), 149–171.

Katzell, R. A., Thompson, D. F., and Guzzo, R. A. (1992). How job satisfaction and job performance are and are not linked. In C. J. Cranny, P. C. Smith, and E. F. Stone (eds.), *Job satisfaction,* 195–217. New York: Lexington Books.

Kealey, D. J. (1996). The challenge of international personnel selection. In D. Landis and R. Bhagat (eds.), *The handbook of intercultural training* (2d ed.). Thousand Oaks, CA: Sage.

Kelley, L., Whatley, A., and Worthy, R., (1987). Assessing the effects of culture on managerial attitudes: A three-culture test. *Journal of International Business Studies, 18*(2), 17–31.

Kennard, R. B. (1991). From experience: Japanese product development process. *Journal of Product Innovation Management, 8,* 184–188.

Kerr, C. (1983). *The future industrial societies: Convergence or continued diversity?* Cambridge, MA: Harvard University Press.

Kerr, S., and Jermier, J. M. (1978). Substitutes for leadership: Their meaning and measurement. *Organizational Behavior and Human Performance, 22,* 375–403.

Khadra, B. (1990). The prophetic-caliphal model of leadership: An empirical study. *International Studies of Management and Organization, 20,* 37–51.

Kilmann, R., Saxton, M., and Serpa, R. (1985). *Gaining control of the corporate culture.* San Francisco: Jossey-Bass.

Kim, H. J. (1991). Influence of language and similarity on initial intercultural attraction. In S. Ting-Toomey and F. Korzenny (eds.), *Cross-cultural interpersonal communication,* 213–229. Newbury Park, CA: Sage.

Kim, U. M. (1994). Significance of paternalism and communalism in the occupational welfare of Korean firms: A national survey. In U. M. Kim, H. C. Triandis, C. Kagitcibasi, S.-C. Choi, and G. Yoon (eds.), *Individualism and collectivism: Theory, methods and applications, Cross-cultural research and methodology 18*, 251–266. Thousand Oaks, CA: Sage.

Kim, W. C. (1987). Competition and the management of host government intervention. *Sloan Management Review, 28*(3), 33–39.

Kim, Y. Y., and Paulk, S. (1994). Intercultural challenges and personal adjustments: A qualitative analysis of the experiences of American and Japanese coworkers. In R. Wiseman and R. Shuter (eds.), *Communicating in multinational organizations,* 117–140. Thousand Oaks, CA: Sage.

Kipnis, D., and Schmidt, S. M. (1983). An influence perspective of bargaining within organizations. In M. H. Bazerman and R. J. Lewicki (eds.), *Negotiating in organizations.* Beverly Hills, CA: Sage.

Kirkbride, P. S., and Westwood, R. I. (1993). Hong Kong. In R. B. Peterson (ed.), *Managers and national culture: A global perspective.* Westport, CT: Quorum Books.

Kirkman, B. L., and Shapiro, D. L. (1997). The impact of cultural values on employee resistance to teams: Toward a model of globalized self-managing work team effectiveness. *Academy of Management Review, 22*(3), 730–757.

Kitchell, S. (1995). Corporate culture, environmental adaptation, and innovation adoption: A qualitative approach. *Journal of the Academy of Marketing Science, 23*(3), 195–205.

Klopf, D. W. (1995). *Intercultural encounters: The fundamentals of intercultural communication.* Englewood, CO: Morton.

Kluckholn, F. R., and Strodbeck, F. L. (1961). *Variations in value orientations.* Evanston, IL: Row, Pearson.

Knapp, M. L., Putnam, L. L., and Davis, L. J. (1988). Measuring interpersonal conflict in organizations: Where do we go from here? *Management Communication Quarterly, 1,* 414–429.

Kogut, B., and Singh, H. (1988). The effect of national culture on the choice of entry mode. *Journal of International Business Studies,* Fall, 411–432.

Kolb, D. M., and Putnam, L. L. (1992). The multiple faces of conflict in organizations. *Journal of Organizational Behavior, 13*(3), 311–321.

Konovsky, M. A., and Pugh, S. D. (1994). Citizenship behavior and social exchange. *Academy of Management Journal, 37,* 656–669.

Kopelman, R. E., Brief, A. P., and Guzzo, R. A. (1990). The role of climate and culture in productivity. In B. Schneider (ed.), *Organizational climate and culture,* 282–318. San Francisco: Jossey-Bass.

Korabik, K. (1993). Women managers in the People's Republic of China: Changing roles in changing times. *Applied Psychology: An International Review, 42*(4), 353–363.

Kotter, J. P., and Heskett, J. (1992). *Corporate culture and performance.* New York: Free Press.

Kozan, M. K. (2002). Subcultures and conflict management style. *Management International Review*, 42(1), 89–105.

Kozan, M. K. (1992). Relationships of hierarchy and topics to conflict management styles: A comparative study. In M. A. Rahim (ed.), *Theory and research in conflict management*. New York: Praeger.

Kram, K. E. (1985). *Mentoring at work*. Glenview, IL: Scott Foresman.

Kram, K. E., and Isabella, L. A. (1985). Mentoring alternatives: The role of peer relationships in career development. *Academy of Management Journal, 28*, 110–132.

Kras, E. S. (1988). *Management in two cultures: Bridging the gap between U.S. and Mexican managers*. Yarmouth, ME: Intercultural Press.

Kroon, M. B., Van Kreveid, D., and Rabbie, J. M. (1992). Group versus individual decision-making: Effects of accountability on gender and groupthink. *Small Group Research, 23*, 427–458.

Kuchinke, K. P. (1999). Leadership and culture: Work related values and leadership styles among one company's U.S. and German telecommunication employees. *Human Resource Development Journal, 10*(2), 135–154.

Laaksonen, O. (1992). *Management in China during and after Mao in enterprises, government and party*. New York: Walter de Gruyter.

Lachman, R., Nedd, A., and Hinings, B. (1994). Analyzing cross-national management and organizations: A theoretical framework. *Managerial Science, 40*(1), 40–55.

Lam, S. K., Hui, C., and Law, K. S. (1999). Organizational citizenship behavior: Comparing perspectives of supervisors and subordinates across four international samples. *Journal of Applied Psychology, 84*(4), 594–601.

Lambert, S. J. (1991). The combined effects of job and family characteristics on the job satisfaction, job involvement, and intrinsic motivations of men and women workers. *Journal of Organizational Behavior, 12*, 341–363.

Lammers, C. J., and Hickson, D. J. (1979). *Organizations alike and unlike*. London: Routledge and Kegan Paul.

Lansing, P., and Ready, K. (1988). Hiring women managers in Japan: An alternative for foreign employers. *California Management Review, 30*(3), 112–127.

Larsson, R., and Lubatkin, M. (2001). Achieving acculturation in mergers and acquisitions: An international case study. *Human Relations, 54*(12), 1573–1601.

Lassere, P. (1988). Corporate strategic management of overseas Chinese groups. *Asia Pacific Journal of Management, 5*(2), 115–131.

Lau, C. M., and Ngo, H. Y. (2001). Organization development and firm performance: A comparison of multinational and local firms. *Journal of International Business Studies, 32*(1), 95–114.

Laurent, A. (1986). The cross-cultural puzzle of international human resource management. *Human Resource Management, 25*(1), 91–102.

Laurent, A. (1983). The cultural diversity of Western conceptions of management. *International Studies of Management and Organizations, 13*(1–2), 75–96.

Lawler, E. E., Ledford, G. E., and Mohrman, S. A. (1995). *Employee involvement and total quality management: Practices and results in Fortune 1000 companies.* San Francisco: Jossey-Bass. .

Lawrence, P. R. (1991). *Management in the Netherlands.* Oxford, UK: Clarendon Press.

Lawrence, P. R., and Edwards, V. (2000). *Management in Western Europe.* London: Macmillan.

Lecraw, D. J. (1984). Bargaining power, ownership and profitability of subsidiaries of transnational corporations in developing countries. *Journal of International Business Studies,* Spring–Summer, 27–43.

Lee, D. J., and Sirgy, M. J. (1999). The effect of moral philosophy and ethnocentrism on quality-of-life orientation in international marketing: A cross-cultural comparison. *Journal of Business Ethics, 18,* 73–89.

Lee, J., Roehl, T. W., and Choe, S. (2000). What makes management style similar and distinct across borders? Growth, experience and culture in Korean and Japanese firms. *Journal of International Business Studies, 31*(4), 631–652.

Lee, K., Allen, N. J., Meyer, J. P., and Rhee, K. Y. (2001). The three component model of organizational commitment: An application to South Korea. *Applied Psychology: An International Review, 50*(4), 596–614.

Lee, M., and Barnett, G. A. (1997). A symbols and meaning approach to the organizational cultures of banks in the United States, Japan and Taiwan. *Communication Research, 24*(4), 394–413.

Lee, S. M., and Peterson, S. J. (2000). Culture, entrepreneurial orientation and global competitiveness. *Journal of World Business, 35*(4), 401–412.

Leiba-O'Sullivan, S. (1999). The distinction between stable and dynamic cross-cultural competencies: Implications for expatriate trainability. *Journal of International Business Studies, 30*(4), 709–725.

Lenartowicz, T., and Johnson, J. P. (2002). Comparing managerial values in twelve Latin American countries: An exploratory study. *Management International Review, 42*(3), 279–307.

Lenartowicz, T., and Roth, K. (2001). Does subculture within a country matter? A cross-cultural study of motivational domains and business performance in Brazil. *Journal of International Business Studies, 32*(2), 305–325.

Lenartowicz, T., and Roth, K. (1999). A framework for culture assessment. *Journal of International Business Studies, 30*(4), 781–798.

Lenway, S., and Murtha, T. P. (1994). The state as strategist in international business research. *Journal of International Business Studies, 25,* 513–535.

Lepper, M., and Greene, D. (1978). Overjustification research and beyond: Towards a means-ends analysis of intrinsic and extrinsic motivation. In M. Lepper and D. Greene (eds.), *The hidden costs of reward.* Hillsdale, NJ: Erlbaum.

Leung, K. (1997). Negotiation and reward allocations across cultures. In P. Barley and M. Erez (eds.), *New perspectives on international industrial organizational psychology.* San Francisco: Jossey-Bass.

Leung, K. (1989). Cross-cultural differences: Individual-level and cultural-level analysis. *International Journal of Psychology, 24,* 703–719.

Leung, K. (1988). Some determinants of conflict avoidance. *Journal of Cross-Cultural Psychology, 19*(1), 125–136.

Leung, K., Au, Y. F., Fernandez-Dols, J. M., and Iwawaki, S. (1992). Preference for methods of conflict processing in two collectivist cultures. *International Journal of Psychology, 27*(2), 195–209.

Leung, K., and Bond, M. H. (1989). On the empirical identification of dimensions for cross-cultural comparisons. *Journal of Cross-Cultural Psychology, 20*(2), 133–151.

Leung, K., and Bond, M. H. (1984). The impact of cultural collectivism on reward allocation. *Journal of Personality and Social Psychology, 47,* 793–804.

Leung, K., and Lind, A. B. (1986). Procedural justice and culture: Effects of culture, gender, and investigator status on procedural preferences. *Journal of Personality and Social Psychology, 50*(6), 1134–1140.

Levanoni, E., and Knoop, R. (1985). Does task structure moderate the leaders' behavior and employees' satisfaction? *Psychological Reports, 57,* 611–623.

Levine, R. V. (1997). *A geography of time: The temporal misadventures of a social psychologist, or how every culture keeps time just a little bit differently.* New York: HarperCollins.

Levinson, H. (1994). Beyond the selection failures. Special issue: Issues in the assessment of managerial and effective leadership. *Consulting Psychology Journal: Practice and Research, 46*(1), 3–8.

Li, H. Z. (1999). Communicating information in conversations: A cross-cultural comparison. *International Journal of Intercultural Relations, 23*(3), 387–409.

Li, J., Xin, K. R., and Tsui, A. (1999). Building effective international joint venture leadership teams in China. *Journal of World Business, 34*(1), 52–65.

Li, M. C., Cheung, S. F., and Kau, S. (1979). Competitive and cooperative behavior of Chinese children in Taiwan and Hong Kong. *Acta Psychologica Taiwanica, 21*(1), 27–33.

Li, Y. M. (ed.). (1992). *Chinese women: Through Chinese eyes.* London: East Gate.

Licuanan, V. S. (1993). Entrepreneurs: Her way. *Asian Manager*, 2, 4–10.

Limlingan, V. S. (1986). *The overseas Chinese in ASEAN: Business strategies and management practices*. Manila, the Philippines: Vita Development Corp.

Lin, R. Y. (1995). How individualism-collectivism influence Asian and U.S. managers in choosing their career goals and tactics. *Journal of Asian Business*, 11(3), 97–116.

Lin, X., and Germain, R. (1998). Sustaining satisfactory joint venture relationships: The role of conflict resolution strategy. *Journal of International Business Studies*, 29(1), 179–196.

Lin, Y. (1935). *My country and my people*. New York: John Day.

Lincoln, J. R. (1989). Employee work attitudes and management practice in the U.S. and Japan: Evidence from a large comparative study. *California Management Review*, Fall, 89–106.

Lincoln, J. R., and Kalleberg, A. L. (1996). Commitment, quits, and work organization in Japanese and U.S. plants. *Industrial and Labor Relations Review*, 50, 35–59.

Lind, E. A., and Tyler, T. R. (1988). *The social psychology of procedural justice*. New York: Plenum.

Lindholm, N. (1999). National culture and performance management in MNC subsidiaries. *International Studies of Management and Organization*, 29(4), 45–66.

Ling, W. Q. (1989). Patterns of leadership behavior assessment in China. *Psychologia*, 32, 129–134.

Ling, W. Q., Chia, R. C., and Fang, L. (2000). Chinese implicit leadership theory. *Journal of Social Psychology*, 140(6), 729–739.

Lippitt, G. L., and Hoopes, D. S. (1978). *Helping across cultures*. Washington, DC: International Consultants Foundation.

Liu, J., and Mackinnon, A. (2002). Comparative management practices and training: China and Europe. *Journal of Management Development*, 21(2), 118–132.

Livinthal, D., and March, J. G. (1993). The myopia of learning. *Strategic Management Journal*, 14, 95–112.

Locke, E. A. (1991). The motivation sequence, the motivation hub, and the motivation core. *Organizational Behavior and Human Decision Processes*, 50, 288–299.

Locke, E. A. (1976). The nature and causes of job dissatisfaction. In M. D. Dunnette (ed.), *The handbook of industrial and organizational psychology*, 901–926. Chicago: Rand McNally.

Loong, P. (1994). China: Political, social and economic overview. Paper presented at the China M and A Market for the Future Conference. *Acquisition Monthly*, 6, 36–37.

Lord, R. G., and Maher, K. J. (1991). *Leadership and information processing: Linking perceptions to performance.* Boston: Unwin Hyman.

Luthans, F., Welsh, D. H., and Rosenkrantz, S. A. (1993). What do Russian managers really do? An observational study with comparison to U.S. managers. *Journal of International Business Studies, 24,* 741–761.

Lynn, S. A., Cao, L. T., and Horn, B. (1996). The influence of career stage on the work attitudes of male and female accounting professionals. *Journal of Organizational Behavior, 17*(2), 135–149.

Ma, L. C., and Smith, K. (1992). Social correlates of Confucian ethics in Taiwan. *Journal of Social Psychology, 132,* 655–659.

MacKenzie, S. B., Podsakoff, P. M., and Fetter, R. (1991). Organizational citizenship behavior and objective productivity as determinants of managerial evaluations of salespersons performance. *Organizational Behavior and Human Decision Process, 50,* 123–150.

Manev, I. M., and Stevenson, W. B. (2001). Nationality, cultural distance, and expatriate status: The effects on the managerial network in a multinational enterprise. *Journal of International Business Studies, 32*(2), 285–303.

Manz, C. C., and Sims, H. P. (1993). *Business without bosses: How self-managing teams are building high performance companies.* New York: Wiley.

Marcoulides, G. A., Yavas, B. F., and Bilgin, Z. (1998). Reconciling culturalist and rationalist approaches: Leadership in the United States and Turkey. *Thunderbird International Business Review, 40*(6), 563–583.

Markus, H. R., and Kitayama, S. (1991). Culture and the self: Implications for cognition, emotion, and motivation. *Psychological Review, 98,* 224–253.

Marsh, R. M. (1996). *The great transformation: Social change in Taipei, Taiwan since the 1960s.* Armonk, NY: Sharpe.

Martinez, J. I., and Jarillo, J. C. (1991). Coordination demands of international strategies. *Journal of International Business Studies, 22*(3), 429–444.

Martinez, Z. L., and Ricks, D. A. (1989). Multinational parent companies' influence over human resource decisions of affiliates: U.S. firms in Mexico. *Journal of International Business Studies, 20*(3), 465–487.

Maslow, A. H. (1943). A theory of human motivation. *Psychological Review, 80,* 370–396.

Massie, J. L., and Luytjes, J. (1972). *Management in an international context.* New York: Harper Row.

Matthias, Z. (2001). Country-of-origin effects, host country effects, and the management of HR multinationals: German companies in Britain and Spain. *Journal of World Business, 36*(2), 107–127.

Maurice, M., Sorge, A., and Warner, M. (1980). Societal differences in organizing manufacturing units: A comparison of France, West Germany and Britain. *Organizational Studies, 1,* 59–86.

Mayer, D., and Cava, A. (1993). Ethics and the gender equality dilemma for U.S. multinationals. *Journal of Business Ethics, 12,* 163–172.

Maznevski, M. L., and DiStefano, J. J. (1995). Measuring culture in international management: The cultural perspectives questionnaire. Paper presented at the Academy of International Business Conference, Seoul, South Korea, November.

McAuley, J. (1994). Exploring issues in culture and competence. *Human Relations, 47*(4), 417–430.

McBain, R. (1997). The role of human resource management and the psychological contract. *Manager Update, 8*(4), 22–31.

McClelland, D. (1976). Power is the great motivator. *Harvard Business Review, 54,* 100–110.

McClelland, D. (1961). *The achieving society.* Princeton, NJ: Van Nostrand.

McCormick, I. A., and Cooper, C. L. (1988). Executive stress: Extending the international comparison. *Human Relations, 41,* 65–72.

McCrae, R. R., and Costa, P. T. (1997). Personality trait structure as a human universal. *American Psychologist, 52,* 509–516.

McCrae, R. R., Costa, P. T., and Yik, M. S. M. (1996). Universal aspects of Chinese personality structure. In M. H. Bond, *The handbook of Chinese psychology,* 189–207. Hong Kong: Oxford University Press.

McGrath-Champ, S., and Yang, X. (2002). Cross-cultural training, expatriate quality of life and venture performance. *Management Research News, 25*(8–10), 135–141.

McGregor, D. (1960). *The human side of enterprise.* New York: McGraw-Hill.

McSweeney, B. (2002). Hofstede's model of national cultural differences and their consequences: A triumph of faith—a failure of analysis. *Human Relations, 55*(1), 89–118.

Meindl, J. R. (1990). On leadership: An alternative to the conventional wisdom. In B. M. Staw and L. L. Cummings (eds.), *Research in organizational behavior.* Greenwich, CT: JAI Press.

Meyer, J. P., and Allen, N. J. (1991). A three-component conceptualization of organizational commitment. *Human Resource Management Review, 1,* 61–89.

Miles, R. H., and Snow, C. S. (1978). *Organizational strategy, structure, and process.* New York: McGraw-Hill.

Miner, J. B. (1980). *Theories of organizational behavior.* Hinsdale, IL: Dryden Press.

Miner, J. B. (1965). *Studies in management education.* New York: Springer.

Miner, J. B., Chen, C. C., and Yu, K. C. (1991). Theory testing under adverse conditions: Motivation to manage in the People's Republic of China. *Journal of Applied Psychology, 76*(3), 343–349.

Misawa, M. (1987). New Japanese-style management in a changing era. *Columbia Journal of World Business, 22*(4), 9–17.

Mishra, R. C. (1994). Individualist and collectivist orientations across generalizations. In U. Kim, H. C. Triandis, C. Kagitcibasi, S.-C. Choi, and G. Yoon (eds.), *Individualism and collectivism: Theory, method, and applications,* 225–238. Thousand Oaks, CA: Sage.

Misumi, J. (1985). *The behavioral science of leadership.* Ann Arbor: University of Michigan Press.

Misumi, J., and Peterson, M. F. (1985). The performance-maintenance (PM) theory of leadership: A review of a Japanese research program. *Administrative Science Quarterly,* June, 198–223.

Mitchell, R. K., Smith, J. B., Morse, E. A., Seawright, K. W., Peredo, A. M., and McKenzie, B. (2002). Are entrepreneurial cognitions universal? Assessing entrepreneurial cognitions across cultures. *Entrepreneurship Theory and Practice,* 26(4), 9–32.

Mobley, W. (1982). *Employee turnover causes, consequences, and control.* Reading, MA: Addison-Wesley.

Mohr, J., and Spekman, R. (1994). Characteristics of partnership success: Partnership attributes, communication behavior, and conflict resolution techniques. *Strategic Management Journal, 15*(2), 135–152.

Moorman, R. H. (1991). Relationships between organizational justice and organizational citizenship behavior: Do fairness perceptions influence employee citizenship? *Journal of Applied Psychology, 6,* 845–855.

Moran, R. T., and Abbott, J. (1994). *NAFTA: Managing the cultural differences.* Houston: Gulf.

Moran, R. T., and Stripp, W. G. (1991). *Dynamics of successful international business negotiations.* Houston: Gulf.

Morris, M. A., and Robbie, C. (2001). A meta-analysis of the effects of cross-cultural training on expatriate performance and adjustment. *International Journal of Training and Development, 5,* 112–125.

Morris, M. W., and Leung, K. (1999). Justice for all? Understanding cultural influences on judgments of outcome and process fairness. *Applied Psychology: An International Review,* 48(4), 28–39.

Morris, M. W., Williams, K. Y., Leung, K., Larrick, R., Mendoza, M. T., Bhatnagar, D., Li, J., Kondo, M., Luo, J. L., and Hu, J. (1998). Conflict management style: Accounting for cross-national differences. *Journal of International Business Studies,* 29(4), 729–747.

Morrison, A. M. (1992). *The new leaders: guidelines on leadership diversity in America.* San Francisco: Jossey-Bass.

Morrison, E. W., and Robinson, S. A. (1997). When employees feel betrayed: A model of how psychological contract violation develops. *Academy of Management Review,* 22(1), 226–256.

Mottaz, C., and Potts, G. (1986). An empirical evaluation of models of work satisfaction. *Social Science Research, 15,* 153–173.

Mouritsen, J. (1989). Accounting, culture and accounting culture. *Scandinavian Journal of Management, 5*(1), 21–47.

Nakamura, H. (1964). *Ways of thinking of Eastern peoples.* Honolulu, HI: East-West Centre Press.

Nakata, C., and Sivakumar, K. (1996). National culture and new product development: An integrative review. *Journal of Marketing, 60*, 61–72.

Namie, G., and Namie, R. (2003). Anti-bullying advocacy: An unrealized EAR opportunity. *Journal of Employee Assistance, 33*(2), 9–11.

Neelankavil, J. P., Mathur, A., and Zhang, Y. (2000). Determinants of managerial performance: A cross-cultural comparison of the perceptions of middle-level managers in four countries. *Journal of International Business Studies, 31*(1), 121–140.

Neil, C. C., and Snizek, W. E. (1987). Work values, job characteristics, and gender. *Sociological Perspectives, 30*(3), 245–265.

Nelson, B. (1998). Motivating workers worldwide. *Workforce, 77*(11), 25–27.

Newman, K. L., and Nollen, S. D. (1996). Culture and congruence: The fit between management practices and national culture. *Journal of International Business Studies, 27*, 753–779.

Nicholls, J. (1993). The paradox of managerial leadership. *Journal of General Management, 18*(4), 1–14.

Nikandrou, I., Apospori, E., and Papalexandris, N. (2003). Culture and leadership similarities and variations in the southern part of the European Union. *Journal of Leadership and Organizational Studies, 9*(3), 61–84.

Nohria, N., and Ghoshal, S. (1997). *The differentiated network: Organizing MNCs for value creation.* San Francisco: Jossey-Bass.

Nonaka, I. (1988). Toward middle up-down management: Accelerating information creation. *Sloan Management Review, 29*, 9–18.

Noor, M. N. (2002). Work-family conflict, locus of control, and women's well-being: Tests of alternative pathways. *Journal of Social Psychology, 142*(5), 645–662.

Nyfield, G., and Baron, H. (2000). Cultural context in adapting selection practices across borders. In J. Kehoe (ed.), *Managing selection in changing organizations: Human resource strategies,* 242–268. San Francisco: Jossey-Bass.

Oetzel, J. G. (1998). Culturally homogeneous and heterogeneous groups: Explaining communication processes through individualism-collectivism and self-construal. *International Journal of Intercultural Relations, 22*, 135–161.

Offermann, L. R., Kennedy, J. K., and Wirtz, P. W. (1994). Implicit leadership theories: Content, structure, and generalizability. *Leadership Quarterly, 5*, 43–58.

Ohbuchi, K., and Takahashi, Y. (1994). Cultural styles of conflict management in Japanese and Americans: Passivity, covertness, and effectiveness of strategies. *Journal of Applied Social Psychology, 24*(15), 1345–1366.

Olian, J. D., Carroll, S. J., and Giannantonio, C. M. (1993). Mentor reactions to protégés: An experiment with managers. *Journal of Vocational Behavior, 43,* 266–278.

Olie, R. (1994). Shades of culture and institutions in international mergers. *Organization Studies, 15*(3), 381–405.

Olson, L. B., and Singsuwan, J. (1997). The effect of partnership, communication, and conflict resolution behaviors on performance success of strategic alliances: American and Thai perspectives. In P. W. Beamish and J. P. Killing (eds.), *Cooperative strategies: Asian Pacific perspectives,* 245–267. San Francisco: New Lexington Press.

Onedo, A. E. O. (1991). The motivation and need satisfaction of Papua New Guinea managers. *Asia Pacific Journal of Management, 8*(1), 121–129.

Ones, D. S., and Viswesvaran, C. (1997). Personality determinants in the prediction of aspects of expatriate success. In Z. Aycan (ed.), *Expatriate management: Theory and research,* vol. 4. Greenwich, CT: JAI Press.

O'Reilly, C. A. (1989). Corporations, culture, and commitment: motivation and social control in organizations. *California Management Review, 31*(4), 9–25.

O'Reilly, C. A., Chatman, J., and Caldwell, D. F. (1991). People and organizational culture: A profile comparison approach to assessing person-organization fit. *Academy of Management Journal, 16*(3), 487–516.

Organ, D. W. (1988). *Organizational citizenship behavior: The good soldier syndrome.* Lexington, MA: Lexington Books.

Oskamp, S., and Costanzo, M. (eds.). (1993). *Gender issues in contemporary society.* Newbury Park, CA: Sage.

Osterman, P. (1994). How common is workplace transformation and who adapts to it? *Industrial and Labor Relations Review, 47,* 173–188.

Ouchi, W. (1981). *Theory Z: How American businesses can meet the Japanese challenge.* Reading, MA: Addison-Wesley.

Pan, L. (1988) *The new Chinese revolution.* Chicago: Contemporary Books.

Park, H., Gowan, M., and Hwang, S. D. (2002). Impact of national origin and entry mode on trust and organizational commitment. *Multinational Business Review, 10*(2), 52–61.

Park, S. H., and Ungson, G. R. (1997). Reexamining national culture, organizational complementarity, and economic motivation on joint venture dissolution. *Academy of Management Journal, 40*(2), 279–307.

Parker, M. (2000). *Organizational culture and identity.* London: Sage.

Parkhe, A. (1993). Partner nationality and the structure-performance relationship in strategic alliances. *Organization Science, 4*(2), 301–324.

Parkhe, A. (1991). Interfirm diversity, organizational learning, and longevity in global strategic alliances. *Journal of International Business Studies,* Fourth Quarter, 579–601.

Parry, M. E., and X. M. Song, (1993). Determinants of RandD-marketing integration in high-tech Japanese firms. *Journal of Product Innovation Management, 10*, 4–22.

Pasa, S. F., Kabasakal, H., and Bodur, M. (2001). Society, organizations, and leadership in Turkey. *Applied Psychology: An International Review, 50*(4), 559–589.

Pascale, R. T. (1990). *Managing on the edge: How the smartest companies use conflict to stay ahead.* New York: Simon and Schuster.

Pavett, C., and Morris, T. (1995). Management styles within a multinational corporation: A five-country comparative study. *Human Relations, 48*(10), 1171–1191.

Pearson, M. M. (1991). *Joint ventures in the People's Republic of China.* Princeton, NJ: Princeton University Press.

Pedigo, S. (1991). Diversity in the work force: Riding the tide of change. *Wyatt Communicator,* Winter, 4–11.

Peng, T. K., Peterson, M. F., and Shyi, Y. P. (1991). Quantitative methods in cross-cultural management research: Trends and equivalence issues. *Journal of Organizational Behavior, 12*, 87–108.

Perry, J. L., and Wise, L. R. (1990). The motivational bases of public service. *Public Administration Review, 50*(3), 367–373.

Peters, E. B., and Lippitt, G. L. (1978). The use of instruments in international training. *Journal of European International Training, 2*(7), 24–25.

Peters, T., and Waterman, R. (1982). *In search of excellence.* New York: Harper Row.

Peterson, M. F., et al. (1995). Role conflict, ambiguity and overload: A twenty-one nation study. *Academy of Management Journal, 38*, 429–452.

Peterson, R. B., and George-Falvy, J. (1993). United States. In R. B. Peterson (ed.), *Managers and national culture: A global perspective.* Westport, CT: Quorum Books.

Peterson, R. M., Dibrell, C. C., and Pett, T. L. (2002). Long vs. short-term performance perspectives of Western European, Japanese, and U.S. countries: Where do they lie? *Journal of World Business, 37*(4), 245–255.

Pfeffer, J. (1994). The costs of legalization: The hidden dangers of increasingly formalized control. In S. B. Sitkin and R. J. Bies (eds.), *The legalistic organization,* 329–346. Thousand Oaks, CA: Sage.

Pillai, R., Scandura, T., and Williams, E. A. (1999). Leadership and organizational justice: Similarities and differences across cultures. *Journal of International Business Studies, 30*(4), 763–779.

Pillai, R., and Williams, E. A. (1996). Performance beyond expectations? A study of transformational leadership, fairness perceptions, job satisfaction, commitment, trust, and organizational citizenship behavior. Paper presented at the National Academy of Management Meeting, Cincinnati, OH, August.

Pleck, J. H., Staines, G. L., and Lang, L. (1980). Conflicts between work and family life. *Monthly Labor Review, 103,* 29–32.

Popp, G. E., Davis, H. J., and Herbert, T. T. (1986). An international study of intrinsic motivation composition. *Management International Review, 26,* 28–35.

Porter, L. W., Steers, R. M., Mowbay, R. T., and Boulian, P. V. (1974). Organizational commitment, job satisfaction, and turnover among psychiatric technicians. *Journal of Applied Psychology, 59,* 603–609.

Porter, M. E. (1990). *The competitive advantage of nations.* New York: Free Press.

Posner, B. Z., Hall, J. I., and Harder, J. W. (1986). People are most important asset but: Encouraging employee development. *Business Horizons,* September–October, 52–54.

Posner, B. Z., and Schmidt, W. H. (1992). Values and the American manager: An update updated. *California Management Review, 34*(3), 80–94.

Potvin, T. C. (1991). Employee organizational commitment: An examination of its relationship to communication satisfaction and evaluation of questionnaires designed to measure the construct. Ph.D. diss., University of Kansas, Lawrence.

Poulton, R. G., and Ng, S. H. (1988). Relationships between Protestant work ethic and work effort in a field setting. *Applied Psychology: An International Review, 37*(3), 227–233.

Poynter, T. A. (1985). *Multinational enterprises and government intervention.* New York: St. Martin's Press.

Prasad, S. B. (ed.). (1990). *Advances in comparative management,* vol. 5. Greenwich, CT: JAI Press.

Preziosi, R. C. (2000). Perception of the relationship between values congruency and organization sustainability in Jamaica. Paper presented at the International Applied Business Research Conference, Puerto Vallarta, Mexico, March.

Preziosi, R. C. (1999). The relationship between employee/organizational values and total quality management in Panama. Paper presented at the International Applied Business Research Conference, Vassa, Finland, March.

Preziosi, R. C., and Gooden, D. J. (2001). Values congruence and its relationship to the new science leadership style among Brazilian executives. Paper presented at the International Applied Business Research Conference, Cancun, Mexico, March.

Pruitt, D. G. (1981). *Negotiation behavior.* New York: Academic Press.

Pruitt, D. G., and Carnevale, P. (1993). *Negotiation in social conflict.* Pacific Grove, CA: Brooks/Cole.

Pruitt, D. G., and Rubin, J. Z. (1986). *Social conflict: Escalation, stalemate, and settlement.* New York: Random House.

Psenicka, C., and Rahim, M. A. (1989). Integrative and distributive dimensions of styles of handling interpersonal conflict and bargaining outcome. In M. A. Rahim (ed.), *Managing conflict: An interdisciplinary approach*, 33–40. New York: Praeger.

Pucik, V., and Saba, T. (1998). Selecting and developing the global versus the expatriate manager: A review of the state-of-the-art. *Human Resource Planning*, 21(4), 40–54.

Punnett, B. J. (1995). Preliminary considerations of Confucianism and needs in the PRC. *Journal of Asia Pacific Business*, 1(1), 25–42.

Putti, J. M., Aryee, S., and Phua, J. (1990). Communication relationship satisfaction and organizational commitment. *Group and Organizational Studies*, 15(1), 44–52.

Pye, L. (1982). *Chinese commercial negotiating style*. Cambridge, MA: Oelgeschlager, Gunn and Hain.

Quarstein, V., McAffee, R., and Glassman, M. (1992). The situational occurrences theory of job satisfaction. *Human Relations*, 45(8), 859–873.

Rabin, B. R. (1994). Benefits communication: Its impact on employee benefits satisfaction under flexible programs. *Benefits Quarterly*, Fourth Quarter, 67–83.

Radford, M. H., Mann, L., Ohta, Y., and Nakane, Y. (1991). Differences between Australia and Japan in reported use of decision processes. *International Journal of Psychology*, 26, 35–52.

Ragins, B. R., and Cotton, J. L. (1993). Gender and willingness to mentor in organizations. *Journal of Management*, 19, 97–111.

Rahim, M. A. (2001). *Managing conflict in organizations* (3d ed.). Westport, CT: Quorum Books.

Rahim, M. A. (1997). Style of managing organization conflict: A critical review and synthesis of theory and research. In M. A. Rahim, R. T. Golembiewski, and L. E. Pate (eds.), *Current topics in management*, 2:61–77. Greenwich, CT: JAI Press.

Rahim, M. A. (1989). Relationships of leader power to compliance and satisfaction with supervision: Evidence from a national sample of managers. *Journal of Management*, 15, 545–557.

Rahim, M. A. (1988). The development of a leader power inventory. *Multivariate Behavioral Research*, 23, 491–502.

Rahim, M. A. (1986a). *Managing conflict in organizations*. New York: Praeger.

Rahim, M. A. (1986b). Referent role and styles of handling conflict: A model for diagnosis and intervention. *Psychological Reports*, 44, 1323–1344.

Rahim, M. A. (1985). A strategy for managing conflict in complex organizations. *Human Relations*, 38, 81–89.

Rahim, M. A., Antonioni, D., and Psenicka, C. (2001). A structural equations model of leader power, subordinates' styles of handling conflict, and job performance. *International Journal of Conflict Management*, 12(3), 191–211.

Rahim, M. A., and Bonoma, T. V. (1979). Managing organizational conflict: A model for diagnosis and intervention. *Psychological Reports, 44,* 1323–1344.

Rahim, M. A., Magner, N. R., Antonioni, D., and Rahman, S. (2001). Do justice relationships with organization-directed reactions differ across U.S. and Bangladesh employees? *International Journal of Conflict Management, 12*(4), 333–349.

Rahim, M. A., Magner, N. R., and Shapiro, D. (2000). Do justice perceptions influence styles of handling conflict with supervisors? What justice perceptions, precisely? *International Journal of Conflict Management, 11*(1), 9–31.

Rajiv, M., Larsen, T., Rosenbloom, B., Mazur, J., and Poisa, P. (2001). Leadership and cooperation in marketing channels: A comparative empirical analysis of the USA, Finland and Poland. *International Marketing Review, 18*(6), 633–667.

Ralston, D. A., Gustafson, D. J., Cheung, F. M., and Terpstra, R. H. (1993). Differences in managerial values: A study of U.S., Hong Kong and PRC managers. *Journal of International Business Studies, 24*(2), 249–275.

Ralston, D. A., Gustafson, D. J., Elsacs, P. M., Cheung, F. M., and Terpstra, R. H. (1992). Eastern values: A comparison of managers in the United States, Hong Kong and the People's Republic of China. *Journal of Applied Psychology, 77,* 664–671.

Ralston, D. A., Gustafson, D. J., Terpstra, R. H., and Holt, R. H. (1995). Pre-post Tiananmen Square: Changing values of Chinese managers. *Asia Pacific Journal of Management, 12,* 1–20.

Ralston, D. A., Holt, D. A., Terpstra, R. H., and Yu, K. C. (1997). The impact of national culture and economic ideology on managerial work values: A study of the United States, Russia, Japan, and China. *Journal of International Business Studies, 28,* 177–208.

Ralston, D. A., Nguyen, T. V., and Napier, N. K. (1999). Symposium: New trends in international and multicultural management: A comparative study of the work values of North and South Vietnamese managers. *Journal of International Business Studies, 30*(4), 655–673.

Ralston, D. A., Yu, K. C., Wang, X., Terpstra, R. H., and He, W. (1996). The cosmopolitan Chinese manager: Findings of a study on managerial values across the six regions of China. *Journal of International Management, 2,* 79–109.

Rao, A., Hashimoto, K., and Rao, A., (1997). Universal and culturally specific aspects of managerial influence: A study of Japanese managers. *Leadership Quarterly, 8*(3), 295–312.

Rao, A., and Schmidt, S. M. (1998). International business negotiations: A behavioral perspective on negotiating international alliances. *Journal of International Business Studies, 29*(4), 665–694.

Reade, C. (2002). Dual identification in multinational corporations: Local managers and their psychological attachment to the subsidiary versus the global organization. *International Journal of Human Resource Management, 12*(3), 405–424.

Reddin, W. J. (1967). The 3–D management style theory: A typology based on task and relationship orientation. *Training and Development Journal, 21,* 11–22.

Redding, S. G. (1992). Capitalist cooking lessons. *Asian Business,* November, 50–52.

Redding, S. G. (1990). *The spirit of Chinese capitalism.* New York: Walter de Gruyter.

Redding, S. G. (1987). The study of managerial ideology among overseas Chinese owner-managers. *Asia-Pacific Journal of Management, 4*(3), 167–177.

Redding, S. G. (1986). Developing managers without "management development": The overseas Chinese solution. *Management Education and Development, 17,* 271–281.

Redding, S. G., and Hsiao, M. (1990). An empirical study of overseas Chinese managerial ideology. *International Journal of Psychology, 25*(5–6), 629–641.

Redding, S. G., and Ng, M. (1982). The role of "face" in the organizational perceptions of Chinese managers. *Organizational Studies, 3,* 201–219.

Redding, S. G., and Tam, S. K. W. (1985). Networks and molecular organizations: An exploratory view of Chinese firms in Hong Kong. In K. C. Mun and T. S. Chan (eds.), *Proceedings of the Inaugural Meeting of the Southeast Asia Region Academy of International Business.* Hong Kong: Chinese University of Hong Kong.

Redding, S. G., and Wong, G. Y. Y. (1986). The psychology of Chinese organizational behavior. In M. H. Bond (ed.), *The Psychology of Chinese People,* 267–295. Hong Kong: Oxford University Press.

Redpath, L., and Nielsen, M. O. (1997). A comparison of native culture, nonnative culture and new management ideology. *Canadian Journal of Administrative Sciences, 14*(3), 327–339.

Reed, D. (2003). Don't abuse sick time, American CEO warns. *USA Today,* January 9, B2.

Reeve, J., Cole, S., and Olsen, B. (1986). Adding excitement to intrinsic motivation research. *Journal of Social Behavior and Personality, 1,* 349–363.

Reeve, J., and Deci, E. L. (1996). Elements of the competitive situation that affects intrinsic motivation. *Personality and Social Psychology Bulletin, 22,* 24–33.

Reilly, A. J. (1974). Individual needs and organizational goals: An experiential lecture. In J. W. Pfeiffer and J. E. Jones (eds.), *1974 annual handbook for group facilitators.* San Diego: University Associates.

Renwick, P. A. (1975). Perception and management of supervisor-subordinate conflict. *Organizational Behavior and Human Performance, 13,* 444–456.

Richardson, P., Trewatha, R. L., and Vaught, B. C. (1995). Labor and management perspectives toward work and job satisfaction in difficult times. *Journal of Management, 12*(3), 325–336.

Risher, H., and Stopper, W. G. (2000a). Paradoxes in Vietnam and America: "Lessons earned" part I. *Human Resource Planning, 23*(1), 7–8.

Risher, H., and Stopper, W. G. (2000b). Paradoxes in Vietnam and America: "Lessons earned" part II. *Human Resource Planning, 23*(2), 9–10.

Risher, H., and Stopper, W. G. (2000c). Paradoxes in Vietnam and America: "Lessons earned" part III. *Human Resource Planning, 23*(3), 8–10.

Robbins, S. P. (1998). *Organizational behavior: Concepts, controversies, applications* (8th ed.). Englewood Cliffs, NJ: Prentice Hall.

Robert, C., Probst, T. M., Martocchio, J. J., Drasgow, F., and Lawler, J. (2000). Empowerment and continuous improvement in the United States, Mexico, Poland and India: Predicting fit on the basis of the dimensions of power distance and individualism. *Journal of Applied Psychology, 85*(5), 643–658.

Roberts, K., and Boyacigiller, N. (1984). Cross-national organizational research: The grasp of blind men. *Research in Organizational Behavior, 6,* 423–475.

Robertson, C. J. (2000). The global dimension of Chinese values: A three-country study of Confucian dynamism. *Management International Review, 40*(3), 253–268.

Robinson, S. L., Kraatz, M. S., and Rousseau, D. M. (1994). Changing obligations and the psychological contract: A longitudinal study. *Academy of Management Journal,* February, 137–152.

Rodriques, C. A. (1990). The situation and national culture as contingencies for leadership behavior: Two conceptual models. In S. B. Prasad (ed.), *Advances in international and comparative management: A research annual,* 5:51–68. Greenwich, CT: JAI Press.

Romzek, B. S. (1990). Employee investment and commitment: The ties that bind. *Public Administration Review, 50*(3), 374–382.

Rondinelli, D., and Berry, M. (2000). Environmental citizenship in multinational corporations: Social responsibility and sustainable development. *European Management Journal, 18,* 70–84.

Ronen, S., and Shenkar, O. (1985). Clustering countries on attitudinal dimensions: A review and synthesis. *Academy of Management Review, 10,* 435–454.

Roney, J. (1997). Cultural implications of implementing TQM in Poland. *Journal of World Business, 32,* 152–168.

Rosen, R. (2000). *Global literacies: Lessons on business leadership and national cultures.* New York: Simon and Schuster.

Rosenbaum, A. (1999). Testing cultural waters. *Management Review, 88*(7), 41–43.

Rousseau, D., and Parks, J. (1992). The contracts of individuals and organizations. In L. L. Cummings and B. M. Staw (eds.), *Research in organizational behavior,* 15:1–47. Greenwich, CT: JAI Press.

Rubin, J, Z., and Zartman, I. W. (1995). Asymmetrical negotiations: Some survey results that may surprise. *Negotiation Journal, 11*(4), 349–364.

Rusbult, C. E., Insko, C. A., and Lin, Y. H. W. (1995). Seniority based reward allocation in the United States and Taiwan. *Social Psychology Quarterly, 58*(1), 13–30.

Ryan, A. M., McFarland, L., and Baron, H. (1999). An international look at selection practices: Nation and culture as explanations for variability in practice. *Personnel Psychology, 52*(2), 359–391.

Ryan, A. M., and Schmit, M. J. (1996). An assessment of organizational climate and P-E fit: A tool for organizational change. *International Journal of Organizational Analysis, 4*(1), 75–95.

Ryan, R. M., and Deci, E. L. (1996). When paradigms clash: Comments on Cameron and Pierce's claim that rewards do not undermine intrinsic motivation. *Review of Educational Research, 66*(1), 33–38.

Sackmann, S. A. (1992). Culture and subcultures: An analysis of organizational knowledge. *Administrative Science Quarterly, 37,* 140–161.

Sager, J. (1994). A structural model depicting salespeople's job stress. *Journal of Academy of Marketing Science, 22,* 74–84.

Scandura, T. A. (1999). Rethinking leader-member exchange: An organizational justice perspective. *Leadership Quarterly, 10,* 25–40.

Scandura, T. A. (1992). Mentorship and career mobility: An empirical investigation. *Journal of Organizational Behavior, 13,* 169–174.

Scandura, T. A., and Viator, R. E. (1994). Mentoring in public accounting firms: An analysis of mentor-protégé relationships, mentorship functions, and protégé turnover intentions. *Accounting, Organizations and Society, 19,* 717–734.

Scarpello, V., and Campbell, J. P. (1983). Job satisfaction: Are all the parts there? *Personnel Psychology, 3,* 577–600.

Schaan, J. L. (1988). How to control a joint venture even as a minority partner. *Journal of General Management, 14*(1), 4–16.

Schaan, J. L., and Beamish, P. (1988). Joint venture general managers in LDCs. In F. J. Contractor and P. Lorange (eds.), *Cooperative strategies in international business,* 279–299. Lexington, MA: Lexington Books.

Schein, E. H. (1996). Culture: The missing concept in organizational studies. *Administrative Science Quarterly,* June, 229–240.

Schein, E. H. (1985). *Organizational culture and leadership.* San Francisco: Jossey-Bass.

Schein, E. H. (1980). *Organizational psychology* (3d. ed.) Englewood Cliffs, NJ: Prentice Hall.

Schein, E. H. (1978). *Career dynamics: Matching individual and organizational needs.* Reading, MA: Addison-Wesley.

Schein, E. H. (1968). Organizational socialization and the profession of management. *Industrial Management Review, 1,* 1–16.

Schermerhorn, J. R. (1999). Terms of global business engagement in ethically challenging environments: Applications to Burma. *Business Ethics Quarterly, 9*(3), 485–505.

Schermerhorn, J. R., and Bond, M. H. (1991). Upward and downward influence tactics in managerial networks: A comparative study of Hong Kong Chinese and Americans. *Asia Pacific Journal of Management, 8,* 147–158.

Schmidt, K. D. (1987). *Doing business in France.* Menlo Park, CA: SRI International.

Schmidt, S. M., and Yeh, R. S. (1992). The structure of leader influence: A cross-national comparison. *Journal of Cross-Cultural Psychology, 23,* 251–264.

Schneider, S. C. (1988). National vs. corporate culture implications for human resource management. *Human Resource Management, 37,* 238–242.

Schneider, S. C., and Barsoux, J. L. (1997). *Managing across cultures.* Englewood Cliffs, NJ: Prentice Hall.

Schwartz, S. H. (1999). A theory of cultural values and some implications for work. *Applied Psychology, 48*(1), 23–47.

Schwartz, S. H. (1994a). Are there universal aspects in the content and structure of values? *Journal of Social Issues, 50,* 19–45.

Schwartz, S. H. (1994b). Beyond individualism/collectivism: New cultural dimensions of values. In U. Kim, H. C. Triandis, and G. Yoon (eds.), *Individualism and collectivism: Theoretical and methodological issues,* 85–119. Newbury Park, CA: Sage.

Schwartz, S. H. (1992). Universals in the content and structure of values: Theoretical advances and empirical tests in 20 countries. In M. P. Zanna (ed.), *Advances in experimental social psychology.* San Diego: Academic Press.

Schwartz, S. H., and Davies, S. (1981). Matching corporate culture and business strategy. *Organizational Dynamics, 8*(2), 30–48.

Schwartz, S. H., and Sagie, G. (2000). Value consensus and importance: A cross-national study. *Journal of Cross-Cultural Psychology, 31*(4), 465–497.

Scott, W. (1997). Personality and self-leadership. *Human Resource Management Review, 7*(2), 139–155.

Scott, W. G., and Mitchell, T. R. (1976). *Organization theory: A structured and behavioral analysis.* Homewood, IL: Richard Irwin.

Segall, R. (2000). Japanese killer. *Psychology Today, 33*(5), 10–11.

Senge, P. (1996). Leading learning organizations. *Executive Excellence,* April, 10–12.

Senge, P. (1990). *The fifth discipline.* New York: Doubleday.

Sergeant, A., and Frenkel, S. (1998). Managing people in China: Perceptions of expatriate managers. *Journal of World Business, 33,* 17–34.

Sexton, D., and Bowman, N. (1985). The entrepreneur: A capable executive and more. *Journal of Business Venturing, 1*(1), 129–140.

Shackleton, V., and Newell, S. (1994). European management selection methods: A comparison of five countries. *International Journal of Selection and Assessment, 2,* 91–102.

Shamir, B. (1992). Attribution of influence and charisma to the leader: The romance of leadership revisited. *Journal of Applied Social Psychology, 22*(5), 386–407.

Shane, S., and Kolvereid, L. (1995). National environment, strategy, and new venture performance: A three country study. *Journal of Small Business Management, 33,* 37–50.

Shane, S., Venkataraman, S., and MacMillan, I. (1995). Cultural differences in innovation championing strategies. *Journal of Management, 21*(5), 931–952.

Shapiro, D. L., and Bies, R. J. (1994). Threats, bluffs, and disclaimers in negotiations. *Organizational Behavior and Human Decision Processes, 60*(1), 14–35.

Sharfuddin, I. (1987). Toward an Islamic administrative theory. *American Journal of Islamic Social Science, 4*(2), 229–244.

Sheer, V. C., and Chen, L. (2003). Successful Sino-Western business negotiation: Participants' accounts of national and professional cultures. *Journal of Business Communication, 40*(1), 50–85.

Sheng, R. (1979). Outsiders' perception of the Chinese. *Columbia Journal of World Business, 14*(2), 16–22.

Shenkar, O., and Ronen, S. (1987). The cultural context of negotiations: The implications of Chinese interpersonal norms. *Journal of Applied Behavioral Science, 23*(2), 263–275.

Shenkar, O., and Zeira, Y. (1992). Role conflict and role ambiguity of chief executive officers in international joint ventures. *Journal of International Business Studies, 23*(1), 55–76.

Sheppard, B. H., Lewicki, R. J., and Minton, J. W. (1992). *Organizational justice: The search of fairness in the workplace.* New York: Lexington Books.

Sheridan, J. E. (1992). Organizational culture and employee retention. *Academy of Management Journal, 35*(5), 1036–1056.

Shieh, G. S. (1989). Black-hands becoming their own bosses: Class mobility in Taiwan's manufacturing sectors. *Taiwan: A Radical Quarterly in Social Studies, 2,* 11–54.

Shim, I.-S., and Paprock, K. E. (2002). A study focusing on American expatriates' learning in host countries. *International Journal of Training and Development, 6*(1), 13–24.

Shuka, A., Sarna, T., and Nigam, R. (1989). Work attitudes of employed men and women who are married. *Psychological Reports, 64,* 711–714.

Shuler, R. S., Dowling, P. J., and De Cieri, H. (1993). An integrative framework of international human resource management. *International Journal of Human Resource Management,* 4(4), 717–764.

Sickler, S., Buschmann, B., and Seim, H. (1996). Recruiting community based preceptors: Money is not the key. *Academic Medicine,* 71(6), 573–579.

Siegrist, J. (1996). Adverse health effects of high-effort/low-reward conditions. *Journal of Occupational Health Psychology, 1,* 27–41.

Siegrist, P. R. (2001). Psychosocial work environment and the risk of coronary heart disease. *Advances in Mind-Body Medicine,* 17(3), 202–203.

Silver, P., Poulin, J. E., and Manning, R. C. (1997). Surviving the bureaucracy: The predictors of job satisfaction for the public agency supervisor. *Clinical Supervisor, 15*(1), 1–20.

Silverthorne, C. (2003a). Individual/organizational fit, organizational culture, commitment and job satisfaction in Taiwan. Paper presented at the European Association of Work and Organizational Psychology, Lisbon, Portugal, May.

Silverthorne, C. (2003b). A test of social power use across cultures. Paper presented at the Western Psychological Association Annual Convention, Vancouver, Canada, April.

Silverthorne, C. (2002). Situational leadership in Taiwan. Paper presented at the American Psychological Society Annual Convention, New Orleans, LA, June.

Silverthorne, C. (2001a). Leadership effectiveness and personality: A cross-cultural evaluation. *Personality and Individual Differences, 30,* 303–309.

Silverthorne, C. (2001b). A test of the path-goal theory of leadership in Taiwan. *Leadership and Organizational Development Journal,* 22(4), 151–158.

Silverthorne, C. (2000). Situational leadership theory in Taiwan: A different culture perspective. *Leadership and Organizational Development Journal,* 21(2), 68–74.

Silverthorne, C. (1998). National culture or corporate culture: An evaluation of the effects of a clash of cultures on organizations. Paper presented at the 24th International Congress of Applied Psychology, San Francisco, CA, August.

Silverthorne, C. (1996). Motivation and management styles in the public and private sectors in Taiwan and a comparison with the United States. *Journal of Applied Social Psychology,* 26(20), 1827–1837.

Silverthorne, C. (1992). Work motivation in the United States, Russia, and the Republic of China (Taiwan): A comparison. *Journal of Applied Social Psychology,* 22(20), 1631–1639.

Silverthorne, C., and Wang, T. H. (2001). Situational leadership style as a predictor of success and productivity among Taiwan business organizations. *Journal of Psychology: Interdisciplinary and Applied, 135*(4), 399–412.

Simon, M. (1996). Suicide rates are rising for the unpopular, harassed police force in Paris. *New York Times,* April 7.

Sims, H. P., and Gioia, D. A. (1986). *The thinking organization.* San Francisco: Jossey-Bass.

Sinangil, H. K. (2002/2003). Building bridges between Europe and Asia: Industrial, work and organizational (IWO) psychology in Turkey. *European Association of Work and Organizational Psychology Newsletter,* Winter, 5–7.

Singelis, T. M., Triandis, H. C., Bhawuk, D. S., and Gelfand, M. (1995). Horizontal and vertical dimensions of individualism and collectivism: A theoretical and measurement refinement. *Cross-Cultural Research, 29,* 240–275.

Sinha, J. B. (1995). *The cultural context of leadership and power.* New Delhi, India: Sage.

Sinha, J. B. (1990). A model of effective leadership styles in India. In A. M. Jaeger and R. N. Kanungo (eds.), *Management in developing countries, 252–263.* New York: Routledge.

Sinha, J. B. (1980). *The nurturant task leader: A model of the effective executive.* New Delhi, India: Concept.

Smart, D. T., and Conant, J. S. (1994). Entrepreneurial orientation, distinctive marketing competencies and organizational performance. *Journal of Applied Business Research, 10*(3), 28–38.

Smith, C. A., Organ, D. W., and Near, J. P. (1983). Organizational citizenship behavior: Leader fairness and task scope versus satisfaction. *Journal of Applied Psychology, 68,* 653–663.

Smith, P. B. (1997). Leadership in Europe: Euro-management or the footprint of history. *European Journal of Work and Organizational Psychology, 6,* 375–386.

Smith, P. B. (1984). The effectiveness of Japanese styles of management: A review and critique. *Journal of Occupational Psychology, 57,* 121–136.

Smith, P. B., and Bond, M. H. (1999). *Social psychology across cultures.* Boston: Allyn and Bacon.

Smith, P. B., Peterson, M. F., et al. (1994). Organizational event management in 14 countries: A comparison of Hofstede's dimensions. In A. M. Bouvy, F. Van de Vijver, P. Boski, and P. Schmitz (eds.), *Journeys in cross-cultural psychology.* Lisse, the Netherlands: Swets and Zeitlinger.

Smith, P. B., and Schwartz, S. H. (1997). Values. In J. W. Berry, M. H. Seagall, and C. Kagitcibasi (eds.), *Handbook of cross-cultural psychology* (2d ed.). Boston: Allyn and Bacon.

Smith, P. B., and Tayeb, M. H. (1988). Organizational structure and processes. In M. H. Bond (ed.), *The cross-cultural challenges to social psychology, 153–164.* Newbury Park, CA: Sage.

Smith, P. B., and Wang, Z-M. (1996). Chinese leadership and organizational structures. In M. H. Bond (ed.), *Chinese psychology.* Hong Kong: Oxford University Press.

Smolowitz, I. (1996). Corporate culture and core competency. *Business and Economic Review,* 42(3), 29–30.

Sniezek, J. A., and May, D. R. (1990). Conflict of interests and commitment in groups. *Journal of Applied Social Psychology, 20,* 1150–1165.

Solomon, C. M. (1995). Global teams: The ultimate collaboration. *Personnel Journal, 74,* 49–50.

Song, X. M., and Dyer, B. (1995). Innovation strategy and RandD marketing interface for Japanese firms: A contingency perspective. *IEEE Transactions on Engineering Management,* 42(4), 360–363.

Song, X. M., and Parry, M. E. (1992). The RandD-marketing interface in Japanese high-technology firms. *Journal of Product Innovation Management, 9,* 91–112.

Sood, J. H. (1990). Equivalent measurement in international market research: Is there really a problem? *Journal of International Consumer Marketing,* 2(2), 25–41.

Sood, J. H., and Mroczkowski, T. (1994). Human resource management challenges in Polish private enterprise. *International Studies of Management and Organization, 24,* 48–63.

Sosik, J., and Jung, D. I. (2002). Work-group characteristics and performance in collectivistic and individualistic cultures. *Journal of Social Psychology, 142*(1), 5–23.

Sousa-Poza, A., and Sousa-Poza, A. A. (2002). Taking another look at the gender/job-satisfaction paradox. *Kyklos, 53*(2), 135–152.

Sousa-Poza, A., and Sousa-Poza, A. A. (2000). Well-being at work: A cross-national analysis of the levels and determinants of job satisfaction. *Journal of Socio-Economics,* 29(6), 517–538.

Spector, P. E. (1997). *Job satisfaction.* Thousand Oaks, CA: Sage.

Spector, P. E., et al. (2001). Do national levels of individualism and internal locus of control relate to well-being: An ecological level of international study. *Journal of Organizational Behavior, 22,* 815–832.

Spencer, D. G., and Steers, R. M. (1981). Performance as a moderator of the job satisfaction-turnover relationship. *Journal of Applied Psychology, 8,* 511–514.

Spreitzer, G. M. (1996). Social structural characteristics of psychological empowerment. *Academy of Management Journal, 39*(2), 483–504.

Stafford, D. (2001). Turnover costs businesses dearly; being ignorant about it costs more. Knight Ridder/Tribune News Service, July 10, pK7522.

Steers, R. M., and Porter, L. W. (1979). *Motivation and work behavior* (2d ed.). New York: McGraw-Hill.

Steyrer, J. (1999). Charisma in organisationen—zum stand der theorienbildung und empirischen forschung. In G. Schreyogg and J. Sydow (eds.), *Managementforschung*, 9:143–197. Berlin: de Gruyter.

Stroh, L. K., and Caligiuri, P. M. (1998). Strategic human resources: A new source for competitive advantage in the global arena. *International Journal of Human Resources Management, 9*, 1–17.

Stroh, L. K., Gregersen, H. B., and Black, J. S. (1998). Closing the gap: Expectations versus reality among repatriates. *Journal of World Business, 33*(2), 111–124.

Su, S. K., Chin, C. Y., Hong, Y. Y., Leung, K., Peng, K., and Morris, M. W. (1999). Self-organization and social organization: American and Chinese constructions. In T. R. Tyler, R. M. Kramer, and O. P. John (eds.), *Psychology of the social self*. Mahwah, NJ: Lawrence Erlbaum.

Sullivan, D. P., and Weaver, G. R. (2000). Cultural cognition in international business research. *Management International Review, 40*(3), 269–297.

Szabo, E., Brodbeck, F. C., den Hartog, D., Reber, G., Weibler, J., and Wunderer, R. (2002). The Germanic Europe cluster: Where employees have voice. *Journal of World Business, 37*(1), 55–68.

Szalay, L. B., Strohl, J. B., Fu, L., and Lao, P.S. (1994). *American and Chinese perceptions and belief systems: A People's Republic of China–Taiwanese comparison*. New York: Plenum.

Tan, B. (2002). The impact of national environment on managerial value systems: A comparative study of Chinese managers in the United States, Singapore and the People's Republic of China. *Management International Review, 42*(4), 473–486.

Tang, S., and Kirkbride, P. (1986). Development of conflict management skills in Hong Kong: An analysis of some cross-cultural implications. *Management Education and Development, 17*(3), 287–301.

Tang, T. L. P., and Ibrahim, A. H. (1998). Antecedents of organizational citizenship behavior revisited: Public personnel in the United States and in the Middle East. *Public Personnel Management, 27*(4), 529–550.

Tansuhaj, P., Wong, J., and McCullough, J. (1987). Internal and external marketing: Effects on consumer satisfaction and banks in Thailand. *International Journal of Bank Marketing, 5*(3), 73–83.

Tata, J. (2000). The influence of national culture on work team autonomy. *International Journal of Management, 17*(2), 266–271.

Tayeb, M. H. (1994). *Organizations and national culture: A comparative analysis*. Beverly Hills, CA: Sage.

Tayeb, M. H. (1988). *Organizations and national culture*. Beverly Hills, CA: Sage.

Taylor, S. (1993). Japan. In R. B. Peterson (ed.), *Managers and national culture: A global perspective*. Westport, CT: Quorum Books.

Teboul, B., Chen, L., and Fritz, L. (1994). Intercultural organizational communication research in multinational organizations. In R. Wiseman and R. Shuster (eds.), *Communicating in multinational organizations,* 12–29. London: Sage.

Terborg, J. R. (1977). Women in management: A research review. *Journal of Applied Psychology,* 62(6), 647–664.

Terpstra, V. (1991). *The cultural environment of international business* (3d ed.). Cincinnati: Southwestern.

Terpstra, V. and David, K. (1990). *Environment of international business* (3d ed.). Cincinnati: Southwestern.

Testa, M. R., Mueller, S. L., and Thomas, A. S. (2003). Cultural fit and job satisfaction in a global service environment. *Management International Review,* 43(2), 129–148.

Thaler-Carter, R. E. (2000). Whither global leaders? *HRMagazine,* 45(5), 82–88.

Thomas, A. S., and Mueller, S. L. (2000). A case for comparative entrepreneurship: Assessing the relevance of culture. *Journal of International Business Studies,* 31(2), 287–301.

Thomas, K. W. (1992). Conflict and negotiation processes in organizations. In M. D. Dunnette and L. M. Hough (eds.), *Handbook of industrial and organizational psychology,* 651–717. Palo Alto, CA: Consulting Psychologists Press.

Thomas, K. W. (1976). Conflict and conflict management. In M. Dunnette (ed.), *Handbook of industrial and organizational psychology,* 889–935. Chicago: Rand McNally.

Thomas, K. W., and Kilmann, R. H. (1974). *Thomas-Kilmann Conflict Mode Instrument.* Tuxedo, NY: Xicon.

Thomas, K. W., and Velthouse, B. A. (1990). Cognitive elements of empowerment: An "interpretive" level of intrinsic task motivation. *Academy of Management Review,* 15, 666–681.

Thomson, A. (1997). *A portrait of management development.* London: Institute of Management.

Tichy, N. M., and Devanna, M. A. (1990). *The transformational leader* (rev. ed.). New York: Wiley.

Ting-Toomey, S. (1988). A face negotiation theory. In Y. Y. Kim, and W. B. Gudykunst (eds.), *Theory and intercultural communication,* 47–92. Thousand Oaks, CA: Sage.

Ting-Toomey, S. (1985). Toward a theory of conflict and culture. In W. B. Gudykunst, I. P. Stewart, and S. Ting-Toomey (eds.), *International and intercultural communication annual,* vol. 9, *Communication, culture and organizational processes.* Newbury Park, CA: Sage.

Ting-Toomey, S., Gao, G., Trubisky, P., Yang, Z., Kim, H. S., Lin, S. L., and Nishida, T. (1991). Culture, face maintenance, and styles of handling interpersonal conflict: A study in five cultures. *International Journal of Conflict Management, 2*(4), 275–296.

Tinsley, C. H. (2001). How negotiators get to yes: Predicting the constellation of strategies used across cultures to negotiate conflict. *Journal of Applied Psychology, 86*(4), 583–593.

Tinsley, C. H., and Pillutla, M. M. (1998). Negotiating in the United States and Hong Kong. *Journal of International Business Studies, 29*(4), 711–727.

Tjosvold, D. (1999). Bridging East and West to develop new products and trust: Interdependence and interaction between a Hong Kong parent and North American subsidiary. *International Journal of Innovation Management, 3,* 233–252.

Tjosvold, D. (1998). The cooperative and competitive goal approach to conflict: Accomplishments and challenges. *Applied Psychology: An International Review, 47,* 285–342.

Tjosvold, D. (1985). Power and social context in superior-subordinate interaction. *Organizational Behavior and Human Decision Processes, 35,* 281–293.

Tjosvold, D., Hui, C., and Law, K. S. (2001). Constructive conflict in China: Cooperative conflict as a bridge between East and West. *Journal of World Business, 36*(2), 166–183.

Tjosvold, D., Hui, C., and Law, K. S. (1998). Empowerment in the manager-employee relationship in Hong Kong: Interdependence and controversy. *Journal of Social Psychology, 138*(5), 624–637.

Tjosvold, D., Sasaki, S., and Moy, J. (1998). Developing commitment in Japanese organizations in Hong Kong: Interdependence, interaction, relationship and productivity. *Small Group Research, 29,* 560–582.

Tjosvold, D., and Sun, H. (2000). Social face in conflict: Effects of affronts to person and position in China. *Group Dynamics: Theory, Research and Practice, 4*(3), 259–271.

Tongren, H. N., Hecht, L., and Kovach, K. (1995). Recognizing cultural differences: Key to successful U.S.-Russian enterprises. *Public Personnel Management, 24*(1), 1–17.

Traves, J., Brockbank, A., and Tomlinson, F. (1997). Careers of women managers in the retail industry. *Service Industries Journal, 17*(1), 133–154.

Triandis, H. C. (1995). *Individualism and collectivism.* Boulder, CO: Westview.

Triandis, H. C. (1993). The contingency model in cross-cultural perspective. In M. M. Chemers and R. Ayman (eds.), *Leadership theory and research.* San Diego: Academic Press.

Triandis, H. C. (1976). Some universals of social behavior. *Personality and Social Psychology Bulletin, 4,* 1–17.

Triandis, H. C., and Albert, R. (1987). Cross-cultural perspectives. In F. Jablin (ed.), *Handbook of organizational communication,* 264–295. Newbury Park, CA: Sage.

Triandis, H. C., Bontempo, R., Villareal, M. J., Asai, M., and Lucca, N. (1988). Individualism and collectivism: Cross-cultural perspectives on self in-group relationships. *Journal of Personality and Social Psychology, 21,* 323–338.

Triandis, H. C., and Gelfand, M. J. (1998). Converging measurement of horizontal and vertical individualism and collectivism. *Journal of Personality and Social Psychology, 74,* 118–128.

Trice, H. M., and Beyer, J. M. (1993). *The cultures of work organizations.* Englewood Cliffs, NJ: Prentice Hall.

Trompenaars, F. (1993). *Riding the waves of culture.* London: Nicholas Brealey.

Trompenaars, F., and Hampden-Turner, C. (1998). *Riding the waves of culture: Understanding cultural diversity in global business* (2d ed.). New York: McGraw-Hill.

Trubisky, P., Ting-Toomey, S., and Lin, S. L. (1991). The influence of individualism-collectivism and self-monitoring on conflict styles. *International Journal of Intercultural Relations, 15*(1), 65–84.

Tse, D. K., Francis, J., and Walls, J. (1994). Cultural differences in conducting intra- and inter-cultural negotiations: A Sino-Canadian comparison. *Journal of International Business Studies, 24,* 537–555.

Tse, D. K., Lee, K.-H., Vertinsky, I., and Wehrung, D. A. (1988). Does culture matter? A cross-cultural study of executives' choice, decisiveness, and risk adjustment in international marketing. *Journal of Marketing, 52,* 81–95.

Tsui, J., and Windsor, C. (2001). Some cross-cultural evidence on ethical reasoning. *Journal of Business Ethics, 31*(2), 143–150.

Tu, W. M. (1985). *Confucian thought: Selfhood as creative transformation.* Albany: State University of New York Press.

Tuch, S. A., and Martin, J. K. (1991). Race in the workplace: Black/white differences in the sources of job satisfaction. *Sociological Quarterly, 32,* 103–116.

Tuncalp, S. (1988). The marketing research scene in Saudi Arabia. *European Journal of Marketing, 22*(5), 15–22.

Tung, R. L. (1998). American expatriates abroad: From neophytes to cosmopolitans. *Journal of World Business, 33*(2), 125–144.

Tung, R. L. (1988a). Career issues in international assignments. *Academy of Management Executive, 11,* 241–244.

Tung, R. L. (1988b). Towards a paradigm of international business negotiations. *Advances in International Comparative Management, 3,* 203–219.

Tung, R. L. (1987). Expatriates assignment: Enhancing success and minimizing failure. *Academy of Management Executive, 1*(2), 117–125.

Tung, R. L. (1984). *Key to Japan's economic strength: Human power.* Lexington, MA: Lexington Books.

Tung, R. L. (1981a). Patterns of motivation in Chinese industrial enterprises. *Academy of Management Review, 12*(2), 3–19.

Tung, R. L. (1981b). Selection and training of personnel for overseas assignments. *Columbia Journal of World Business, 16,* 68–71.

Turban, D. B., and Keon, T. L. (1993). Organizational attractiveness: An interactionalist perspective. *Journal of Applied Psychology, 78,* 184–193.

Turban, D. B., Lau, C.-M., Ngo, H.-Y., Chow, I. H. S., and Si, S. X. (2001). Organizational attractiveness of firms in the People's Republic of China: A person-organization fit perspective. *Journal of Applied Social Psychology, 86*(2), 194–206.

Tyler, T. R. (1989). The psychology of procedural justice: A test of the group value model. *Journal of Personality and Social Psychology, 57,* 830–838.

Unsworth, K. L., and West, M. A. (2000). Teams: The challenges of cooperative work. In N. Chmiel (ed.), *Introduction to work and organizational psychology.* Oxford, UK: Blackwell.

Valentine, S. (2000). International person-organization fit: The role of national culture. *International Journal of Management, 17*(3), 295–302.

Vandenberghe, C. (1996). Assessing organizational commitment in a Belgium context: Evidence for a three-dimensional model. *Applied Psychology: An International Review, 45,* 371–386.

Van Deusen, C., Mueller, C. B., Jones, G., and Friedman, H. (2002). A cross-cultural comparison of problem solving beliefs and behaviors: Helping managers understand country differences. *International Journal of Management and Decision Making, 3*(1), 52–66.

Van de Vliert, E. (1997). *Complex interpersonal conflict behavior: Theoretical frontiers.* Hove, UK: Psychology Press.

Van de Vliert, E., Euwema, M. C., and Huismans, S. E. (1995). Managing conflict with a subordinate or a superior: Effectiveness of conglomerated behavior. *Journal of Applied Psychology, 80,* 271–281.

Van de Vliert, E., and Kabanoff, B. (1990). Toward theory-based measures of conflict management. *Academy of Management Journal, 33,* 199–209.

van Oudenhoven, J. P. (2001). Do organizations reflect national cultures? A 10-nation study. *International Journal of Intercultural Relations, 25,* 89–107.

Varona, F. (1996). Relationship between communication satisfaction and organizational commitment in three Guatemalan organizations. *Journal of Business Communications, 33,* 111–140.

Vecchio, R. P. (1987). Situational leadership theory: An examination of a prescriptive theory. *Journal of Applied Psychology, 72*(3), 444–451.

Veenhoven, R. (1991). Is happiness relative? *Social Indicators Research, 24,* 1–34.

Veiga, J. F., Yanouzas, J. N., and Buchholtz, A. K. (1995). Emerging cultural values among Russian managers: What will tomorrow bring? *Business Horizons, 38,* 20–27.

Verespej, M. A. (1999). Global quandary. *Industry Week, 248*(21), 9–10.

Voronov, M., and Singer, J. A. (2002). The myth of individualism-collectivism: A critical review. *Journal of Social Psychology, 142*(4), 461–480.

Vroom, V. H. (1964). *Work and motivation.* New York: Wiley.

Wagner, J. A. (1995). Studies of individualism-collectivism: Effects on cooperation in groups. *Academy of Management Journal, 38,* 152–172.

Waley, A. (1938). *The analects of Confucius.* New York: Random House.

Waller, M. J., Conte, J. M., Gibson, C., and Carpenter, M. (2001). The impact of individual time perception on team performance under deadline conditions. *Academy of Management Review, 26,* 586–600.

Walton, R. E. (1987). *Managing conflict: Interpersonal dialogue and third-party roles* (2d ed.) Reading, MA: Addison-Wesley.

Walumbwa, F., and Lawler, J. (2002). Building effective organizations: Transformational leadership, collectivist orientation and outcomes. Paper presented at the Academy of Management Conference, Denver, CO, August.

Wang, Z. M. (1994). Culture, economic reform, and the role of industrial and organizational psychology in China. In H. C. Triandis, M. D. Dunette, and L. M. Hough (eds.), *Handbook of industrial and organizational psychology* (2d ed.), 4:689–725. Palo Alto, CA: Consulting Psychologists Press.

Wang, Z. M. (1992). Managerial psychological strategies for Chinese-foreign joint ventures. *Journal of Managerial Psychology, 7*(3), 10–16.

Warner, M. (1993). Managing human resources in East Asia. *International Journal of Human Resource Management, 6*(1), 34–51.

Warrington, M. B., and McCall, J. B. (1983). Negotiating a foot into the Chinese door. *Management Decision, 21*(2), 3–13.

Wasti, S. A. (1999). A cultural analysis of organizational commitment and turnover intentions in a collectivist society. Paper presented at the Academy of Management Conference, Chicago, IL, August.

Wederspahn, G. M. (2002). Expatriate training: Don't leave home without it. *Training and Development, 56*(2), 67–70.

Wederspahn, G. M. (1992). Costing failures in expatriate human resource management. *Human Resources Planning, 15*(3), 27–35.

Weider-Hatfield, D., and Hatfield, J. D. (1995). Relationships among conflict management styles, levels of conflict, and reactions to work. *Journal of Social Psychology, 135,* 687–698.

Wellins, R., and Byham, W. (2001). The leadership gap. *Training, 38*(3), 98–106.

Wellins, R., Wilson, R., Katz, A., Laughlin, P., Day, C. R., and Price, D. (1990). *Self-directed teams: A study of current practice.* Pittsburgh: DDI Press.

Welsh, D. H., Luthans, F., and Sommer, S. M. (1993). Managing Russian factory workers: The impact of U.S.-based behavior and participative techniques. *Academy of Management Journal, 36*(1), 58–79.

Westwood, R. I., Tang, S. F., and Kirkridge, P. S. (1992) Chinese conflict behavior: Cultural antecedents and behavioral consequences. *Organization Development Journal, 10*(2), 13–19.

White, M. M., Parks, J.M., McLean, J., and Gallagher, D.G. (1995). Validity evidence for the organizational commitment questionnaire in the Japanese corporate culture. *Educational and Psychological Measurement, 55*(2), 278–290.

Wilkof, M. V., Brown, D. W., and Selsky, J. W. (1995). When the stories are different: The influence of corporate culture mismatches on interorganizational relations. *Journal of Applied Behavioral Sciences, 31*(3), 373–388.

Willmott, B. (2002). Bullying needs monitoring for the sake of work harmony. *Personnel Today*, January 15, 10.

Wilmot, W. W., and Hocker, J. L. (2001). *Interpersonal conflict* (6th ed). New York: McGraw-Hill.

Wilson, M. G., Norcraft, G., and Neale, M. (1985). The perceived value of fringe benefits. *Personnel Psychology, 38*, 309–320.

Witt, L. A., and Nye, L. G. (1992). Gender and the relationship between perceived fairness of pay or promotion and job satisfaction. *Journal of Applied Psychology, 12*, 910–917.

Woffard, J. C., and Liska, L. Z. (1993). Path-goal theories of leadership: A meta-analysis. *Journal of Management, 19*(4), 857–876.

Wong, A., Tjosvold, D., Wong, W., and Liu, C. K. (1999). Relationships for quality improvement in the Hong Kong China supply chain: A study of the theory of cooperation and competition. *Journal of Quality and Reliability Management, 16*, 24–41.

Wong, C. S., Hui, C., Wong, Y. T., and Law, K. S. (2001). The significant role of Chinese employees' organizational commitment: Implications for managing employees in Chinese societies. *Journal of World Business, 36*(3), 326–339.

Wong, S. L. (1985). The Chinese family firm: A model. *British Journal of Sociology, 36*(1), 58–71.

Wren, J. T. (1994). Teaching leadership: The art of the possible. *Journal of Leadership Studies, 1*(2), 73–93.

Wright, I., Bengtsson, C., and Frankenberg, K. (1994). Aspects of psychological work environment and health among male and female white-collar and blue-collar workers in a big Swedish industry. *Journal of Organizational Behavior, 15*, 177–183.

Wright, P. M., and McMahan, G. C. (1992). Theoretical perspectives for strategic HRM. *Journal of Management, 18*, 295–320.

Wu, N. (1992). State-owned enterprises: No longer state run. *Beijing Review*, November 16–22, pp. 17–21.

Xu, L. C. (1989). Comparative study of leadership between Chinese and Japanese managers based upon PM theory. In B. J. Fallon, H. P. Pfester, and J. Brebner (eds.), *Advances in organizational psychology*, 42–49. Amsterdam: Elsevier.

Yamada, H. (1990). Topic management and turn distributions in business meetings: American versus Japanese strategies. *Text, 110*, 271–295.

Yamagishi, T., Jin, N., and Miller, A. S. (1998). In-group bias and culture of collectivism. *Asian Journal of Social Psychology, 1*, 315–328.

Yang, C. Y. (1984). Demystifying Japanese management practices. *Harvard Business Review, 62*(6), 172–182.

Yang, K. S. (1988). Will societal modernization eventually eliminate cross-cultural psychological differences? In M. H. Bond (ed.), *The cross-cultural challenge to social psychology*. Newbury Park, CA: Sage.

Yang, K. S., and Bond, M. H. (1990). Exploring implicit personality theories with indigenous or imported constructs: The Chinese case. *Journal of Personality and Social Psychology, 58*, 1087–1095.

Yates, J. F., Lee, J. W., and Shinotsuka, H. (1996). Beliefs about overconfidence, including its cross-national variation. *Organizational Behavior and Human Decision Processes, 65*, 138–147.

Yeh, R. S. (1995). Downward influence styles in cultural diversity settings. *International Journal of Human Resource Management, 6*(3), 626–641.

Yeh, R. S., and Granrose, C. S. (1993). Work goals of Taiwanese men and women managers in Taiwanese, Japanese and American owned companies. *International Journal of Intercultural Relations, 17*(1), 107–123.

Yeh, R. S., and Lawrence, J. J. (1995). Individualism and Confucian dynamism: A note on Hofstede's cultural root to economic growth. *Journal of International Business Studies, 26*(4), 655–669.

Yeung, A. K., and Ready, D. A. (1995). Developing leadership capabilities of global corporations: A comparative study in eight nations. *Human Resource Management, 34*, 529–547.

Yeung, I. Y. M., and Tung, R. L. (1996). Achieving business success in Confucian societies: The importance of *guanxi* (connections). *Organizational Dynamics, 24*(3), 54–65.

Yukl, G. (1994). *Leadership in organizations* (3d ed.). Englewood Cliffs, NJ: Prentice Hall.

Zahra, S. A., and Pearce, J. (1990). Research evidence on the Miles-Snow typology. *Journal of Management, 16*(4), 751–768.

Zhang, M. (1993). Taking stock of women in management in the People's Republic of China. *Proceedings of Women in Management in Asia Conference* (Chinese University of Hong Kong, November), 18–26.

Zhou, J., and Martocchio, J. J. (2001). Chinese and American managers' compensation award decisions: A comparative policy capturing study. *Personnel Psychology,* 54(1), 115–145.

Zhu, Y. L. (1991). *Confucian ideal persona and Chinese culture.* Shenyang, China: Liaoling Educational Press.

Zucker, L. G. (1986). Production of trust: Institutional sources of economic structure 1840–1920. In B. M. Staw and L. L. Cummings (eds.), *Research in Organizational Behavior, 8,* 53–111.

Name Index

Subject Index